W9-CEI-269

INSIGHT GUIDES

AUSTRIA

Discovery CHANNEL

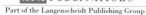
APA PUBLICATIONS

Part of the Langenscheidt Publishing Group

INSIGHT GUIDE
AUSTRIA

ABOUT THIS BOOK

Editorial
Project Editor
Freddy Hamilton
Editorial Director
Brian Bell

Distribution

UK & Ireland
GeoCenter International Ltd
The Viables Centre, Harrow Way
Basingstoke, Hants RG22 4BJ
Fax: (44) 1256 817988
United States
Langenscheidt Publishers, Inc.
46–35 54th Road, Maspeth, NY 11378
Fax: 1 (718) 784 0640
Canada
Thomas Allen & Son Ltd
390 Steelcase Road East
Markham, Ontario L3R 1G2
Fax: (1) 905 475 6747
Australia
Universal Press
1 Waterloo Road
Macquarie Park, NSW 2113
Fax: (61) 2 9888 9074
New Zealand
Hema Maps New Zealand Ltd (HNZ)
Unit D, 24 Ra ORA Drive
East Tamaki, Auckland
Fax: (64) 9 273 6479
Worldwide
**Apa Publications GmbH & Co.
Verlag KG (Singapore branch)**
38 Joo Koon Road, Singapore 628990
Tel: (65) 6865 1600. Fax: (65) 6861 6438

Printing

Insight Print Services (Pte) Ltd
38 Joo Koon Road, Singapore 628990
Tel: (65) 6865 1600. Fax: (65) 6861 6438

©2003 **Apa Publications GmbH & Co.
Verlag KG (Singapore branch)**
All Rights Reserved
First Edition 1991
Third Edition 2001
Updated 2003

CONTACTING THE EDITORS
We would appreciate it if readers
would alert us to errors or out-
dated information by writing to:
**Insight Guides, P.O. Box 7910,
London SE1 1WE, England.**
Fax: (44 20) 7403-0290.
insight@apaguide.co.uk

This guidebook combines the interests and enthusiasms of two of the world's best-known information providers: Insight Guides, whose titles have set the standard for visual travel guides since 1970, and Discovery Channel, the world's premier source of nonfiction television programming.

The editors of Insight Guides provide both practical advice and general understanding about a destination's history, culture, institutions and people. Discovery Channel and its popular website, www.discovery.com, help millions of viewers explore their world from the comfort of their own home and encourage them to experience it first hand.

How to use this book

This updated edition of *Insight Guide: Austria* is structured to convey a rich understanding of the country and its culture as well as to guide readers through its best sights and activities:

◆ The **Features** section, indicated by a yellow bar at the top of each page, covers the history and culture of Austria in a series of essays.

◆ The main **Places** section, with a blue bar, is a complete guide to all the sights and the areas worth visiting. Places of special interest are coordinated by number with the maps.

◆ The **Travel Tips** listings section, indicated by an orange bar, provides a handy point of reference for informa-

tion on travel, hotels, shops, restaurants and more, throughout Austria.

The contributors

This fully revised edition of *Insight Guide: Austria* was masterminded in the series' editorial headquarters in London by **Freddy Hamilton**.

Playing indispensable roles in this edition were two writers with wide experience of Austria and travel writing. **Louis James** lives in Vienna and has written extensively on Austria and the Austrians. His book *The Xenophobe's Guide to the Austrians* is a light-hearted dig at the people of his adopted land. For this guide, he reworked the history section and contributed new chapters on the Austrian people, recent history, Vienna, and the country's rich traditions in arts and music, as well as a new feature on Sigmund Freud. **Paul Karr** has contributed to numerous Insight Guides, including those on Switzerland, Vienna and Montreal, and has travelled extensively in Austria. He updated and reworked the rest of the book, including the Travel Tips, and contributed new features on hiking and the Salzburg Festival, as well as the picture stories on Melk Abbey, Winter Playgrounds and *The Sound of Music*.

This book builds on the success of earlier editions, the first of which was put together in the original German by Frankfurt-based Austrian author **Wilhelm Klein**. The first English translation was edited by **Tony Halliday**, and later editions were overseen in London by **Dorothy Stannard** and **Clare Griffiths**.

Contributors to the earlier versions of *Insight Guide: Austria* – and a great deal of their work still appears in this edition – included **Rowlinson Carter** (History), **Marton Radkai** (The Austrian Muse), **Ute Fischer** (Baroque Masterpieces), **Dr Jutta Kohout** (Austrian Cuisine), **Christian Neuhold** and **Alfred Kölbel** (The Great Outdoors), **Evelyn Feichtenberger** and **Kurt Feichtenberger** (Lower Austria, Burgenland, Styria, Upper Austria, the Salzkammergut, Carinthia and East Tyrol), **Dr Dieter Maier** (Salzburg, Salzburg Province, Tyrol, Vorarlberg) and **Chris Clouter** (updates).

The entire book was updated in 2003 by Vienna resident **Margaret de Fonblanque**. Additional editorial assistance was provided by **Lesley Gordon**, **David Isaacson**, **Tom Le Bas**, **Siân Lezard** and **Graham Meikleham**. Thanks go also to **Pam Barrett**, who proofread this edition, and to **Elizabeth Cook**, who indexed it.

Map Legend

▬ ▪ ▬	International Boundary
▬ ▬ ▬	Province Boundary
▪ ▪	National Park/Reserve
Ⓤ	U–Bahn
✈ ✈	Airport: International/Regional
🚌	Bus Station
❶	Tourist Information
✉	Post Office
✝ ✝ ✝	Church/Ruins
✝	Monastery
☾	Mosque
✡	Synagogue
⌂ ⌂	Castle/Ruins
∴	Archaeological Site
∩	Cave
⌶	Statue/Monument
★	Place of Interest

The main places of interest in the Places section are coordinated by number with a full-colour map (e.g. ❶), and a symbol at the top of every right-hand page tells you where to find the map.

INSIGHT GUIDE
austria

CONTENTS

Introduction

History

Features

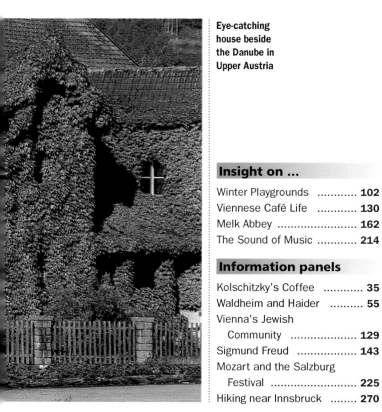

Eye-catching
house beside
the Danube in
Upper Austria

Insight on ...

Information panels

Travel Tips

Places

ALPS, VINES AND VIENNA

Austria offers fabulous mountains, quiet rural backwaters and

a capital city both quaintly historic and robustly enjoyable

Austria has a knack of looking both backwards and forwards. So in 2002, more than 80 years after the collapse of the Empire and the abdication of the last Emperor, the Republic marked the 90th birthday of his son, Dr Otto von Habsburg, with a service in the Stephansdom and a ceremony at the Hofburg. The birthday was a chance to celebrate Habsburg's career as a member of the European Parliament and an advocate of the enlargement of the European Union. Two years earlier a new Austrian coalition government had been formed that included Jörg Haider's far-right Freedom Party. This provoked riots in Vienna and the temporary imposition of sanctions by the selfsame European Union. Four days after the birthday celebrations, however, the Freedom Party's vote fell heavily in national elections, and its influence on Austrian politics waned accordingly.

It was unfortunate that Haider's short-lived grasp on the reins of power had tempted so many observers to decry the Austrian people as a whole, as they are some of the friendliest and most down-to-earth in Europe. And the land they inhabit is a spectacular one, containing everything from cowbell-tickled meadows and slim-pointed mountain chapels to deep gorges and ranges of dark, high peaks.

In the far west, Bregenz touches the shores of Lake Constance at the junction of three nations. Ignoring the casino and heading into the Bregenzerwald, one begins to know an earthy, outgoing people. The sense intensifies in Salzburg – with its impressive position between hill and river, and its lingering echoes of Mozart – and Innsbruck, wedged between high alps, a base for hiking, skiing and adventure.

Some of the world's best spas, and a load of fine vistas besides, pack themselves into the intervening folds and lakes of the Salzkammergut region. At length, as one gets off the main train line and moves up through the Danube Valley's bountiful vineyards – best explored by riverside bike trail, at harvest time – one realises that the Austrian character has been misapprehended. With a bit more time before reaching the capital, further exploration might include side trips to places such as Graz and Klagenfurt, all but unknown except to the Austrians.

And then there is Vienna. Visitors are always surprised by the Viennese – gregarious and hedonistic, they enjoy ice cream, coffee, good talk and dining as much as anyone. And their city, forgotten for a time, now finds itself at the cutting edge of historic change: the fall of the Iron Curtain has brought a flood of new people and ideas through the city gates, and noisy construction projects to all but the oldest quarters. Like Austria as a whole, it is not altogether what you had expected, and that is the joy of it. ❏

PRECEDING PAGES: Johann Strauss Jr in Vienna's Stadtpark; carriage-driver and his horses; traditional fare in the Pinzgau; Café Schwarzenberg in Vienna.
LEFT: Pallas Athena statue at Vienna's parliament building.

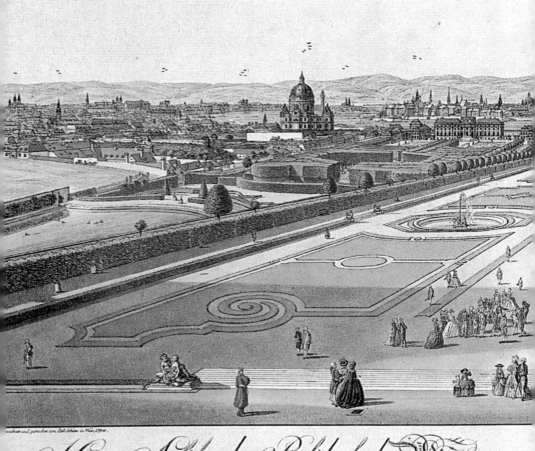

radirt und gestochen von Carl Schütz in Wien 1784.

Haupt Ansicht der Residenzstadt Wien,
nd des größten Theils ihrer Vorstädte, von Belvedere anzusehen.

- *Maria Hilf.*   - *St. Ulrich.*   - *Kirche.*   - *Augustiner Hofkirche.*
- *Paulaner auf der Wieden.*   - *Burgten in der Josephstadt.*   - *Pfarrkirche in der Alstergasse.*

Vüe De la Capitale de Vienne, et d'une grande partie de ses Fauxbourgs, prise du coté du Belvedere.

Decisive Dates

BEGINNINGS

circa 25,000 BC The Danube Valley is inhabited – the Venus of Willendorf dates from this era.

800–400 BC The Hallstatt Culture inhabit the Salzkammergut, working salt mines that are still in operation today.

circa 450 BC The Celts begin to arrive and establish the kingdom of Noreaia.

15 BC The Romans come to the Danube. They set up a garrison town of 6,000 soldiers at Vindobona, the future Vienna.

circa AD 280 Systematic viticulture is introduced to the Danube region.

5th–6th centuries The *Völkerwanderung* (migration of the peoples) takes place across Central Europe; Slavs and Bavarians immigrate into the region. In 433 the Romans are forced to abandon the area around the Danube.

798 Salzburg becomes an archbishopric.

799–800 Charlemagne repulses the advancing Avars and establishes a territory known as the *Ostmark* (Eastern March) in what is now Upper and Lower Austria.

907 The Magyars conquer the *Ostmark*.

955 At the Battle of Lechfeld, the Saxon king Otto the Great defeats the Magyars.

THE BABENBERG ERA

976 Otto II puts the Babenbergs in charge of the *Ostmark*.

996 The first official record of the name Ostarrichi.

1114–33 Babenberg leader Leopold III founds monasteries at Klosterneuburg and Heiligenkreuz.

1156 Heinrich II Jasomirgott moves the seat of the Babenbergs to Wien (Vienna).

1192 On his return from the Third Crusade, Richard the Lionheart is imprisoned and held hostage by Leopold V.

1246 Duke Friedrich II is killed in the Battle of Leitha against the Hungarians, marking the end of the Babenberg dynasty. Control of Austria passes to Ottakar II of Bohemia.

THE HABSBURGS

1278 Ottakar is killed at the Battle of Dürnkrut by the forces of Rudolf of Habsburg, the Holy Roman Emperor. Rudolf gives his sons Austria in fief, thereby founding the Habsburg dynasty, which would rule the country until 1918.

1365 Vienna University is founded by Rudolf IV.

1421 Albrecht V institutes a devastating pogrom against Jews, driving them from Vienna and demolishing the city's ghetto.

1493–1519 Cleverly exploiting several marital alliances, Maximilian I extends the Habsburg domains to include the Netherlands, Burgundy and Spain and also makes preparations for the unification of Austria, Bohemia and Hungary. During his reign the Reformation reaches the country.

1521 The Edict of Worms denounces Martin Luther.

1526 Ludwig II of Hungary dies fighting the Turks. Hungary and Bohemia fall to the Habsburgs.

1529 The Turks, under Sultan Suleiman I, reach the gates of Vienna. They almost take the city but are forced to withdraw after the early onset of winter.

1550s Protestantism spreads, and by the late 16th century most of Austria's population has converted. The Catholic Habsburgs summon the Jesuits to Vienna.

1619–48 Fanatical Catholic Ferdinand II takes on the Protestants. The conflict spreads to the rest of Europe, resulting in the Thirty Years' War.

1620s–1730s With the Counter-Reformation comes the Baroque, which sweeps the country, reaching a peak with Vienna's Karlskirche (1739).

1683 Vienna is besieged by Kara Mustapha and his 250,000-strong Turkish army. The city is liberated by Imperial forces.

1697 Prince Eugene becomes supreme commander of the army. His successes on the battlefield extend

Habsburg control in Hungary, modern-day Croatia and large swathes of Western Europe. Austria becomes prime mover on the European mainland.

1713 Pragmatic Sanction introduced, providing legitimacy for female succession.

1740 Maria Theresa ascends the throne.

1756 Wolfgang Amadeus Mozart is born in Salzburg.

1765 Maria Theresa's son Joseph II becomes co-regent and rules jointly with his mother.

THE AUSTRIAN EMPIRE

1805 Napoleon's troops occupy Vienna (as they would again in 1809).

1806 Franz II declares the end of the Holy Roman Empire to prevent Napoleon becoming its Emperor.

1814–15 After the fall of Napoleon, the Congress of Vienna is convened, at which Europe's princes and statesmen rearrange the political map. Under Chancellor Metternich, Austria sinks into the deathly stillness of the Biedermeier era.

1848 The March Revolution is crushed by Imperial troops; simple-minded Ferdinand I abdicates in favour of his 18-year-old nephew, Franz Joseph.

1857 Work begins on Vienna's Ringstrasse.

1870s Austrian anti-semitism begins to spread.

1890s *Fin-de-siècle* Austria (especially Vienna) sees a flowering of intellectual and artistic activity, with the appearance, among others, of Sigmund Freud, Gustav Mahler, Arthur Schnitzler, Otto Wagner and Gustav Klimt.

1914 The assassination in Sarajevo of Archduke Franz Ferdinand, the heir to the Imperial throne, ushers in World War I.

1916 Emperor Franz Joseph dies.

1918 After defeat in the war Karl I abdicates – the fall of the Habsburgs.

POST-IMPERIAL AUSTRIA

1918 The Republic of Austria is declared. In the post-war treaty Austria is forced to shrink to a twelfth of its pre-war size.

1930 Robert Musil begins his epic novel of the Habsburg decline, *The Man Without Qualities.*

1934 Chancellor Engelbert Dollfuss is assassinated in an attempted putsch by Austrian Nazis.

1938 The Nazis take over – Anschluss with Germany. Hitler is welcomed in Vienna. Thousands of Jews (including Sigmund Freud) flee Austria.

PRECEDING PAGES: View of Vienna from the Belvedere in 1784. **LEFT:** Kara Mustapha, leader of the Turks during the siege of Vienna in 1683. **RIGHT:** the Austrian coat of arms.

1939 Outbreak of World War II.

1944–45 Bombing raids by the Allies destroy 30 percent of Vienna.

1945 Vienna is taken by the Red Army. Austria and its capital are divided into four occupation zones.

1955 The *Staatsvertrag* (State Treaty) between Austria and the Allied Powers, guarantees Austria's sovereignty and neutrality.

1970 Socialist chancellor Bruno Kreisky is elected.

1979 Vienna becomes the third seat of the United Nations, after New York and Geneva.

1986 During his campaign to become president of Austria, former UN secretary-general Kurt Waldheim is accused of being involved in war-time atrocities.

1992 Thomas Klestil is elected president. Six years later he would win a second term.

1994 Austrians vote to join the European Union.

2000 Jörg Haider's far-right Freedom Party joins a coalition government, provoking rioting in Vienna and consternation abroad. As a result, the EU imposes, and later drops, sanctions on Austria. The country's first holocaust memorial is erected in Vienna. In the worst alpine disaster in history, 155 skiers are killed when a fire breaks out on an underground funicular train above Kaprun.

2002 The Austrian Schilling is replaced by the Euro, giving Austria the same currency as eleven other European countries. In parliamentary elections the Freedom Party's vote falls heavily. ❑

Noch nun auff die zeit Otto des kaysers pm ko
men so wil ich von den dingen sagen die zu sei
nen zeytten zu auffspurg gestrechen send Do sich d
kayser otto beraittet wider berengarium den künig vo
lamparden als wider ain wietrich vnd geitigen vn
der alle gerechtikait vmb gelt gab Doch so forcht
m der selb wietrich van er die machtikait des kay
sers wol wißet vnd durch ratt des herßogen vo luth
ringen kam er zu dem kayßer vnd begeret frid Do

CELTS, ROMANS AND INVADERS FROM HELL

The early history of central Europe is marked by tribal migrations, grand empires and disputed successions

Comparatively little is known about the earliest inhabitants of Austria; the Danube Valley was settled by around 25,000 BC, and the salt mines of the Salzkammergut were being worked from 800 BC, but it was not until the Celts began to arrive after about 450 BC that the region began to develop. At this time, Athens had just passed the apex of its power and was about to be engulfed by the Macedonians under Alexander the Great. While the Macedonians pushed east through Persia towards India, the Celts drove in the opposite direction. In coats of mail, armed with huge shields and iron swords, equally happy fighting on foot, horses or from chariots, the Celts were unstoppable as they tore through Austria, Northern Italy, Gaul, Spain and Britain.

For all their ferocity in battle, the Celts were evidently quite benign in victory and quickly assimilated. The indigenous people introduced them to their well-developed techniques of iron and salt mining, while the Celts brought a new language, religion, viticulture and a taste for urban settlement. Noreaia, the name given to the Celtic "kingdom", corresponded with all but the western extremities of modern Austria.

Germanic tribes to the north were a constant threat to Noreaia but it was eventually to the Romans that it lost its independence. Possibly because they feared the Germanic tribes more than the Romans, the Noricans were pleased to be included in plans for an empire which would stretch from the Rhine in the west to the Danube in the east.

Roman Noricum

For 50 years or so the Romans were content to let the Noricans run their own affairs under traditional leaders, but incessant harassment by northern tribes necessitated putting the province, re-named Noricum, on a more military footing. Settlements were fortified; the future Vienna (known as Vindobona) received an earth rampart and a garrison of 1,000 cavalry from Britain (Ala I Britannica).

Rome kept up a lively trade with all corners of the empire and beyond, and as the Danube was the principal eastern artery, Noricum was bound to be in the thick of it. The supplementary network of roads and mountain passes carried a heavy traffic in Austrian gold, iron, salt and cattle south. Rome supplied olive oil and wine, introduced bee-keeping and systematised and extended existing viticulture.

Christianity was another import. Legend attributes the first teaching to St Florian, a soldier and early convert who escaped with 40 followers from Diocletian's persecution in Rome. Hoping that Noricum would be more tolerant, he sat down to explain his religious convictions

LEFT: the Battle of Lechfeld, 955.
RIGHT: Venus of Willendorf, ancient fertility symbol.

to the governor. The governor's response was to have him drowned. The statue still to be seen in many Austrian villages of a saint pouring water over a burning house is of St Florian.

The collapse of the Roman empire caused a power vacuum in central Europe, and the ensuing *Völkerwanderung* (migration of the peoples). Noricum first fell prey to Germanic tribes from the north, who were in turn eclipsed by Baltic peoples, who were said to eat roots and raw meat, leading to the assumption that they could only have originated in hell. Some of these tribes remained for a generation or two and then moved on, but there

guished him from the eastern emperor in Byzantine Constantinople. In more familiar terms, he became "Holy Roman Emperor".

After Charlemagne's death in 814 the empire disintegrated, but the idea behind it lived on. The German nobility, the hard core of Charlemagne's support, decided among themselves who would be their overall monarch under the title of King of the Romans. The throne was not hereditary – although reigning kings of the Romans were forever scheming to make it so – but it was the recognised stepping stone to becoming emperor, a transition which required the pope's endorsement and a coronation.

were always others waiting to fill their space. Vandals and Huns were followed by Langobards, Avars and, later, Slavs.

Charlemagne and the Ostmark

In the 8th century the Franks established an empire under Charlemagne to impose Christian order on a Europe of squabbling kingdoms and marauding tribes. The Eastern March, or *Ostmark*, corresponding to modern Upper and Lower Austria, was their buttress against the unruly eastern tribes. In return for helping Pope Leo III in his difficulties with rebellious Langobards, Charlemagne was crowned Emperor of the Romans in 800 AD, a title which distin-

Over the centuries, the rules of succession were modified. The election of the king was vested in an electoral college (or Diet) of seven princes, membership of which was a fiercely contested honour. A new king of the Romans was elected and kept in the wings during an emperor's lifetime in order to speed up the eventual succession. Any Christian ruler, not merely a German one, became eligible for the throne, and this tended to make the competition hotter and less manageable.

Not to appreciate the prestige and complications of the imperial succession is to run the risk of being thoroughly confused by the flow of European history which was central to the making of modern Austria. It caused many more wars than anything else over 1,000 years, and the chance to become Holy Roman Emperor was a mouth-watering prospect even for a hardened atheist like Napoleon *(see page 36)*. A perennial claim to the imperial throne, abetted by a talent for arranging useful marriages, was the mainspring of the House of Habsburg.

The Babenberg dynasty

The lengthy build-up to the Habsburgs' near monopoly of the throne began in 955 when the Holy Roman Emperor Otto the Great defeated the Magyars at the historic Battle of Lechfeld.

adept at making the most of the chronic three-cornered power struggle between the Pope in Rome, the Holy Roman Emperor, who was supposed to be loyal to him but often had other ideas, and the German princes who effectively put the emperor where he was.

The Babenberg policy of supporting the king of the Romans, in other words the emperor-elect, at a critical point in this contest earned them a duchy in 1156. The Babenberg in question was Heinrich (Henry), better known as "Jasomirgott", a contraction of his favourite saying: "God help me!" Heinrich moved the Babenberg seat to Vienna.

The rescued eastern marches were in 976 put in the charge of Count Leopold of Babenberg. A document of 996 makes reference to his lands as "Ostarrichi", only a short cry from the later "Österreich".

By then the Babenbergs were well on their way to laying the foundations of a dynasty which was to last 300 years. The Habsburg fortunes were built on claims to the Babenberg inheritance. The Babenbergs were particularly

His son, Leopold V, was incensed by Richard the Lionheart, King of England, who removed a Babenberg banner at the crusade siege of Acre. Richard was captured and imprisoned at Dürnstein Castle, and the money received for his release paid for, amongst other things, the city walls of Vienna. Inevitably, such wealth attracted predators. The last of the Babenbergs, known as Friedrich "the Quarrelsome", was caught between a Holy Roman Emperor threatening the duchy from the west, warlike Magyars from the east, and jealous princely rivals all around. He lost Vienna to the first, his life to the second (at the Battle of Leitha in 1246), and his dominions to Ottakar II of Bohemia. ❏

FAR LEFT: Iron Age figure.
LEFT: Charlemagne, Holy Roman Emperor.
ABOVE: the death of Duke Friedrich II ("the Quarrelsome"), last of the Babenbergs.

ENTER THE HABSBURGS

From the 13th to the 15th centuries, the Habsburgs survived war, rivalry and penury to become the undisputed masters of central Europe

The Babenberg dynasty was just one victim of a period of utter anarchy in central Europe. Pope Gregory became so alarmed by the "Terrible Times" that in 1273 he warned that if the princes and barons did not settle their differences for long enough to elect a new king of the Romans to restore order, he would impose one himself.

The obvious choice was King Ottakar of Bohemia, but while the nobles felt obliged to obey the pope, a king actually able to call them to order was the last thing they wanted. They cast around for a suitable nonentity who would not impede their rampaging ways, and their eyes settled on a minor count, Rudolf of Habsburg, who was duly elected in 1273.

Rudolf was not a charismatic figure; his complexion was pale, his expression grave, and he tended to wear peasant dress, a notable eccentricity in an age of resplendent feudal regalia. He was not well-off. But his election as king would change that. "I am not he that once before ye knew," he declared ominously as he rose from his knees after the coronation.

Habsburg expansion

His first success was to defeat Ottakar at the battle of Dürnkrut northeast of Vienna in 1278 and take over all his lands. As the undisputed master of the Austrian provinces, Rudolf parcelled them out to his sons and went off in pursuit of "more acres". He bought out the residual Babenberg claims in the region, persuaded Henry of Bavaria to cede him land above the Enns, and took over Carinthia.

His dynastic ambitions took a significant step forward in 1282 when the electors agreed at the Diet of Augsburg that Austria, Styria, Carinthia and Carniola would pass to his two sons as a joint inheritance. Swabia, Alsace and Switzerland were earmarked for a third son, Hartman, but on a journey to England with a view to

LEFT: portrait of Maximilian I.
RIGHT: the Herzogsstuhl ducal throne on Carinthia's Zollfeld plain.

marrying Joanna, Edward III's daughter, Hartman fell into the Rhine and drowned.

The pacification of the pugnacious German barons was a formidable task, and in one year alone Rudolf destroyed 70 castles belonging to them. Encouraged by his success, Rudolf advanced on the Counts of Burgundy and Wurt-

temberg, who appealed to Philip IV of France for protection. The French king sent ambassadors to tell Rudolf to get off French territory. "Tell Philip," he replied languidly, "that we await his arrival, and will convince him that we are not here to dance or make merry, but to give law with the sword." In reality, his army had run out of supplies, was practically starving and about to be defeated. With an unerring talent for the morale-boosting gesture, Rudolf pulled a turnip out of the ground and ate it raw, saying he could not remember a better meal.

Rudolf was invigorated at the age of 64 by a second marriage to Agnes of Burgundy, a lovely girl of 14. But his last desire on reaching the age of 73 was to secure his son Albrecht's future. The plum would have been to get him elected as king of the Romans and therefore in line to become emperor, but the electors were not keen on Albrecht. Their rejection is said to have broken Rudolf's heart so that he died soon afterwards in deep depression.

But in time Albrecht managed to win election as king of the Romans on the strength of his own merits in putting down revolts in Vienna and Styria. Pope Boniface VIII hesitated

> ### LONG-TERM RULE
>
> Rudolf's accession to the throne in 1273 marked the beginning of 640 years – right up to the outbreak of World War I – of almost unbroken Habsburg dynastic rule within Austria.

Counterfeit glory

Rudolf IV, then head of the Habsburg House, retaliated with the discovery of a cache of documents which proved that the Habsburgs were the most illustrious family in Christendom, so exalted in fact that they outranked even the collective authority of the electors. The documents were forgeries, of course, but the various Habsburgs wore their windfall of new titles with considerable aplomb. Rudolf let it be known that if the electors continued to bar

before confirming the election, but Albrecht did not live long to enjoy the throne. He lost his life in a war with the Swiss, whose numbers included the celebrated William Tell. The imperial crown slipped off Habsburg heads and was not to be regained for a century.

Alarmed at the thought that in Rudolf and Albrecht they had inadvertently sown the seeds of a power beyond their control, the princely electors set about cutting the Habsburgs down to size. During his reign, Karl of Bohemia published a Golden Bull which stripped the Habsburgs of their vote in the electoral college, an almost essential platform from which to mount another bid for the throne.

his path to the imperial throne, he was empowered by God to establish a new one.

The contest for the title of king of the Romans became a battle between Rudolf and his father-in-law, Karl of Bohemia. The construction of St Vitus's Cathedral in Prague goaded Rudolf into reconstructing St Stephen's in Vienna on an even grander scale in 1359. A university in Prague? Vienna must have one too, and better: Vienna University was founded in 1365.

Years of crisis

The Hussite uprising in Bohemia at the beginning of the fifteenth century was the first intimation of religious revolt which, under Martin

Luther, still lay another century ahead. It was recognised at once, though, as a threat to much of what the empire stood for, and the Bohemian Emperor Sigismund was grateful for any help, even from the Habsburgs. Albrecht V, then head of the house, was willing to give it, but at the price of marriage to Sigismund's daughter and, on Sigismund's death, the Hungarian kingdom. With the extra crown firmly on his head, Albrecht could no longer be denied the coveted title and the Habsburgs regained the imperial throne in 1438.

In his dual capacity as king of Hungary and Holy Roman Emperor, Albrecht was immediately called upon to defend his lands against a threat from the Turkish Ottomans. They had already conquered much of Asia Minor, laid siege to Constantinople and invaded Serbia. Hungary was next in line, and any doubts the Hungarians might have harboured about their new king were overshadowed by the need to rally round him. The actual confrontation, however, fizzled out because dysentery laid both sides low. Albrecht himself contracted it. "I shall recover," he declared confidently, "if I can only once more behold the walls of Vienna." He couldn't and he didn't, however, dying on his way back to the city. Immediately after he died the Hungarians snatched back their throne.

Albrecht may have been politically successful, but during these years Vienna seethed with economic unrest. Blame for hardship fell on the Jews, who were then persecuted and massacred in fearful numbers in the terrible pogrom of 1421, the *Wiener Geserah*. Albrecht's decision to persecute the Jews has never been fully explained, being at odds with the tradition of Babenberg and Habsburg protection of the people who were regarded as a vital source of finance. It is likely to have been inspired by an increase in anti-semitic dogma from the Catholic Church, a possible reaction to the threat from the heretical Hussites.

Conditions hardly improved under Friedrich III. Crowned Holy Roman Emperor in 1452, he had only a limited hold on power within Austria. He was at loggerheads with his neighbour, Matthias Corvinus of Hungary, fought wars against his brother and was besieged with

LEFT: Walther von der Vogelweide, poet at the time of the Babenbergs.

RIGHT: Rudolf IV, claimed to be empowered by God.

his family in the Hofburg by the Viennese themselves. The wretched royals were forced to eat the palace pets and even vultures, which gathered hungrily but unwisely on the roof.

Friedrich was sustained by sublime confidence in the efficacy of his royal blood. As ingenious in matters of geneology as Rudolf IV had been, Friedrich was able to trace his line to Augustus Caesar and thence to King Priam of Troy. Steeped in magic and the occult, he had all his possessions engraved enigmatically with the letters A E I O U. To the untrained eye, these looked like the alphabet vowels, but Friedrich was able to reveal with smug

satisfaction that they stood for *Austriae Est Imperare Orbi Universo*, or "Austria (by which he meant the House of Austria, the Habsburgs) is Destined to Rule the Whole World".

The practical side of Friedrich's nature knew that if the Habsburgs were going to rule anything at all their coffers would have to be replenished massively and without delay. Moreover, the previous bloodline was in jeopardy. All but two of his children were dead. The only hope lay in negotiating an advantageous marriage for his son Maximilian Paulus Aemilius, whose name he had invented through some astrological formula, a combination of Fabius Maximus and Paulus Aemilius.

Maximilian and marriage

Maximilian, then 14, was taken along to wait in the wings while Friedrich negotiated for Marie, daughter of Charles the Bold, the Duke of Burgundy and the richest man in Europe. Innumerable suitors were jostling for Marie's hand, and Charles was in no mood to let her go for an iota less than she was worth. On financial grounds, Friedrich would have stood absolutely no chance, but he had something in his gift (Charles believed), the only thing which was more important than money: Friedrich could make him king of the Romans, his heir-apparent. As such, in one glorious bound, he

LOUIS XI

Fils de Charles VII, né à Bourges en 1423.
Très jeune, il eut la soif du pouvoir, se révolta contre son père
et à sa mort, en 1461, se fit sacrer à Reims. Malgré ses défauts,
Louis XI reste un des créateurs de l'unité nationale.
Nul ne connut mieux les ruses de la politique, les passions des hommes,
et les moyens de les dominer. Grâce à sa ruse, à sa patience,
et sa mauvaise foi, il abaissa les grands, surtout le Duc de Bourgogne,
Charles le Téméraire et réussit non seulement à leur enlever leurs pouvoirs,
mais à accroître le territoire de la Couronne.
Il mourut en 1483, au Château de Plessis-lez-Tours,
livré à toutes les Terreurs du remords et de la superstition.

4   ND

A RENAISSANCE MAN

Maximilian's reign represents the bridge between the world of the Middle Ages and that of the Renaissance. The atmosphere in the capital also attracted intellectuals and artists, who brought a spirit of learning and aesthetics derived from Italy, and indeed Maximilian himself is often regarded as the quintessential Renaissance man. He was well versed in Latin, French, German and Italian, skilled in various arts and sciences and the author of works on such diverse subjects as religion, military matters, hunting, hawking and cookery. He was also an able administrator who established local government in the 10 districts of empire, overhauled the legal system and abolished many oppressive taxes.

would soar in rank over the despised king of France. Confident that Friedrich would have to accept his terms, Charles called in his jewellers to have his head measured for a crown.

But Charles over-estimated Friedrich's ability to influence the electors. They were as usual open to bribery, but Friedrich was in no position to bribe them. The whole purpose of marrying Maximilian to Marie was to make money, not give it away.

Stuck with an unbetrothed daughter and a half-finished crown, Charles seemed to lose his senses, launching himself into a series of gravely misjudged and ultimately ruinous wars. Friedrich sat and waited for the inevitable. By 1476 Charles was a broken man, willing to let Marie go to Maximilian unconditionally. In order to forestall any designs the son of Louis XI of France might have on Marie, the Duke Ludwig of Bavaria played the part of the proxy groom in a ceremony which required him to lie next to her on a bed with one leg bare. The rest of his body was covered, awkwardly it would seem, in armour.

Marie gave Maximilian an heir, Philip, and a daughter, Margaret, and was then killed in a riding accident. Maximilian was devastated, his gloom compounded by news that the skinny Dauphin who had once been his rival for Marie's hand was now Charles VIII of France and lobbying furiously for the kingdom of the Romans which Maximilian considered his own.

With France looking even more dangerous than the Turks, Maximilian surveyed the options among states capable of making the king of France think again. As he could hardly marry another Burgundy, he looked at the next best, and that was Brittany. Anne, the 15-year-old heiress to Brittany, fitted the bill perfectly. The necessary arrangements were concluded without fuss and an ambassador despatched to lie in bed with Anne, a leg bared.

Desperate search

Charles VIII, the proverbial bad penny, understood what was going on and refused to acknowledge the pre-emptive rights of the proxy marriage. While Maximilian was detained in Frankfurt on electoral college business, he marched into Brittany, seized Anne, summoned a priest for a perfunctory ceremony, and consummated the marriage there and then. Still desperately short of money, Maximilian was forced to think again and lower his marital sights. In the eyes of his peers, his sights could not have gone much lower than his next quarry, Bianca Sforza, niece of the Duke of Milan. The Sforzas were regarded as jumped-up peasants; still, they appeared to be rich. The Sforzas were keen on the marriage, and Maximilian must have noted with some satisfaction that even the preparations for the proxy wedding were entrusted to Leonardo da Vinci.

Getting to know Bianca was full of surprises which seemed to confirm misgivings about her background. She had to be taught, first of all, not to eat her meals on the floor. Perhaps most

In retrospect, the most breathtaking feature of Maximilian's reign is the way he manipulated marriages, not only his own but also those of his relatives. He could be relied upon to come up with a suitable bride or groom for almost any situation. By the end of his reign he had secured a member of his family in almost every royal house in Europe.

Maximilian's last official function as emperor was to attend the Diet of 1518. In characteristic fashion, he used the occasion to ensure that the imperial succession went to his grandson, the future Karl V. In equally characteristic fashion, he did so by buying the

disconcerting of all, however, was the dawning truth that Bianca was not nearly as rich as he had imagined and, moreover, that any money she had was spent with frivolous abandon. On a journey through the half-starved Netherlands, she insisted on goose tongues for every meal.

It was noted at court that Maximilian took to seeing other women, and it was not long before they formed a queue at his door clutching the illegitimate issue. One of these was a future Archbishop of Salzburg.

LEFT: Maximilian's opponent, Louis XI of France.
ABOVE: Vienna in 1530.

requisite number of votes with money he did not possess. Two other items of business on the Diet's agenda that year were ominous. One was the Turkish threat, then looming so large that the Pope was calling for another crusade. The other, which Maximilian did not consider of great significance, concerned a meddlesome Augustinian monk who the previous year had affixed to the door of the church at Wittenberg 95 propositions condemning the Church's dubious raising of funds through the sale of indulgences. Maximilian died with little intimation of what the Turks and Martin Luther would mean to the Habsburg fortunes his arranged marriages had nurtured. ❏

Turkish and Protestant Infidels

Despite religious upheavals, Turkish sieges and French aggression,
the Habsburgs were stronger than ever by the mid-18th century

Karl V, Maximilian's heir, grandson and a Habsburg of the Spanish branch, was forced to spend millions on bribes to see off challenges for the imperial throne from Francis I of France, Henry VIII of England, Lajos of Hungary and Sigismund of Poland. In victory, however, he could survey the fruits of

Maximilian's matchmaking: in addition to his Spanish inheritance, which included Naples and Sicily, he had an aunt Margaret who was regent of the Netherlands, sisters who were queens of France, Portugal, Hungary, Bohemia, Denmark, Norway and Sweden and another aunt, Catherine of Aragon, who was married to the King of England. Karl ceded his German-speaking lands to his brother, Archduke Ferdinand, as he realised that one man could not successfully rule an empire on which "the sun never set". Karl presided over the Diet at Worms in 1521 whose outcome was the famous Edict of Worms that denounced Martin Luther and was famously ignored by him. With Karl frequently

distracted by other imperial business, the Archduke Ferdinand was left to grapple with the intractable problem of Protestantism in Austria not only among the masses, who rose in what became known as the Peasants' Wars of 1525–26, but also at the University of Vienna and among the aristocracy.

Turkish breakfast

An even more dangerous threat to the faith that Karl was pledged to defend came in 1526 with the news that a Turkish army "sufficient to exterminate the world" under the command of Suleiman the Magnificent had advanced to the Hungarian border. This time Suleiman withdrew but he was back three years later with the intention of taking Vienna. His army reached the walls of the city with only trifling opposition and laid siege. "On the third day," a message to the motley defenders promised, "we will breakfast within your walls." Turkish sappers moved their trenches forward and tunnelled under the walls to lay mines. If Vienna fell, there was no knowing where or how the Turks could be stopped.

As days and then weeks passed with the situation unchanged, the Viennese commander was emboldened to signal the Turks: "Your breakfast is getting cold." So was the weather, and the Turks knew better than Napoleon would about the perils of feeding 250,000 mouths in frozen conditions hundreds of miles from home. With the first snow of winter, the Turks struck their tents and departed.

Even so, by 1555 Karl was a broken man. The Turkish and French threats, coupled with German princes who saw Lutheranism as a tool to undermine the central authority of the empire, sapped him of the will to continue in office. He resigned the crowns of the Netherlands and Spain to one of his sons, and took the unprecedented step of abdicating the imperial throne as well. He then retired to a monastery.

While the Counter-Reformation was pursued vigorously, not to say brutally, in the Spanish half of the empire, Karl's easy-going heir

Maximilian was far more tolerant of Protestants. An ambassador commented that in Austria "the question is seldom asked whether anyone is Catholic or Protestant". The relative calm lasted until 1618 when a political altercation in Prague ended in defenestration, a dignified term for the business of throwing people out of windows.

The victims in this instance were two Roman Catholic imperial envoys who had gone to Prague for a meeting with Protestant leaders. Tempers frayed and the two envoys in full regalia were hoisted out of a window of the Hradcany castle 18 metres (60 feet) above the ground. They managed to cling to the window ledge by their finger tips for a while, but a bang on the knuckles broke their hold and sent them plunging in howling descent. They landed, as luck would have it, in a pile of dung and made good their escape to report the insult to Vienna. The result was the Thirty Years' War, a conflict which engulfed Europe as never before.

Behind the rhetoric of the battle as Protestant versus Catholic, an underlying cause of the war was the house of Habsburg settling old scores with France, and it only ended through the sheer exhaustion of all concerned.

Leopold I and the Siege of Vienna

When the dust of the Thirty Years' War settled, the Habsburg fortunes were in the hands of a 14-year-old who had impressed his Jesuit teachers in his nursery by making little chapels out of wooden blocks and pretending to be a priest celebrating mass. His personal qualities were not otherwise alluring – young Leopold was small, weak, ugly and devious. Nonetheless the sickly youth rallied to log one of the longest reigns in Austria (1640–1705), and against two of the wiliest opponents of all time – Louis XIV of France and Kara Mustapha, Grand Vizier of Turkey – he steered his domain into joining the first rank of European powers.

The early years of Leopold's career were occupied by what might be described as routine business. His Jesuit advisers were let loose to conduct the Counter-Reformation, he sur-

---

LEFT: Martin Luther, seen as a Protestant threat.
RIGHT: officer cadet in the Thirty Years' War.

vived an attempt on his life by Hungarian Protestants and Turks who sent him a poisoned pigeon pie, Vienna was struck by plague in 1679, and all the time Louis XIV was trying to encroach on his territory.

The passage of Halley's comet in 1682 heralded something extraordinary, the nature of which Leopold did not yet know. "May God will that I do nothing wicked," he wrote, "for I know myself as a great sinner, and just now it is high time to appease the godly majesty, who

shows his anger, for we see a comet ... a warning to make atonement before our new sins are punished with a well-deserved lash..."

The lash in question was wielded by the Grand Vizier Kara Mustapha. He would not relax, he announced, until his horses were stabled under the dome of St Peter's in Rome, and with that objective in mind a Turkish army 250,000-strong began the long march through the Balkans.

By July 1683 the Turks were only hours away from Vienna and blind panic set in. The sight of the Carmelite convent on the Kahlenberg burning told the population just how close the Turks were. Peasants poured into the capital and the nobility began to flee. Surrounded by subjects imploring him not to desert them, Leopold wept and held out a hand to be kissed even as he backed into a carriage. Palace courtiers and servants bolted from the Hofburg in such haste that they neglected to close the gates.

The lives of the 60,000 people left in Vienna rested on a mixed force of 20,000 infantry and armed civilians backed up by artillery of untested quality. The city was enclosed by the walls on three sides, the river took care of the fourth, and the bridge across it was destroyed as the Turks approached. The imperial army, such as it was, was held in reserve further up the

the city by force, but he preferred to wait for a capitulation. It was a mistake. Before then a salvo of rockets from the Kahlenberg signalled the approach of the relief column. As a mixture of Saxons, Swabians, Bavarians and Bohemians charged down the Kahlenberg on 12 September, Polish cavalry executed a brilliant manoeuvre which ended the siege that day.

Leopold was on a boat on the Danube when he learned of the lightning victory. His immediate orders were to postpone any celebrations until he got to Vienna. He was candid about the reason: "It is true I have commanded that I must be the first to enter the city, for I fancy

Danube under the command of Leopold's brother-in-law, Duke Charles of Lorraine. Luckily, King John Sobieski of Poland, recognising that the fall of Vienna would leave the road open to Poland, offered to help.

On 4 September a tremendous explosion destroyed part of the wall near the Hofburg. Thousands of Turks protected their heads with sacks as they scaled the walls crying "Allah! Allah!". They were able to plant two standards on the wall before being driven back. The defenders patched up the hole in the wall with rubble, furniture, wine-presses, mattresses – anything that came to hand.

The Grand Vizier could probably have taken

that otherwise the love of my subjects for me would be diminished, and their affection for others increase."

The Grand Alliance

On the other flank of the empire, the problem was, as usual, France. Louis XIV was determined to win for his son, Philip, the Spanish crown which the Habsburgs had come to regard as family property. England was absolutely opposed to a union between France and Spain, the newly imported King William of Orange

ABOVE: the siege of Vienna.
RIGHT: Prince Eugene, Austria's greatest soldier.

especially so. In the War of the Spanish Succession, the ensuing Grand Alliance between Austria and England was effective, in part due to the military prowess of the English Duke of Marlborough, and the Austrian Prince Eugene. Of course, the English objective was to defeat France, not to win Spain for the Habsburgs, and as soon as the French were beaten, England broke off the alliance. Karl VI, Leopold's successor, therefore did not get Spain, although under the Treaty of Utrecht he was compensated with Spanish possessions – Naples, Milan, the Spanish Netherlands and Sardinia, the last later exchanged for Sicily. The French Philip did get Spain, but only on the condition that he forfeited rights to the French throne.

As if to make up for his disappointment over Spain, Karl introduced what was to become an enduring feature of the Habsburg court in Vienna. Etiquette and ritual followed Spanish custom, and king and courtiers wore Spanish dress. The other preoccupation was to improve on anything the wretched French could do. Fischer von Erlach, the young architect largely responsible for rebuilding Vienna following the siege, conceived the Baroque Schloss Schönbrunn to outdo Versailles. But such extravagance drew attention to the yawning gulf between rich and poor; the disparity was particularly glaring in Bohemia where confiscated land belonging to Protestants had been parcelled out to the Roman Catholic noblility, who were expected to reciprocate with unswerving loyalty to the Habsburgs and not decamp with their estates into the arms of some rival power. As time went by, the Habsburgs had to sweeten the bonds by exempting the nobility from taxation.

A PERFECT MATCH

The Grand Alliance between England and Austria in the War of Spanish Succession created one of history's most famous military partnerships, the Duke of Marlborough, Winston Churchill's ancestor, and little Prince Eugene, destined to become Austria's most famous soldier. Yet the two men could not have been more different. When Marlborough once spotted some of his men apparently leaving the field of battle, he extended an arm and cried out: "Gentlemen, the enemy lies that way." In exactly the same circumstances, indeed during the same battle, Eugene whipped out a gun and shot his men. As a team, however, Marlborough and Eugene were devastating.

The problem of succession

As the empire was held together by the pampered self-interest of the respective nobilities rather than geographical or cultural links, Karl, even at the age of 28, was fretting over his apparent inability to produce the male heir without which the whole thing would very likely fall apart. There was no provision for the throne going to a daughter, so the empress's bed-chamber was stuffed with male charms of the type which could well have been supplied by a witchdoctor. When these failed to work, Karl resorted, in 1713, to the "Pragmatic Sanction", a loophole which enabled him to pro-

mulgate certain laws without reference to the Electoral Diet. In this instance, the Pragmatic Sanction went against all precedent by permitting the crown to pass to a daughter if necessary – a solution that raised a chorus of objection from those countries keen to see the Austrian Empire disintegrate. As Karl was to learn, the willingness of some to turn a blind eye came at a price.

Karl wanted to see Maria Theresa, his threatened heiress, secured as far as possible by a good marriage. The Prussian Crown Prince Frederick was considered, as was a Spanish Bourbon prince, but the 15-year-old archduchess was single-minded about marrying

Franz Stephan, the heir to the Duchy of Lorraine and grandson of the commander at the siege of Vienna. France rubbed its hands at the prospect; it was time to play its Pragmatic Sanction card. The bridegroom would have to surrender his Lorraine inheritance to France. Franz Stephan was appalled at the blackmail. On being told to sign, he thrice picked up the pen, stopped himself, and threw it down. "No renunciation, no archduchess," taunted one of Karl's ministers. He signed.

The couple were married in 1736 and within four years they produced three children, all girls. During those four years, the emperor went

from bad to worse. The Pragmatic Sanction imbroglio dragged him into two disastrous wars. He had grown fat and suffered from gout. His final act was to raise his arms in a gesture of benediction towards the ante-room where Maria Theresa was waiting.

An Empress rules

"I found myself," Maria Theresa wrote of her succession, "without money, without credit, without an army, without experience and knowledge…" Especially without money. The funds in the exchequer stood at 100,000 florins, her army had not been paid for months, and the national debt did not bear thinking about. Fab-

ulously rich subjects who could have settled her financial needs at a stroke were the nobility who paid no taxes and expected things to remain that way. The peasants who did pay tax had already been bled dry. Added to the gloomy economic prognosis was a new phenomenon in European politics: the rise of Prussia under the man once thought a suitable husband, the future Frederick the Great. Frederick had just succeeded his father and was busy studying the map of Europe for opportunities for Prussian aggrandisement. "Silesia is the portion of the imperial heritage to which we have the strongest claim and which is most suitable," he declared to his aides.

Maria Theresa never forgave Frederick for the invasion of Silesia (present-day southern Poland), the opening move in the War of the Austrian Succession. But her geriatric advisers failed to see far worse writing on the wall. France was preparing to dismember the Habsburg empire: "There is no more House of Austria," Cardinal Fleury announced prematurely. The French plan was to give Bohemia and Upper Austria to the Elector of Bavaria, who would then be crowned emperor; Moravia and Upper Silesia to Saxony; Lower Silesia and Glatz to Prussia; and Lombardy to Spain.

In the meantime Maria Theresa gave birth to the child she had been carrying at the time of her succession. Recent Habsburg failure in the matter of male heirs was reversed with spectacular emphasis: the boy, Joseph, was a 7-kg (16-lb) giant at birth and apparently normal in every respect. Clutching the infant, Maria Theresa set off on a last desperate gamble to fend off imminent invasion by both Bavaria and France. Theresa appealed to her Hungarian subjects for help. Her speech, in Latin, was a classic example of playing to ingrained Hungarian chivalry.

The Hungarians voted her six regiments, enough to repel the Bavarians and persuade the French to make peace. Maria Theresa never regained Silesia, but she did retrieve the crown of the Holy Roman Empire. She considered herself ineligible to wear it, and instead her husband was elected emperor in 1745. Their strapping son, Joseph II, was elected "Roman king" in 1764, and the following year became emperor after the death of his father. ❑

LEFT: the formidable Maria Theresa.

Kolschitzky's Coffee

In 1683, the Turkish siege had reduced Vienna to the verge of capitulation. Every day the Viennese commander climbed the tower of St Stephen's to scan the horizon for signs of the relief column. What he saw instead was a Turkish camp larger and more populous than Vienna itself, "crowded not only by soldiers but by the merchants of the East, who thronged thither as to a fair deal in the plunder of the Christians".

The man who was given the dangerous task of crossing Turkish lines to run messages to and from the beleaguered city was a Pole named Kolschitzky. A Turkish speaker, he mingled easily with the Ottomans, cheerfully accepting numerous invitations to stop for coffee. The drink was unknown in 17th-century Vienna, but Kolschitzky had developed a taste for it on his travels. As he sipped at endless cups, he studied the Turkish deployments.

Kolschitzky's observations were passed on to the Duke of Lorraine and King Sobieski, and were to be of inestimable value in the plans drawn up by the Polish king for a lightning cavalry strike. Once the Turks were routed, the besieged population rushed out and fell on the food stores the Turks had left behind. One of the crowd, Kolschitzky knew exactly what he was looking for – sacks of a certain brown bean. Those who saw them asked whether they were best eaten baked, boiled or fried. The Pole knew otherwise and was rewarded for his services with a licence, the first of its kind in the Holy Roman Empire, to open his Kaffee Schrank ("Coffee Cupboard"), later the Blue Bottle in Singerstrasse. The coffee house was born. There was hardly a business deal, illicit romance or diabolical plot in Central Europe thereafter that was not hatched in one of hundreds of imitations.

In the department of diabolical plots, Vienna's Café Central ran true to form in 1913. One of the regulars during an especially cold winter was a Herr Bronstein, who frequently played chess against an opponent noticeable for his bushy moustache. If their true identities had been known, they would not have meant much to the secret police, but their patronage was recalled when news of the Russian Revolution broke. The joke in Vienna was that it had been cooked up in the Café Central. Bronstein was Trotsky; his partner, Stalin.

RIGHT: Turkish soldiers besieging Vienna in 1683 unwittingly introduced coffee to the city.

There were 4,000 coffee houses in Vienna before World War II; today there are some 400. Coffee-house connoisseurs have strong, if often perplexing, views on what constitutes a worthy establishment. Staff with character is important. Attractively-wrapped Amazonian waitresses are considered a plus, but the thoroughbred is a waiter with the right combination of "a harrassed manner and a hint of cynical rapacity". The Bräunerhof has waiters who, it is approvingly said, could try the patience of a saint.

Correct deportment in the august surroundings is essential, and visitors ought to be aware that the Austrians' interest in their coffee "amounts almost

to a scientific discipline, in which every possible combination of milk and coffee is obsessively categorised". Simply to order "a coffee" would be considered unimaginative, if not imbecilic. The progression from pitch black to milky goes through three stages: *Mokka* to *Kapuziner* to *Franziskaner*. Poised somewhere between the last two is the *Melange*, and the tricky choice between a precise measure of milk or a blob of cream. An *Einspanner* is definitely cream, masses of the whipped variety.

Herr Kolschitzky might have persuaded the Turks to go home by serving them the *Kaiser Melange* – black coffee and two egg yolks. A tourist was asked his opinion of the concoction: "Rather..." he began weakly, "no, not rather... *unbelievably* vile." ❏

METTERNICH

Metternich's diplomatic acumen served Austria well in post-Napoleonic Europe,

but heavy-handed repression at home brought rebellion and chaos

Joseph, the boy on whom the hopes of the empire rested, grew up to share the throne with his mother as co-regent. The gulf between them was apparent. She always believed in absolute rule. He was a student of radical French philosophy and wished to revolutionise the entire empire. On becoming Joseph

II he put his liberal theories into practice. The press was given unprecedented freedom, Jews no longer had to identify themselves by wearing yellow stripes and sleeves, and education was made compulsory for all, including women. By the time of his death in 1790, Europe was confronted with what appeared to be the logical conclusion to unfettered liberty, the French Revolution. The only way to avoid that ghastly scenario in Austria amounted to a backlash.

Austria and France were poles apart: a conservative Roman Catholic monarchy versus a brash, atheistic republic. Both were championed at the beginning of the 19th century by young

men who were born within a year of one another in foreign parts. Franz II, the Habsburg emperor, was born in Tuscany, Napoleon in Corsica. Each dreamed of expansive empires; Europe was clearly not big enough for both of them.

Napoleon's occupation of Vienna in 1805 after his lightning victories in Italy was a terrible shock and sent the imperial family packing with all its treasures and archives to the fortress of Olmutz. The stunning French victory over Austria at Austerlitz was handled by Franz with remarkable, although not uncharacteristic, stoicism. A note to his wife read: "A battle was fought today which did not turn out well. I pray you consequently to withdraw from Olmutz to Teschen with everything that belongs to us. I am well."

End of the Holy Roman Empire

Napoleon had crowned himself Emperor of the French in 1804, with the clear intention of appropriating from Franz the symbolic title of Holy Roman Emperor; indeed, after a group of German princes seceded to join him in the Confederation of the Rhine, he controlled much of the Empire's territory. In response, Franz declared that the Holy Roman Empire was finished. He would henceforth be Franz I of Austria, a Habsburg empire which owed nothing to the Holy Roman one. The title which had fomented countless cunning marriages and numerous wars for 1,000 years dropped out of currency as simply as that.

Franz's immediate concern was to check Napoleon before he could do further damage to the redefined empire. Emboldened by French reverses in Spain, Austrian forces mobilised and, against all odds, inflicted a single-handed defeat at Aspern. Franz watched the victory from a nearby hill. He could be as laconic in triumph as he was in despair. All he said after the battle was: "Now we can, I think, go home."

There then emerged in Austrian affairs a man whose first actions in office bore the stamp of his style. Prince Clemens von Metternich bought peace with Napoleon – "the Corsican ogre" – by persuading him to marry Marie

Louise, Franz's daughter. A proxy wedding took place in Vienna in March 1810. It was quintessentially Metternich's doing that, having bought peace with the marriage, Austria then declared war on France.

The Congress of Vienna

Napoleon was, of course, defeated at Waterloo, and immediately afterwards the Austrian, Russian, Prussian and British allies set about carving up his conquests at the Congress of Vienna. Metternich's diplomatic skill secured Austria a generous territorial settlement from the peace conference, acquiring Salzburg and Venice and

imbecile in the clinical sense of the word. With Ferdinand on the throne, Metternich could look forward to running the empire with a free hand. It remained to get Ferdinand on to it and keep him there. In short, Metternich had to preserve the monarchy in order to exploit it.

Assisted by Joseph Sedlnitzky, the Chief of Police, Metternich sought to preserve the existing social and political order with draconian controls. The freedom of the press was swept away and political activity totally prohibited. The effect of the repression on ordinary people was to make them banish serious issues from their minds. They settled for *Gemütlichkeit* and

regaining much of northern Italy. The new order established at the congress proved enduring and helped to ensure relative peace in Europe for several decades.

Metternich had larger ambitions than could be satisfied by the congress settlement, but for the moment it served his purposes to remain dutifully at the foot of the throne and bide his time. A glance into the Hofburg nursery was enough to see that the next-in-line was a totally hopeless case. The heir Ferdinand, everyone agreed, was a friendly little fellow but an

LEFT: Joseph II is crowned.
ABOVE: Napoleon rides through.

THE PRICE OF HOSPITALITY

While Vienna benefited from the prestige and fast-flowing money of 100,000 visitors and princely delegates to the 1815 Congress, the cost and complications of putting up all the reigning sovereigns, their families and servants were awesome. The guests were fed each day at 40 banqueting tables, and a transport pool of several hundred carriages was kept in readiness in the Hofburg palace stables. Many of the guests had quirks: the Czar Alexander had some unexplained need for a regular supply of large blocks of ice to his room; the king of Württemberg, too fat to reach the table, required a semi-circular hole cut out of it to accommodate his stomach.

the trivial diversions of the so-called Bieder-meier age. Superficially, it was the emergence of a prosperous, urban middle class swept along by crazes for the waltz, floral wallpaper, beer and sausages. No fewer than 65 factories churned out pianos in Vienna, which then had a population of 200,000.

In the spring of 1831, Metternich blandly announced that there was no reason why Ferdinand should not marry (he thought it would make him more plausible Imperial material). He had the perfect wife standing by. She was the extremely plain and virtuous Princess Marianna of Sardinia. On clapping eyes on her imminent

plenty of it. The Family Law promulgated in 1839 was breathtaking. It first defined the family as all the archdukes (plus wives and widows) and all the archduchesses descended in the male line from Maria Theresa. They were to observe a code of conduct which amounted to undebatable obedience to the emperor's will. If they failed to do so they would forfeit all imperial honours, titles, privileges – and income. If they married without the emperor's permission, they lost all rights for themselves and their children.

The ordinary citizens of Austria were hardly better off than the besieged members of the

husband, Marianna turned white. Even the doddering Emperor Franz was heard to mutter at the wedding, "May God have mercy."

Foreign ambassadors were aghast at the prospect of having to do business with the new emperor. The cleverest thing he ever said, one of them remarked, was "I am the emperor and I want dumplings." Yet Vienna genuinely loved him; he was such a guileless, good-natured antidote to Metternich and his secret police.

Repression and revolution

With the dim-witted emperor in his pocket, Metternich could use the emperor's personal power as his own, so he made sure he had

family. Writers were the first to stick their heads above the parapet, and they did so in 1845 with a petition against censorship. Their defiance broke the false tranquillity of Biedermeier and people took to the streets. The National Guard was called out, but the students of Vienna kept up the pressure. The Paris Revolution and the numerous other revolts of 1848 inspired the population to stage a general uprising. Metternich quickly packed and escaped, reputedly hidden in a laundry basket, to England.

It became clear to the Habsburgs that their survival depended on more ingenuity than Ferdinand could bring to the task. The whole clan assembled in his apartment in the early morning of 2 December 1848 and told him he would have to go. A deed of abdication was put before him. Franz Joseph, who stood beside him to take over the throne, had just turned 18. Ferdinand, who had once complained that governing was easy, "what is difficult is to sign one's name", took up a pen and laboriously scratched out his name.

A monarch of the old school

Franz Joseph reigned from 1848 to 1916, a Habsburg record. It was only with the humiliating help of 200,000 Russian troops that he restored order in his unruly inheritance, and for 68 years thereafter, a period of momentous change in Europe, he mostly rowed against the tide, attempting to preserve his empire by repression although he was occasionally prepared to use negotiation and concession.

On paper, the empire included nine kingdoms, and in time-honoured Habsburg fashion he was in every instance the king as well. This was at a time when groups of people who spoke the same language and had a common culture were beginning to think of themselves as separate nations who, if they wanted a king at all, preferred to make their own arrangements.

The Austrian empire was held together by a number of pins, primarily bureaucracy, the army and the German language. But this last was double-edged. The feeling among the urban classes that they were, or had become, "German" was to drive a wedge between them and the more conservative peasants who clung to their ethnic roots. As time went by, the rift grew ever wider. Ultimately, it gave Hitler an excuse for the Austrian Anschluss and the seizure of the mainly urban and industrial (and therefore "German") Czech Sudeten. All these people, Hitler said, were really Germans. Some agreed with him.

The seeds of Hitler's theory were sown in Maria Theresa's reign, when the rise of Prussia under Frederick the Great offered the German Austrians an alternative spiritual home. Prior to that, Germany only existed in a nebulous sense as a jumble of states that could not singly or even collectively hold a candle to the mighty Habsburgs. As the 19th century progressed and nationalist pressures increased within the empire, German Austrian intellectuals looked increasingly to a solution involving incorporation with Prussia and, later, with Bismarck's powerful Germany. This *deutschnational* or *grossdeutsch* solution appealed across classes and political parties, but was not to reflect the majority view until after 1918.

The Austrian empire, on the other hand, was gradually ceding its Germanic nature to Hungary and to Slavic influence in the east, or so people thought. Following the loss of Lombardy to the French in 1859, renewed demands for Hungarian independence pushed Franz Joseph into conciliatory mode. However,

the establishment of a parliament, with 85 Hungarian representatives, failed to placate the rebels. After another military defeat, this time against Prussia at Sadowa, had further weakened Austria and further enhanced Hungarian claims, a compromise known as the *Ausgleich* was reached. Hungary and Austria, which is to say Hungary as opposed to the rest of the empire, would each have their own parliaments, however perfunctory. The new set-up was to be called the Dual Monarchy of Austria-Hungary.

Yet the army, foreign affairs and finance would remain under Austrian control. In other words, there was still a pyramid and the emperor was at the top of it. ❑

LEFT: the 1848 Revolution was crushed by troops.
RIGHT: an Austrian passport in Franz Joseph's reign.

A DYNASTY IN RETREAT

Increasingly determined nationalist forces, and the related outbreak of World War I,
destroyed the old European order and, with it, the unwieldy Austro-Hungarian Empire

The late 19th century was a time of rapid change in Austria, and particularly in Vienna. The demolition of the city walls in 1857 ushered in the construction of the Ringstrasse – a magnificent boulevard lined with fabulous buildings including a new City Hall, opera, theatres and stock exchange. By the 1870s the city had been transformed into a modern metropolis, with much-needed infrastructural development – including major improvements in sanitation and drainage, the building of several bridges across the Danube, and the introduction of a city tram service.

On the negative side, there was a marked rise in anti-semitism in both Vienna and the wider Austrian German population. The city Jews were blamed for the traumatic financial crash of 1873; through the 1880s and 1890s, the influential and popular Karl Lueger managed to give anti-semitism a kind of mainstream respectability, at first from his position as head of the Christian Social party, and later as mayor of Vienna. Despite this, *fin de siècle* Vienna was a colourful city with a flourishing artistic and intellectual community – Mahler, Klimt and Freud all lived here at this time.

Trouble at the top

Meanwhile, back at the Hofburg, Emperor Franz Joseph's marriage to a vivacious Bavarian Wittelsbach called Elisabeth had been the 22nd between the two families and there was some concern about the blood running too thin, especially when their son Rudolf proved a sickly child. By the age of 10, however, Rudolf had banished doubts about any congenital flaws. He was bright, articulate and said to have excellent manners. "I hear you exercise yourself with history," he remarked to an eminent historian, "history is my favourite subject too, but I have not got further than Servius Tullius." At 14, he unsettled his tutor with opinions which did not bode well for a future emperor.

LEFT: Emperor Franz Joseph, longest-reigning Habsburg.
RIGHT: Rudolf, his problematic son.

"The aristocracy and the clergy manipulated the masses," he wrote in an essay, "through enforced ignorance and superstition."

Not many years later he was party to an anonymous pamphlet portentously entitled "The Austrian Aristocracy and its Constitutional Function. A Warning to Aristocratic

Youth". The warning was, bluntly, that they were stupid, lazy and no competition for the bourgeoisie. But Rudolf continued to collect compliments from all sides. "Most easy to get on with," Queen Victoria of England noted.

An ill-fated marriage

Rudolf's marriage to Stephanie of Coburg-Gotha (the daughter of King Leopold II of Belgium) got off to a good start, and by the end of a year he brought himself round to saying that he loved her. He was genuinely pleased when in 1883 she gave birth to a daughter. But Stephanie was evidently a poor conversationalist, and the search for more convivial company steered Rudolf towards what Franz Joseph considered the worst conceivable circle of friends and drinking companions – journalists, many of whom were Jews.

Although Franz Joseph's creation of the Dualism with Hungary was an implicit acknowledgement of the loss of German supremacy to the Prussians, Rudolf felt much more strongly that the empire's future lay in the east. Like his mother, he felt a strong affinity with the Hungarians and they, sensing that, sounded him out on the possibility of assuming the Hungarian throne. As Franz Joseph happened to be the reigning Apostolic King of Hungary, the

slightest suggestion of any such thing was dynastic treason of the worst possible kind. Under the strain of being party to this kind of talk, Rudolf cracked up.

Rudolf's breakdown was apparent to his wife. "Not only was his health undermined," she wrote, "but his restlessness had also increased." The word "restlessness" may have been her euphemism for the pursuit of other women.

Rudolf, Mary and Mayerling

The marriage disintegrated, although in public they kept up appearances. They thus appeared together at a reception given by the German ambassador on 27 January 1889 in honour of Kaiser Wilhelm II's birthday. In a blaze of hindsight because of what followed, everyone present had something to say about the occasion. The British ambassador's wife thought Rudolf looked "dejected, sad, and only just fought back his tears". Someone else remembered Rudolf bowing with exaggerated deference to the emperor. Everyone claimed to remember the Baroness Mary Vetsera. They argued about which was more eye-catching: the ripe "development" of one so young – she was 17 – or the seductive sway when she walked.

Mary Vetsera was the daughter of the Baroness Helene Vetsera, *née* Baltazzi, who was determined that Mary should do better than marry a lightly-titled obscure diplomat as she herself had done. Once launched into Vienna's social whirl, it was inevitable that Mary and Rudolf would eventually cross paths. Such a meeting in fact occurred at the Burgtheater in October 1888, three months before Kaiser Wilhelm's birthday party. This was an introduction her mother would not have sought to develop. Rudolf was the crown prince, but as long as the apparently robust Stephanie lived, he was in no position to marry Mary. Some weeks after that meeting, Mary was approached by Countess Marie Larisch-Wallersee, Rudolf's cousin and occasional procuress. Mary was soon afterwards smuggled into Rudolf's rooms at the Hofburg.

Shortly afterwards, Rudolf organised a shooting trip. He invited some friends along. They would meet up at his shooting lodge, Mayerling, southwest of the captial. What he didn't tell the others was that Mary Vetsera was also invited. His brother-in-law, Prince Philip of Coburg, and Count Hoyos were Rudolf's shooting guests. There was no sign of Mary's presence when they arrived at Mayerling, and Rudolf said nothing to indicate that she had arrived at the lodge.

Rudolf and Philip were due to return to Vienna overnight for a family dinner, while Hoyos was to stay at Mayerling – not in the lodge itself but in a cottage about 500 yards from it. Rudolf and Philip would be back in time for breakfast. Rudolf then cried off. He said he did not feel strong enough for the journey and asked Philip to extend his apologies both to the emperor and Stephanie, who was expecting him to join her.

Loschek got up, dressed, and made his way to the stables. He had not gone far when he heard two shots. Racing back to the lodge, he could smell powder. The door was locked; he managed to smash a hole large enough to reach in and unlock the door from the inside.

"What an appalling sight," he said in a memorandum taken down by his son many years afterwards. "Rudolf, fully dressed, was lying on his bed, dead; Mary Vetsera, likewise fully dressed, on her bed. Rudolf's army revolver was by his side. The two had not gone to bed at all… It was clear at first sight that Rudolf first shot Mary Vetsera and then killed himself."

Philip having left, Rudolf and Hoyos sat down to dinner. After Hoyos went off to the cottage, Mary emerged from hiding. When Rudolf and Mary withdrew to the bedroom, it was with instructions to the valet Loschek not to allow anyone in, not even the emperor.

Staying in the next room, Loschek could hear Rudolf and Mary talking late into the night but not what they were saying. His next recollection was of Rudolf walking into his room fully dressed at about 5.40 am with the request that he get horses and a carriage ready right away.

LEFT: Baroness Mary Vetsera.
ABOVE: the Crown Prince with Bratfisch, his coachman.

The Crown Princess Stephanie printed Rudolf's farewell letter to her in her memoirs. "Dear Stephanie: You are rid of my presence and plague; be happy in your own way. Be good to the poor little girl [their daughter] who is the only thing that remains of me. Give my last regards to all friends… I am going calmly to my death which alone can save my good name. Embracing you most warmly, your loving Rudolf."

A controversial marriage

Franz Joseph's heir had been shot out from under him, so to speak, and in 1898 the unthinkable happened to his beloved though frequently absent Sisi, as he called Elisabeth. While on hol-iday in Switzerland with her lady-in-waiting she was assassinated by a half-crazed Italian anar-chist, who, deliberately bumping into the empress, slid a sharpened file through her rib-cage. Sisi did not appear to feel it, but it had gone through her heart.

Franz Joseph never got over the shock of his wife's death, but ever the conscientious emper-or he focused his attention on his remaining heir, his nephew the Archduke Franz Ferdinand. Of particular concern were his marital prospects, which would clearly have to conform to the still active Family Law.

locket of the kind in which lovers kept minia-ture portraits of their dearest. Isabella prised open the locket and stared at the portrait in total disbelief. It was Countess Sophie Chotek von Chotkova und Wognin, her lady-in-waiting.

Sophie was sacked on the spot, and the emperor would not hear of Franz Ferdinand marrying her. Her family had a respectable Bohemian background and her father was a Czech diplomat but that was not enough, and Franz Joseph wheeled out the Family Law. Eventually, under pressure from Pope Leo XIII, Kaiser Wilhelm and Czar Nicholas, he agreed to a morganatic marriage, which meant that a

The Archduke Friedrich and Archduchess Isabella's bevy of lovely daughters had the nec-essary qualifications, so when Franz Ferdinand made a practice of spending weekends at their Pressburg estate the only question in the arch-duchess's mind, and a nagging one, was not knowing which of the daughters he preferred. He seemed to be remarkably even-handed in dealing with them, but Isabella liked to think it was her eldest, Marie Christine.

The solution to the mystery seemed at hand when Franz Ferdinand inadvertently left his watch behind at Pressburg. Instead of a normal chain, it was attached to a string of the trinkets he collected and one of them was seen to be a

wife would not assume her husband's title, rank or privileges, nor would any children. The emperor boycotted the wedding, but relented slightly in promoting Sophie to princess of Hohenberg. The title was small compensation for slights at court, such as not being allowed to share her husband's box at the theatre or sit next to him at dinner if more authentic Habsburgs were present. Despite these restrictions, Franz Ferdinand was delighted with his choice.

The road to Sarajevo

Franz Ferdinand's preoccupation while he waited to step into his uncle's shoes was to make up for the loss of power to Prussia in the west by consolidating the empire's hold in the east, in particular on Bosnia and Herzegovina, acquired from Turkey at the 1878 Congress of Berlin. He envisaged a multiplication of the Dual System with Hungary so that other parts of the empire could enjoy a certain degree of self-rule within the umbrella of empire.

The ironic flaw in Franz Ferdinand's thinking was that he had enemies who believed it might work, that scattered peoples would settle for limited autonomy and drop demands for full independence. These misgivings were especially acute among extremists in Bosnia's large Serb population who wanted full independence

entice him to visit their shops. Franz Ferdinand fell for the ruse and decided to visit the antique shops of Sarajevo that very day. At one point during their walk to the bazaar they passed close to, but probably did not notice, a thin-lipped, pale youth who was not cheering.

Gavrilo Princip was 19 years old, born the fourth of nine children to the postman in the village of Oblej in the wild, mountainous region separating Bosnia from the Dalmatian coast. An ethnic Serb, he was by nationality Austro-Hungarian and had been to school in Sarajevo. In 1912 he had gone off to live in the Serbian capital, Belgrade, and had returned to Sarajevo

in order to break away and join up with Serbia to form Greater Serbia. The archduke was aware of rumblings in Bosnia and was therefore delighted to receive an invitation to observe military manoeuvres which were to be held there in the summer of 1914.

The royal party arrived at Ilidze on 25 June 1914. The trip had been publicised well in advance and the resort was festooned with flags and bunting. Fully aware of Franz Ferdinand's antique collection, the Sarejevo dealers had craftily decorated his hotel with their wares to

only four weeks prior to the archduke's visit. Only a handful of people knew that his time in Belgrade had been spent with the Black Hand, Serbian nationalists who, in the interest of a Greater Serbia, had made the assassination of Franz Ferdinand their top priority. Princip's mission in Sarajevo was to do just that, three days later on Sunday 28 June, the anniversary of Turkey's victory over Serbia at Kosovo in 1389. The choice of this date was to signify a recovery from that defeat.

The first attempt on the archduke's life that Sunday was bungled by one of Princip's accomplices. Franz Ferdinand saw the bomb tossed at the imperial carriage as they made

LEFT: removing the bodies from Mayerling.
ABOVE: Karl Lueger, Vienna's mayor, 1904.

their way to the civil ceremony at the town hall and deflected it into the road, where it injured a handful of spectators. With considerable *sang-froid* the outraged duke carried on to the reception, where the mayor, completely thrown by the assassination attempt, could not bring himself to deviate from the prepared text of his speech.

Franz Ferdinand's reply showed more command of the situation: "It gives me special pleasure to accept the assurances of your unshakable loyalty and affection for His Majesty, our Most Gracious Emperor and King. I thank you cordially, Mr Mayor, for the

resounding ovations with which the population received me and my wife, the more so since I see in them an expression of pleasure over the failure of the assassination attempt..."

War is triggered

While the Princess Sophie went upstairs to talk to a delegation of Muslim ladies, the archduke received local dignitaries in the vestibule. He was assured that the bomber had been arrested. Under the circumstances, however, aides suggested that the archduke should take an alternative route to the city museum, the finale to his tour. Inexplicably, they failed to inform the driver.

After the first bomb attack the assassins further down the route either thought the job had been done or panicked; in any case they scattered – all but Princip. Seeing another chance, he stepped forward, drew his revolver, and at a range of 1.5 metres (5 ft) fired two shots. One hit Franz Ferdinand in the neck, the second hit Sophie in the stomach. Within minutes they were dead.

Not far beneath the outpouring of public and family grief over the couple's death were intimations of cataclysmic consequences. In saying privately that "world peace will not be any worse off", the Italian foreign minister could not have been more wrong. An Italian journal took a different line: "Hail to the gun of Princip and to the bomb of Cabrinovic." The author was the young Benito Mussolini.

The assassins were quickly rounded up and under questioning revealed the part played in the assassination by senior Serbian officials and the Black Hand in particular. On 23 July Vienna presented Serbia with an ultimatum: no more anti-imperial activities on its soil and the arrest of one of the implicated officials. The official in question was arrested but even more quickly "escaped", never to be found again. On 28 July, exactly one month after Franz Ferdinand's death, Austria declared war.

The stage was now set for a major European conflict, as the alliance system swung into action. War on Serbia brought in Russia, which was pledged to defend the interests of the Slavs. In mobilising against Austria, Russia triggered the Austro-Germanic mutual defence pact of 1879. Germany duly declared war on Russia and, knowing that this would activate an alliance between Russia and France, decided to get in first with an attack on France. Great Britain was still technically neutral, but when Germany invaded Belgium in order to attack the French flank, Britain could not countenance the threat to the Channel coast and threw in its lot with France and Russia. At the end, with the United States also drawn in, the body count was some 10 million with another 20 million seriously wounded.

As far as the Habsburgs were concerned, World War I effectively spelled the end. ❏

LEFT: Archduke Franz Ferdinand and Sophie coming down the town hall steps in Sarajevo.
RIGHT: the archduke's blood-spattered uniform.

ANSCHLUSS AND HITLER

The Great Depression, incorporation into the Third Reich, and the ravages of World War II made the 1930s and '40s a traumatic period for Austria

A large number of Austrians sprang a surprise on the architects of the new Europe after World War I. They did not want independence, not on their own; they wanted to be incorporated either into the German Weimar Republic or in some kind of union with Bohemia and Moravia, which the architects insisted belonged to the new Czechoslovakia. Others, mainly the land-owning Roman Catholic peasants, did not want democracy if it meant the country being run by the Social Democrats, who were seen to be against the Church and against private property.

To a considerable degree the division was "Red Vienna" versus the rest of the country, and both sides formed paramilitary organisations, the pro-socialist Schutzbund against the Roman Catholic Heimwehr, one of whose leaders was Goering's brother-in-law.

The impasse had not really been resolved when the Great Depression took hold in 1931. It was particularly severe in Austria because no adequate substitutes had yet developed for its former industrial base, now part of Czechoslovakia, or its mineral and agricultural wealth, which had vanished with the loss of Hungary. The army and the Schutzbund fought a pitched battle in February 1934. The fighting lasted four days, the army won, the Social Democrats were banned. Austrian democracy had lasted all of 15 years.

Bad allies

To Austria's most notorious émigré across the border in Germany, these developments were excellent news. By suppressing democracy and the labour movement, the right-wing Chancellor Engelbert Dollfuss unwittingly removed the natural opposition to pro-Nazi Austrians, who were banging the drum of annexation to Germany more loudly than ever, saying it was the only hope of setting the economy right. Adolf

Hitler agreed completely. Dollfuss saw the threat to Austria's independence and sought to safeguard it with a foreign alliance. He could hardly have chosen a worse ally – Benito Mussolini.

Dollfuss did not live to see the gravity of his error. He was assassinated by Nazis in 1934; Hitler and Mussolini reached their understand-

ing two years later. Dollfuss's successor as chancellor, Kurt Schuschnigg, tried to appease the Austrian Nazis with the offer of a couple of ministries in the government. Hitler was adamant that one of these should be the Ministry of State Security, which he proposed to hand over to Austria's leading Nazi (after himself), Artur Seyss-Inquart. Schuschnigg was summoned to Berchtesgaden and made to understand that he had no choice in the matter.

Schuschnigg handled the meeting with a tempestuous Hitler with quiet aplomb. When he reached for a cigarette, Hitler screamed that smoking was not permitted in his presence. Schuschnigg lit up anyway and casually flicked

LEFT: Austria's most infamous son.
RIGHT: a poster advertising a Hitler speech in Vienna in 1938.

the match across Hitler's table. On returning to Vienna, Schuschnigg lifted the ban on the socialist parties and announced that Austria was definitely in favour of democracy and independence. He invited the country to confirm that commitment in a plebiscite to be held on 13 March 1938.

Hitler did not want any such damaging signal to reach the outside world. Two days before the plebiscite, Germany closed its borders with Austria. The following day, Hitler invaded.

> **THE OSTMARK RETURNS**
>
> Austria gave up even its name on being absorbed into the Reich, reverting to "Ostmark", as it had been known under Charlemagne. Hitler knew a thing or two about history and, especially, conquerors.

other quarters was different. The Catholic Bench of Bishops under Cardinal Innitzer issued a proclamation praising the "splendid services of Nazism in the social field" and calling on all Christians to "proclaim themselves as Germans for the German Reich".

For the majority, however, a few weeks of Anschluss were enough to convince them that, as demonstrated by the way a generous dosage of Slavic blood had altered their facial features, they were not perhaps quite

Predictably, the Jews were the first victims of the invasion. A British newspaper described scenes in Leopoldstadt, where the majority of Vienna's 200,000 Jews lived. "Now day after day, Nazi storm-troopers, surrounded by jostling, jeering and laughing mobs of 'golden Viennese hearts', dragged Jews from shops, offices and homes, men and women, put scrubbing brushes in their hands, splashed them well with acid and made them go down on their knees."

Strong reactions

From the moment of Hitler's entry into Vienna and for weeks afterwards, more than 100 people a day committed suicide. The reaction in

so German after all. "The sweep of the Nazi scythe continued to cut down ruthlessly the flower of the intellectual and professional life in Vienna," the British report continued, "impatient to destroy the last traces of that cultured civilisation which for 500 years had marked out the distinction between Austria and Germany." A great number of Jews and anti-Nazis managed to escape, but within the first 10 days of Nazi occupation 90,000 Austrians were rounded up; most of them ended up in Dachau and Buchenwald.

The country went to war in 1939 as an integral part of Germany, and while the loyalty of the Austrian officer corps to the Third Reich was considered suspect, Austrians were conscripted into the army like everyone else.

Little is said about Austrian resistance, the nature of which varied according to which group was responsible. Communists on the left and monarchists on the right both attempted active resistance; socialists in the middle were more inclined to be passive. Factory workers were encouraged to compete to see who could do their jobs worst, and the Vienna fire brigade managed to achieve such a high level of incompetence that the Gestapo transported more than 700 of its members to a firing range to watch two of the most hopeless cases being shot.

issued orders for the dissolution of the SS when it was learned that the putsch in Germany had failed. The incarcerated commanders managed to get themselves released and immediately ordered arrests. Many executions followed.

Szokoll, the officer who had "dissolved" the SS, not only survived the reprisals but managed to get himself promoted to the rank of major in the Wehrmacht. As such, he produced forged postings and contrived other tricks which resulted in packing the Wehrmacht ranks in Vienna with secret resistance sympathisers. As the end of the war approached, the idea was that these units would coordinate with whichever of

The various resistance groups gradually pooled their resources, a process accelerated by the Moscow Declaration of 1943 which said that whether Austria was judged after the war to have been willingly on Nazism's side or forced on to it would be determined by "her own contribution to her own liberation". Undercover agents in Vienna took the brave gamble of snatching a number of senior Nazi commanders and locking them up in the former Imperial War Ministry on the Ringstrasse. A Captain Szokoll had even

the Allied armies arrived to liberate Vienna and attack the SS divisions. In the event, the Russians got to Vienna first and the plot failed when one of the Austrians lost his nerve.

Nevertheless, Vienna was promptly liberated. The Allies partitioned Austria into four zones, Vienna having a bit of each of them. The harsh attitude adopted by the Soviet troops was one of the explanations offered for the poor communist showing in the elections held in November 1945: four seats out of 165. The Allied victory had persuaded people that they would rather be Austrians than Germans; meeting the Russian troops evidently persuaded them that they'd rather be in the Western camp. ❏

LEFT: dismantling a border post between Austria and Germany following Anschluss in 1938.
ABOVE: German troops on the Ringstrasse, 1938.

AUSTRIA IS FREE

*The post-war period began uncertainly, but the subsequent decades have
seen Austria emerge as a prosperous, stable and democratic nation*

For the first decade of the Cold War there was considerable concern about Austria's ability to stay neutral. Russia had shown in Czechoslovakia that the Iron Curtain could be lifted, moved west, and dropped again – with a new acquisition squirming behind it. In 1955, however, Molotov announced that the

Russians would evacuate Austria on receiving adequate guarantees that there would be no future Anschluss between Austria and Germany. These were quickly given and Austria was again independent, as the Second Republic. This may have been effected just in time. Events in Hungary the following year revealed a very different mood in Moscow.

On 15 May 1955, the *Staatsvertrag* (State Treaty) was signed in the marble hall of the Upper Belvedere Palace, and displayed from the balcony to jubilant crowds below. In October the four-power occupation forces withdrew and the Austrian parliament unanimously passed a constitutional amendment establishing Austria's permanent neutrality. This has become a matter of controversy since the fall of the Iron Curtain in 1989, but then served the all-important purpose of reassuring the Russians. It stood the country in good stead in 1956 when 180,000 Hungarians, fleeing from Soviet suppression of the revolution, streamed over the border and were generously accommodated.

Stability and corruption

From the start, the Second Republic showed a strong determination to learn from recent political history, and in particular from the fatal dispute between the Conservative Christian right and the Social Democratic left that had led to civil war in the 1930s and had paved the way for Nazism. Although the system is now showing signs of strain, the *Sozialpartnerschaft* (Social Partnership) was for 40 years a highly effective device for reconciling the interests of capital and labour. Vital issues such as wages and prices were resolved informally before they could become a matter of open political dispute, and the government accepted the agreed compromise. Strikes were so rare in Austria they could often be counted in minutes per year.

This stability was also reflected in government, where coalitions between the Austrian People's Party (OVP) and the Socialist Party of Austria (SPO) lasted until 1966. With so long a period in power, it was inevitable that the coalition partners would carve out their own fiefdoms in the state sector and *Parteibuch* (party membership) or at least sympathy, was often a determinant factor of employment. At first this didn't matter too much, since the more cynical burghers could simply join the party with the best patronage in the desired area of employment, but gradually cronyism and corruption began to pervade the system.

On the whole the Socialists tended to be more corrupt, a legacy of the lax rule of the "Sun-King" Bruno Kreisky, who came to power in 1970 and was chancellor for 13 years. Kreisky modernised Austria's image abroad and brought in technocrats whose ideological allegiance, if any, was more influenced by mammon than Socialist principle. Eventually the cult of greed engulfed the upper echelons of the party, Kreisky's vice-chancellor and erstwhile anointed heir (Hannes Androsch) actually ending up before the courts for tax evasion. Other scandals erupted with monotonous regularity under Kreisky's successors: the building of a new general hospital for Vienna cost the taxpayer 21 billion Austrian Schillings, far too much of which was kickbacks and illegal payments, as a decade-long court case revealed. Politicians were then found to have been implicated in an insurance scam involving the

International prestige

Despite the deteriorating ethics of his party, Kreisky raised Austria's standing in the world by making Vienna a centre of international diplomacy, beginning with the Strategic Arms Limitation Talks in 1979. The International Atomic Energy Authority had been set up in Vienna in 1957 and in 1967 the United Nations Industrial Development Organisation was to follow, making it the third "UNO city" after New York and Geneva. A special Vienna International Centre was created (1979) beyond the Danube at a cost of 700 billion Schillings and now caters for some 3,000 international civil

deliberate sinking of a freighter with considerable loss of life, and also in the illegal export of arms to Iran. Worst of all from the point of view of the credibility of democratic politics, a general secretary of the Socialist Party was found to have abolished tax-free payments for everyone in the party except himself, and to have avoided tax on 1,800,000 Austrian Schillings. He had plenty of imitators in the regions who awarded themselves sinecures and salaries for invisible input of time or labour.

LEFT: Bruno Kreisky, chancellor from 1970 to 1983.
ABOVE: Jimmy Carter and Leonid Brezhnev at the SALT talks in Vienna, 1979.

servants. Vienna also hosts the Organisation of Petroleum Exporting Countries (OPEC), which first made it the target of terrorist attack in 1975, when the delegates were held hostage and two people were killed.

Nor did Kreisky's pro-Palestinian policy spare Vienna from Palestinian terrorists, who murdered a city councillor in 1981 and bombed the synagogue, killing two. In 1985 a bloody attack was launched on the El Al desk at Schwechat International Airport. On the other hand, the status of the city was further enhanced with the establishment (1986) of the Organization for Security and Co-operation in Europe, which was set up following the Helsinki agreements designed to give human rights activists in the Eastern Bloc more leverage and to draw the communist governments into a continuing dialogue on the issue.

Modern times

Corruption and terrorism are hardly peculiar to Austria, and these isolated incidents did not alter the basic peacefulness, stability and residual piety of a country one pope had called "the island of the blessed". The actual experience of the average citizen from the 1960s to the 1980s was one of steadily increasing living standards, price stability being guaranteed by tying the

worries about human rights preoccupying outsiders. For example, an attack was made on the practice of taking an early pension with full benefits. However, elections in November 2002, which saw a substantial rise in the Peoples's Party vote and a fall in that of the Freedom Party, left future developments unclear.

Many countries would no doubt like to have the problems that Austria has; it is a fact that people who have enjoyed perks and privileges over a long period come to see themselves as entitled to them as of right, so that the removal, say, of a "thirteenth" or even "fourteenth" month of a bureaucrat's salary produces disproportionate

Schilling to the Deutschmark. Austria entered the European Union in 1995 with a robust economy and became its fifth most prosperous member, by 1999 almost level pegging with Germany in terms of per capita GDP. Austria has to come to terms with a number of unpalatable realities, including the relatively high cost of its social net, which threatens its competitiveness, and the ever-growing number of longer-living pensioners with a decreasing workforce to pay for them. The conservative coalition of People's Party and Freedom Party *(see opposite)*, formed early in 2000 to a chorus of abuse from EU partners, made itself unpopular domestically on bread-and-butter issues that had little to do with the

indignation. During this period of adjustment, older Austrians in particular are having to come to terms also with the carefully nurtured half-truth of their nation having been "Hitler's first victims" and to understand that it has to be tempered with a perspective that includes the other half-truth of "Hitler's willing accomplices".

So while the last two decades of the 20th century were, on the whole, economically successful, they were also a time when the nation suffered repeated traumatic shocks as the past came back to haunt it.   ❑

ABOVE: the European Union colours projected onto a concert hall in Klagenfurt

Waldheim and Haider

Towards the end of negotiations with the ambassadors of the occupying powers before the State Treaty was signed in 1955, the Austrian delegation succeeded in having a reference to Austria's own responsibility for participation in Hitler's war removed from the proposed text. From this moment on, the convenient myth of Austria as "Hitler's first victim" became a support for the Second Republic's legitimacy, but also a future diplomatic and political liability.

When Kurt Waldheim, the ex-General Secretary of the United Nations, was elected President of Austria in 1986, some curious omissions in his campaign biography prompted a closer look at his wartime record (he had been an intelligence officer in a part of Yugoslavia notorious for Nazi atrocities). While Waldheims's lapses of memory and professed ignorance of events such as the deportation of Jews suggested (as one commentator acidly put it) that he must have been the "worst informed intelligence officer in history", more revealing was his assumed or actual incomprehension of the qualitative distinction between Nazi aggression and its opponents. This incomprehension was epitomised in his exculpatory remark "I merely did my duty". The resultant scandal revealed the price that Austria (which now began hastily to make payments to Israel, years after West Germany had done so) was obliged to pay for avoiding the unvarnished truth about the past.

President Waldheim became an isolated figure, shunned by Austria's European neighbours and placed on the American watch-list. Yet there was no concrete evidence that he had participated in atrocities and the Americans were unable or unwilling to supply evidence to justify their action. On the other hand, Waldheim's inability to see the dimensions of his problem and his miserably self-serving attempt to identify the country with his own moral ambivalence, placed Austria in an impossible position.

On the domestic political scene, the Waldheim affair coincided with the beginning of the meteoric rise of the Freedom Party (FPO) under Jörg Haider. After the war, its predecessor party had been set up to bring ex-Nazis into the democratic process, but had also inherited a wing of old-fashioned free-market liberals. With considerable brilliance and unscrupulous populist rhetoric, Haider

fashioned a new and powerful coalition out of these elements. He carefully played on the self-righteous rejection of Nazi-era guilt by some of the older generation, and widespread (if completely hypocritical) resentment against "immigrants", a particularly emotive issue following the fall of the Iron Curtain in 1989. The FPO vote increased under his leadership from just 5.5 percent in 1986 to 27.2 percent in 1999, when the party entered government in coalition with the People's Party (OVP), which had exactly the same voter share.

The entry of a far-right party into government provoked Austria's EU partners into a policy of sanctions against the country. Haider's history of

praising aspects of Nazi rule, including the statement made in 1991 that "the Third Reich had a decent employment policy", caused great concern. But the EU seemed unclear as to what its hasty tactic was designed to achieve, given that the coalition government was the result of legitimate elections. In 2000, Haider resigned from leadership of the party, and the EU retreated and dropped the sanctions. However the position changed again in 2002, when disagreements within the Freedom Party led to a break-up of the coalition. In subsequent elections to the Federal Parliament, the People's Party increased their share of the vote to 42 percent, while the Freedom Party's share fell to just 10 percent. ❑

RIGHT: Jörg Haider, ex-leader of the Freedom Party.

Durch ein hur betrogn
beim sein Macht aus
zogn, ward geblendt
namb bösslich Endt.

Fleischerei

Hercules verbrant
an dem kleid welch
es im sein weib het
gschickt zur freit

THE AUSTRIANS

The Austrian national identity is complex. It has a fragmented historical background that is rich in its ethnic and cultural diversity

L ike all nation states, Austria is the product of diverse geopolitical developments and "Austrian" is a concept encompassing historical, cultural and ethnic diversity. The most distinctively individual province of the country is Vorarlberg, whose population is largely of Alemannic origin (with a second influx from the Valais in the 14th century), speaking a dialect that is similar to Schweizerdeutsch.

It is not therefore very surprising that many Vorarlbergians wanted to join Switzerland after World War I. The core population of "German Austrians", however, are mostly the descendants of ancient migrants from Bavaria, who arrived from the 8th century onwards: it was their tongue that established itself as the language of the Austrian territories.

As in Bavaria, this Austrian version of South (or "High") German has a number of idiosyncrasies – enough to justify the two or three "Austrian-German" dictionaries and phrasebooks published for the enlightenment of tourists from North Germany. This language has also been influenced, as has Austrian culture, by six centuries of Habsburg empire-building. The standard German spoken from the North Sea to the Alps is thus mingled with corruptions of, or phrases from, French, Italian, Hungarian and Slav languages, to name but a few.

A rich diversity

Modern Austria still contains a small number of ethnic minorities, the largest and oldest being that of the Slovenes (about 20,000) in Southern Carinthia, where the schools are bilingual. Of more recent (16th-century) origin is the Croat minority of Burgenland, descended from families fleeing the Turkish advance into Dalmatia and Slavonia, although only about 3,000 use Croatian as their first language. Far greater in number than either of these historical minorities are the "legal aliens", chiefly Slav *Gastarbeiter*,

PRECEDING PAGES: a Renaissance house decorated with sgraffito in Gmünd, Lower Austria. **LEFT:** the Opera Ball in Vienna. **RIGHT:** snowball target.

but also Turks and other nationalities, who constitute 737,000 out of Austria's population of 8.1 million. In Vienna they are officially 17 percent of the population, but the figure is considerably higher if illegal residents are added. In fact Austria, or at least Vienna, has always been an immigrant destination, and would have been

the poorer without it. One has only to contemplate the empty spaces in Austrian culture to understand this – if Beethoven and Brahms had not settled in Vienna; or if the Jewish forebears of Freud, Mahler, Wittgenstein, Stefan Zweig and many others had not migrated to Austria; or if the Habsburg *Residenzstadt* had not attracted the Hungarian master of operetta, Franz Lehàr, or the Italian masters of the Baroque age.

However, ethnicity is only a part of Austrian diversity: the historical and cultural traditions of the nine provinces are far more significant. The local patriotism of the Tyrolese, for instance, rests on a mistrust of the central power that goes back at least to the betrayal of their leader, Andreas Hofer, by the Habsburg ruler in the Napoleonic war. Salzburg, with its long history of independent rule by prince-bishops, was so indifferent to the notion of Austria that it made a vigorous attempt to amalgamate with Germany after World War I. Then again the Viennese are *sui generis* the product of an ethnic melting pot and marked by centuries of servility and opportunism employed in seeking the "protection" of those with influence at court or in the bureaucracy. Although the Viennese are keen to promote their narcissistic image of "the golden Viennese heart" (which does indeed exist), others see them as two-faced, *Schlampig*

(sloppy – especially in carrying out tasks) and whingeing. The high-pitched nasal whine and exaggerated "l"s of the Wienerisch dialect are a gift to the cabaret artiste, who uses it to convey the aggressive self-pity and disingenuous behaviour of the Viennese at their worst.

Religious disillusionment

Since the Counter-Reformation stamped out Protestantism as a serious force, a central focus of Austrian identity has been the Catholic Church. One Pope even referred to Austria as "the isle of the blessed", but the present incumbent's policy of packing the Austrian hierarchy

THE MAKING OF AUSTRIA

Precise definitions of "Austrians" and "Austria" are problematic. The word *Ostarrichi*, meaning Eastern Territory (now Upper and Lower Austria), first appeared in a land registration of 996. Styria was added in 1192 and in 1278 these became "hereditary lands" of the Habsburgs, expanded through peaceful means. Carinthia was added in 1335, Tyrol in 1363 and Vorarlberg from 1309 to 1814.

Salzburg came directly under Habsburg rule as late as 1816. These acquisitions always united under the imperial ruler, but divided between branches of the Habsburg dynasty until 1665. The newly founded Republic of Austria added Burgenland, formerly part of Hungary, in 1919. For

most of its existence therefore, "Austria" has been a salmagundi of Babenberg, then Habsburg possessions which, during the period of the Austro-Hungarian Empire (1867–1918) lacked even a constitutional name, until that of "Cisleithania" was concocted and "Austria" was used in common parlance. With the end of the Habsburg Empire in 1918, the Austrian Republic was created with nine federal states, corresponding roughly to the hereditary lands.

Lower and Upper Austria, Salzburg, Styria, Tyrol and Vorarlberg are Christian Conservative strongholds, Vienna is Socialist, Burgenland Socialist and the Governor of Carinthia is the Freedom Party's former leader, Jörg Haider.

with reactionary prelates has had disastrous consequences. After various scandals in the 1990s, including one involving the Cardinal Archbishop of Vienna, thousands have left the church and many of those remaining are disillusioned by the authoritarian hierarchy's insincere pretence of "dialogue" with its critics. At the same time, the opposing ideological bunker of Socialism has crumbled in a welter of shameless corruption and greed resulting from 30 years in power. The old certainties no longer suffice, and modern Austrians therefore look both for narrower parochial and broader global allegiances to underpin their identity.

country *Missgeburt* (a misconceived freak). The average Viennese is doubtless unimpressed by much of this intellectual posturing. In the days of Habsburg absolutism, Austrians learned the art of "happiness in a quiet corner", of maintaining a low profile, while nurturing a quiet contempt for the higher-ups they had to humour and pretended to obey. Doubtless the playwright Nestroy thought of this when he wrote: "Of all nations, the best nation is resignation…"

Austrians have had, with some justification, a tendency to pessimism and resentment. Once plagued by the notoriously ungrateful nations of the Empire, they were severely penalised by

Questions of identity

The resultant insecurity (notwithstanding that Austria remains one of the world's most prosperous countries) is a new catalyst for the Austrian's traditional self-irony: Armin Thurnher entitled his book *A Trauma is Life* parodying a famous Grillparzer play *(A Dream is Life)*; Robert Menasse called his book *The Land without Qualities*, parodying Musil's *The Man without Qualities*. The populist politician Jörg Haider thinks it not incongruous to call his

LEFT: a religious procession in the Stubai Valley, Tyrol. **ABOVE:** a fiacre-driver waiting for custom in Seefeld.

the Versailles peace treaty, became (according to them) the "first victims" of Hitler's aggression, and were the losers in two world wars (as well as several wars preceding them); now they are cruelly misunderstood when they elect Kurt Waldheim as president, or the Freedom Party into government. For the new generation, however, these burdens of historical grievance and guilt are increasingly irrelevant, as they look to a pan-European future. The Freedom Party's contradictory politics of "*Lederhosen* and laptops" (socially reactionary and technically sophisticated) struck a chord for a while; but while the *Lederhosen* may have the last word, the laptops have the future. ❏

THE AUSTRIAN MUSE

Art and music have always flourished in Austria, from Romanesque frescoes and Mozart symphonies to Hundertwasser's postmodern architecture

Austria has provided the world with legions of musicians, painters, sculptors, writers and architects: Salzburg is synonymous with Mozart; the capital, Vienna, has been home to more geniuses per acre than perhaps any other place on earth, and – for better or for worse – it was the birthplace of psychoanalysis. Furthermore, it has supplied the world with a string of geniuses in science, economics and the arts by making life intolerable for them in Austria – this to the great benefit of university faculties in America and arts institutions everywhere.

Cultural legacies

Austria's cultural wealth owes much to its receptiveness to artistic movements originating elsewhere in Europe. Crusaders who crossed Austrian territory to reach the Holy Land and returned the same way brought valuable booty and Byzantine culture, although the influence of the latter in the fine arts probably filtered up from Italo-Byzantine art centred on Ravenna. Notable Romanesque frescoes with pronounced Byzantine traits may be seen in the Johanneskapelle at Pürgg (Steiermark), at Lambach between Salzburg and Linz, and at Friesach in Carinthia; Salzburg and other centres have illuminated Byzantine manuscripts and other treasures.

Around the middle of the 13th century, an ascetic Gothic architecture, introduced by the Augustinians and especially the Cistercians from France, and Gothic painting brought by wandering artists from Italy or Germany, began to replace the hitherto dominant Romanesque style. Church towers grew to ever greater heights, culminating in the spire of St Stephen's Cathedral in Vienna (built 1359–1433), which reached 137 metres (450 ft). Structural innovations enabled solid stone walls to be replaced by walls with massive glass windows, through which light poured into the churches. The altar developed

from a functional table into a complex structure with wings and rear panels.

At least from the high-Gothic period onwards, the most talented artists and architects ceased to be merely anonymous members of workshops or guilds, although these bodies remained powerful. They became instead recognised mas-

ter craftsmen, and some of the best known were Austrians: Hans Puchsbaum, Michael Knab, Anton Pilgram (all working on churches in Vienna), and painters and sculptors such as Michael Pacher (whose magnificent winged altar can be seen at St Wolfgang in the Salzkammergut), as well as other artists (Konrad Laib, Rueland Frueauf) whose work is on display in the Gallery of Austrian Medieval Art in the Orangery of the Lower Belvedere in Vienna.

Increased trade brought greater prosperity to the towns. The wealthy burgher was keen to exhibit his financial standing, which he might do by adding beautiful Gothic features to his house. At this time, the craftsmen guilds were

PRECEDING PAGES: staircase in the Kunsthistorisches Museum, Vienna. **LEFT:** poster design by Oskar Kokoschka. **RIGHT:** 11th-century fresco depicting Christ, at the Benedictine Abbey in Lambach.

generously patronised by the court, the nobility or the church. Much money was spent on fortresses *(Burgen)*, at first to make them siege-proof, and then (in the late-Gothic and Renaissance periods) to make them into sumptuous residences for powerful owners. Among the most impressive are Hohensalzburg, Hochosterwitz in Carinthia, the late 16th-century Hohenwerfen (Land Salzburg) and Rosenburg (Lower Austria).

Gradually the formal elements in Gothic art gave way to a new sense of realism; natural

BAROQUE BEQUEST

The age of the Baroque, beginning around the 1620s, has left the most impressive legacy in Austria *(see next chapter, pages 77–81).*

themes (especially background landscapes) became important in painting, while historical events were represented in contemporary terms. Painters from Austria and southern Germany, collectively belonging to the so-called Danube School, such as Albrecht Altdorfer (1480–1538), who painted the altar in St Florian, Lukas Cranach the Elder (1472–1553) and Jörg Breu (1480–1537), sometimes carried the naturalist approach to extremes. Their chilling depictions of the more violent scenes of Christian martyrdom can shock even the modern viewer accustomed to routine violence of a more synthetic kind.

In part, this violence reflected the troubled times that followed the particularly rich late-

Gothic period, when money was plentiful in much of Austria due to silver mining and many wonderful artefacts were produced, especially the winged altars of Upper Austria. However, the Turks had been making increasingly serious incursions since the 14th century, and by 1529 were at the gates of Vienna; in addition, the proto-Protestant Hussite movement of Bohemia of the 15th century was followed by the Lutheranism of the 16th, that very rapidly gained ground both among the nobility and the artisans.

All this happened just as scientific discoveries started to shake Catholicism's fundamental postulates. The ongoing troubles hindered the rapid spread of the Italian Renaissance on Austrian soil, although there are some examples of military architecture (e.g. the stellar bastions erected round Vienna in the mid-16th century) which reflect Italian influence. Otherwise, Renaissance and Mannerist art and architecture is notably exiguous in an Austria that needed money for defensive warfare rather than grandiose building. Exceptions are the extraordinary Mannerist mausoleum built (1614–38) for Ferdinand II in Graz by the Italians Pietro de Pomis and Peter Valnegro, and another (built 1609–14) for the Eggenburg lords at Ehrenhausen (Styria).

The Italian jobs

With the onset of the exuberant Baroque style, which reflected an increasing confidence in a favourable outcome of the dual war against the Turkish infidels and the Protestant heretics, Italian influence became overwhelming.

Not only in architecture, but also in the fine and performing arts of the mid-17th century to the early 18th century, it was Italians who dominated. They built nearly all the earlier Baroque palaces for the nobility in Vienna and dominated the court music scene (Metastasio, Cesti, Porpora), until their stranglehold was broken by Christoph Willibald Gluck in the mid-18th century. Yet even Gluck had studied in Italy, as did the first great Austrian architects of the Baroque, Fischer von Erlach and Hildebrandt.

Enthusiasm for opera

The marriage of Leopold I (known as the first Baroque emperor) to Margherita of Spain in 1667 had been celebrated by an opera held in the main courtyard of the Hofburg, a wildly extravagant spectacle entitled *Il Pomo d'Oro* with music by Pietro Antonio Cesti.

The stiff and intensely unnatural Italian style of opera prevailed until Maria Theresa discovered Gluck (1714–87), whose reformist works (starting with *Alkestis*, 1767) subordinated the music to dramatic requirements.

Gluck's *Orpheus* is musically one of the finest operas ever written, but he has been overshadowed by Wolfgang Amadeus Mozart, who left the employ of the prince-archbishop of Salzburg (literally being booted out by the chamberlain) and settled in Vienna in 1781. His most suc-

Haydn and Beethoven

Mozart's mentor was "old papa Haydn", a former chorister at St Stephen's, who worked for the Esterházy princes as Kapellmeister and was treated more or less like a butler. His trip to London, however, not only brought him European acclaim, but made him a lot of money. His operas (most rather dull) written for his patron at Esterháza were (mostly) enjoyed by Maria Theresa, but are now seldom played. However, his marvellous masses, oratorios, symphonies and chamber music have ensured him enduring fame. He outlived Mozart and died during the second Napoleonic occupation of Vienna in 1809.

cessful opera in his homeland was *The Magic Flute*, still regarded as the quintessential Viennese opera; however, he was less successful at court, the emperor complaining ironically that *The Seraglio* was "too beautiful for our ears… and with very many notes". Eventually he did succeed Gluck as court composer – but downgraded to a salary of 800 Gulden a year, as compared to the 2,000 Gluck received. "It is," said Mozart, "too much for what I do, and not enough for what I can do."

LEFT: the famous Renaissance figures at Maximilian I's mausoleum in Innsbruck's Hofkirche. **ABOVE:** Franz Schubert. **RIGHT:** playwright Franz Grillparzer.

The officers of the French garrison not only gave Haydn a hero's burial, they also crowded into the Theater an der Wien to hear the premiere of Beethoven's *Fidelio* – an irony not lost on the great composer. A German from Bonn, Beethoven spent most of his productive life writing for Viennese patrons, and indeed his work is a development of the Wiener Klassik, quite apart from the local inspiration that he found – for instance, in the Wienerwald, which can be heard in the bird song sequence of the *Pastoral Symphony*. Beethoven was hero-worshipped by Franz Schubert, in whose wonderful chamber music and *Lieder* gentle lyricism alternates with deep and sometimes melancholy passion, and whose Schubertiades (musical soirées at which he played his latest compositions to friends) are seen as typical of the burgher idyll of the Biedermeier period (1814–48).

The absolutism of the Biedermeier period provoked the "inner emigration" of the now closely watched bourgeoisie, treated like children by the police-state run by Metternich on behalf of the "good" Emperor Franz (in fact one of the dimmest and nastiest of the Habsburgs). It produced a distinctive style in furniture (influenced by the French empire), in painting (idealised family portraiture and sentimental realism) and one great novel (*Indian Summer* by Adalbert Stifter).

complete expression of Biedermeier values that may still frequently be encountered among Austrians – the cultivation of personal virtue, political quietism, "happiness in a quiet corner".

After the post-revolutionary repression had lifted with the initiation of the Ringstrassen era, for which Franz Joseph fired the starting gun in 1857, a new and garish ambience prevailed in Vienna. Even before the revolution, the waltz (based on peasant dances called *Ländler*) had begun to sweep the country; by the mid-century it had become a craze warned against by doctors for its supposed dangers to health and by moralists for its supposed sexual provocation. In the

The theatre was dominated by two towering figures: Ferdinand Raimund (1790–1836), who evoked a fairy-tale world into which his audience could escape from a disagreeable contemporary reality; and the master comic, Johann Nestroy (1801–62), whose brilliant ad-libbing often mocked the authorities and would never have got past the censor if committed to paper.

From Revolution to Ringstrasse

Stifter's novel was actually retrospective, even nostalgic, being written in 1857, a decade after the 1848 revolution had swept away the world of Biedermeier, with its political and personal restraint. It is regarded, however, as the most

three decades before 1848, Josef Lanner and Johann Strauss Sr (a Habsburg loyalist and composer of the memorable *Radetzky March*) had attracted increasingly large audiences; but it was Johann Strauss Jr (1825–99) who became the first pop star of Europe, organising his bands on a commercial basis (they played at several fashionable cafés) and even having to fend off besotted female fans who wrote asking for locks of his hair (he sent them clippings from his poodle).

The Ringstrassen era brought in the fashion for Historicism in painting (huge historical canvases by Hans Makart) and in architecture. The great symbolic buildings of the city's new boulevard, designed in a medley of styles and sometimes (quipped the coffee house wits) in "no style at all", were not, as sometimes claimed, mere copies of Renaissance, Baroque or Classicist buildings. At their best (for example, in the designs of Theophil Hansen, Heinrich von Ferstel and Friedrich Schmidt) they constituted a second Renaissance in architecture and a confident affirmation of a liberal future expressed in *saxa loquuntur*, or stones that made a statement, as Schmidt called them. Yet, although the architects may have exhibited a seriousness

OPERETTA'S ORIGINS

Operetta first reached Vienna with performances of Jacques Offenbach's works in the 1850s. The genre contained a good deal of clever political satire, though this escapes today's audiences.

to-do bourgeois men assuaged such feelings by consorting with poor (often immigrant) girls. These compliant *süsse Mädl* (sweet girls, as they were sentimentalised) had by no means a sweet life, often being left to cope, poverty-stricken, with an illegitimate child.

Flats being damp, dark and cold, writers, artists and intellectuals resorted to the coffeehouse to pass the time reading the witty *feuilletons* (newspaper essays) and plot the next step in their feuds with rival factions.

of purpose, the Ringstrassen era is also a byword for frivolity, excess and irresponsibility, often summed up in the line from a Strauss operetta: "Happy is he who forgets all about what anyway cannot be changed..."

Operetta was the first and only joint cultural product of the Austro-Hungarian Empire, equally popular in Lemberg, Laibach or Ludenz. But it was all of a part with the world of lax sexual morals – at least in the capital, where (as Arthur Schnitzler so well described in plays and novellas) alienation and aboulia prevailed. Well-

LEFT: an evening with Johann Strauss Jr.
ABOVE: Johannes Brahms.

Most memorable of these was that between the journalist Karl Kraus (who wrote and published his own satirical journal) and Sigmund Freud, on whose theories he remarked: "Psychoanalysis *is* the disease it pretends to cure."

Brahms versus Bruckner

A different kind of feud was raging in the music world: its two protagonists were Johannes Brahms, the last representative of Romantic Viennese Classicism in the tradition of Beethoven, and Anton Bruckner, a mild-mannered, even saintly individual, who was taken up by the standard-bearers of Wagner. Arrogance and malice, fuelled by the acidulated musical pope of Vienna, Eduard Hanslick (who was memorably pilloried by Wagner as the pretentious and talentless Beckmesser in *The Mastersingers*) was entirely on Brahms's side.

The irony was that Bruckner, brought up as a choirboy at the monastery of St Florian and later the abbey organist, was deeply and naively religious. The cloudy majesty and discordant drama of his symphonies express the heights and angst-ridden depths of the traditional Austrian piety in which he was reared in his beloved Upper Austria. Brahms dismissed his symphonies, with their unfamiliar pauses and shattering brass climaxes, as "symphonic boa-constrictors, the

amateurish, confused and illogical abortions of a rustic schoolmaster". Even Bruckner's religious faith was denigrated as "priest-ridden bigotry". Franz Joseph could not help with Bruckner's personal request to him at an audience to "stop Hanslick", but he did give him a grace and favour residence in the grounds of the Belvedere for the last few years of his life.

Mahler's influence

One of Bruckner's pupils at the Conservatory (although they were ill-suited) was Gustav Mahler, who has become one of the most fashionable late-Romantic composers. However, his symphonies were not appreciated in Austria during his lifetime; furthermore, as a single-minded disciplinarian, he also made enemies during his tenure of the directorship of the opera.

That tenure (1898–1907) coincides with the golden age of the Wiener Secession *(see page 138)*, the movement founded in 1897 and headed by the painter Gustav Klimt until 1905. The Secession, which produced art nouveau-influenced architecture, applied art and painting, and was a fierce reaction against academicism and above all against the hitherto dominant Historicism in the arts. However, its sensuous flowing lines and gilded or vegetative ornamentation did not meet with universal approval.

Schoenberg's breakthrough

A revolutionary advance was made by the theorist and composer Arnold Schoenberg, who began developing atonality and the 12-tone technique; he had two distinguished followers in what became known as the Second Viennese School: Anton von Webern, whose pieces were

ROBERT MUSIL (1880–1942)

Musil, a contemporary of Freud, is an unusual writer of fiction, in that his educational background was in engineering, followed by studies in philosophy and experimental psychology. His books are marked by a tension between scientifically precise description of behaviour and the counterposing forces of the unconscious and the irrational. His first novel *Young Törless* (1906) is a penetrating portrait of adolescent turmoil in a military academy similar to one that Musil had attended.

Although he published brilliant novellas (*Three Women*, 1924), two dramas, essays and criticism, his life's work was the huge unfinished novel *The Man without Qualities*

(1930–43), a picture of the Habsburg Empire in decline. Its ironic hero, Ulrich, is a study in the creative tension between extreme rationalism and spiritual, even mystical, inclinations. His relationship with his sister charts the reconciliation of these apparently irreconcilable elements (the logical outcome of which is incest), while his external life passes in cloudily absurd preparations for a great celebration of the doomed dynasty. A contrasting relationship (Walter and Clarisse) juxtaposes the unhealthy intoxication of Wagnerian and Nietzschean ideas to the aspirational asceticism of Ulrich, an intoxication that ends in insanity. Two translations of this masterpiece are available in English.

noted for extreme brevity (No. 4 of *Five Pieces for Orchestra* lasts only 19 seconds) and Alban Berg, the composer of two major operas in the new style, *Wozzeck* (1922) and *Lulu* (unfinished at his death in 1935, but later completed and now a mainstay of the repertoire).

Literary movements

In literature, the new spirit at the turn of the century was heralded by the formation of a group known as *Jung Wien* and led by the cultural propagandist, Hermann Bahr. However, both Bahr and Peter Altenberg, the writer of impressionistic sketches that are something of a Viennese

self-realisation. Stefan Zweig's vivid memoir *The World of Yesterday* also documents this spiritual exhaustion in describing the louche, lush world of Vienna in decline.

Twentieth-century Austria produced several other writers of immensely ambitious scope, including Sigmund Freud (who some regard as much a literary as a scientific figure); Heimito von Doderer, technically one of the most sophisticated writers of German, whose novels brilliantly decribe the Austrian psyche buffeted by the trauma of military defeat and oppression; and Hermann Broch, whose great experimental novels (*The Death of Virgil, The Sleepwalkers*)

cult, tend to be a closed book to non-Austrians and do not translate well. It is the novelists who charted the demise of the old empire who have made more impact, especially Joseph Roth with his trilogy concerning three generations of the Trotter family of Habsburg loyalists; and Robert Musil (*see panel opposite*), whose monumental *The Man Without Qualities* combines a scientific precision of language with ironic perspective in charting the spiritual exhaustion of the old order and the search for a new form of

LEFT: a self-portrait by Egon Schiele (1890–1918).
ABOVE: Robert Musil. **RIGHT:** Klaus Maria Brandauer in *Jedermann* at the Salzburg Festival.

remain a minority taste. On the stage, the traumatic experiences of Austrians (notably the poorer classes) in the early 20th century are evoked with anger and compassion in the fiercely anti-fascist plays of Ödön von Horváth.

Post-war experimentalism

Of the writers prominent after World War II, Ingeborg Bachmann has become something of a feminist icon through her novels, dramas and fine lyric poetry; Thomas Bernhard became extremely controversial towards the end of his life, as his searingly provocative plays at the Burgtheater castigated his fellow-countrymen for their hypocrisy concerning the Nazi past and the Catholic Church for its disingenuousness (he also wrote excellent but less controversial novellas); Peter Handke and Robert Menasse have, in their different ways, continued the tradition of coruscating analysis of the Austrian way, Handke from a philosophical and abstract standpoint, Menasse in long, sardonic essays. If Handke is the literary experimentalist with the highest international profile, Vienna has also maintained its reputation for avant-garde art with a variety of movements such as "Actionism", "Magical Realism" (Ernst Fuchs)

> **AUDEN LIVED HERE**
>
> Just west of Neulengbach is the village of Kirchstetten, where the English poet W. H. Auden lived out the last 15 years of his life.

can still surprise with unconventional gestures. By contrast Hans Hollein's postmodern Haas-Haus, opposite the Stephansdom, is altogether less *outré* – which didn't stop protests at the sacrilege of placing a building in modern style opposite the city's most revered and symbolically important edifice.

The top festivals

Austria continues its great tradition of performance with the world-famous Salzburg Festival, but also *inter alia* the summer arts festivals at Bregenz in Vorarlberg and an operetta season at Mörbisch on the Neusiedlersee. Vienna holds the Wiener Festwochen in the early summer and also has festivals of modern music and film. The death of Herbert von Karajan was a milestone, when one considers that his generation had included such major conductors as Karl Böhm (a great Mozartian), Erich Kleiber (who, unlike Böhm and Karajan, was a resolute opponent of Nazism) and the Strauss specialist, Willi Boskovsky.

Perhaps the most impressive of the current generation is the conductor Nikolaus von Harnoncourt, great-great-grandson of the enlightened Archduke Johann of Habsburg, who married a Styrian postmistress. If the current crop of Austrian singers are not as impressive as a generation that included Irmgard Seefried, Gundula Janowitz and the peerless Elisabeth Schwarzkopf, it is clear that music remains in the Austrians' blood and it is only a matter of time before another *Wunderkind* appears as performer or composer.

A culture of criticism

Such a figure can expect to suffer. Austrian adulation of artistic greatness has always gone hand in hand with backbiting and controversy; but that's because Austrians care about their culture – financially as well as artistically, given the high level of public subsidy. Culture is a live issue, and an Austrian who has given up demolishing the latest *Blödsinn* (idiocy) at the theatre or opera house, or swooning over some hitherto undiscovered diva, is generally considered ripe for the graveyard.   ❏

and Hermann Nitsch's extraordinary "happenings" involving simulated blood sacrifice. This modern form of Dionysianism has been given the rather portentous name of the "Theatre of Orgiastic Mysteries".

Quite different is the work of the fashionably "green" architect and painter, Friedensreich Hundertwasser, whose colourful social housing draped with greenery in Vienna has become a tourist attraction (complete with souvenirs produced by a thriving Hundertwasser industry), and is every bit as popular as the nobler Baroque palaces. Hundertwasser's golden-globed tower for the municipal rubbish burner in Vienna is also a dramatic landmark and a sign that the city

LEFT: Hundertwasser's 1987 decoration of the parish church in Barnbach, Styria. **RIGHT:** art nouveau mosaic window at Vienna's Kirche am Steinhof.

BAROQUE MASTERPIECES

From the 1620s to the 1730s, the zeal of the Counter-Reformation spawned the
sensual extremes of Baroque and some of Austria's finest architectural treasures

All of Austria has something of the Baroque about it: the cuisine and its delicatessens, the effusive kissing of hands, the oldeworlde atmosphere of the coffee houses. But it's the architecture that forms the backdrop for this "Baroque experience". No other country in Central Europe displays a comparable abundance of constructions in the Baroque style. Spires and steeples sit like dabs of whipped cream on succulent wedding cake churches. Pompous portals, over-sized sculptures and expansive flights of stairs characterise the mansions of the period.

Jesuit propaganda

An acquired taste for the average northern European brought up with a Protestant mistrust of lushness and excess, the Baroque soon seduces the senses. This is exactly as the Jesuits (the greatest protagonists of the Baroque in ecclesiastical architecture) had intended: its sensuality was a major weapon in the counter-attack of the one true faith of Catholicism against heretical Protestantism, proffering a powerful, didactic "culture of the senses" against the Protestants' bleak and iconoclastic "culture of the word".

Austrian Baroque is often monumental in structure, theatrical in effect and transcendental in content, as can be seen from its most remarkable examples. It produced some of Europe's greatest architects: Jakob Prandtauer (1660–1726), who designed the fabulous monasteries of St Florian and Melk; Johann Lukas von Hildebrandt (1668–1745), who built the magnificent Belvedere Palace in Vienna for Prince Eugene of Savoy; and the Fischer von Erlachs, father (1656–1723) and son (1693–1742), whose greatest work is the Vienna Karlskirche. Also influential in Austrian Baroque was the Italian Carlone family: the father, Pietro Francesco, the sons Carlo Antonio and Giovanni Battista.

PRECEDING PAGES: the grand Marmorsaal (Marble Hall) at St Florian Abbey. **LEFT:** the pilgrimage church at Sonntagberg *(see page 201)*. **RIGHT:** Baroque architect Johann Bernhard Fischer von Erlach.

Swept along in the wake of these giants was a host of major and minor masters specialising in stucco (a technique of decorative plastering brought to its greatest refinement in Austrian and Bavarian Baroque), sculpture and fresco painting. Outstanding among these were the sculptor Georg Raphael Donner, whose Providentia

JOHANN BERNHARD
FISCHER v. ERLACH.

Fountain is on the Neuer Markt in Vienna, and painters such as J.M.Rottmayr or the prolific Franz Anton Maulbertsch, whose work spans the High Baroque, Rococo and Neoclassical styles.

From 1705 there was an Austrian Academy of Fine Arts (founded by Peter Strudl), and it was here that Maulbertsch was taught by Paul Troger, perhaps the greatest master of colour and illusionism in Austrian Baroque fresco painting (as at Stift Altenburg). The illusionism *(trompe l'oeil)* was of course designed to overwhelm the viewer with effects of heightened plausibility, so that transcendental scenes of the Assumption in distant cupolas really suggested a spiritual idea made apprehensible, or marbled columns and pilasters recreated the illusion of solid marble, like a brilliant stage set. Equally important was the fact that artists employed illusionism to show off their virtuosity, so that the celebration of God proceeded hand in hand with the celebration of artistic genius. Austrian Baroque reached an apotheosis with the completion of the Karlskirche by the younger Fischer von Erlach in 1739.

Thereafter there was a relatively brief fashion for Rococo, no doubt following the lead of Maria Theresa who decorated (after 1765) the interior of her Schloss Schönbrunn with plush satin, gilded wood and exotic Chinoiserie. Under her

Heading east, in the Salzkammergut, the parish church in Traunkirchen is notable in that it was built in so-called Jesuit Baroque style. It also contains the "fisher pulpit" representing the miraculous haul of fish in the New Testament.

One very important example of Baroque is in Kremsmünster, between Wels and Steyr (not to be confused with the small city of Krems on the Danube). Founded in the year 777, the Benedictine Abbey here is one of the oldest cultural centres in the Bavarian-Austrian area. Its Baroque renovation, as well as the construction of new monastery buildings, was carried out between 1613 and 1731; the architects were

son, Joseph II, the ultra-rational style of Classicism came into fashion, a product of the Enlightenment that was opposed to the Jesuit *Weltanschaung* (the order itself was dissolved in 1773) and put paid to the Baroque altogether.

The Baroque Road

Most visitors to Austria entering the country via the Salzburg border drive along the so-called "Baroque Road" that leads via Vienna to the South of Austria. Salzburg itself is a Baroque city extraordinaire. Under the influence of Archbishop Wolf Dietrich von Raitenau (1587–1612) and his successors, the city was transformed into a Baroque treasure trove.

Jakob Prandtauer and Carlo Antonio Carlone. Where the monastery meets the secular buildings there is an architectural jewel: the so-called Fischkalter (Fish Tank), a Prandtauer-designed set of ornate fountains, receptacles and statues. At the edge of the minster compound stands the oldest high-rising building in Europe, the 50-metre (160-ft) "mathematical tower", dating from the year 1759.

Melk Abbey

Other Prandtauer buildings can be found further east, in Lower Austria. His pilgrimage church first planned in 1706 in Sonntagberg, for instance, was completed in 1732 by his nephew, the Tyrolean architect Joseph Mungge-nast. But his masterpiece is the abbey at Melk.

Melk Abbey *(see pages 162–3)* towers heavenwards. Prandtauer is said to have located his architectural works of art in the landscape in such a manner that nature and art combine in perfect harmony. Here the sacred aspects are especially emphasised. In contrast to other Baroque monasteries, it is the church itself that dominates the complex.

For almost 40 years – between 1702 and 1736 – Prandtauer summoned the most important Baroque artists to Melk. Paul Troger painted the ceiling fresco in the library. Here belief is depicted allegorically: a woman holds the book with the seven seals and the lamb of the Apocalypse in one hand, in the other a shield. Around her hover the four cardinal virtues – wisdom, justice, strength and moderation. Troger also painted the ceiling frescoes in the Marmorsaal (Marble Hall). In a chariot drawn by lions, Pallas Athena leaves the realm of dark, evil and brutality to enter the realm of light, goodness and beauty.

Rhapsody in blue

Also overlooking the Danube River, some 30 km (18 miles) to the east, the former Augustinian monastery in Dürnstein is another of the highlights of a journey through Baroque Austria. The ruins of the castle in which King Richard I (Richard the Lionheart) was kept prisoner from 1192 to 1193 stand sentinel above the town, while the monastery church clings to the cliff above the Danube. Despite objections from some quarters, renovation included restoring the church to its original blue colour, which over the years had been covered by many layers of yellow.

Dürnstein is actually the only monastery that was built in accordance with the religious concepts of a monk. The abbot, Hyronium Übelbacher, kept precise diaries about the design and the progress of the building. He himself supervised the execution of his plans. Almost all architectural features can be sub-divided into four: four seasons, four continents, four gospels, four elements, four portals. Unusually, the main entrance is not in the middle axis of the church

but rather on the northern side. An additional entrance hall is intended to highlight the contrast between the dark courtyard and the lightness of the interior. By entering the church, man enters life, the four continents.

To the south is St Pölten, where Prandtauer spent the final 34 years of his life; his presence drew a circle of students and fellow artists, and the city is filled with examples of the Baroque style. Apart from various churches, columns and squares, there is a Bishop's residence, the attractive Institut der Englischen Fräuleins and the City Hall (Rathaus) with its splendid mayor's chamber.

Capital of Baroque

Nearer to Vienna, the Augustinian Monastery in Klosterneuburg is a very interesting structure, featuring a lovely altarpiece from the enigmatic Nicolas of Verdun. The monastery later received a Baroque makeover by Giovanni Battista Carlone and Andrea de Retti.

Beyond Klosterneuburg is Vienna, Baroque capital of Central Europe. Among the oldest of the city's early Baroque buildings is the Kirche am Hof dating from 1662. Carlo Carlone was responsible for the facade. Vienna's most important clergymen have preached from the pulpit of this church, which is one of the oldest Jesuit churches in the city. Built in the style of

LEFT: Salzburg's Mirabell Gardens, laid out by Fischer von Erlach. **RIGHT:** the church tower (1733) at the monastery in Durnstein.

the Jesuit establishments in Rome, it is a jewel of the early Baroque.

Johann Bernhard Fischer von Erlach took over as chief architect in Vienna in 1682. He had already been working on the Plague Column for 10 years, and applied to become the architect of the triumphal gate in honour of the entry of Joseph I to Vienna. The designs he submitted were judged to be superior to those of his Italian competitors.

This event was regarded by his contemporaries as being a veritable victory for German art. Fischer von Erlach received his commissions from the Emperor himself, as well as the aristocracy. According to his own statements he

In 1733 Hildebrandt completed the Peterskirche. Immediately afterwards he designed what is now the residence of the Federal Chancellor, a building which took only two years to complete. Fischer von Erlach was successful again with his plans for the Karlskirche, but he died in 1723, and his son, Joseph Emanuel, completed the church, the design of which is heavily influenced by St Peter's in Rome – thus lending further credence to the idea that Vienna was supposed to become another Rome. The mighty dome serves as an ecclesiastical symbol, and the crowns on the columns are signs of secular power. The pond in front of the church was

often worked on as many as 14 buildings simultaneously. But then his fortunes took a sudden turn for the worse. His plans for Schloss Schönbrunn were rejected and he subsequently lost favour with Prince Eugene. Johann Lukas von Hildebrandt took over as leading architect.

At around this time many splendid aristocratic palatial buildings were constructed. The dual-winged Belvedere Palace was built between 1714 and 1723 for Prince Eugene who, it was reported, lived in greater splendour than the Emperor. Schloss Schönbrunn was built 20 years after Fischer von Erlach's death by Nikolaus Pacassi and the plans were influenced by the new Rococo style.

intended to mirror the splendour of the building, but because of the ever-prevailing winds that ruffle its waters, that seldom happens.

East and south of Vienna

Around Vienna there are a number of other important edifices. Johann Lukas von Hildebrandt built Schloss Halbturn, about 60 km (37 miles) southeast of Vienna, in the Burgenland. This is where you'll find the masterpiece of the Baroque painter Franz Anton Maulbertsch, the

ABOVE: the Upper Belvedere Palace in Vienna.
RIGHT: cherubs on a choir stall in the church at St Florian Abbey.

Allegory of Time and Light. In Eisenstadt, the capital of the Burgenland, is Schloss Esterházy, built in the style of the upper Italian early-Baroque, as represented by Carlo Martino Carlone. The humanoid gargoyles on the inner facades of the courtyard are based on the faces of the servants who supplied victuals to the construction workers, lining their pockets to the detriment of the artisans in the process.

Styria and Carinthia

The province of Styria contains the impressive pilgrimage church in Mariazell, with its famous high altar with a globe as a tabernacle. It was designed by Johann Bernhard Fischer von Erlach. The so-called Gnadenaltar (the altar of divine mercy) was designed by his son Joseph Emanuel. Graz, capital of Styria, has its own plethora of Baroque buildings; in Schloss Eggenberg, built by Laurenz van der Sype (1623–33), there is a Baroque museum.

To the west in Carinthia, the Baroque style flourished more modestly. Some pretty parish churches can be seen in Wolfsberg and St Veit an der Glan. The highlight, though, is the church of the former monastery in Ossiach, a Baroque-revised Romanesque basilica. Concerts are held here in the summer. ❑

WHERE ELSE TO SEE BAROQUE IN AUSTRIA

- Benedictine Monastery, **Altenburg** (1735): unsung masterpiece by Joseph Munggenast.
- Benedictine Monastery, **Göttweig** (1718): rebuilt according to the plans of Johann Lukas von Hildebrandt.
- Pilgrimage Church Maria Trost, **Graz** (1714–24): by Andreas and Johann Georg Stengg.
- Benedictine Monastery, **Lambach** (1690s): contains the only extant Baroque monastery theatre.
- Pilgrimage Church, **Lockenhaus** (1669): by Italian master builder Pietro Orsolini.
- Parish Church, **Mondsee** (1679–1730): in former Benedictine monastery; early Baroque interior.

- Augustinian Monastery, **St Florian** (1686-1751): by Carlo Antonio Carlone and Jakob Prandtauer.
- Schloss Hohenbrunn, **near St Florian** (1722-32): Prandtauer-designed castle, now a museum.
- Schloss Mirabell, **Salzburg**: actually a 19th-century reconstruction of a 1720s Hildebrandt design.
- Dreifaltigkeitskirche (Trinity Church), **Stadl-Paura** (1725): built by Johann Michael Prunner.
- Abbey Church, **Stams** (1699): remodelled after 1593 fire.
- Winter Riding School and Hofbibliothek, **Vienna** (1726-34): both completed by Joseph Emanuel Fischer von Erlach after his father's death.

AUSTRIAN CUISINE

Most famous for their deliciously calorific pastries, Austrian cooks also create a spectacular array of savoury dishes with a distinctly international flavour

Fashionable refinements notwithstanding, Austrian cooking is firmly based on a collection of traditional recipes handed down over generations. Occasionally, as the empire expanded, these were supplemented by dishes from neighbouring cooking pots: damson dumplings from Bohemia, paprika goulash from Hungary, spicy braised peppers from the Balkans and rich pasta dishes from Italy. The Austrians zealously imitated all these specialities and in the end confidently claimed to have invented them.

The best example of this culinary plagiarism is the world-famous Wienerschnitzel, the breaded escalope of veal which every self-respecting Austrian housewife insists was discovered by her great-grandmother. Historical research in the National Archives reveals, however, that when Field-Marshal Radetzky returned from Italy in the year of the 1848 Revolution, he brought back tidings not only of the quashing of the uprising, but also of a certain *costoletto alla Milanese*, a recipe which he immediately passed on to the chefs at the Imperial Court – as a closely guarded secret, of course. Ever since then, the breadcrumb coating for veal, pork, chicken or fish has been regarded as typically Austrian.

The Austrians love to eat. This devotion to gastronomic pleasures has been cultivated across the centuries. Tyrolean eagle with dumplings, roast squirrel with salad, or hedgehog in vinegar sauce with noodles were all great delicacies. During times of war and pestilence, when most of the people were starving, the nobility hardly noticed. When Empress Maria Theresa and her entourage visited the Monastery of Melk for just one day, the cook's duties were awesome. His shopping list included 266 kg (587 lbs) of beef, 337 kg (743 lbs) of veal, 9 calves' heads, 40 calves' feet, 2 kg (4 lbs) of marrow and 4 ox tongues. He also required 1,404 eggs, 138 litres (30 gallons) of

dripping, 9 sticks of cinnamon and 5 new roasting spits.

Two and a half centuries later, even ordinary folk can enjoy a feast fit for an empress. Yet the average Austrian is as suspicious of nouvelle cuisine as a medieval cup-bearer faced with a goblet of hemlock. Fortunately, however,

the variety of specialities on offer between Lake Constance and the Neusiedlersee is so extensive that even the most cosmopolitan guest will find plenty of novelties to sample.

Viennese specialities

Vienna, the nation's capital, has a centuries-old culinary tradition, including the rustic inn-styled *Beisl (see page 84)*. In addition to the Wienerschnitzel, the most famous speciality in this city of gourmets is the *Tafelspitz*. This lean cut of beef is cooked in broth and served – surrounded by roast potatoes – with chive sauce, spinach and horseradish and apple purée.

Boiled beef and vegetables can be found on

LEFT: Austria is renowned for its cakes.
RIGHT: a little helping of *Kaiserschmarrn*.

the menu of every modern restaurant, from the smallest *Beisl* (bistro) to the temples of haute cuisine. A true Viennese gourmet, incidentally, is a great soup fan. A lunch menu without a steaming bowl of broth with semolina dumplings, liver dumplings or sliced pancake lurking in its depths is not a proper meal. To follow, choose roast pork with bread dumplings and sauerkraut. Or – better still – eat *Beuschel*, with veal heart, lots of root vegetables, herbs and spices. The favourite beverage is more than likely to be a cool "G'spritzer", equal quantities of white wine and sparkling mineral water. Pudding will be an apple strudel, made with a dough stretched out so thinly that you can read the newspaper through it, filled with a mixture of sliced apple, cinnamon and raisins, rolled up and baked crisply.

Alternatively, a meal may end with a choice of *Torten* (cakes). *Sacher Torte (see page 86)*, the rich dark chocolate cake named after the place of its invention, Hotel Sacher in Vienna, is the best known, but others include *Dobos Torte*, with a caramelised top and *Linzer Torte*, with nuts. Then there are little Czech yeast dumplings, made of yeast dough, filled with damsons, painted with melted butter and served with vanilla sauce.

THE BEISLN

There is no more distinctive food institution in Vienna than the *Beisl*, a delightful combination of pub-style grub, served in Viennese style in a beer-garden atmosphere. A good *Beisl* (*Beisln* in plural) has a handful of simple ingredients: a panelled bar and brightly polished taps for draught beer; a "parlour" with chequered tablecloths and a handwritten menu with different daily specials.

You'll get a good plain meal here alongside the locals (and a few tourists): a clear soup (with pancake, liver or semolina dumplings), followed by goulash or roast beef with vegetables, fish on Friday or even home-made noodles, followed by sweet plum or apricot dumplings.

Provincial delicacies

In the Vorarlberg, the most westerly province, many inns still serve meals prepared from recipes handed down across the generations. *Kässpätzle*, for instance, are home-made noodles prepared with flour, milk and egg and served with butter and cheese. A generous portion of Gouda or Emmenthaler cheese is an essential ingredient in the *Marend*, the Vorarlberg mid-afternoon snack; traditionally it is served with bread and a mug of cider. Special delicacies are trout, whitefish and pike – some weighing as much as 10 kg (22 lbs) – from Lake Constance, where the Romans once fished for their supper.

The cuisine of Tyrol is both substantial and nourishing. The province, through which travellers have passed for centuries on their journey northwards or southwards across the Alps, has a long tradition of hospitality. The region's bacon and cured pork are used in Tyrolean bacon dumplings or a hearty Tyrolean snack. The latter is usually accompanied by a measure of gentian spirit, fruit schnapps or rowan *eau-de-vie* (home-distilled and guaranteed to knock your hat off). It tastes best served in a remote mountain hut after an arduous hike.

For the truly ravenous there is the traditional *Bauernschöpsernes*, tender braised lamb. It is

Travellers should leave some time to visit the historic inns of the Old Town; here, beneath ancient vaulted ceilings or in a shady inner courtyard, you can try Salzburg braised beef, cooked in beer, or a larded veal olive – followed by bilberry soufflé or a sweet baked pudding. No-one should miss the excellent local beer, which is usually served in half-litre *Krügerl* or tankards. In times past the archbishops of Salzburg acquired brewing rights in order to improve their precarious financial situation; for many years now, beer production has been a flourishing economic sideline in this enterprising city.

first seared with fried onion rings, then braised for half the required cooking time. Quartered potatoes are added, with parsley, a bay leaf and a glass of red wine as flavouring, and it is cooked until tender. The meal ends with special doughnuts or freshly stewed apple, and a final tot of fruit schnapps for the road.

The neighbouring province of Salzburg attracts visitors from all over the world, not least for its scenic beauty and works of art. But the region has far more to offer than Mozart, the festival and its celebrated churches.

LEFT: Café Hawelka in Vienna.
ABOVE: *Sachertorte* and coffee at Hotel Sacher.

Sweet music

Confectionery is another Salzburg speciality. Even the revered Wolfgang Amadeus is celebrated by balls of marzipan and plain chocolate – the famous and delicious *Mozartkugeln*.

A detour into the nearby Salzkammergut is always worthwhile, especially a visit to Zauner, the baker in Bad Ischl near the former villa of the Emperor Franz Joseph. It is a paradise for the sweet-toothed, bursting with gâteaux, *Stollen*, sweets and chocolate.

Upper Austria was once an exclusively agricultural region, as can be seen in its typical specialities. Cured pork, *Sauerkraut* and dumplings are an essential component of every menu, as is the substantial *Bauernschmaus* – which also includes sausages and bacon.

The province is considered to be the true home of the dumpling; many an inn holds an annual Dumpling Week, during which every imaginable form of the fluffy dough – savoury, piquant or sweet – will be served. The region's dumpling capital is the Innviertel, where any lunch without dumplings, however lavish it may be, is considered at best a paltry snack.

In the Mühlviertel no meal is complete unless it includes a generous measure of cider or perry. This fermented juice of apples or pears is not really intended for refined palates, for it is rather rough in texture. Many farmers still ferment their own cider; the juice is squeezed from the fruit in autumn, and allowed to settle in oak barrels. Traditionally, cider is served in a stone tankard, accompanied by a thick slice of bread topped by moist bacon.

In Carinthia, the southernmost province of Austria, game is served in every imaginable form, often cooked in red wine. Fish from the clear waters of the lakes, and milk and cheese specialities adorn the menus of restaurants between Villach and Klagenfurt. Best known and best loved are the *Käsnudeln*, pockets of dough filled with curd cheese and mint leaves,

THE SACHERTORTE WARS

Nothing put Vienna on the culinary map like *Sachertorte*. This sinful *Torte*, which alternates layers of chocolate cake with apricot jam, topped with bittersweet chocolate icing, was created by a chef at Hotel Sacher in – well, the dates get a bit fuzzy. In fact, there is little documentation to prove who baked or tasted the first true example of this cake.

But the Sacher so strongly identifies with its eponymous confection that it has even gone to court to protect the name. Only in this Inner Ring hotel, coffee shop or gift shop can you order a true *Sachertorte* (one word), the legally protected name; everywhere else, the *Konditoreien* (bakeries) must sell a *Sacher Torte*, which is virtually identical but whose two-word name is supposed to indicate an inferiority. The tourists don't care, of course. The rival Demel coffee house – a former royal pastry supplier located not far away, which is indisputably the city's finest bakery – certainly does. The Demel maintains it invented the *Torte*, using the dubious argument that one of the Sacher chefs came to work for the Demel and created it there. And, to be fair, the Demel fashions a wonderful *Torte* of its own.

A hugely scandalous lawsuit was undertaken during the 1960s, resulting in much misery for both cafés and a sort of gentleman's agreement not to scuffle over the subject any more. That hasn't stopped them, of course.

served with brown butter and fried diced bacon. A sweet variation is stuffed with prunes and chopped dried pears. The district around the Wörthersee is a busy tourist centre, but a few miles outside town the traveller can find peaceful meadows and little inns offering good plain cooking of excellent quality.

If you are lucky the landlady may even bake the bread herself, from a mixture of wheat and rye flour. One of these rustic loaves may weigh as much as 3–4 kg (6–7 lbs), with a diameter of up to 50 cm (20 inches). A thick slice topped with bacon or dripping, or just fresh farmhouse butter and honey, makes a substantial snack.

local pumpkin specialities earn eulogies from visiting gourmets.

If the salad you ordered tastes different here from elsewhere in the world, you must ascribe the exotic flavour to the use of black pumpkin oil. For a long time it was scorned as "carriage grease"; today the darkly shimmering oil with its inimitable nutty flavour is found in the fashionable restaurants of Vienna, where it adds the finishing touch to an elegant salad buffet.

Mushroom goulash and braised cabbage, poulardes and pork in every variation are other tempting – and fattening – specialities of Austria. If you decide on a fruit diet, head for the

In Styria, locals and visitors alike feast on the hearty, down-to-earth dishes. Characteristic is the *Heidensterz*, fried dumplings and crackling prepared from buckwheat flour, pork dripping and water. Another classic is *Klachlsuppe*, a soup prepared from slices of leg of pork, herbs and vegetables, juniper berries and peppercorns. It is seasoned generously and served with boiled potatoes and grated horseradish. Guests who insist on something lighter, however, will find that the local market gardens can supply a huge range of fresh vegetables. The

southern part of the province, along the border with Slovenia. Fruit trees form guards of honour along the roads; their harvest goes to make apple juice and warming pear schnapps.

Wine and woods

In Lower Austria, the region, like the wine, is measured in quarters: those lying above and below the Manhartsberg, those above and below the Vienna Woods, and the Wine and Woodland Quarters. The cuisine of the region is just as varied. Many dishes have been handed down from the former woodland dwellers to the present-day inhabitants.

The River Danube and the region's lakes and

LEFT: Pinzgau specialities.
ABOVE: delicious apricot dumplings.

streams are teeming with fish. A perennial favourite is trout *à la meunière*, in which the fish is fried in butter, seasoned with lemon and served garnished with sprigs of parsley. Game dishes – from "pheasant in a bacon jacket" to roast wild boar – are a culinary sensation. For dessert, the sweet cream *Strudel* has achieved national fame. As a *digestif*, try a fine liqueur or apricot brandy from the Wachau, with its excellent country inns and ambitious cooks.

Ancient spice

The culinary skills of the Burgenland, Austria's youngest province, are as colourful as its

population. Here live Croats, Hungarians and Gypsies whose traditional dishes are gathered together under the collective title of "Pannonian cuisine". Many specialities – such as the Esterházy Roast – can trace their names back to the ancient aristocratic families of the region. Hungarian cooking is not only represented by its spicy *Gulyas* (goulash) and other stews, but also by delicious sweet and savoury pancakes, *Palatschinken*. The heady local wine can best be sampled as an accompaniment to a crispy fried *Fogosch* (freshwater fish). The Burgenland specialises in sweet wines; those from the shores of Neusiedler See, "Vienna's sea", are particularly fine.

Refreshing drinks

Austria's spectacular variety of food, is helped along by particular refreshments. In the Arlberg a perfect day is capped by a *Jagatee*, a brew of schnapps, wine and a drop of tea. Similarly, an essential part of the grape harvest are the open-air lunches of bacon, sausages and freshly pressed grape juice. It is at this time that town-dwellers flock to the Neusiedler See, southern Styria, the Weinviertel or the hills surrounding Gumpoldskirchen to help with the hard labour in the vineyards.

Try to avoid the potent fermented brew known as *Sturm* at all costs. From grape juice via the *Sturm* it is only a small step to the *Heurige*, the Austrian's favourite cure all. The *Heurige*, or new wine, is best sampled in an establishment of the same name, a *Heuriger* – in the vicinity of Vienna, in Grinzing, Salmannsdorf, Kahlenbergerdorf or Nussdorf.

If you see a low vintner's cottage, with the sound of laughter and the clinking of glasses echoing from the little inner courtyard, then you will have found a likely place. Some wine growers also invite travellers to a tasting in their cool cellars, among the acid smell of wooden barrels and fermented grapes, where the candle-light flickers romantically against the vaulted ceilings. Equally inviting are the attractive whitewashed houses in the vintners' districts in the Weinviertel and in southern Burgenland.

The coffee houses

The secret recipe for a genuine coffee house has still not been fathomed. It should, if possible, be situated in Vienna – although Salzburg, Linz or Graz are acceptable alternatives. Red velvet banquettes and marble tables, mirrors and crystal chandeliers, and a grumpily superior head waiter are pretty well vital, as is the smell of fresh coffee, butter croissants and poppyseed cake, and the rustling of newspapers from all over the world. It is a mixture to which one can easily become addicted.

In Vienna, you are spoiled for choice. Many of the coffee houses are open late into the evening, and not just in the city centre. Why not skip dessert in a restaurant and adjourn to a coffee house for a slice of *Sacher Torte*, a cup of coffee and a glass or so of schnapps? ❏

LEFT: the grape harvest in the Wachau.
RIGHT: a sign in a Vienna flea market.

THE GREAT OUTDOORS

*The Alps are famous for their skiing, but the Austrian countryside has a great
deal more to offer, from paragliding in Kössen to ice-sailing on the Neusiedler See*

Austria is, quite simply, one of Europe's prime spots for outdoor recreation. The hills, valleys, lakes and mountains here are astonishingly full of opportunities to commune with nature in a sporting environment – and local guides, associations and tourist offices are nearly always at the ready to help you find them.

Better yet, Austria's charms are not as well-known or touristy as those of neighbouring Switzerland. As such, you'll often find resorts and hikes pleasantly uncrowded in comparison with those further west.

A nation of skiers

This is the home of modern skiing. At the beginning of the 20th century, in the little village of Lilienfeld in Lower Austria, the ski pioneer Matthias Zdarski invented the now world-famous stem turn which even today causes every fledgling skier so many problems.

Since then Austria has become one of the finest winter sports centres in the world. The resorts are strung out like pearls on a necklace right across the Alps: Lech am Arlberg, St Anton, Innsbruck, Kitzbühel, Saalbach, Obertauern, Schladming. Only Switzerland can look back on a similarly long tradition of winter sports. But in Austria, skiing is not just a winter sport. The country possesses the greatest density of all-year-round glacial ski regions. Areas like the Dachstein, the Kaunertal, the Pitztal or the Mölltal offer skiing with all amenities whatever the weather. It is possible to ski in a swimming costume in the summer.

In 2000, in Kitzbühel, aficionados celebrated the 60th anniversary of the notorious Hahnenkamm downhill race on the Streif Run, the most difficult and dangerous descent in the world. In skiing circles a victory in this race is more prestigious than a gold medal in the world championships. All great downhill skiers have

stood on the starting line at the top of the run, which is over 2 km (1½ miles) long. The winners' names have gone down in the annals of skiing history: Toni Sailer, the first man to win a gold medal in all three alpine ski disciplines, Karl Schranz, the Austrian downhill champion of the 1960s, and the Olympic medallist from

Carinthia, Franz "The Emperor" Klammer, who once completed the course just one-thousandth of a second faster than the famous Italian skier, Gustav Thoeni.

During the past decade, off-piste skiing in powder snow has become increasingly popular in Austria. Ski touring was for many years treated with derision as the hobby of a handful of extremists; but today it is definitely considered one of the most exciting winter sports. It should always be undertaken in the company of experienced guides, however; in view of the high risk of avalanches in the Austrian mountains, it would be extremely dangerous to venture out without their help.

PRECEDING PAGES: snowboard acrobatics.
LEFT: ice-climbing is not for the timid.
RIGHT: cross-country skiing in Austria
guarantees spectacular scenery.

The Dachstein offers the country's best off-piste skiing *(see panel)*. Remember that, to avoid damaging young saplings when skiing in this fashion, try not to use the sides of your skis more than necessary. Trees in the central Alps are of vital importance; they provide avalanche protection in winter and prevent mountainslides and mudflows in summer. Austria claims the highest number of deaths from avalanches in the world.

For ski acrobats

During the past few years the innovative branch of the ski industry has invented a number of demanding alternatives to alpine skiing.

The fun element is undoubtedly greater in the case of the snowboard. Wearing normal mountain boots, one stands in overshoes which are mounted directly on the snowboard. Centrifugal force enables the expert snowboarder to take spectacular curves, braking as he does so with his fists; on humpbacked slopes he can even leap in the air. Both items of equipment are suitable for beginners. For some years now, virtually all Austrian ski schools have offered courses in snowboarding, and an increasing number of resorts are installing half-pipe runs (grooved trails specifically for snowboarders) to capture the young market segment that craves the sport.

OFF PISTE IN THE DACHSTEIN

Austria's best – and perhaps most challenging – off-piste skiing is probably in the Dachstein, and it should only be attempted by extremely seasoned skiers. To experience it, take the first cable-car of the day up to the Dachstein glacier, as it is a long haul to reach the starting point. At the top shoulder your skis and trudge uphill through deep snow for over an hour to a snowy gully just 100 metres (320 ft) below the Dachstein peak. The incline is steeper than 60 percent, and a mixture of deep drifts of powder snow and treacherous ice. The gully itself is about 50 metres (160 ft) wide, bordered by high walls of rock and littered with jagged rocky outcrops and ridges through which you must pick your way.

Leaning backwards as far as possible, and making short, rapid swings to left and right in order not to gain too much speed, you will experience an intoxicating sense of euphoria as you descend into the valley. Usually one guide leads the group whilst a second brings up the rear, ready to assist those who need help. The deep-snow adventure will last all of 10 minutes, during which you may often sink up to your neck in snow. You may feel weak at the knees from exertion, but the experience of skiing through deep snow is simply far more exhilarating than that on the manicured pistes. The rest of the descent runs fairly gently through a beautiful mountain forest.

It's interesting to note the trend towards more exotic and dangerous outdoor sports. Specialists such as the Dachstein-Tauern Region Adventure Club have abandoned alpine skiing altogether. Apart from the snow sports mentioned above they also provide an introduction to snow rafting, in which the boldest sports enthusiasts hurtle down the pistes in huge inflatable rafting boats. The descent takes place at breakneck speed, but unfortunately there is absolutely no way of steering the snow raft. Every excursion inevitably ends with a tumble. Canyoning, equally foolhardy *(see below)* is the latest thrill-of-the-moment.

other ice sports. From the end of December until the beginning of February you can usually skate across the lake from Pamhagen to Rust. Neusiedler See also serves as the national centre for ice-sailing. Although they are fragile vessels weighing only a few kilograms and supported on blades, ice yachts can reach top speeds of more than 80 km (50 miles) an hour in a good wind, which makes them faster than any other form of sailing boat. Ice-sailing requires a high degree of technical proficiency as a sailor. The sport is not without hazard for participants; dangers include sudden gusts of wind and a capsize if the ice sheet suddenly gives way.

Ice pursuits

Austria has a long history of skating. Skating rinks such as Engelmann, or the Stadhalle or the Southern Ice Rink in Vienna or the stadia in Graz, Klagenfurt or Villach, are well patronised during the winter months. But Austria's lakes provide the most exciting skating to be had.

When there is a hard frost Neusiedler See is transformed into a huge ice-sheet, frozen to a depth of several metres and offering an area of almost 40 sq. km (15 sq. miles) for skating and

The Weissensee in Carinthia is the location of Europe's only golf course on ice – when the weather is cold enough. Golfers putt on the "white" instead of on the "green". There is just one disadvantage – once the ball is in the hole it is lost for ever, for the Weissensee is over 100 metres (330 ft) deep in places. Once a year the Weissensee is transformed into the setting for the Carinthian Ice Marathon, during which skaters must complete a course of over 200 km (125 miles) on ice.

South of the main Alpine ridge, ice hockey is the most popular sport. The matches of KAC (Klagenfurt) and their perpetual challengers from Villach always attract large crowds.

LEFT: a common experience for the novice skier.
ABOVE: ice-sailors on Neusiedler See can reach speeds of over 80 kmh (50 mph) on a windy day.

Anyone and everyone can try their skill at curling. This sport has many thousands of enthusiasts, especially in the western provinces of Austria. There are two kinds of curling: firstly, long-distance curling, in which the aim is to slide the curling stone – a metal plate weighing some 5 kg (11 lbs) with a handle – as far as possible across the ice. The present world record is held by an Austrian, who achieved a distance of over 200 metres (650 ft). In the more sophisticated version of the game the curling stone must be placed as close as possible to the tee. In winter the Sunday curling match is one of the highlights of the week.

Most tourist-oriented villages have a curling pitch where visitors may join in.

Much smaller, and therefore more exclusive, is Austria's circle of bobbers. Nonetheless, the Austrians often occupy top places in the world rankings. The real heroes of Innsbruck are, however, the skeleton riders. The town's skeleton club may lack the cosmopolitan flair of the skeleton club in St Moritz, whose membership includes jet-set personalities like Gunter Sachs, but the steep walls of the Innsbruck run result in record times. The public particularly appreciates races on natural toboggan runs, which are usually narrow defiles or forest tracks with an

CLIMBING THE GROSSGLOCKNER

The first hour of this challenging hike and climb is spent crossing the Pasterze Glacier, passing crevasses up to 25 metres (80 ft) deep. When the surface ice is thawing one must wade the last metres through slush.

But that's just the beginning. An exhausting climb of seven and a half hours through the Leitertal to the Salmhütte refuge follows. The overnight hut sits at an altitude of 2,644 metres (8,673 ft); it is advisable to engage a guide for the next day's climb. The remaining 1,000 metres (3,300 ft) include several sections calling for expert climbing skills. The terrain to the "Eagle's Nest" (3,400 metres/11,150 ft) becomes progressively steeper, often with a gradient of 50

percent. After one hour you reach the steep wall below the Eagle's Nest, one of the key sections of the ascent. It takes a good 30 minutes to scale the wall in order to reach the summit ridge, and a further half hour walking along the path – barely 40 cm (16 inches) wide – to reach the lowest of the summits of the Grossglockner.

After a short rest, continue to the "Little Glockner", separated from the summit proper only by the "roof", a relatively flat ridge. To the left and right, clefts fall away almost vertically. Much of the remaining way is difficult; only the path near the summit flattens out a little before the top at 3,798 metres (12,460 ft) – the highest point in all Austria.

artificial surface of ice. Here the sledges achieve top speeds of over 60 km (38 miles) per hour. Throughout Austria, sledging is a popular alternative to skiing as well as a much-loved après-ski pastime. Many an evening of merrymaking in one of the numerous ski huts culminates in a toboggan ride by torchlight along woodland paths to the valley.

The newest winter sport trend, dog sledging, imported from Canada and the US, has become one of the most popular spectator sports in Austria. The country's mushers are some of the continent's best. Horst Maas, the sportsman-adventurer from Linz, was the first man to cross

climbers, but native mountaineers more than made up for this in the 20th century. Some of them – Habeler, Fritz Morawetz, Heinrich Harrer and Edi Koblmüller – have achieved world fame; together, they have conquered all the 8,000-metre (26,250-ft) giants of the Himalayas. All the country's climbing heroes began with the mountains on their back doorstep, the peaks of the Eastern Alps, the Karawanken or the Totes Gebirge. Most of them passed their first baptism of fire on difficult sections such as the south wall of the Dachstein. All of them have tackled the king of Austrian mountains, the Grossglockner.

the Himalayas and the previously almost unknown kingdom of Sanskar with a dog sledge and also one of the few European dog sledgers to take part in the notorious Iditarod race in Alaska.

The call of the mountains

Austria is one of the cradles of mountaineering. During the 19th century, most of the country's 3,000-metre (9,850-ft) peaks were conquered for the first time by English

At 3,798 metres (12,460 ft) the Grossglockner is the most majestic of all the country's peaks. It is notorious above all for its rapidly changing weather conditions as well as the panoramic road completed during the 1930s, the first of its kind in the world. It enabled the general public to penetrate the heart of the Austrian Alps. Yet the Alpine Highway is actually just the approach road to the real world of the Grossglockner.

To really explore the area you should park your car at the Franz-Josephs-Höhe near the Pasterze Glacier – at the spot where hordes of tourists in sensible shoes clamber out of their air-conditioned coaches to gaze at the marmots.

LEFT: dog sledging.
ABOVE: a high-level tour in the Ötztaler Alps, Tyrol region.

Apart from the Glockner, mountaineers should head for the Grossvenediger, the Silvretta group, the Dachstein, the Ötscher in Lower Austria, the Wilder Kaiser and the precipitous peaks of the Karawanken in Carinthia.

Learning to climb

Climbing is taught in Austria's many mountaineering schools. The Alpine School in Kaprun is run by the Austrian Climbing Association. It lies in a picturesque high mountain valley by the top reservoir of the Kaprun hydroelectric scheme. The school uses the rock faces of the Glockner as practice walls and is famous

for its children's courses, which give youngsters a first taste of alpine sports.

Austria's mountaineering schools also offer courses in free climbing, a popular pursuit in the Alps. Free climbers are not interested in a 3,000-metre (9,800-ft) peak, but in the trickiest rock face in one of Austria's increasing number of climbing parks (one of the best known is in Bad Ischl in the Salzkammergut). Most routes are in the limestone Alps, in the Gastein Valley or in the Salzkammergut.

Another variation gaining popularity among mountaineers is ice or waterfall climbing. Equipped with two ice picks and exceptionally large crampons, experienced mountaineers make the ascent of frozen waterfalls and ice-covered mountain slopes. Their only grip is by means of the axes embedded in the ice; the crampons only serve to support some of their weight. One false blow, and the fragile ice shatters – and the climber is alone. The ice climbing centre is the Gastein valley. Here, at temperatures many degrees below zero, the frozen waterfalls offer a variety of climbing opportunities.

Water sports

The most famous sailing regions are Neusiedler See in Burgenland, the Attersee and Wolfgangsee in the Salzkammergut, the Bodensee in Vorarlberg and the Achensee in Tyrol. Small, agile sailing dinghies are the most popular as they adapt more quickly to the wind conditions, which often tend to extremes. The national windsurfing centre is on Neusiedler See.

Windsurfing has overtaken sailing in popularity throughout Austria; many stars of the international windsurfing scene first tacked into the wind across Neusiedler See. Another popular venue is the "New" Danube in the Lobau, whose mirror-calm waters and stable wind conditions make it ideal for beginners.

For decades now Austria has been one of the European white-water centres. The most attractive rivers for kayak and canoe trips are the Enns, the upper reaches of the Salzach, the Isel in East Tyrol, the Drau, the Gail, the Steyr and the Kamp in the Waldviertel of Lower Austria. Numerous white-water schools have been set up along the banks of all these rivers; all offer instruction as well as touring programmes. Adequate training is essential, especially in spring, when the melting snows make the country's mountain torrents highly dangerous and difficult to navigate.

During the past few years rafting has overtaken canoeing in popularity. The formula for what may well be the most exciting adventure on Austria's mountain rivers is a heavy-duty rubber dinghy, nine people, nine wooden paddles, steel safety helmets, life jackets, wet suits and a raging torrent. Even this, however, is not extreme enough excitement for some.

The very latest fad is canyoning, a variation on rafting whereby participants swim down the rushing torrent with only a life jacket or light raft to keep them afloat. It is a sport that requires considerable courage – or at least foolhardiness. In Switzerland in 1999 a flash flood swept down a steep gorge and killed 21 canyoners caught in the valley. But there is little sign of the sport's popularity waning.

The lovely, crystal-clear Alpine lakes offer some of Europe's finest diving experiences. A wide variety of freshwater fish, an unspoilt underwater world and the remarkable flora may not compare with the wealth of colour of tropical coral reefs, but diving in mountain lakes at heights of 2,000–2,500 metres (6,550–8,200 ft) can present a challenge of quite a different sort. Diving centres in Austria include the Hallstätter See, which is home to the most famous div-

centres are the Rax-Schneeberg area with its landing fields and small airfields in the Vienna Basin, as well as the Inn Valley in the Tyrol, and Carinthia. Glider pilots require an internationally recognised licence to take off over Austrian airspace; they must also register their flight with the airport authorities.

During the summer, thousands of brightly coloured hang-gliders hurl themselves down the steep rock faces, but when it comes to popularity, paragliding has long overtaken hanggliding in Austria. The paragliding centres are Kössen in Tyrol and the Garstner Valley in the Phyrn-Priel region. The sport is practised all

ing school in Austria, run by the Zauner family. Other centres include the Attersee, the Grundlsee, the Fernsteinsee near the Fernpass in Tyrol and the Erlaufsee in Lower Austria, near the pilgrimage village of Mariazell.

Airy alternatives

The Alps make Austria a glider's heaven. Perfect thermal conditions are created by the steep mountain slopes during the summer months, permitting the motorless machines to hover for hours above the mountain tops. The gliding

over the country, however. Other favourite starting points are the mountains surrounding Hallstatt in the Salzkammergut or the Zettersfeld, near Lienz in East Tyrol. Scattered across the country are more than 30 hang-gliding and paragliding schools.

Mountain biking

The Burgenland, Austria's easternmost province, is the ideal setting for a cycling tour. The region offers a well-developed network of cycle tracks with inns and service stations offering special services for cyclists. Well-maintained tracks also run along the Danube, from the Strudengau in Upper Austria, and through the

LEFT: climbing a frozen waterfall.
ABOVE: paragliding is popular all over Austria.

Wachau – Austria's most famous wine-growing area – to Vienna. In Upper Austria cycling tours are organised whereby luggage is transported to the next overnight stop whilst the visitors cycle unencumbered along the Danube valley.

The mountain-bike boom has taken Austria by storm. There are plenty of opportunities for mountain biking in all regions of Austria, although the owners of some private woods have banned bikes; in the province of Salzburg, on the other hand, many forest tracks and paths have been made available. Their use is permitted in most woods managed by the Federal Forestry Commission.

Hiking and gentle strolls

The Austrian passion for hiking began in 1825, when an official at the Viennese court by the name of Josef Kyselak applied for absence, shouldered his rucksack and set off to walk the length and breadth of the land. Wherever he arrived he wrote his name to prove the point – on walls, on rocks, on towers, churches and bridges. He went on to write up his experiences in a two-volume work. It was the first book to describe the pleasure of walking in Austria and was published simultaneously in Europe and the United States.

Many people have followed in his footsteps. The slogan invented a few years ago by the National Tourist Authority – "Austria is wander-bar!" – is not so much a challenge as a statement. During holidays or sunny weekends large numbers of Austrians leave the towns for the countryside; they are joined in their wanderings by many of their country's numerous visitors.

Any list of suggestions for mountain walks will inevitably lead to disagreement, but particularly recommended are the Bregenzer Wald and the Montafon in the Vorarlberg and the Kitzbühel Alps in Tyrol. In Salzburg province, the best hiking areas include the Österhorn Mountains (between the Salzkammergut and the Dachstein), the Pinzgauer Mountains (Saalbach, Zell am See, Uttendorf) and the head of the Rauris Valley (Kolm-Saigurn), where gold mining and glacier trails have been devised.

In Carinthia, the gently rolling Nockberg Mountains are worth a mention, as are the Low Tauern, the Hochschwab and the Koralpe in Styria. In Upper Austria, favourite recommendations include the Warscheneck Mountains in the Totes Gebirge, the Salzkammergut and the hills of the Muhlviertel. Popular in Lower Austria are the Otscherland, the Ybbstal Alps and the Waldviertel.

One route that is especially rewarding is the footpath from the Bokstein in Salzburg province (Gastein Valley) across the Korntauern Mountains to Mallnitz in Carinthia. Parts of the pass have existed for 5,000 years. On the north side of the steep, narrow pass the ascent is via steps formed by flat stone slabs that were probably placed there by the Celts.

There are a few precautions to remember before setting out on any walk. Always seek advice in the local tourist office as to a walk's degree of difficulty (staff are well-informed); some mountain footpaths are steep tracks over rocky terrain requiring surefootedness and a head for heights.

One of the pleasures of walking in Austria are the mountain refuges offering high-altitude refreshment and accommodation. In some regions, however, especially in Styria, the refuges in the medium altitude districts close in mid-September because hunting takes priority. Otherwise, long periods of fine weather make the early autumn an ideal time. ❑

LEFT: a mountain biker taking the fresh air in the mountains near Kitzbühel.
RIGHT: hiker looking towards the Sonnenspitze.

AUSTRIA'S WINTER PLAYGROUNDS

Austria has long been one of Europe's winter hot spots. There's lots to do, including helicopter skiing, snowboarding and ample après-ski

Skiing in Austria doesn't necessarily entail frigid weather; normal daytime temperatures in January can reach –5°C (23°F). The varied terrain of high Alps, sharp glaciers and graceful mountain meadows has led to the development of both Alpine and Nordic skiing here, and most resorts offer a variety of trails. The country food and mountain-town hospitality are also legendary, though it's best to try and avoid the busy school holidays. December may be the beginning of good snow, but it is usually still fine in March and can last almost until summer.

The snowboard, relatively new to the scene, is becoming popular. Among the early converts are lesser-known resorts – Fieberbrunn, Alpbach and Ischgl (in Tyrol), Badgastein (in Salzburg Province) and Kleines Walsertal (in Vorarlberg) – looking to carve out new identities as snowboard meccas. December brings countless competitions to Tyrol and Salzburg Province. Still more dangerous pursuits are at hand: helicopters and parachutes, if one has the stomach for them, will quickly carry a skier to fields of fresh virgin snow.

▽ **LIVELY APRÈS-SKI**
The après-ski scene rivals neighbouring Switzerland in opulence and likely outpaces it in sheer *joie de vivre*.

▽ **CROSS-COUNTRY**
Lermoos (in Tyrol) and Ramsau (in Styria) maintain perhaps the best-kept Nordic skiing fields in Austria.

SPECTATOR SPORT

Spectating is a major sport in Austria: there are three World Cup events each year. The most significant of these are the annual Hahnenkahm competition in Kitzbühel and the Kandahar Race in St Anton am Arlberg, a resort that also hosted the World Alpine Ski Championships in 2001.

▷ **INSTRUCTION ON THE NURSERY SLOPES**
Even the smallest resort will invariably possess its own ski school, perfect for the novice and experienced skier alike.

△ THRILL SEEKERS

One of the most thrilling ways to experience a fresh snowfield is to fly to one by helicopter. Tourist offices have details of heli-skiing guides.

▽ THE WORLD CUP

The Hahnenkahm World Cup race is Austria's most famous. Skiers like Mario Reiter ski down the near vertical run at Kitzbühel each January.

△ SNOW-CAPPED RESORT

High, sunny and blessed with plenty of snow, the town of Lech am Arlberg is one of Vorarlberg's popular resorts.

△ DOWNHILL ALL THE WAY

Downhill powder skiing was first devised in the Arlberg region – which overlaps bits of Tyrol and Vorarlberg – towards the end of the 19th century.

▷ AT THE CUTTING EDGE

Tyrol has always been at the cutting edge of snowboarding. Austria's first club was founded in 1984 in St Johann in Tirol.

TAKING CARE ON THE SLOPES

Skiing can be fun and invigorating, but take care that a day on the slopes doesn't lead to trouble. First, get fit before you go – skiing requires exertion. Next, be sure to wear insulated clothing. Don't forget sunscreen, and sun goggles to spare your eyes from the glare of the sun.

When you do hit the slopes, pay attention to the markers. In Austria, pistes are marked using disks on a pole: blue denotes an easy run, red indicates medium difficulty and a black marker is for experts only. A system of plastic globes steers you towards the run should you stray off course: green indicates a run, combined green and red globes mark its edges and red indicates areas outside the run. Finally, remember that avalanches are a rare but serious risk in the high mountains of Europe so don't go off piste without a guide.

PLACES

A detailed guide to the entire country, with principal sites clearly cross-referenced by number to the maps

I f one feature characterises Austria more than any other it is its towering mountains. "Land of Mountains" is the opening line of the country's national anthem, and today the people of Austria have even more reason to eulogise their landscapes. The upland pastures, which once made life so difficult for highland farmers, are now criss-crossed by ski lifts and cable-cars, evidence of the booming summer and winter tourist industry that accounts for the largest slice of the national economy.

Nestled amongst the wild Alpine scenery are hundreds of mountain lakes and idyllic watercourses that exercise an attraction of their own, especially in summer. The gentle charms of both the Salzkammergut and the lakes of Carinthia are underlined by the majestic backdrop of the mountains.

To the east, the foothills of the Alps gradually peter out in the Vienna Woods, reaching to the very suburbs of the nation's capital. Along the Danube, which crosses northeast Austria for 350 km (220 miles) of its course, stood the outposts of the Roman Empire. It was here, too, that Irish monks brought Christianity to Central Europe. Upper Austria, Lower Austria and eastern Styria have been cultivated by man since time immemorial and have been the scene of many episodes of Central European history.

Vienna, once the seat of the Babenberg dynasty and for over 600 years the centre of the vast Habsburg empire, is today one of the loveliest cities in the world and the repository of a wealth of art treasures.

Every period of European cultural history is reflected in Austria. Romanesque, Gothic, Renaissance and Baroque buildings are scattered across the land. Statues, frescoes, ceiling and wall paintings document more than 1,000 years of history.

Austrians have a reputation for being a hospitable and amenable race. The tradition stretches back a long way. For centuries Austria has been crossed by foreign peoples and tribes, by soldiers and traders. Many of them made their homes here. The inhabitants of the eastern provinces, in particular, reveal a mixture of Germanic and Slavic characteristics. In Salzburg and Tyrol, by contrast, the people are very like Bavarians. The natives of Vorarlberg, however, are of Alemannic and Rhaetian descent, and are related to the Swiss inhabitants of the Engadine and Upper Rhine.

In spite of these differences they are all proud Austrians. Since the fall of the Habsburgs and the testing period of the Third Reich they have forged a new, specifically Austrian, identity. ❑

PRECEDING PAGES: footprints in the virgin snow; traditional procession on a Tyrolean mountainside; cyclists in the Wachau.
LEFT: Alpine idyll near Goldegg, in Salzburg Province.

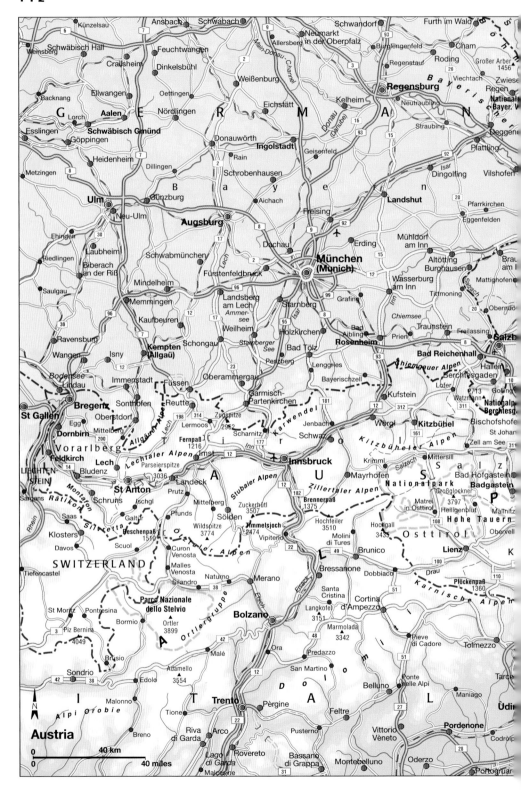

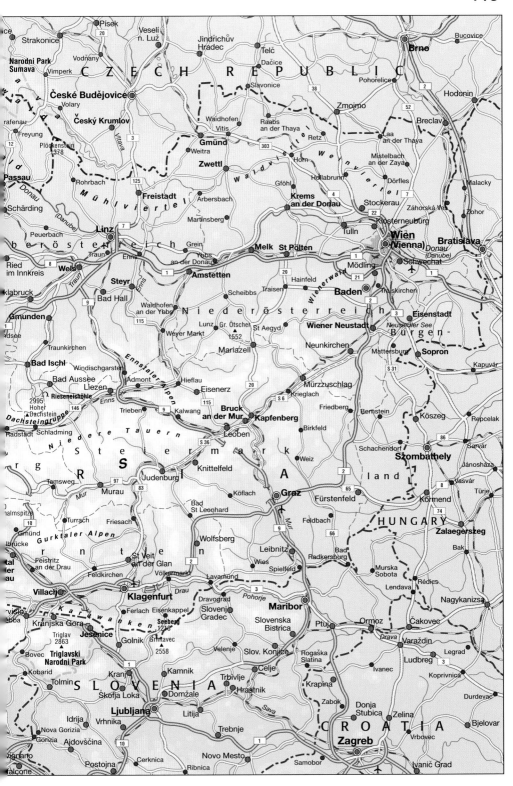

VIENNA: THE OLD CITY

Vienna's compact historic centre is a treasure trove of secular and sacred gems, from the famous cafés and grand Habsburg palaces to the magnificent Gothic cathedral at its heart

Map on page 120

Vienna (Wien) is a world-famous metropolis that has never quite shed its provincial image. Even when it was the administrative centre for an empire of more than 50 million subjects, Johannes Brahms remarked that he lived in Vienna because he could work well only in a village. Of its many contradictions, Vienna's ability to be profoundly conservative and extraordinarily progressive at the same time is something that stands out: you see it in the architectural mix of Baroque and Gothic with Secession, Jugendstil and now ecological postmodern; and in the attitudes of the people, scornful of innovation but demanding the most sophisticated modern infrastructure. This can be summed up in the Viennese tram, a means of transport abolished in many other cities, but here reborn in the 1990s when sleek, futuristic wagons, replacing the old models, began to carry people through the traffic jams reliably and in comfort.

Conservatism and flexibility also clash in the eternal question of immigration, which causes racist moaning, even while the moaner is in search of a reliable Serb cleaning woman, or a Polish carpenter, or a Croatian construction worker. Some of these "immigrants" are temporary *Gastarbeiter* ("guest workers"), but many, according to an old tradition, are the parents of children who will join the Viennese melting pot. Vienna is a city where the temporary and provisional transform imperceptibly into the permanent and traditional. A Viennese, remarked one close observer, "is and remains a somewhat ungraspable character – a sketch, a draft, never a completed whole...".

PRECEDING PAGES: Old City rooftops from the west. **LEFT:** the National Library in the Hofburg. **BELOW:** hussar figure high above the Kohlmarkt.

Moments in Viennese history

Vienna owed its rise to its position at a commercial crossroads. The north–south axis was identified with the amber trade route, running from the Baltic to Aquilea (on the Adriatic), that existed from prehistoric times. The east–west axis is represented by the River Danube, one of Europe's great trading arteries, which runs from the Black Forest 2,850 km (1,770 miles) to the Black Sea. The river served as the Romans' northern frontier, and their defensive forts along its banks often had garrisons and civilian settlements attached. One such was Vindobona, a Roman forerunner of Vienna dating from 15 BC and occupying part of today's **Altstadt** (Old City).

Around this garrison town, the Romans resettled the indigenous Celtic inhabitants from the strategic Kahlenberg and Leopoldsberg *(see page 147)*, which make up the last eastern stretch of both the Alps and the **Wienerwald** (Vienna Woods). The square plan of the Roman town bounded an area now marked by the Graben to the south, the Rotenturmstrasse to the southeast and the Tiefer Graben to the northwest. To the south and west of the garrison lay the Roman rest-and-recreation

area, remains of which have been discovered and exposed on the Michaelerplatz in front of the Michaelertor of the Hofburg (former Habsburg residence).

Following the retreat of the Romans in the early 5th century, Vindobona somehow survived the Dark Ages but in a much reduced state. It was revived when the Babenberg Margrave (incorporating much of modern Austria) was set up by the German Emperor, Otto II, in 976 as a buffer against the insurgent Hungarians. By then it was known as Wenia, later Wien, after the old Celtic name for the small river that ran from the Wienerwald into the Danube. This name first appears in an 881 document specifying land rights, but Vienna become important only when the Babenberg Margraves moved their court here in 1156, the year in which their territory was elevated to a dukedom. This was a defining moment for the city: the ducal court was set up in the area still known as Am Hof (At the Court), and Irish monks were summoned from Regensburg to found their Benedictine monastery here.

Under the Babenbergs, many of Austria's greatest abbeys and cloisters were founded along the Danube, and an agreement with the powerful bishopric of Passau led to a new parish church dedicated to St Stephen just outside Vienna's city boundary to the east. This predecessor of the great Stephansdom was consecrated in 1147 in a ceremony attended by Emperor Konrad III and his crusaders. Under Leopold VI (1198–1230), Vienna became wealthy on the backs of visiting merchants, who were obliged to sell their wares in the city, thus guaranteeing the Viennese the lion's share of the downstream Danubian trade.

The Babenberg line died out when Friedrich II was killed in battle in 1246. Austria was then ruled by Ottokar II of Bohemia, and it was he who built the first fort that was to be extended gradually over the next 600 years by his

Paradoxically, the monastery founded by Irish monks in Vienna in the 12th century is called the Schottenstift or Scots Abbey (see page 128) – Ireland was known at the time as Scotia Maior.

BELOW: a 1609 view of Vienna, showing the 16th-century ramparts.

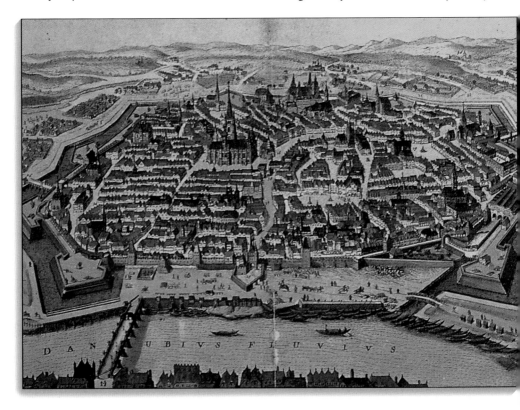

successors, the Habsburgs, and which we know today as the Vienna Hofburg. After Rudolf of Habsburg defeated Ottokar in 1278, Vienna became the imperial residence of one of history's greatest dynasties.

The pious Babenbergs had already initiated the first religious building boom, which was to be repeated twice under the Habsburgs. In the late Middle Ages the city was flooded with religious orders, who built their cloisters and churches in Gothic style. A few of these, like the Minoritenkirche *(see page 127)*, have retained their Gothic aspect, but most were transformed into Baroque affairs in the second great wave of religious architecture during the Counter-Reformation from 1622. If we (wrongly) think of Vienna as primarily a Baroque city, it is no doubt because of the powerful impression made by the architecture at a time when Prince Eugene built the fabulous Belvedere (as well as a fine winter palace within the city walls), and other great noble families – Liechtensteins, Starhembergs, Lobkowitzes, Dietrichsteins – changed the face of the city.

Map on page 120

Victory over Lutherans and Turks

This great building boom took place after the second Turkish siege of 1683 was repulsed at the last moment by armies under Jan Sobieski of Poland. After the double victory over Lutheranism (Vienna had been 80 percent Protestant in the late 16th century) and the Turks, both the Church and the nobility began to build in a spirit of triumph. Nobles built summer palaces outside the inner city walls and, later, the burghers also began to escape to the suburbs and villages that have gradually been incorporated into the city over the past hundred years. The furthest urban periphery was the *Linienwall*, built in the 18th century to protect against marauding Hungarian freedom fighters and demolished in 1893. Now it has been replaced by a ring road, with traffic jams by day, and prostitutes, garish lights and tacky bars by night.

By contrast, the narrow confines of the inner city present a kaleidoscopic architectural and social impression of Vienna through the ages. Much of Viennese life was clustered around an artificially confined court – after the first Turkish siege of 1529, elaborate defensive bastions in a star formation girdled the medieval town. These were not removed until the Ringstrassen boulevard *(see page 135)* was created to replace it by order of Emperor Franz Joseph in 1857.

Any modern building in this microcosmically focused environment has inevitably been controversial, whether it be the notorious house built by Adolf Loos on the Michaelerplatz in 1911, which was deemed an unfitting accompaniment to the Michaelerkirche and the Hofburg; or Hans Hollein's bold Haas-Haus (1990), which faces the Stephansdom, itself a building that embodies all that the Viennese hold sacred. Yet people often seem to forget that Vienna has always been a jumble of old and new, outward- and inward-looking, reactionary and progressive, ascetically pious and lustily sybaritic. Today the area of nightlife known as the Bermuda Triangle shares space with the city's oldest standing church (Ruprechtskirche) and the synagogue, while the Stephansdom is a stone's throw from the Graben and Kärntner Strasse with their fashionable, expensive shops.

BELOW:
Stephansdom on fire in 1945.

A further incongruity is the fact that the Socialists have been in power in the city since 1918, yet no-one has been more assiduous in assisting the preservation of churches, palaces and monuments – the heritage of their traditional enemies. Still, not all would regard their tenure as benign: the wealthy were taxed until the pips squeaked in the 1920s period of "Red Vienna", a policy that ensured the provision of the high-quality mass housing that remains a feature of the city.

A Martian coming to earth would unhesitatingly land at Vienna, thinking it the capital of the planet.

– BILL BRYSON

The heart of the Old City

The **Stephansdom ❶** (open daily; entrance fee for towers only) is the focal point of the inner city, and indeed of Vienna. The glorious Gothic south tower (known affectionately as the *Steffl* to the Viennese) was finished in 1435 and should have been complemented by a north tower, of which only a stump remains. The earliest part of the church is the west facade with two Romanesque towers known as Pagan Towers (*Heidenturme*), although their supposed resemblance to minarets is not apparent to the modern eye.

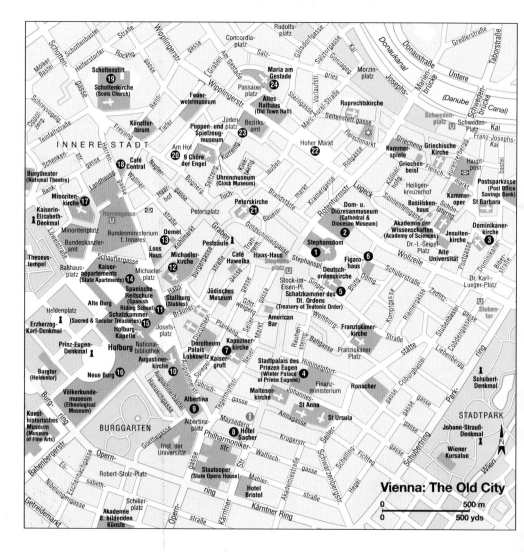

Vienna: The Old City

It is worth walking round the outside to admire the monumental effect of the whole, and the intricacies of the architecture of the **South Tower** from which Count Starhemberg directed operations against the Turks during the siege of 1683. You should also look up at the colourful tiled roof that bears the Habsburg double-eagle on one side, and the coats of arms of Vienna and Austria on the other. The entire roof of the cathedral burned out in the last days of World War II, and all the Austrian provinces contributed to its rebuilding, together with the recasting and installation in the north tower of the great bell (known as the *Pummerin*), which was partly made from abandoned Turkish cannons. Against the northeastern external wall of the cathedral is the pulpit from which the Dominican Giovanni Capistrano preached during the crusade against the Turks of 1454–55.

The interior is remarkable for the many Baroque altars that replaced Gothic ones during the Counter-Reformation. Two particular highlights are the **Albertine Choir**, initiated by the Habsburg Albrecht II and completed under his successors in 1340, and, not far from the west door, Anton Pilgram's **pulpit** (*circa* 1500), whose side panels show the fathers of the Church represented as the four humours. The Pilgram self-portrait below shows him leaning out of a window, and he is also represented under the organ loft on the north wall.

Walking northeast round the church from here, you pass the entrance to the **catacombs**, where the embalmed entrails of many Habsburg rulers were deposited. At the end of the north nave is the **Wiener Neustadt Altar** (1447), with its sculptured groups showing the life of Christ and of the Virgin Mary. The Baroque high altar (1640) by Tobias Pock depicts the martyrdom of St Stephen, and beyond it, at the souteastern corner, is the fine late-Gothic **Tomb of Emperor Friedrich III** (1467) by Niclaes Gerhaert van Leyden. For a close look you have to join a guided tour, which is certainly worthwhile for this is one of Austria's best sepulchral monuments. Many of the cathedral's other treasures are displayed at the **Dom- und Diözesanmuseum ❷** (Cathedral and Diocesan Museum) (open Tues–Sat; entrance fee; tel: (01) 51 552-3689), which is at Stephansplatz 6, to the north of the cathedral.

Exploring on foot

The rest of this chapter is arranged as three walking tours, each of which starts and ends at the Stephansdom. The passageway leading north from the entrance to the cathedral museum brings you to the Wollzeile, which features attractive antiquarian bookshops and the recommended Café Diglas at No. 10. Continuing north, the passageway that leads to the Köllnerhofgasse contains Vienna's most famous Wienerschnitzel restaurant, **Figlmüller**, which is somewhat touristy, but nonetheless atmospheric and moderately priced. The waiters are famed for their sarcasm. To avoid falling victim to it, don't order a beer; it's not done here – drink the tindery Grüner Veltliner wine and be happy!

Continuing on Köllnerhofgasse, you pass the entrance (from Grashofgasse) to the tranquil oasis of the Heiligenkreuzerhof, a former monastic complex. Veer right on to the Fleischmarkt and you will reach the impressive **Greek Orthodox Church**, redesigned by Theophil Hansen in the 1860s. Continuing east past

In the high season, Mozart impersonators wander the Old City selling concert tickets.

BELOW: the tiled roof of the Stephansdom.

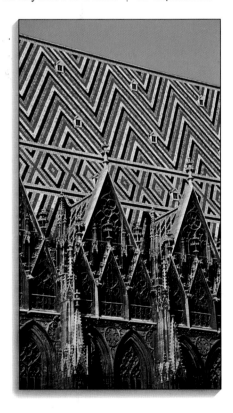

The twin steeples of the Jesuit Church tower above the surrounding streets.

BELOW: Adolf Loos's American Bar, off Kärntner Strasse.

the newly renovated Central Post Office with its trendy cyber shop, you come into the Postgasse where, at No. 4, is the **Dominican Church ❸**. The church features a fine Baroque interior, the highlight of the frescoes being Johann Spillenberger's *Adoration of the Shepherds* next to the pulpit.

Turn right at the end of Postgasse and you will arrive, via Bäckerstrasse, in Dr-Ignaz-Seipel-Platz. In front of you is the Academy of Sciences, facing the Old University across the square. To the north is the **Jesuit Church** (1631), with a later interior by Andrea Pozzo and exotic barley-sugar columns recalling the main altar of St Peter's in Rome. If you head south from the square (recrossing the Wollzeile and heading along the Riemergasse and the Seilerstatte), a right turn brings you into the Himmelpfortgasse, in which is the **Winter Palace of Prince Eugene of Savoy ❹** (1709, now the Ministry of Finance), designed by the two great rivals of the Austrian Baroque, J.B. Fischer von Erlach and Lukas von Hildebrandt. Fischer laid claim to the overall concept, with the implication that Hildebrandt's contribution was mere tinkering. The impressive stairway, with Atlas figures by Giovanni Giuliani, may be glimpsed if you ask the porter.

One block to the north is the Franciscan Church, which has some startling illusionistic effects in its Baroque interior. Further east on Weihburggasse, the street that runs along the southern side of the church, is the **British Bookshop**, a long-standing Viennese institution that has a good selection of books about Austria. Back at the church, exit the northern side of the Franziskanerplatz into the Singerstrasse; at No. 7 (to the west) is the **Deutschordenskirche und Schatzkammer ❺** (Church and Treasury of the Teutonic Knights) (open Mon, Wed–Sat; Mon and Thur am only; Wed and Fri pm only; entrance fee; tel: (01) 512 1065). The highlight here is the treasury overlooking an attractive cobbled

courtyard, at the foot of whose stairway is a painted, 18th-century *sala terrena*. This ecclesiastical collection, which includes secular objects relating to the crusades, when the order of knights was founded, is a lot more interesting than most comparable exhibitions. The last stop on this walk, one street to the north, is the **Figarohaus** ❻ (Domgasse 5; open Tues–Sun; entrance fee; tel: (01) 513 6294), where Mozart lived (1784–87) and wrote *The Marriage of Figaro*. You can listen to Mozart's works on headphones, but there is not much to attract the casual visitor, save for a few manuscript copies and similar memorabilia. Two minutes' walk brings you back to Stephansplatz to the west.

Map on page 120

The doormen keep up appearances at the Hotel Sacher.

South and west of Stephansdom

From the cathedral, Stephansplatz merges to the south with Stock-im-Eisen (Iron-in-Wood) Platz, named after the tree stump on its periphery, where visiting iron-trade apprentices would knock in a nail for luck. **Kärntner Strasse** is a fashionable pedestrian shopping zone leading south towards the opera house and the Ringstrasse. In a narrow street to the right (Kärntner Durchgang) is Adolf Loos's celebrated **American Bar,** a symphony of mirrors and marble that measures only 5 metres (16 ft) by 2.5 metres (8 ft), but seems considerably larger, and which has a coffered ceiling of yellow and white marble.

The next right turn off Kärntner Strasse brings you into the Neuer Markt, on the southwestern side of which is the **Kapuziner Kirche und Kaisergruft** ❼ (Capuchin Church and Imperial Crypt) (open daily; entrance fee; tel: (01) 512 6853). Of the crypt's Baroque sepulchres, Balthasar Moll's tomb of Emperor Franz Stephan I and his wife, Maria Theresa, is probably the finest, but those of Empress Elisabeth, and Zita, the last empress, buried here in 1989, are more popular. In the centre of the square is a copy of Georg Rafael Donner's **Providentia Fountain**, whose naked figures shocked Maria Theresa's Chastity Commission, and which was removed in 1773.

BELOW: Providentia Fountain, too risqué for Maria Theresa.

Tegetthoffstrasse leads to the corner of Albertinplatz, passing on the right the Tirolerhof Café, much favoured by the locals. The Mozart Café on the left featured in Graham Greene's screenplay for *The Third Man*, since when it has lost its shabby genteel character. Adjacent to it and facing the back of the opera *(see page 139)*, is the **Hotel Sacher** ❽, famous not only for its *Sachertorte*, but also for its tradition as a watering hole of the *beau monde*. The most illustrious of its 20th-century regulars was the playwright Thomas Bernhard (1931–89), whose coruscating plays about the Austrian character caused scandals when staged at the Burgtheater in the 1980s. Sacher remains steadfastly traditional (ties are still required for the Red Bar and jackets for the restaurant), yet is surprisingly unstuffy, as befits a place where aristocrats and the new rich used to conduct discreet affairs with ballet dancers in Imperial times, while the cigar-smoking proprietress stood at the back door feeding the poor with leftovers.

West of Sacher is the Albertinaplatz with Alfred Hrdlicka's monument against war and fascism at its centre. Also on the square is the **Albertina** ❾ (open daily; Wed until 9pm; entrance fee; tel: (01) 534 830). This famous museum houses a huge collection of graphic art

TIP

The evening performances of the Spanish Riding School need to be booked months in advance by writing to Spanische Reitschule, Hofburg, A-1010, Wien, fax: (01) 535 0186. Tickets for the morning training sessions are sold on the day at the entrance to the school.

BELOW: a Lipizzaner stallion performing a *Levade*.

(including drawings by Dürer, Rubens and Picasso). It was reopened in 2003 after major renovations. To the north is the striking **Lobkowitz Palais**, with a facade by Fischer von Erlach. The Palais now houses the **Theatre Museum** (open Tues–Sun; Wed until 8pm; entrance fee; tel: (01) 512 8800). Further north, at Dorotheergasse 11, is the **Jewish Museum** (open Sun–Fri; Thur until 8pm; entrance fee; tel: (01) 535 0431), which has permanent displays on Viennese Jewish culture and regularly puts on temporary exhibitions. On the same street, at No. 6, is the dim and smoky **Café Hawelka**, a longtime favourite of Viennese intellectuals and celebrities.

Walking northwest along the Augustiner Strasse, you pass the entrance on your left (on Josefsplatz) to the 14th-century **Augustinerkirche** ⑩, formerly the parish church of the court. The interior is austere, but it does contain Antonio Canova's much admired Neoclassical tomb for Marie Christine, Maria Theresa's favourite daughter, as well as the Herzgruftel (Little Crypt of the Hearts), the hearts in question being those of the Habsburgs. On Sundays at 11am, Mass is celebrated here with a full orchestra and choir – worth experiencing, but the church is very cold, so dress up warmly. At Josefsplatz you enter the precincts of the **Hofburg** itself: on your left is the Hofbibliothek (the court library designed by Fischer von Erlach, with a marvellous Baroque interior).

Ahead is the **Redoutensaal**, and to its right the **Spanish Riding School** ⑪ (open for training Mar–Jun, Sept–Oct, Dec: Tues–Sat am only; entrance fee; tel: (01) 533 9031). A relatively new attraction is the **Lipizzaner Museum** (open daily; entrance fee; tel: (01) 52 524-416) in the former pharmacy (entrance between the Hofburg and the arcaded **Stallburg**). This is the place to buy souvenirs, literature and tickets for morning training and to view the horses through windows giving onto some of the boxes. The history of the Lipizzaners is interestingly displayed.

Mummies in open coffins

Continuing northwest onto the Michaelerplatz, the **Michaelerkirche** ⓬ is on your right. This is a Romanesque and Gothic church with a Neoclassical facade and a dramatic Baroque backdrop to the high altar *(St Michael Expelling the Rebellious Angels)*. Take a guided tour of the crypt (tel: (01) 5538 0000), which features mummified figures in open coffins. Opposite the church on the north side of the square is the **Loos Haus** (1911), whose plain facade is said to have so dismayed the emperor that he kept the curtains drawn in the Hofburg opposite. The house (now a bank) is accessible in working hours and for exhibitions, and has a beautiful marbled interior. The Kohlmarkt runs northeast from here to the Graben, passing Vienna's best map and guide shop (Freytag Berndt) on the right; on the left is the famous **Demel** ⓭, a former "royal and imperial" confectioner with an elegant neo-Rococo interior. The prices are high, but the cakes are legendary – it's worth braving the connoisseurs to take your pick from the display counter. The long-running dispute with nearby Hotel Sacher over the *Sacher Torte* recipe was settled with a compromise in 1965 – only Sacher can use the one-word name *(Sachertorte)* and call its product "original".

The **Hofburg** may be entered from the Michaelerplatz through the Michaelertor under a green and gilded cupola; a right turn in the large courtyard (known as "In der Burg") beyond brings you to the Kaisertor and the entrance to the **Kaiserappartements** ⓮, as well as the Silver and Porcelain Collection (both open daily; entrance fee; tel: (01) 533 7570). The latter is redolent of elegance and wealth, the former a rather dreary trudge through rooms occupied by Emperor Franz Joseph and Empress Elisabeth, their ambience going some way to explaining why the empress was so depressed.

Map on page 120

The infamous Sacher Torte *is just one of the many delectable cakes at Demel.*

BELOW: statue representing Habsburg power, on Michaelerplatz.

THE SPANISH RIDING SCHOOL

This world-famous equestrian spectacle has its origins in the foundation in 1572 of an Imperial school of horsemanship. A stud farm was set up in Lipizza near Trieste, hence the name "Lipizzaner stables", and was moved to its present location in Piber *(see page 181)* when Lipizza became part of Slovenia after World War I.

Originally an Arab, Berber and Spanish hybrid, the horses were imported from Spain and bred for their qualities of grace and stamina. The dressage steps of the trained horses might look somewhat artificial but they actually derive from Renaissance battle manoeuvres. These include the *Capriole* – a leap into the air with the hind legs kicking out; the *Levade* – a rear-up with the hocks of the hind legs almost touching the ground; and the *Croupade* – a leap into the air with all four legs tucked under the belly.

Of the 40 or so foals born at the stud farm every year, only a handful of males are considered worthy of admission, at the age of four, to the Riding School, where the training process takes an average of eight years. The training of riders is done without textbooks or written orders and is based on knowledge passed down by word of mouth from generation to generation.

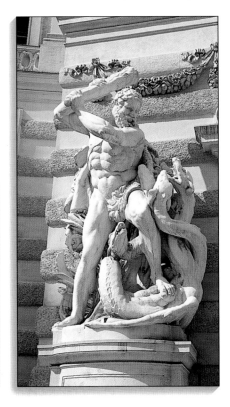

TIP

To book seats for a performance of the Vienna Boys' Choir, write at least 10 weeks in advance to Hofburgkapelle, Hofburg, A-1010 Wien, fax: (01) 216 3942-53. Otherwise, standing-room tickets are sold at the chapel between 3pm and 5pm on the preceding Friday.

BELOW: the President's suite in the Hofburg.

Of greater interest are the **Sacred and Secular Treasuries** ⓯ (open Wed–Mon; entrance fee; tel: (01) 52 524-0), reached through the Swiss Gate on the southeast side of the same courtyard. The entrance is below the steps to the **Burgkapelle**, where the Vienna Boys' Choir sings mass (Sep–June: every Sun at 9.15am). Although some of the claims made for the "relics" in the Sacred Treasury may seem unlikely and other items, such as the agate bowl once claimed to be the Holy Grail, are crusaders' loot, the rarity, exoticism and sheer glamour of many of the items on display make this a unique museum. Moreover, this may be the only chance you'll ever have to see the horn of a unicorn.

To reach more museums in the ponderous **Neue Burg** ⓰, retrace your steps to In der Burg and turn southwest through an arch onto the Heldenplatz. It was on this square that thousands turned out to welcome Hitler in 1938, when he addressed them from the balcony of the National Library after the Anschluss. More recently it has seen demonstrations against Kurt Waldheim and the right-wing coalition incorporating the Freedom Party *(see page 55)*. In addition to the National Library, there are three museums in the Neue Burg (all open Wed–Mon; entrance fee; tel: (01) 52 524-484): the Ephesus Museum displays the finds from excavations in Ephesus and Samothrace; the Collection of Arms and Armour is considered the most impressive in the world; the Collection of Ancient Musical Instruments is a fitting homage to a musical nation (several Habsburgs were accomplished composers).

If you leave the Heldenplatz at the north corner, you will pass the Austrian President's suite in the Leopold Wing of the Hofburg on your right, and the Volksgarten followed by the offices of the Chancellor and the Foreign Office (on Ballhausplatz) on your left. The Bruno-Kreisky-Gasse leads to the Minoriten-

platz and the **Minoritenkirche** ⑰, with its elaborate Gothic portal. This is the church of the city's Italian community – most of the long-standing foreign communities in Vienna have their own churches, which hold services in their native tongue. There are imposing Baroque palaces (mostly ministries) on the west and north sides of the square, which you leave at the northwest, turning right into Bankgasse, which is likewise lined with Baroque facades.

Map
on page
120

The street of lords

Bankgasse leads into Herrengasse (the Street of Lords, referring to the nobles who lived near the court in imperial times) almost opposite **Palais Ferstel**. This palace (built 1856–60) is named after its Ringstrassen architect, Heinrich Ferstel, who built it to house the stock exchange, as well as fancy shops and the subsequently celebrated **Café Central** ⑱. Vienna's *fin de siècle* literati started coming here in 1897 after the Café Griensteidl (now reopened) on the Michaelerplatz was closed amid much wailing and gnashing of teeth. The writer Alfred Polgar described the Central as "a true asylum for people who want to kill time so as not to be killed by it". It is now a tourist trap, but the neo-Gothic interior is nevertheless impressive. Don't be deceived by the astonishing life-like mannequin just inside the door. This model of a man reading a newspaper represents Peter Altenberg, a cult writer of *fin de siècle* Vienna who spent a lifetime living on credit in coffee houses and sponging off friends. In truth his talent was minor, his reputation grossly inflated by the narcissistic Viennese.

Adjoining Palais Ferstel to the north is the imposing Harrach Palais, whose regular exhibitions often feature artefacts from the Kunsthistorisches Museum *(see page 140)*. The Harrach looks out on the **Freyung**, on the north side of

Traditional fiacres (open carriages) with bowler-hatted drivers give tours of the city.

BELOW: Viennese resting the legs in the Volksgarten.

Map
on page
120

which are the **Schottenkirche** and **Schottenstift** ⑲. The latter (Freyung 6; open Thur–Sun; entrance fee; tel: (01) 53 498-600) is worth a visit for its picture gallery. Two panels *(The Flight to Egypt, The Visitation)* of a 15th-century winged altar feature the earliest known views of Vienna. The church contains the tomb of the first Babenberg duke (Heinrich II, the first ruler to make Vienna his official home, in 1156) and a fine neo-Renaissance altar by Ferstel.

Heading southeast out of Freyung, you pass the Kunstforum of Bank Austria (which puts on first-rate exhibitions) and enter the space known as **Am Hof** ⑳, which was the site of the first ducal court in the 12th century. The dissolution of the Holy Roman Empire was announced from the balcony of the church on the east side in 1806. The empire had existed since the crowning of Charlemagne by the pope in AD 800, but Napoleon was now in the ascendant and there was no room for other would-be European emperors. To the left of the church a narrow street leads to the **Clock Museum** (Schulhof 2; open Tues–Sun; entrance fee; tel: (01) 533 2265), whose fascinating collection features 3,000 timepieces from the 15th to the 20th century. From here it is a short walk southeast to Stephansplatz.

The northwest corner

The main thoroughfare running west of the cathedral is the fashionable **Graben**, whose ornate Trinity Column, also known as the Pestsäule (Plague Column), celebrates the city's deliverance from the disease in 1679. Just off the Graben, the Baroque **Peterskirche** ㉑ (1733) is one of the finest works attributed to Lukas von Hildebrandt. A right turn along Tuchlauben brings you to the **Hoher Markt** ㉒, at the eastern end of which you'll find the Jugendstil **Anker Clock** where models of historical figures parade across the clockface every day at noon.

BELOW: the Anker Clock (1913).

To the northeast, in the nightlife area known as the Bermuda Triangle, is the Ruprechtskirche, Vienna's oldest church. The treasures of the nearby Seitenstettengasse synagogue can be seen in the Jewish Museum *(see page 124)*. This area is where the young, but not terribly hip crowd hang out at jazz bars like the Roter Engel, bounce to the flavourless pop at Ma Pitom and sample the endless varieties of beer at Krah Krah.

Northwest of the Hoher Markt, Wipplingerstrasse runs past the Old City Hall, whose Salvatorkapelle has a fine Renaissance entrance, and past (on your left) the **Judenplatz** ㉓, with Rachel Whiteread's controversial **Holocaust Memorial**. Opposite the memorial, the statue of Gotthold Lessing, whose poem *Nathan the Wise* (1779) was a plea for tolerance of Jews, was re-erected in 1982 after the Nazis had removed it. Excavations in the area, which served as the Jewish ghetto until 1421, revealed the remains of the old synagogue, now incorporated into a museum illustrating mediaeval Jewish Vienna (Judenplatz 8; open Sun–Thur, and Fri am; entrance fee; tel: (01) 535 0431).

Further northwest a right turn brings you to **Maria am Gestade** ㉔, Vienna's loveliest Gothic church, built by Michael Knab at the start of the 15th century, whose open-work steeple is especially fine. It is now the church of the Czech community. From here it's a short walk west to the trams on the Ringstrasse, if you don't want to retrace your steps to Stephansplatz. ❑

Vienna's Jewish Community

There has been a Jewish presence in Vienna for around 1,000 years, but it was not until the 19th century that the community was able to prosper in a culture of relative tolerance and freedom. In fact, from the late 1800s until the advent of Austrian Fascism in the 1930s, the Jewish community in Vienna was one of the most visible, vibrant and assimilated in Western Europe. The progressive Emperor Joseph II had granted Jews substantial rights in his Edict of Tolerance in 1781. After the 1848 revolution, thousands arrived from the *shtetls* (traditional village communities) of Galicia and Bukovina (in modern-day Poland, Ukraine and Romania). In District 2, in Leopoldstadt, the *Mazzesinsel* (Orthodox community) established all the institutions needed to supply a full Jewish way of life, including Torah schools, synagogues and kosher butchers.

It was in Vienna more than anywhere else that Jewish intellectuals shaped the development of *fin de siècle* art, science, literature and journalism. The author Arthur Schnitzler (1862–1931) described in his novels and plays the world of the enlightened Jewish bourgeoisie. In keeping with a zeitgeist best expressed by another Viennese Jew, Sigmund Freud, his works are underpinned by psychological analysis.

Freud had his practice in the Berggasse. Opposite, at No. 6, the founder of Zionism, Theodor Herzl, worked on his book *The Jewish State*, which detailed his vision of a mass Jewish exodus to Palestine. Other Viennese Jews prominent in the early 20th century include writers Robert Musil and Stefan Zweig and composers Johann Strauss, Gustav Mahler, Arnold Schönberg and Alban Berg.

By 1910, some 10 percent of the city's population (about 180,000) were Jewish, from small traders to the wealthy middle class. In the same year, of the 174 editorial posts in daily Viennese newspapers, 123 were held by Jews.

But from as early as the stock market crash of 1873, Gentiles had begun to blame their problems on Jewish success. Anti-semitism was further promoted by Karl Lueger, mayor from 1897 to 1910, and by the time Hitler marched into Vienna in 1938, thousands of Jews had already fled. Nevertheless, around 65,000 Viennese Jews died in the Holocaust.

Today the community numbers barely 7,000. The renowned Nazi-hunter Simon Wiesenthal's documentation centre is in the former Jewish textile quarter, and the Jewish Welcome Service tries to maintain ties with emigrants all over the world. Recently, despite fears over the rise of the far-right Freedom Party, political developments have encouraged a cautious renaissance of Jewish culture in Vienna. Austria's first Holocaust memorial has been erected in the city, the synagogue in the Seitenstettengasse reports rising attendance figures and the Jewish Museum charts the community's achievements. But the wounds have not completely healed – as one young Viennese Jew puts it: "You never know when you'll have to pack again." ❑

RIGHT: Orthodox Jews in the Jewish cemetery in Seegasse, north of the Old City.

INTELLECTUAL HAUNTS: THE CAFÉS OF VIENNA

In Vienna's old coffee houses you can fantasise about debating with famous figures who once sat in your place. In Konditorei, *just concentrate on the cakes*

Some of Vienna's cafés are famous landmarks, like the Café Landtmann, the Griensteidl, the Central, the Hawelka, and of course the Sacher. Others are less well known, but remain more authentic. There are still a vast number of them, but they are a pale imitation of Viennese café culture of the early 20th century. The superb coffee, rich assortment of cakes and wide range of newspapers can still be enjoyed, but they have lost their old intellectual buzz.

No longer do their patrons sit at the same marble tables each day to discuss, and in many cases shape, the future of international politics, literature, medicine, psychoanalysis or music. No longer do they draw up party manifestoes and plot revolutions as they play chess, indulge in slanderous gossip about one another, or stave off imminent starvation by persuading the waiter to supply food on credit. All the big names in Vienna in the early 20th century had their own particular favourites.

END OF AN ERA

This highly sophisticated form of popular culture was destroyed by the Nazis because it was dominated by Jewish intellectuals, and it never recovered from this terrible blow. But in one respect at least, Vienna's cafés are in a stronger position than they were 100 years ago: they are havens of tranquillity in contrast to the frenetic pace of life outside, and are greatly envied by visitors. A bonus is to sit outside in summer and watch the world go by while sipping a speciality coffee.

CAFÉ DEMEL ▷
The traditional and elegant Demel *Konditorei* is famous for the elaborate formality of its waiters (I, Kohlmarkt 14). But be warned: in season it's always packed with tourists.

◁ KURKONDITOREI OBERLAA STADHAUS
Opinion is split: is the Oberlaa Stadhaus (I, Neuer Markt 16) or the Demel the best café in Vienna?

HOW TO ORDER YOUR COFFEE

◁ CAFÉ CENTRAL

In the early 1900s, this was the haunt of the Viennese literati; a lot has changed since then, including the prices. However, it still has one famous regular: the writer Peter Altenberg, who died in 1919 and is represented by a papier mâché model (I, Herrengasse 14).

△ DAZZLING CREATIONS

Apple strudel, *Sacher Torte*, mini-pralines, "bishop's bread", cream cakes... Everything on display is of exceptional quality at the Demel, which used to be the official supplier to the Imperial court. This fabulous café is still a place of pilgrimage for foodies.

◻ CAFÉ HAWELKA

The owner of this former artists' café, Mr Hawelka, has been serving customers himself for decades. Today, its wonderful (though smoky) atmosphere makes it especially popular with students and tourists (I, Dorotheergasse 6).

FOOD AND FRESH AIR ▷

Here is a typical summer scene outside St Stephen's Cathedral. Each year, the café waiters put tables and chairs on the pavement or on pedestrianised streets. When consumed outdoors, the coffee and *Torte* seem to taste better than ever.

Since the first Viennese cafés opened in the late 17th century, coffee-drinking has practically become a religion. You don't just go into a café to slurp down a quick cup of coffee and scoff a slice of cake. You go there to gossip, exchange *bons mots*, read the paper, play chess, come up with brilliant ideas, show what a cultured person you are, and not least to refuel before returning to the fray. Therefore, although the coffee may seem somewhat expensive, you are also paying for the privilege of sitting in pleasant surroundings and enjoying the unique and unhurried atmosphere.

Ordering a coffee is a rather more complicated process than you might expect. It is important to get it right to maintain your credibility in the eyes of the waiter! Rather than asking for a *Kaffee* (Austrians stress the first syllable), try getting your mouth around a *kleiner* or *grosser Brauner* (small or large white coffee), a *Kapuziner* (coffee with cream, sprinkled with cocoa or chocolate), an *Einspänner* (black coffee with whipped cream, served in a glass), or one of any number of other varieties. Any good café will automatically serve you a glass of water as well, and you can ask for this to be refilled for free as many times as you like.

VIENNA: THE RINGSTRASSE AND BEYOND

Map on pages 136–7

Circling the inner city, Franz Joseph's grand boulevard, the Ringstrasse, is lined with notable edifices. Beyond it, the outer districts of the city hold delights both historic and modern

The Altstadt (Old City) or Innere Stadt of Vienna is also the First District (out of 22). To the north it is bordered by the Danube Canal (built in the 1870s to prevent constant flooding of the land around Brigittenau and Leopoldstadt to the north and east). Recently incorporated city districts include two beyond the Danube itself, Floridsdorf and the Donaustadt, the latter including Vienna International and the offices of the United Nations agencies.

The Leopoldstadt was the Jewish quarter in the 19th and 20th centuries, until the Nazis deported all of Vienna's 180,000 Jews who had not fled or could not buy their freedom. Its main attraction is the **Prater** ❶ (open daily) with its giant Ferris wheel, funfair and sporting attractions. Originally an imperial hunting ground, the Prater was opened to the public by Joseph II (1780–90), and its promenade became fashionable among the bourgeoisie in the 19th century. Another park worth visiting in the Leopoldstadt is the **Augarten**, an attractive open space despite the presence of one of Hitler's huge bunkers.

The periphery of the Altstadt not touched by the Danube Canal is marked by the pompous **Ringstrasse**, built after 1857, when Emperor Franz Joseph ordered the demolition of the old bastions. The idea was to create a broad boulevard, on the model of Haussmann's Paris, with buildings symbolising the aspirations of liberal democracy. Conversely, the Neoclassical **Parliament** building and the **Rathaus** (City Hall), modelled on their counterparts in the merchant cities of the Middle Ages, can be seen as the narcissistic projection of a wealthy and propertied class. The importance of the historical allusions is evident in Ferstel's neo-Renaissance university, the neo-Gothic Votivkirche, the elaborate symbolism of the parliament statuary and the statue of Athena in front of it.

PRECEDING PAGES: Jugendstil facade by Otto Wagner. **LEFT:** the Giant Wheel in the Prater. **BELOW:** the 19th-century City Hall.

"Ornament is Crime"

The Ringstrasse was criticised by those who didn't share the complacent assumptions behind its creation, but it remains an impressive example of urban planning and often noble symbolic architecture. It transformed Vienna into a modern metropolis, even though its pretensions provoked a hostile reaction at the end of the 19th century. This was most mordantly expressed by the architect Adolf Loos, whose 1908 pamphlet *Ornament is Crime* contemptuously described the petit bourgeoisie as living insignificant lives behind neo-Baroque facades that were feebly reminiscent of princely grandeur.

Trams 1 (clockwise) and 2 (anti-clockwise) run along the Ring and can conveniently be used to visit the sights. Proceeding clockwise from Schwedenplatz,

you pass on your right Otto Wagner's remarkable **Postsparkasse** ❷ (Post Office Savings Bank), a somewhat forbidding example of a functional style that highlights building elements as part of the design. Across the Ring is the War Ministry, fronted by an equestrian statue of Marshal Radetzky, Franz Joseph's most successful general in the fight against Italians rebelling against the Habsburg yoke.

Next on this side of the Ring are the University of Applied Arts and the **Museum für angewandte Kunst** ❸ (Museum of Applied Arts; open Tues–Sun; Tues until midnight; entrance fee; tel: (01) 71 136-0). Here you'll find samples of periods, styles and objects in sets designed by contemporary artists. Most interesting are the excellent exhibits of furniture and Secession artefacts, but there are also temporary exhibitions by modern artists. The excellent café-restaurant is a fashionable place for the art crowd and intellectuals to lunch.

An extended but worthwhile detour to the east brings you to **Hundertwasserhaus** ❹, on the corner of Löwengasse and Kegelgasse. This quirky apartment block was designed by artist and architect Friedensreich Hundertwasser, whose innovative structures dispense with straight lines and often incorporate eco-friendly touches such as a grass-covered roof. The nearby **KunstHaus Wien** has a permanent exhibition devoted to his work, plus a shop and café in his idiosyncratic style (Untere Weissgerberstrasse 13; open daily; entrance fee; tel: (01) 71 204 9512).

Bust of the Waltz King

Back on the Ring, south of MAK is the **Stadtpark** ❺, a green oasis studded with composers' busts, most strikingly that of Johann Strauss, "the Waltz King", near the southwestern end. The River Wien, popular for lovers' trysts, meanders through the park in a sunken bed. Schwarzenbergplatz is beyond the park to the southwest, and a walk up the Rennweg past the Polish Gardekirche brings you to the entrance to the **Lower Belvedere** ❻. This part of the palace, built in 1714–23 for Prince Eugene of Savoy by Lukas von Hildebrandt, houses the Austrian Baroque Museum.

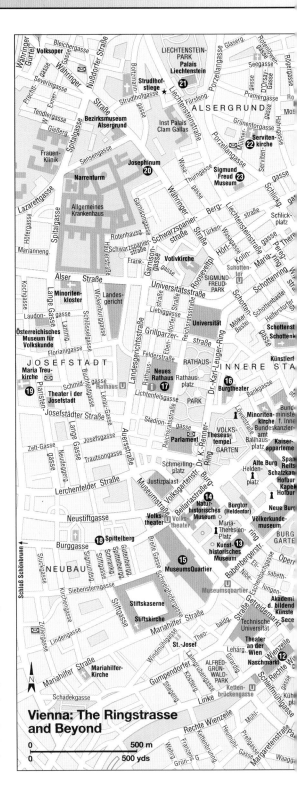

Vienna: The Ringstrasse and Beyond

0   500 m
0   500 yds

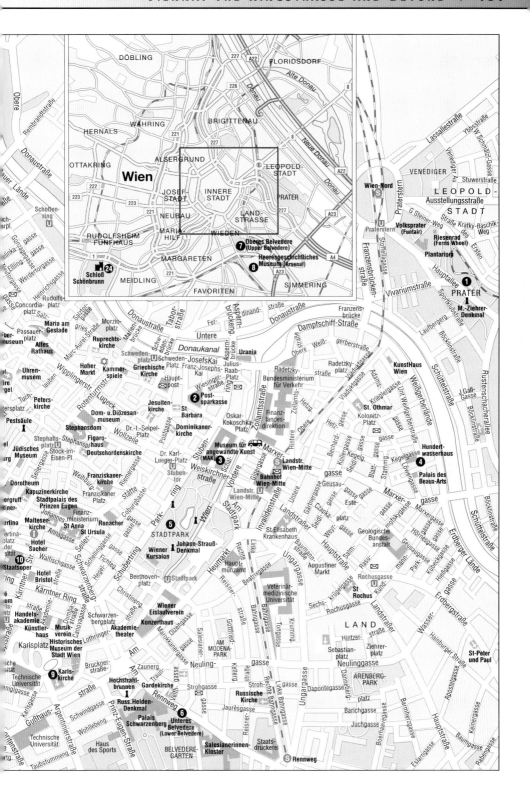

The park that links the two Belvedere palaces is adorned with terraces, statues and fountains.

BELOW: street-cleaners on the Stubenring.

The adjacent **Orangery** contains the excellent Museum of Austrian Medieval Art. The palaces and park were conceived to honour their patron, which is evident in the Baroque Museum's allegorical references to Prince Eugene as Apollo and in Balthasar Permoser's sculpture *The Apotheosis of Prince Eugene*. A stroll up the spacious park brings you to the **Upper Belvedere ⑦** and the Austrian Gallery, whose collection of major works by the likes of Klimt, Schiele and Kokoschka is essential viewing (all Belvedere museums open Tues–Sun; entrance fee; tel: (01) 79 557-134).

South of the Upper Belvedere, Prinz-Eugen-Strasse leads you to the *Gürtel* (ring road), across which and some way to the southeast is the vast military complex of the **Arsenal ⑧**, whose Museum of Military History (open Sat–Thur; entrance fee; tel: (01) 79 561) makes the trek worthwhile. Here you can see the car in which Franz Ferdinand was riding when he was shot in Sarajevo on 28 June 1914, and the mayor of Sarajevo's settee, on which he bled to death. The most moving exhibit is the Tyrolean painter Albin Egger Linz's picture of *The Unknown Soldier*.

Monument to the Unknown Plunderer

A tram ride down Prinz-Eugen-Strasse returns you to Schwarzenbergplatz, passing on the right the Schwarzenberg Palace – now a luxurious hotel with a gourmet restaurant – and the Russian War Memorial. After 1989 there was talk of removing what the Viennese call the "Monument to the Unknown Plunderer" (among ruder appellations), but a treaty obliges the Austrians to maintain it.

A turn to the west on Lothringer Strasse brings you to the Karlsplatz and the **Vienna History Museum** (open Tues–Sun; entrance fee; tel: (01) 505 8747). The glory of the square is the magnificent **Karlskirche ⑨** (1739, by Fischer von

THE SECESSION IN VIENNA

The Austrian Secession paralleled other *fin de siècle* movements – art nouveau in Paris and New York, Jugendstil in German-speaking lands, and the Glasgow Four in Scotland. All displayed a refreshing, sensual vigour expressed in fluid decorative lines and vivid colour.

Members of the Künstlerhaus in Vienna who "seceded" from the art establishment in 1897 were led by the painter Gustav Klimt, who became the Secession's first president. Emblazoned on the walls of the Secession Building, designed by Joseph Maria Olbrich, was the defining slogan "To the Age its Art, to Art its Freedom".

In architecture the Secession spirit is represented by Otto Wagner, designer of the rapid transit railway stations, the Post Office Savings Bank and several villas. His work also incorporated a functionalist element that eschewed the fake decorative grandeur of the prevalent neo-Gothic and neo-Baroque styles. In the applied arts Josef Hoffmann made furniture in the distinctive Secessionist style. He also created whole unified interiors known as *Gesamtkunstwerke*.

Since then, Secessionist art and architecture has become a distinctive feature of the Vienna landscape. To follow the Secessionist trail, see Christian Nebehay's excellent book *Vienna 1900: Architecture and Painting*.

Erlach, father and son), fronted by two free-standing columns modelled on Trajan's Column in Rome. Their corkscrew friezes celebrate the life and work of Saint Carlo Borromeo, renowned for his heroism in the Milan plague. Emperor Karl VI commissioned the church in thanksgiving for the end of the plague that hit Vienna in 1713. The interior is also impressive, but the best view is of the exterior, across the pond with Henry Moore's sculpture *Hill Arches* in the middle. Karlsplatz has an enticing air of faded gentility and in summer office workers can frequently be seen eating their sandwiches on its benches.

Map
on pages
136–7

Mahler by Kitaj

Crossing under busy Lothringer Strasse, the **Künstlerhaus** (a late 19th-century exhibition hall and artists' association) lies ahead and, to the east, the **Musikverein**, home of the Wiener Philharmoniker. Stroll up Dumbastrasse, turn left on the Ring and you come to the **Staatsoper** ❿ (State Opera; tours daily: 2pm and 3pm), scene of many a Mahler and von Karajan triumph, and many a memorable feud. A portrait of Mahler by R. B. Kitaj hangs in the upper lobby.

The Secession Building is topped with a globe of gilded laurel leaves, which locals refer to as the "Golden Cabbage".

Further along the Ring westwards you pass on your left the **Academy of Fine Arts** at Schillerplatz 3, behind which (walk along Makartgasse) is the famous **Secession Building** ⓫ (open Tues–Sun; Thur until 8pm; entrance fee; tel: (01) 587 5307) built by Joseph Maria Olbrich in 1898 *(see opposite)*. Apart from exhibitions of contemporary work, the Secession has the *Beethoven Frieze*, a not entirely successful homage by Klimt inspired by the *9th Symphony*. Labelling in English explains its complicated imagery. If you're hungry, stop off at the clean and modern **Naschmarkt** ⓬ between Linke and Rechte Wienzeile. The market is particularly good for fruit, vegetables and traditional Viennese products.

BELOW: the Künstlerhaus.

Returning to the Ring, continue west, passing the Burggarten on your right. On the left is the imposing **Kunsthistorisches Museum ⑬** (Fine Art Museum; open Tues–Sun; Thur until 9pm; entrance fee; tel: (01) 5252 4403), which contains a vast collection of antiquities and pictures that once belonged to the Habsburgs. On the first floor are the renowned picture galleries, which would take a day to visit thoroughly. Brueghel's depictions of the seasons, Raphael's *Madonna in the Meadow,* Giorgione's *Three Philosophers* and Habsburg portraits by Velasquez are among the major works on display. The Greek, Roman, Sculpture and Decorative Arts sections are currently closed for renovation, though some of their most important pieces are on show in the picture galleries.

The best way to circumnavigate the Ringstrasse is on the regular and efficient trams, which circle it completely in both directions.

The Venus of Willendorf

Opposite the Kunsthistorisches Museum is the **Naturhistorisches Museum ⑭** (Natural History Museum; open Wed–Mon; Wed until 9pm; entrance fee; tel: (01) 52 177). Its contents are also based on Habsburg collections, notably that of Maria Theresa's husband, Franz Stephan. Its most celebrated item is a 25,000-year-old limestone fertility symbol, the Venus of Willendorf *(see page 160).*

To the southwest, what was once the Imperial stables has been transformed into the huge **MuseumsQuartier ⑮** (tel: (01) 0820 600 600), which brings together a number of major collections. It includes the **Leopold Museum** (open Wed–Mon; entrance fee; tel: (01) 525 700), which contains the world's largest collection of works by Egon Schiele, and a new modern art museum, the MUMOK (open Tue–Sun; entrance fee; tel: (01) 52 500-1313). Both are housed in striking new buidings, the Leopold's white limestone contrasting with the MUMOK's dark grey basalt. Other features of the MuseumsQuartier include the Kunsthalle,

BELOW: coffee in the sun at Café Landtmann, near the Burgtheater.

which houses contemporary art exhibitions and includes a theatre in the former Winter Riding School; a children's museum; a tobacco museum and arts centre; an architecture centre; and a number of very modern shops, bars and restaurants.

Moving on round the Ring, you pass the **Parlament** (tours Mon–Fri: 11am and 3pm) designed by Theophil Hansen, opposite the Volksgarten. The park's northwest gate leads to the **Burgtheater ⓰**, designed by Gottfried Semper and Carl von Hasenauer and with attractive painted ceilings over the lateral stairways by the Klimt brothers and their partner, Franz Matsch (for tours, tel: (01) 51 444 4140). Opposite the Burgtheater is Friedrich Schmidt's imposing neo-Gothic **Neues Rathaus ⓱** (tours Mon, Wed and Fri: 1pm), in front of which a Christkindlmarkt of trinkets, oddities, snacks and drinks takes place in Advent. In summer opera films are screened in the park in front of the building.

To the north is the **University**, designed by Ferstel. The Festsaal is not open to the public, but is sometimes accessible: its ceiling features Matsch's *Triumph of Light over Darkness*, and copies of Klimt's *Jurisprudence*, *Medicine* and *Philosophy* surround it (the originals were destroyed in the war). North of the university is Ferstel's austere neo-Gothic **Votivkirche**. To the east, on Schottenring, is the last great Ringstrassen building, Hansen's **Börse** (Stock Exchange).

West and north of the Ring

The **Spittelberg ⓲** between Burggasse and Siebensterngasse (in the 7th District) is an area (stretching to Neustiftgasse in the north) that has become increasingly trendy. In summer the pedestrian zone of the Spittelberggasse is lined with small restaurants and taverns. To the north, **Josefstadt** (8th District), one of Vienna's most desirable residential quarters, is full of enticing small eateries

Map on pages 136–7

TIP

After wandering the hip streets of Josefstadt and the Spittelberg, take a coffee from the famously rude waiters at Café Hummel (Josefstädter Strasse 66). Later on, check out cool bars such as Wirr (Burggasse 70).

BELOW: statue on Beethoven's house in Heiligenstadt, a *Heuriger* village.

HEURIGEN

Along the edge of the city are 7,000 vineyards, the wine from which (all white – usually a Riesling blend) is traditionally drunk in the year following the harvest. The most famous wine villages (now suburbs of Vienna) are Heiligenstadt and Grinzing. The villages are picturesque, and an evening spent at a *Heuriger* (wine tavern) such as Mayer (Pfarrplatz, Heiligenstadt) or Reinprecht (Cobenzl Gasse 22, Grinzing) is an authentic Viennese experience, although you may have to share it with busloads of tourists.

In these popular villages, the larger *Heurigen* also offer *Schrammelmusik* (featuring accordion, guitar and fiddle), which is mostly sentimental and often about death. The wine is an acquired taste, but the buffets, featuring roast pork, fried chicken, sausages, dumplings, cold cuts and a huge salad selection, are usually excellent.

To find *Heurigen* less populated with tourists venture further afield to Neustift am Walde and Salmannsdorf (Tram 38 from Schottentor to Krottenbach/Silbergasse, then Bus 35A), or across the Danube to Jedlersdorf, Stammersdorf (Tram 31 from Schottenring) and Strebersdorf (Tram 32) in the north. The village of Gumpoldskirchen, not far from Baden in the southwest, produces prized white wines and has wine festivals in June and August.

Map on pages 136–7

(try the Alte Backstube at Lange Gasse 34). The **Maria Treukirche** ⑲ on Jodok-Fink-Platz features a superb cycle of Baroque frescoes (1753) with biblical themes by Franz Anton Maulbertsch. The nearby **Schönborn Palais** (Laudongasse 15–19; open Tues–Sun; entrance fee; tel: (01) 406 8905) was designed by Hildebrandt and contains the Museum of Austrian Folklore.

To the north is the 9th district (Alsergrund). Here, in the grounds of the old general hospital, is the **Narrenturm**, or Fools' Tower (enter at Spitalgasse 2), which used to house lunatics but now contains the gruesome Museum of Pathological Anatomy (open Wed pm & Thur am; May–Sept: also first Sat am in month; entrance fee; tel: (01) 406 8672). At Währinger Strasse 25 is the **Josephinum** ⑳, with its Museum of Medical History (open Mon–Fri; entrance fee; tel: (01) 42 776 3401). This former school for military doctors has fascinating life-size anatomical models made by Florentine craftsmen in 1780.

Cross Währinger Strasse, head up Boltzmanngasse and turn right into the Strudlhofgasse to reach the **Strudlhofstiege**, attractive art nouveau steps dating from 1910. Descend here to reach the **Palais Liechtenstein** ㉑ (open daily; entrance fee; tel: (01) 319 5767-0). The Palais opens in March 2004 as the new home of the Liechtenstein Princely Collections. These include paintings by Rubens, van Dyck and Cranach, together with weaponry, porcelain and bronzes.

The Grünentorgasse leads east from the museum past the **Servitenkirche** ㉒. If the doors are open, check out the remarkable stucco in the porch. There's also a fine pulpit by Balthasar Moll, showing the evangelists and allegories of the virtues. From here walk along the Servitengasse and turn right into Berggasse. At No. 19 is the **Freud Museum** ㉓ (open daily: entrance fee; tel: (01) 319 1596). The collection includes Freud memorabilia, souvenirs, books and a video show; the famous divan, however, is in London's Freud Museum. A short walk southeast along Schickgasse or Liechtensteinstrasse brings you back to the Ring.

BELOW: fountain at Schloss Schönbrunn.

Maria Theresa's Rococo cottage

Most visitors to Vienna make the trip out on underground line U4 to **Schloss Schönbrunn** ㉔ (open daily; entrance fee; tel: (01) 81 113-239), the huge palace that Maria Theresa hoped would rival Versailles in its grandeur. Highlights include the Hall of Mirrors where the child prodigy Mozart played for the imperial family, the Blue Chinese Room, reflecting the Rococo taste for chinoiserie, and the Grosse Galerie, where Guglielmi's ceiling frescoes glorify the house of Habsburg and Lorraine.

There is also a chapel, a Rococo theatre and a Carriage Museum, but perhaps Schönbrunn's finest feature is its park, with the Neptune Fountain, "Roman Ruins" and the Gloriette monument (marking Maria Theresa's resistance to the aggression of Frederick the Great). At the Hietzing end of the park is the wrought-iron and glass Palmenhaus and the zoo (open daily; entrance fee; tel: (01) 877 9294). The oldest zoo in the world, it retains the radial Baroque design (1752) of Franz Stephan's original menagerie. The park is popular, especially at weekends, but is easily large enough to accommodate all the joggers, family groups, botanists, bird watchers and pensioners. ❑

Sigmund Freud

Sigmund Freud (1856–1939), the eldest son of an itinerant Jewish textile merchant, was born in Moravia and brought to Vienna aged three. The family settled in the Jewish quarter (the Leopold-stadt). Despite difficult financial circumstances, Freud's parents made sure he had a good education – his childhood heroes apparently included Hannibal and Oliver Cromwell.

An outstanding student, Freud became a neuropathology *Privatdozent* (unsalaried lecturer) in 1885. He travelled to Paris to study under the famous Jean-Martin Charcot, who had pioneered the use of hypnosis in medicine. The encounter with Charcot marked the beginning of Freud's career as the explorer of the unconscious and of therapies to deal with psychological disorders. Back in Vienna Freud worked with Josef Breuer on hysteria but was subject to the opposition of numerous rivals.

For his part Freud observed in 1914 that mankind's flattering view of itself had suffered three great blows since the Middle Ages: first Copernicus put paid to the vain presumption that man is at the centre of the universe, Darwin challenged the belief that mankind is a uniquely elevated species, and psychoanalysis showed that man is not even the master of his own soul.

When Freud's pioneering *The Interpretation of Dreams* appeared in 1900, it went largely unnoticed by a society in decline. Freud remarked that the writer Schnitzler knew by instinct what he himself discovered through empirical enquiry. But just as Schnitzler was pilloried for his candour, so Freud was often lambasted by his colleagues. In 1910 a fellow doctor denounced him at a medical congress with the claim: "Freud's theories have nothing to do with science; they are rather a matter for the police."

Today's revolutionaries found tomorrow's orthodoxies, and over the years Freudianism has bred its own orthodoxy, with the usual accompanying "heresies" and intellectual witch-hunts. Even as his influence was burgeoning across the globe, Freud was being hounded from his native Austria by the Nazis. He left in 1938, and the following year died in exile in England.

Today Freud remains a highly contentious figure and arguments still rage over the scientific nature of his far-reaching experiments. It is unlikely that Freud would have been surprised by this – controversy could have been his middle name. He blithely weathered any number of professional and personal storms for his science. Two of his most bitter arguments were with his distinguished colleagues Alfred Adler (who coined the phrase "inferiority complex") and Carl Gustav Jung, once his heir apparent.

Perhaps it was as much an insight into his own nature as into the human subconscious that provoked his bleak observation: "It really seems as though it is necessary for us to destroy some other thing or person in order not to destroy ourselves."

Despite the sceptics, Freud's monumental achievement in establishing psychoanalysis as a "religion" of the 20th century and beyond, has so far resisted demolition. ❏

RIGHT: Sigmund Freud, the ever-present father-figure of psychoanalysis.

LOWER AUSTRIA

The country's largest province is a subtle landscape of rolling hills and verdant vineyards, peppered with monasteries and castles and bisected by the mighty Danube

Map on page 148

Lower Austria (Niederösterreich) completely surrounds Vienna, so it is the first region you come across as you leave the capital. Here are a few landmarks to enable you to get your bearings: Lower Austria is the River Danube, it's Richard the Lionheart's prison, it's moated castles and thermal springs, bustards and slow-worms, streams and rivers, a place for hiding in haystacks and playing tag in the meadows. You will find something of everything here – forests and vineyards, plains and mountains. The province's most picturesque region is the Wachau – a section of the Danube between the towns of Krems and Melk *(see pages 159–61)*.

The Vienna Woods

As you leave Vienna in a northwesterly direction following Road 14, you will see the city's twin local mountains: the **Kahlenberg** and the **Leopoldsberg**. The road leads past them to **Klosterneuburg ❶**, where the principal sight, visible from far away, is the imposing **Augustinian Monastery**, its church topped by a dome in the form of the Imperial Crown (monastery open daily; fee for obligatory tours; museum open May–Nov: Tues–Sun). The monastery was founded in 1114 by Margrave Leopold III of Babenberg, also known as Leopold the Pious. The church is Romanesque in style and dates from the early 12th century, with a number of later additions. The present interior is of 17th-century origin. The highlight of the tour is the magnificent 12th-century enamel-and-gilt Verdun altar. The town is also home to the new **Essl Collection** of modern Austrian and international art (open Tues–Sun; entrance fee; tel: (0800) 232 800).

The picturesque road between Klosterneuburg and Hütteldorf is known as the **Vienna High Road**; it leads back along the upper slopes of the Kahlenberg and the Leopoldsberg, both of which have cafés and panoramic terraces with magnificent views of Vienna, the Danube and the Marchfeld beyond.

The way leads over the **Sophienalpe**, with its pretty rustic café and picnic meadows (and all only a few minutes' drive from Vienna), through fairy-tale woods to **Mauerbach**, which has the remains of a Carthusian monastery founded in 1313. The combination of the Baroque church, added some three centuries later, and the monks' cells built on to the outside presents an interesting architectural ensemble.

Purkersdorf ❷, just south of Mauerbach, was the site of the first staging post on the old Imperial Road to Linz. The post house, built in 1796 in an early Neo-classical style, is decorated between the windows with reliefs depicting in symbolic manner the secrecy of the postal service. Recently created near this town,

PRECEDING PAGES: sphinx at Schloss Greillenstein. **LEFT:** dawn in the hills. **BELOW:** the grape harvest.

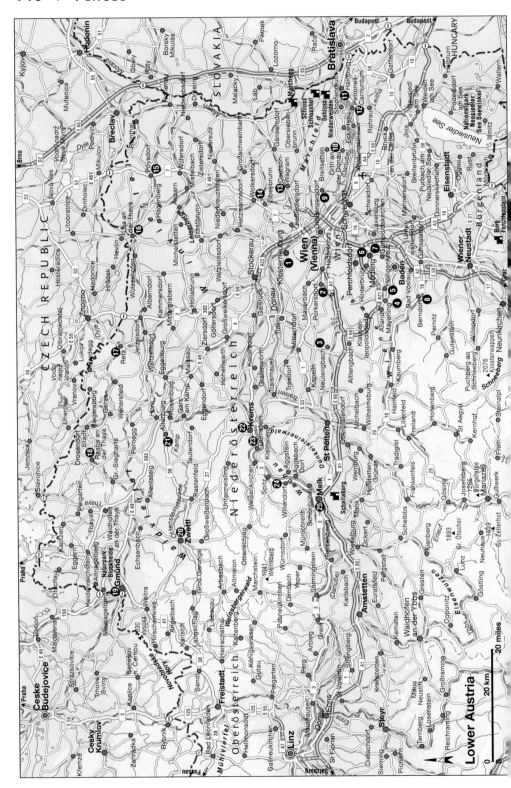

which still retains much of its 19th-century charm, is the **Sandstein-Wienerwald Nature Park**, which includes wildlife enclosures.

Just west of Purkersdorf is a reservoir, the **Wienerwaldsee**. It is surrounded by a district which is elegantly discreet as regards both landscape and inhabitants. Tullnerbach, Pressbaum and Rekawinkel are typical of the recreation areas in the vicinity of the capital. Further west is **Neulengbach** ❸, the "Pearl of the Vienna Woods". It lies on the western fringe, nestled between the Buchberg and the Kohlreith, two mountains that are popular excursion destinations. The town centre was built in about 1200 around the castle of the lords of Lengbach. Its present-day countenance is characterised by well-maintained Renaissance buildings. It is well worth walking from **Altlengbach**, which lies to the south and which is dominated by a 16th-century late-Gothic church, to the **Schöpfl**. Its 895-metre (2,935-ft) summit makes it the highest eminence in the area, hence affording a spectacular panoramic view across the entire Vienna Woods.

Circling back east from here along the Schwechat River via **Klausen-leopoldsdorf** – where the main defile of the Schwechat with its twin wooden attendants' huts provides an attractive scene – one eventually reaches **Alland** and **Mayerling** ❹, on Road 210. Alland was once the home of the Babenbergs and the birthplace of Friedrich of Austria. Today its main attraction, apart from a wide range of sporting facilities, is its stalactite cave. Mayerling became a household name when it rocketed to fame as the setting for the tragic suicide of Crown Prince Rudolf *(see pages 42–43)*, which occurred in the hunting lodge here. On the spot where the prince shot first his mistress, Baroness Mary Vetsera, and then himself, there now stands a Carmelite convent of atonement, founded by the Emperor Franz Joseph.

A stroll through history and nature

From this point it is possible to drive directly along the romantic and much-sung **Helenental** to the neighbouring town of Baden bei Wien; before doing so, however, it would be a pity not to make the acquaintance of some of the other villages in the Vienna Woods which lie on an alternative route.

At **Heiligenkreuz** ❺, the Cistercian abbey of the same name is an architectural gem (open daily; entrance fee). The basilica, begun in 1135, has Austria's oldest example of ribbed vaulting; the Gothic hall chancel was a model for many South German hall churches. Beyond the Romanesque cloisters on the south side is the well house, its lead well glinting mysteriously. The chapter house, which has the tombs of 13 rulers – including the last of the Babenbergs – is moving in its simple perfection.

Nearby **Mödling** ❻, which has been a settlement for almost 8,000 years, has attracted a wide range of interesting personalities over its long history. From Adolf Loos to Oskar Kokoschka, from Johann Strauss to Arnold Schönberg, countless artists, writers and composers have escaped Vienna to paint, write and compose here. Ludwig van Beethoven lived at Hauptstrasse 79 from 1818 to 1820.

Visits to the Romanesque charnel house of St Otmar, the magnificent Plague Column and the Town

Map on page 148

The neo-Gothic Burg Liechtenstein is north of Mödling in Brunn am Gebirge.

BELOW:
the abbey church at Heiligenkreuz.

Mountain-biking is a popular weekend activity in the Vienna Woods.

BELOW: the rolling hills of the southern Vienna Woods.

Hall on the Schrannenplatz, a stroll to the Black Tower, to the mysterious Lake Grotto or through the pedestrian area of the Old Town, make a visit to Mödling well worthwhile. A tip for avid mountaineers: the almost vertical rock faces – for example, on the way to Hinterbrühl – serve as popular practice crags for enthusiasts and climbing schools.

Further east is **Schloss Laxenburg** (grounds open daily; entrance fee). The 18th-century palace (not open to the public) is resplendent in gleaming "Schönbrunn Yellow". The surrounding park has been designed to look as natural as possible. A large artificial lake stretching from the central area towards the east invites visitors to take a boat trip or to visit the Franzensburg on an islet. Reached by ferry or via the Roman bridge, this medieval-style folly, built by Franz II in 1798, houses a museum and a café. At the end of a long, straight avenue of poplars, beside a canal, lies a recreation centre with a restaurant, swimming pool, mini-golf course and camp site.

Just south of Mödling is **Gumpoldskirchen** ❼, the most popular wine-growing village to the south of Vienna. The hilly stretch through the vineyards conveys something of the district's convivial atmosphere and serves as an ideal preparation for the pleasures of the world-famous Gumpoldskirchner vintages.

With its thermal baths, theatre and casino, the spa town of **Baden** has a nostalgic air of faded empire. A slightly decadent, 19th-century charm continues to pervade the architecture and the spa park; this impression is underlined by events such as the Operetta Summer.

After a splash in the thermal waters of **Bad Vöslau**, 5 km (3 miles) south – where the spa complex is worth visiting for its architecture alone – the visitor should end this tour of the Vienna Woods just west on Road 212 at **Berndorf** ❽. The undisputed cultural focal point, not only of the town, but of the entire valley, is the magnificent Municipal Theatre, built in the spirit of Vienna's Ringstrasse architecture and with an interior which resembles the Rococo stage at the court of a minor prince.

The neo-Baroque Church of St Margaret, whose gleaming green cupola tops the roofs of the town, is also worth attention. The church building is flanked by two apparently unremarkable school buildings constructed in 1808, but their interiors are anything but everyday: the 12 classrooms have been decorated in 12 important architectural styles, ranging from Moorish to Gothic and from Egyptian to Doric.

An abundance of castles

Heading east of Vienna, any journey through the March-Donauland is an excursion back through history, as the visitor leaps from castle to castle and wends through unspoilt countryside. Most of the little villages in the northern part of the Marchfeld have retained their charming rural character. A favourite first port of call is **Grossenzersdorf** ❾, which is about 12 km (7 miles) east of Vienna. First mentioned in 1158, it is an attractive little town which has managed to retain a large proportion of its medieval fortifying wall. The town hall, a former monastery church and numerous meticulously restored old houses testify to Grossenzersdorf's rich past.

From here, continue east on Road 3 to **Orth an der Donau** ❿, the site of a moated castle straight out of a fairy tale. The forbidding complex was built in the 12th century, but acquired its present-day appearance about 1550. The New Castle, which lies on the western flank, was added in 1784. Orth Castle became the property of the Habsburg family in 1824, subsequently becoming one of the favourite residences of Crown Prince Rudolf. Today it houses the **Danube Park Centre and Fishing Museum** (open Apr–Oct: Wed–Sun; entrance fee; tel: (02212) 2555). To fortify yourself, repair to the "Uferhaus" (at Uferstrasse 20), where the speciality – Serbian-style carp – has made the restaurant a great favourite amongst Viennese fish-fanciers.

Next on our eastward journey is the hunting lodge at **Eckartsau**, the last Austrian home of the last Emperor in 1918, reached via Wagram an der Donau. It was destroyed in 1945 but has since become an example of superb restoration work. The original 12th-century castle was completely rebuilt in the 18th century; the creation of what was, in effect, a new building, testifies to the consummate skills of such great masters as Fischer von Erlach, Johann Lukas von Hildebrandt, Lorenzo Mattielli and Daniel Gran.

Further east is **Stopfenreuth**, where the Danube meadows have attracted much public attention, as a result of local initiatives and WWF campaigns. An observant and careful walker will find a unique biotope which is home to kingfishers, beavers and cormorants as well as herons and freshwater turtles. It is one of the last primeval forests to be found in Europe.

Near the junction of Roads 3 and 49 is **Schloss Niederweiden** (open Apr–Oct: Tues–Sun), a magnificent building that reveals the unmistakable guiding hand of Fischer von Erlach, despite its subsequent reconstruction in

Map on page 148

Surprisingly, the staid town of Baden is the setting for the famous erotic novel Venus in Furs *(1870), by Leopold Sacher-Masoch, who gave his name to masochism.*

BELOW: support and sustenance for walkers.

BELOW: Schloss Schlosshof, close to the Slovak border.

accordance with the instructions of Empress Maria Theresa. The master builder designed the hunting lodge at the end of the 17th century for Count Ernst Rüdiger Starhemberg, as a replacement for Grafenweiden Castle, which had been destroyed by the Turks.

Three kilometres (2 miles) away, off the main route, is **Schloss Schlosshof** (open Easter–Oct: Tues–Sun), the real centre of royal and aristocratic life in the Marchfeld. Prince Eugene acquired a 17th-century fortress here, and in 1729 Johann Lukas von Hildebrandt completed the extensive alterations. With the addition of two wings and the resulting courtyard, the beautiful fountain and the sweeping staircases, the building was intended to be the most lavish and magnificent summer residence far and wide. It was also intended that it should be capable of being defended in an emergency. After the castle passed into the possession of Maria Theresa in 1755 she immediately embarked upon a programme of alterations and extensions, which rapidly made Schlosshof a favourite residence of the Imperial court. Following a laborious restoration programme, the castle today provides an elegant setting for special exhibitions. A few kilometres further north lies the charming hunting lodge of **Marchegg**, which is home every summer to a large colony of white storks.

Retracing the route back to Road 49, you pass Niederweiden again and cross the Danube, this time to reach the well-fortified citadel of **Hainburg ⓫** on the south bank. The erstwhile fortress of the Babenberg empire lies to the left. Situated on the Braunsberg, it is a pretty little town which has retained much of its original character – a fact best appreciated by the present-day visitor arriving from the west, whose approach will be through the attractive Wienertor, the 13th-century town gate. There are two other town gates: the Ungartor and the Fischertor.

Apart from sections dating from the 11th century, the forbidding fortress on the Schlossberg still has a massive round-arch gateway and a keep with ribbed vaulting constructed in 1120, and an entrance hall built in 1514. The complex has been uninhabited since the 17th century, but has nevertheless been constantly modernised and restored. Visitors yearning for wider horizons should continue their journey along the panoramic road (E 58) on the **Braunsberg**. The view is breathtaking, especially at sunset, and will bring you very nearly to Bratislava at the Slovakian border.

Map on page 148

Roman ruins

If you now turn back west and stay on the south bank of the Danube, you will shortly come to **Petronell-Carnuntum** ⓬ (open Mar–Nov: daily; entrance fee; tel: (02163) 3377), the site of the most extensive Roman excavations in Central Europe. During its heyday the town of Carnuntum had a population of 70,000; including a military camp, it covered an area of 10 sq. km (4 sq. miles). The open-air museum includes exhibits showing the floor plans of an entire section of the town, indicating the position of houses, baths and workshops. The highlights include the main baths, the palace ruins, an amphitheatre and the Heidentor, once more than 20 metres (65 ft) high and now reduced to 12 metres (40 ft), but still imposing.

From Petronell, Road 211 leads south to **Rohrau**. It was here that Joseph Haydn was born on 31 May 1732; today his birthplace houses the **Haydn Museum** (open Tues–Sun; entrance fee). Also here is **Schloss Harrach** (open Easter–Oct: Tues–Sun; entrance fee), which dates from the 16th century but has been rebuilt several times. It now contains the largest private gallery in

BELOW: tranquil river scene near Hainburg.

The fertile Weinviertel north of Vienna is Austria's chief wine-producing region.

BELOW: bucolic scene in the Weinviertel.

Austria; its collection represents a complete cross-section through the Dutch, Flemish, Italian, Spanish and French schools of painting.

Wine country

The village of **Deutsch-Wagram** , 20 km (12 miles) from Vienna in a north-easterly direction, actually lies on the edge of the Marchfeld. It is, however, on the way to the **Weinviertel** (Wine Country). The little community is first mentioned in records as long ago as 1250, and the church belfry is actually 1,000 years old. The village owes its fame, however, to no less a personage than Napoleon Bonaparte. He established his base camp here in 1809 in the Battle of Deutsch-Wagram. The memorial stone on the relevant spot, as well as numerous mementoes in the local museum, provide information concerning this period. Here, too, is the ever-popular **Marchfelderhof**, which provides culinary delights in an opulently rustic environment.

Roughly 10 km (6 miles) north via a series of back roads, **Wolkersdorf** ⓴ is often mentioned as the true gateway to the Wine Country. Here, too, the Battle of Deutsch-Wagram left traces: first of all, the Emperor Franz I set up his base camp in the priest's backyard; shortly afterwards, following the victory of his army, Napoleon took up residence in the castle. Nowadays the main building, originally built in 1050 as a moated castle and subsequently converted into a hunting lodge in 1720 by Karl VI, has become the landmark of this attractive little town.

There is an entire museum village (open Apr–Oct: daily; entrance fee; tel: (02534) 333) in **Niedersulz**, 23 km (14 miles) northeast. The open-air collection includes about 30 complete original buildings in representative vernacular style: two chapels, various workshops, a wine-pressing shed, a water mill and the

obligatory tavern complete with bowling alley – all presenting a picture of a Weinviertel village before industrialisation.

The market town of **Wilfersdorf**, lying in the midst of a fertile agricultural and wine-growing region to the north, presents a completely different character. As early as the 14th century it was the seat of the local assizes; its history as a thriving trading and business centre is still apparent today. The most eye-catching element is undoubtedly the bright yellow **Liechtenstein Castle**.

Head 10 km (6 miles) north of here to find the wine market at **Poysdorf** ⑮, with its picturesque alleys and fine vintages – a highlight for wine buffs. Twenty wine-growers from the municipality have joined together to form the Poysdorf Wine-Growers' Syndicate. This permits an expert selection from a total of approximately 100 different wines, predominantly Grüner Veltliner, Welschriesling, Rhine Riesling and white Burgundy, but also several red wines of excellent quality.

You could continue west instead on Road 40 to **Mistelbach**, an ideal place in which to relax. It possesses a large sports centre offering a wide range of facilities, an open-air swimming pool and a mini-golf course. A Gothic hall church, a 12th-century charnel house, a former Barnabite cloister (with frescoes by Maulbertsch) and a small Baroque castle provide cultural interest.

Asparn an der Zaya lies just west in the foothills of the Leiser Mountains. The heart of the old wine-growing and market town is undoubtedly the fortress complex, complete with moat, church, battlement walk and monastery. Housed in sections of the castle, which is one of the most attractive historic monuments in the country, is a wine museum (open Apr–Oct: Sat pm and Sun) and a museum of prehistory (open Apr–Nov: Tues–Sun).

Map on page 148

Gross-Schweinbarth, east of Wolkersdorf, is home to the unlikely-sounding International Shepherds' Museum.

BELOW: milk churns drying in the sun.

North of Asparn, at the Czech border, is a settlement with a 5,000-year history. **Laa an der Thaya** was fortified as a bulwark against Bohemia by the Babenbergs around 1200. Sections of the town walls and the town's general appearance both date from this time. So, too, does the castle – now the home of a **beer museum** (open May–Oct: Sat and Sun pm; entrance fee). Also worth more than a cursory glance are the Gothic pillory, the Plague Column on the main square, and the local churches.

Finally, some 42 km (25 miles) west via Roads 45 and 30, is the town of **Retz** ⓥ. The ground under Retz has an important inner life of its own: an extensive cellar complex (the largest historic wine cellar in Austria) criss-crosses beneath the town. The subterranean network actually covers a larger area than the streets and alleys above ground; the tunnels often extend three storeys deep into the underlying sand. Guided tours of the vaults (Mar–Dec: daily; Jan–Feb: Sat & Sun; entrance fee) only encompass 5 percent of the system, but still include 900 metres (2,955 ft) of tunnel. The town also possesses a large number of Baroque and Renaissance buildings; its landmark is a 1772 windmill which is still in working order.

The Waldviertel

The **Waldviertel** (Woodland Country) possesses a singular, austere charm of its own. One becomes particularly aware of its northerly latitude at night, when jackets are automatically buttoned a little higher on account of the persistent cool breeze. One will seldom experience here the riotous outdoor activity which characterises the balmy summer nights of Southern Austria. In any case, the visitor comes here in search of peace and quiet.

Northwest of Retz, on the Czech border, is the hamlet of **Hardegg**. Perched on a high mountain ridge overlooking it is a forbidding castle dating from the 12th century. Here, the bridge over the river Thaya will make the heart of every fisherman beat faster, for the waters below are teeming with trout.

A few miles to the west lies the magnificent Baroque castle of **Riegersburg** (open Apr–mid-Nov: daily; entrance fee; tel: (02916) 400), which one should not fail to visit on the way to **Geras**. The latter, a peaceful holiday village, owes the abbot of the local monastery a debt of gratitude for reviving the local tourist industry. The courses he runs in painting rustic furniture and glass-blowing techniques have proved very popular with visitors.

The next town of any size, **Raabs an der Thaya** ⓼ has been nicknamed "The Pearl of the Thaya Valley". If you look down on the attractive little town from above, you'll agree that the name is justified. The best bird's-eye perspective can be gained from the picturesque 11th-century castle (open July–Sept: Fri, Sat and Sun; entrance fee) which is perched on a steep cliff high above the confluence of the German and Moravian Thaya rivers.

West of Raabs, the situation of the market town of **Thaya im Waldviertel** was determined by the sunny climate and healthy, bracing air. Two Renaissance fountains adorn the market place, surrounded by

BELOW: timeless country character.

beautifully renovated merchants' houses and a Romanesque parish church. In a wood just beyond the town boundary you will find the excavations of the medieval village of **Hard**.

Further west, a massive moated castle (open Apr–Oct: Tues–Sun; entrance fee) lends a fairy-tale aura to the general appearance of the romantic town of **Heidenreichstein**, first mentioned in records in 1205. The fortress is still approached via medieval drawbridges.

Of slightly later date is the castle in **Gmünd** ⓳, the main town in the northwest district of the province. With two border crossing points into the Czech Republic and its position as an administrative and educational centre, Gmünd is an important regional hub. It is also the terminus of the Waldviertel Narrow Gauge Steam Railway, which runs south from here to Grossgerungs. The principal attraction, however, is the almost mystical sandstone formations found in the nearby **Blockheide Eibenstein Nature Park**. A tip for food-lovers: the gourmet restaurant Hackl (at Schubertplatz 11), provides fine examples of the region's cuisine.

Many of the towns and villages around Gmünd, including **Alt-** and **Neu-Nagelberg**, **Angelbach** and **Hirschenwies**, are home to the famous Waldviertel glass cutters. They are the best places to buy good-quality glassware.

Heading south on Road 41 through **Weitra**, Austria's oldest brewing town and home to the country's smallest brewery, the Brauhotel, we turn southeast to begin our journey back towards the Danube. Some 24 km (15 miles) away is the romantic town of **Zwettl** ⓴, where the brewing theme continues – this is the seat of the largest privately-owned brewery in Austria, and the beer is worth sampling. Apart from this, the most important places to see include the medieval town walls and the 11th-century Presbytery Church. On the outskirts lies a magnificent

Map on page 148

BELOW: waiting for custom at a butcher's shop in Weitra.

Burg Ottenstein, situated on the reservoir of the same name, has frescoes dating from 1200.

Cistercian abbey (Stift Zwettl; open May–Oct: daily; entrance fee) built in 1138; a little further out of town in the opposite direction is the Baroque **Schloss Rosenau** (open daily; entrance fee), where an initiation into the mysteries of Freemasonry awaits the curious visitor. The castle's restaurant serves hearty fare.

Just east at the very heart of the Waldviertel lies **Ottenstein Reservoir**, with its countless fjord-like inlets. Rastenfeld is an ideal starting point for this water sports centre, which attracts anglers, swimmers, sailors and surfers; for landlubbers there are 35 km (20 miles) of signposted footpaths, bicycle rental, a fitness circuit, tennis courts and bowling greens.

Baroque treasures

About 25 km (15 miles) northeast of Rastenfeld, via Road 38, is a truly impressive Baroque masterpiece, **Stift Altenburg ㉑** (open Easter–Oct: daily; fee for obligatory tours). Primarily the work of Josef Munggenast, the monastery displays the splendours typical of the more famous abbeys – a wonderful library and plenty of frescoes by Paul Troger, who lived here for many years. Not far from the abbey is **Schloss Greillenstein** (open Apr–Oct: daily; entrance fee), which is noted for its exotic Baroque statuary.

Southeast of Altenburg, we soon catch sight of **Schloss Rosenburg** (open Mar–Oct: daily; April & Nov: Tues–Sun; entrance fee), idyllically situated high above the River Kamp. First mentioned in 1175, the magnificent structure possesses a unique jousting yard and houses a large number of works of art, including weapons and examples of Renaissance furniture.

South of Rosenburg, Road 34 brings you to **Gars am Kamp**, a pretty village lying at the foot of a ruined castle that once belonged to the Babenbergs. High-

BELOW: the unheralded but stunning monastery of Altenburg.

lights of the village include the Romanesque-Gothic Church of St Gertrude, a number of fine patrician houses and an exhibition documenting the local excavations, which have revealed that the Gars district has been a site of human settlement for at least 5,000 years. Another attraction is Willy Dungl's Bio-Training Hotel, a health spa run by Niki Lauda's former fitness guru.

Map on page 148

The Wachau

South of Gars, you enter the Wachau, the most charming river region in Austria – a land of apricot blossoms, ruined castles, rolling vineyards and, of course, the waves of the Danube. Every visitor should taste the region's fine wines and in particular, its apricot brandy. On its eastern extremity is **Krems** ㉒, the "Model Town for the Preservation of Historical Monuments". A considerable proportion of its buildings are beautiful old houses. The town itself lies nestled among terraced vineyards, clinging to the bank of the Danube.

Immediately west of Krems is the hamlet of **Und** (And). This tiny community, with its odd name, includes a former monastery housing a wine-growers' college with enormous cellars containing the choicest vintages from Austria's wine-growing valleys; visitors are able to taste and purchase them to their heart's content.

Across the river lie two of the best restaurants in Austria. Chef Lisl Wagner-Bacher wields her wooden spoon at the Bacher in **Mautern**, fully justifying her three "chef's hat" symbols in the *Gault-Millau* guide. A few kilometres south, in **Kleinwien**, is Schickh, a restaurant run by her sister Gerda, whose apricot dumplings seem to capture the unique taste of the Wachau.

On a hilltop overlooking Kleinwien is one of the highlights of the area, the fine **Stift Göttweig** (open Apr–mid-Nov: daily; entrance fee; tel: (02732) 8558-1231), a once-mighty 11th-century monastery which was later reworked in Baroque style after a series of fires. The hand of several builders and designers is apparent here, but the plans of Johann Lukas von Hildebrandt were only ever partly realised. His masterly Kaiserstiege (Imperial Staircase) and the frescoed banqueting hall known as the Altmannsaal can be seen on the guided tour.

Back at the river, head west to **Dürnstein** ㉓, probably the most popular town in the whole Wachau. It also enjoys what must be one of the most beautiful locations, overlooked by a towering ruined castle.

Dürnstein was made famous by the legend of King Richard the Lionheart and Blondel, his minstrel. At the end of the 12th century, the king of England, captured by Leopold V on his return from the Third Crusade, languished as a prisoner in the dungeons of the town's impregnable castle. Only one faithful follower, his minstrel Blondel, refused to believe that his beloved master was no longer alive. He took his lute and set off to find him. Eventually, striking up the first bars of Richard's favourite song beneath Dürnstein Castle, he was answered by the familiar voice of his master. Soon afterwards, Richard was released upon payment of a huge ransom by the English. (The money was used to finance the construction of Vienna's first city wall.)

The popular Grüner Veltliner wine.

BELOW: the old town, Krems.

Terracotta reliefs dating from 1573 adorn the arcades at Schloss Schallaburg.

BELOW: Durnstein is dominated by its monastery tower.

Apart from the castle on the hill, other sights in Dürnstein include a beautiful Baroque monastery church, whose stunning blue-and-white steeple is best viewed from the river, plus a 17th-century castle built to a square ground plan and a former Clarissan cloister dating from around 1300, which now houses a hotel. The entire village is pervaded by an unusual charm to which it is easy to succumb.

The road to Melk

Beyond Dürnstein is **Weissenkirchen**, a very picturesque village with narrow alleys, historic houses and ancient gleaning yards. The entire community is dominated by an imposing fortified church which dates from 1190. It is well worth planning a stopover in **Joching**, and in particular at Josef Jamek's wine cellars and restaurant. His wines are featured on the menus of the best gourmet restaurants in the country; no visitor should miss the chance to taste them on home territory.

After Joching, the road heads for **Spitz**, a famous wine-growing town that sprawls around the Tausendeimerberg. The mountain's name refers to the claim that, during a good year, the yield from its vineyards will total 1,000 buckets of wine. Romantic souls among the town's visitors are bound to fall heavily in love with Erlahof Castle and the ruined Fortress of Hinterhaus. The late-Gothic parish church has a triple nave and a Baroque high altar with an altarpiece by Kremser Schmidt.

Upstream from Spitz is **Willendorf** ㉔, famous for the discovery of the "Venus of Willendorf", a neolithic limestone statue. The soil here is the repository of many a fascinating historical detail; it has revealed, for instance, that a camp of mammoth hunters was situated here during the Ice Age.

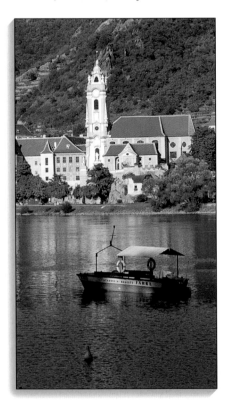

THE VENUS OF WILLENDORF

When archaeologist Josef Szombathy, digging in the town of Willendorf, unearthed the so-called Venus of Willendorf in 1908, he wasn't sure exactly what he had found. The limestone figure, just 10 cm (4 inches) high but fashioned with disproportionately large hips, breasts, buttocks and sexual parts, hadn't even been made from local rock. It had most likely been crafted elsewhere, then brought here by trading. After a number of false starts, carbon dating established a possible age for the figurine. It turns out to date from Paleolithic times, approximately 25,000–30,000 BC, making it one of the oldest pieces of sculpture ever found. It is thought to have been created by the same Aurignacian peoples who produced the famous cave paintings at Lascaux in southwestern France.

The figure's graphic sexuality suggests that it may have been a fertility figure. Other recent theories include its possible use as a totemic hunting object or good-luck charm – Venus' braided hair is bunched in seven rings, a number which may have been chosen in an early form of numerology. But these are only theories; the overarching mysteries about the enigmatic statue – who carved it, and why – remain unsolved. To see it for yourself, head for Vienna's Naturhistorisches Museum *(see page 140)*.

Across the river from Willendorf are the awesome ruins of **Aggstein Castle** (open Mar–Nov: daily), almost 700 years old, and perched about 300 metres (985 ft) above the Danube. Here it was that the Kuenringers, a lawless tribe of robber barons, barricaded the river with chains in order to plunder passing ships. Today the main attraction is undoubtedly the fine panoramic view: upstream towards Melk, south to the foothills of the **Dunkelsteiner Wald** and north to the highland plateau of the Waldviertel.

Staying on the same side of the river, it is worth allowing yourself time to explore the next village, **Aggsbachdorf**, at leisure. It contains a former Carthusian monastery dating from the 14th–16th centuries as well as the tombs of the founding Maissau family, embellished with coats of arms. About 5 km (3 miles) further upstream lies **Schloss Schönbühel**. The castle, dating from the 12th century, occupies a dominant site on a 40-metre (130-ft) high cliff above the river. On one of its exterior walls is an interesting relief depicting the Last Supper.

Without a doubt the most impressive sight in the Wachau is the magnificent **Stift Melk** ㉕, set on a steep hill above the Danube (open Easter–Oct: daily; Nov–Easter: guided tours only, at 11am and 2pm daily; entrance fee; tel: (02752) 555 225). Best viewed initially from the river, the monastery's yellow-and-white walls stretch for an extravagant 362 metres (1,187 ft) on its southern facade. *(See pages 162–63 for a full description of the monastery).*

Just a few kilometres south, beyond the A1 to Vienna, crumbling **Schloss Schallaburg** (open May–Oct: daily; entrance fee; tel: (02754) 6317) is worth a visit. Its most impressive feature is the miraculously preserved 16th-century interior courtyard, which recalls the glories of Florence or Venice. Every year the castle puts on an archaeological or historical exhibition. ❑

Map on page 148

BELOW: dawn haze, southwest of Melk.

MELK ABBEY: A BAROQUE TREASURE

The Abbey of Melk is among Austria's most prized architectural treasures. A brief glimpse from the train en route to Vienna just doesn't do it justice

The Benedictine Abbey of Melk (known in German as Stift Melk, *see page 161*), which stands high above the Danube River, is among Austria's most prized Baroque treasures. It can be seen from the window of a train passing through the town en route to Vienna, but a full day is required to appreciate it.

The abbey was rebuilt in its present form after the Turks burnt it down in 1683. The abbot at the time, Berthold Dietmayr, was an enthusiastic supporter of Baroque master Jakob Prandtauer, but other monks were reluctant to commit large funds to the rebuilding. Dietmayr prevailed and Prandtauer produced a masterpiece. Especially impressive are the ceiling frescoes by J.M. Rottmayr in the abbey church, a breathtaking depiction of the life, death and ascension of St Benedict.

IN THE ABBEY LIBRARY

The frescoes are a mere appetizer to the abbey library. One of the finest in the world, it is said to have inspired Umberto Eco to write his medieval thriller *The Name of the Rose*. Some 85,000 ancient hand-copied books and illuminated manuscripts – carefully rebound in leather and leafed in gold – line the wooden shelves of the enormous room. The abbey also possesses important religious items, such as a piece (the monks claim) of the Calvary cross and the rarely shown St Koloman's bones.

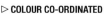

△ **BEST FACE FORWARD**
The Gutenberg Bible was once sold by the Melk order to finance the renovation of the abbey's aging facades. Depicted above is the west facade, which faces the river.

▷ **EUROPE'S FINEST**
The 61-metre (200-ft) octagonal dome sits atop the abbey church at the centre of the complex, a fine example of Baroque design.

▷ **COLOUR CO-ORDINATED**
The Prälatenhof courtyard unifies the monastery buildings. Its ornate fountain dates from the early 19th century.

A MODERN MONASTERY

△ **THE SAINT'S ASSUMPTION**
The ceiling frescoes in the church depict the combat of good and evil, and Benedict's assumption into heaven, as seen by two monks in a vision.

▽ **FINE FRESCOES**
There is little marble in the Marmorsaal (Marble Hall), whose columns are faux, but it is worth a visit for the splendid Paul Troger frescoes.

Originally a castle stood on the site of Melk Abbey – the Babenberg family's first residence after they gained power in 976. The Order of Benedictines was given the land by Leopold II in 1089, and monks have lived and worked here ever since.

While most of its two to three dozen monks do not live on the grounds, the abbey continues to operate much as it always has. Monks still carry out agricultural tasks; they still brew beer; and nearly 1,000 children attend the religious schools here – a grammar school, a secondary school and a boarding school – which are collectively known as the Stift Gymnasium. There is a strict emphasis on biblical scholarship, and the monks are renowned throughout Europe for their instruction. There is also the ongoing task of maintaining the huge structure, which has long been a concern.

The monks also run a busy museum, commission modern artists to add new frescoes and curate occasional art exhibits inside the abbey walls.

◁ **ITALIAN DESIGN**
Antonio Galli-Bibiena created the magnificent high altar in marble and pure gold. The central scene is of Peter taking leave of Paul.

▷ **MONASTIC LAW**
Benedictines follow the tenets written down by Italian monk St Benedict (c. 480–547).

BURGENLAND

Map
on page
168

*Austria's easternmost province has a distinctly Hungarian feel and
still shows signs of Turkish occupation. Visitors come for the
beaches of Neusiedler See and the fine wines produced nearby*

I t is possible that visitors to the Burgenland might be tempted to believe that
the region derives its name from the numerous castles *(burgen)* within its
boundaries. Their theory, however, is false. Before putting the record straight
here, though, it should be pointed out that even the majority of Austrians cannot explain the real origins of the name.

Once upon a time, there was a large area of land called German West Hungary.
It consisted of four administrative districts: Pressburg, Wieselburg, Ödenburg
and Eisenburg, each with a county town bearing the same name. The inhabitants
were predominantly German-speaking. After World War I the victorious and
defeated powers sat down together to negotiate the new national boundaries.
Peace conferences were held – among other places, at the Trianon in Paris –
which is where Austria's territorial claims with respect to Hungary were debated.
In the Venice Protocol the eastern boundary of Austria was finally agreed –
with the proviso that the inhabitants of Ödenburg themselves should decide to
which country they wished to belong.

Austria's agreement to the 1921 plebiscite was, in fact, tantamount to a surrender at the outset, for the area in question was inhabited predominantly by
Hungarians. There was no alternative, however, for this was the price Austria
had to pay in order to gain the rest of the territory.

After the plebiscite, most of German West Hungary
was ceded to Austria. It was named the "Burgenland"
after the suffix "Burg" which formed part of the former names of the constituent districts. Of the former
county towns, three now lie in Hungary and one –
Pressburg (now Bratislava) – in Slovakia.

The community of Ödenburg – now called Sopron –
forms a "peninsula" which appears to jut into Austria
and which, had it not been for the plebiscite, would
probably have become the "natural" capital of the
Burgenland. And so, since 1925 the province's capital – succeeding Mattersburg – has been Eisenstadt.
Five years later the regional government of the Burgenland was also transferred there.

The Esterházys

Eisenstadt ❶ is small, as provincial capitals go,
claiming a population of about 10,000 people. It is
dominated by the names of its most famous inhabitants: the Esterházy family and Haydn *(see page 169)*.

It is a town where the visitor is best served by
exploring on foot. All notable sights are easily accessible. Instead of merely admiring the facades of the
fine old houses, it is worthwhile stealing into the lovely
inner courtyards of some of them.

Dominating the town is the magnificent **Schloss
Esterházy** (open Apr–Oct: daily; Nov–Mar: Mon–Fri;

PRECEDING PAGES:
the town of Rust,
overlooking
Neusiedler See.
LEFT: a Turk's head
in St Margarethen.
BELOW: chimney-
top stork's nest.

entrance fee; tel: (02682) 719 3000). Reconstruction of the existing medieval fortress for Paul I, the son of Nikolaus Esterházy von Forchtenstein, began in 1663 under the direction of Carlo Carlone, the Italian master builder. His French successor, Charles Moreau, added pyramid-shaped roofs to the corner towers, previously topped by onion-shaped domes. He also designed a number of porticoed constructions and completely rearranged the garden, even filling in the moat that had surrounded the castle. He was also responsible for the **Leopoldine Temple**, built to house a marble statue that had earlier stood in the castle: a likeness, created by Antonio Canova, of Princess Leopoldine of Esterházy, who subsequently married into the Liechtenstein royal family. When the work was complete the complex comprised a total of more than 200 spacious rooms and six ballrooms.

Near the castle, in pretty Haydngasse, is the so-called **Haydnhaus** (open mid-Apr–Oct: daily; entrance fee; tel: (02682) 719 3900), where the composer lived from 1766 to 1778. It displays artefacts relating to both Haydn and another son of Burgenland, Franz Liszt.

Neusiedler See

Not far away, the sun shines down on the powerful colours of an oil painting, massive and clear. Above the golden yellow belt of reeds a heron prepares to land, its wings beating ponderously... Images from a strange, exotic world? Not at all. Just a few miles east of Eisenstadt and barely 70 km (45 miles) from Vienna, on the shores of **Neusiedler See** – Europe's largest steppe lake (320 sq. km/125 sq. miles) – can be found one of the last major breeding grounds for almost 300 rare species of bird. The lake has no outflow and loses most of its water through evaporation. Only a handful of more celebrated regions in the world can stand comparison with this region as a bird haven. There are 15 nature conservation areas to choose from, a real paradise. One can even tour the lake via a circular cycling path that takes you into Hungary before completing the circuit.

Here the last foothills of the Alps subside into the Pannonian plain, creating a steppe-like climate, which ranges from very hot summers to bitterly cold winters. Low rainfall and a steady breeze are other characteristics of this particular micro-climate. Sun-worshippers might like to note that in some of the lakeshore communities the average temperatures in July and August lie only one degree below those of the French Riviera. This Mediterranean characteristic, combined with the varying saline levels of the ponds and lake (made up of soda, Glauber's salt, Epsom salts and common salt), provide ideal conditions for unique flora and fauna.

Map on page 168

A tour of the lake

The main road around the lake heads northeast from Eisenstadt and soon reaches the wine-making village of **Donnerskirchen** ❷. Those lucky enough to visit the area between mid-April and the beginning of May will be able to witness a splendid natural spectacle – the cherry blossom. The thousands of cherry trees laden with white blossom on the slopes of the Leitha Mountains surrounding Donnerskirchen are truly spectacular. The sight puts local inhabitants in festive mood, too. The entire village takes to the streets for a high-spirited celebration of the arrival of spring. Donnerskirchen is also famous for its highly successful village restoration project, which accounts for its well-cared-for appearance.

Since the parish church here is dedicated to St Martin, it seems appropriate to mention a few facts about the patron saint of the Burgenland. The local version of the legend has it that St Martin, pursued by a number of persecutors, sought refuge here but was betrayed by the loud gabbling of some geese. However it came about, 11 November is the day of the traditional St Martin's goose dinner – not only in the Burgenland, but also in Lower Austria and Vienna. And

BELOW: wine-tasting in the cellar.

JOSEPH HAYDN

Joseph Haydn was born in 1732 in Rohrau, just over the border in Lower Austria. After struggling as a freelance musician in the 1750s, he was appointed Kapellmeister to the Esterházy family in Eisenstadt in 1761. He kept the post for 30 years and wrote some of his best symphonies, operas and chamber music here. Twelve of these years (1766–78) were spent at what is now Haydngasse 21.

Prince Esterházy allowed the maestro to retire to Vienna in 1792. In 1795, however, he was summoned back to the castle once more, where he composed two masterpieces, his oratorios *The Creation* and *The Seasons*.

Haydn died in Vienna in 1809. Eleven years later his body was transferred to Eisenstadt. During the process it was discovered that the skull was missing. Haydn's friend, Joseph Rosenbaum, had appropriated the composer's head in order to study it, and it eventually ended up on display at the Society of the Friends of Music in Vienna. In 1954, however, it was borne with due ceremony back to Eisenstadt and reunited with the rest of his body in the Bergkirche.

Nowadays the composer is celebrated by a series of top-rate musical performances in the city. An annual highlight is the International Haydn Festival, which is usually held in September in Schloss Esterházy.

since the Burgenland is one of Austria's foremost wine-producing areas, 11 November is also the day on which the new wine, *Heuriger*, is broached – to wash down the roast goose dinner.

There is one more point of interest in Donnerskirchen: the **Wine Forum** in the Leisserhof – a documentation and communication centre devoted to the viti-culture of the Burgenland. In the so-called Wine Vault there's an exhibition assembled by dozens of vineyards offering more than 100 wines. In the Wine Exchange are stored tens of thousands of bottles of rare vintages. You can even rent a private wine safe here. And whoever can keep their eye on the ball in spite of a glass or two can try their hand on the magnificent local golf course.

All the villages lying on the lakeshore share a typical infrastructure, including a bathing area, boat rental, sailing and windsurfing facilities, a camp site and bicycle rental. There is a simple explanation for the predominance of sailing and wind-surfing; the lake is very shallow – mostly only 1–2 metres (3–7 ft) deep – and on most days you can be sure of finding a Force 6 wind whipping across its surface.

Northeast of Donnerskirchen is **Purbach**, the site of an 8-hectare (19-acre) camp site as well as a sailing school and a wide range of leisure activities. This community suffered badly during the Turkish Wars. In 1683 it was virtually razed to the ground. The marks of charring dating from this event explain the origin of its Hungarian name, Feketevaras, which means "Black Town". Rare relics dating from the Turkish era and still standing today are parts of the city wall and gates. According to local legend, the stone figure peeping out of the chimney of the Türkenkeller represents a single remaining Turk.

In **Breitenbrunn** ❸ near the northern end of the lake a friendly atmosphere greets the visitor. The 30-metre (98-ft) high watchtower known as the Türken-

TIP

Beware of stormy weather on Neusiedler See. It is a mistake to underestimate the lake, as even experienced sailors often struggle with incredibly high waves, despite the shallow depth.

BELOW: Oggau, on the western side of the lake.

turm is another relic of the wars against the Turks. It is the town's principal landmark and figures prominently on every postcard. From the balcony of the free-standing edifice there is a fine panoramic view of the lake. Baroque farmhouses and dark, picturesque alleys complete the picture of this pretty village set in the water meadows. As in all the other lakeside villages of any size, the sports-oriented holidaymaker will find a yachting marina and windsurfing school in Breitenbrunn.

At nearby **Jois**, a Roman double grave containing the skeletons of a mother and daughter was discovered in 1982. Another skeleton discovered a few years later, the so-called Lame Woman of Jois, showed evidence of two badly healed breaks in the lower leg. One of the most gruesome finds, however, is the family grave of a Bronze Age prince. It was flanked on all sides by 12 further graves containing male skeletons. All the skulls had been smashed, indicating unequivocally the barbaric customs of the Scythians, who were wont to dispatch a number of courtiers into the next world to accompany a dead ruler.

The eastern shore

Just east of Jois, we come to the tiny town of **Neusiedl am See ❹**. This was once home to the **Pannonisches Heimatmuseum**, a quirky private museum devoted to all things rural and old-fashioned. The museum's future is uncertain, as its proprietor, the eccentric Karl Eidler, is now too old and frail to continue its upkeep.

Southeast of Neusiedl, at the foot of a geological formation known as the Parndorfer Platte, is the wine village of **Weiden**, which has retained its true rural character. Every day in summer the peasant women sit on plain wooden chairs in front of their houses along the main road, offering all sorts of produce for sale: fresh fruit and vegetables from their own gardens, and hand-made items of straw woven during the long evenings of the previous winter.

Before continuing one's journey along the lake shore, a short detour 10 km (6 miles) southeast to the village of **Halbturn ❺**, just before the Hungarian border, is recommended. The castle here (open May–Oct: Tues–Sun; entrance fee; tel: (02172) 8577) is one of the most famous Baroque buildings in Burgenland, and served the Habsburg family as a hunting lodge and summer residence for over 300 years. Given by the Empress Maria Theresa to her favourite daughter, the Archduchess Maria Christina, as a wedding present, the castle with its gardens and park remained in the private possession of the Habsburg-Lothringen branch of the family, from whom the present owner is descended. The castle, situated on the edge of the village, was built at the beginning of the 18th century by Lukas von Hildebrandt for Count Harrach. Emperor Karl VI joined hunting parties here, and it served his wife Elisabeth as a dower residence. Empress Maria Theresa finally had it rebuilt, and it is thanks to her that it contains priceless frescoes by Maulbertsch. Extensively damaged during World War II, and in a disastrous fire in 1949, the structure underwent a major restoration campaign beginning in 1971. Today the building serves as an attractive venue for exhibitions and concerts.

Map on page 168

BELOW: grapes ready for pressing.

Back beside the lake, head south along the eastern shore to the tourist centre of **Podersdorf** ❻, the "Pearl of Neusiedler See". The largest camp site in Austria, a yachting marina and a total of 3 km (2 miles) of reed-free shoreline account for its popularity. An integral part of its charm is one of the last working windmills in the Burgenland whose sails continue to turn in spite of an advanced age of 200 years.

South of Podersdorf, in the elbow of the lake, is the village of **Illmitz** ❼. It is at the centre of a bird watcher's paradise known as the Seewinkel. Exploratory trips into the wildlife reserves lying along the shore of the lake, guided by knowledgeable ornithologists from the National Park Centre at the edge of town (open Apr–Oct: daily; Nov–Mar: Mon–Fri; tel: (02175) 3442), can be made by horse-drawn carriage, bicycle or even on foot. A well-signposted nature trail provides interesting information about the scientific work of the Biological Field Station. Lange Lacke, the conservation area near **Apetlon**, is closed to the public but you can walk or cycle along a footpath skirting its perimeter.

Generally considered the prettiest house in Illmitz is the **Florianihaus**, with its original thatched roof and narrow Baroque courtyard. Almost as old is the **Pusztascheune**, a Magyar-style barn and now a well-known *Heuriger* often resounding to impassioned dance rhythms.

Storks and wine

Back on the western side of the lake is **Rust** ❽, which is world famous as the summer retreat for families of storks. In conjunction with the World Wide Fund for Nature a Stork Post Office (postal code A-7073) has been set up here. It is open all year round, and the special postmark depicting a stork is much

TIP

The great bustard, Europe's heaviest bird, is a local inhabitant but is difficult to spot. One of the best places to see it is in the marshland southeast of Tadten, a village east of Illmitz.

BELOW:
summertime
activities on
Neusiedler See.

sought-after among philatelists and animal lovers. You can also buy special "stork" envelopes and postcards in the town's shops. With the proceeds, the local inhabitants and the WWF aim to acquire new food sources for the long-legged visitors, and to create additional breeding places on the roofs of the houses in the Old Town, their traditional nesting sites. These measures will, it is hoped, secure stocks of the much-loved bird at their present levels – or possibly even manage to increase them.

Rust is at least as famous for its wine as for its storks. Pleasantly full-bodied, it is well-rounded and easily digestible. No other Austrian community has such a large number of special-quality wines; every cork bearing the brand-marked "R" guarantees the Rust origins of the wine. Wine buffs can become connoisseurs at the town's **Burgenland Wine Academy**. One should also find time to visit what is – artistically and culturally speaking – the most significant building in the town: the **Fischerkirche** (Fishermen's Church). Romanesque in origin, it later acquired a Gothic extension. With a bit of luck you may even be able to enjoy a romantic concert by candlelight.

Also worthwhile is a short detour west to the Roman quarries at **St Margarethen**, 4 km (2 miles) away (open daily). Stone from here was used to build Carnuntum *(see page 153)* and Vindobona (Roman Vienna). In the summer artists from all over the world converge here for an international sculpture school.

Operetta on the lake

South of Rust is **Mörbisch** ❾. The town has been famous since 1957 as the site of the Mörbisch Lakeside Festival, which takes place on a pontoon built out over the lake. The themes chosen are those from light music; every year a dif-

Map
on page
168

BELOW:
a street in Rust.

ferent operetta is performed during July and August. In order that nothing should spoil the evening's entertainment, here is a tip: it is advisable to smear yourself liberally with insect repellant, for the pesky mosquito also enjoys warm evenings on the water.

The Hungarian border, only 2 km (1¼ miles) south of Mörbisch, makes its proximity felt in the appearance of the old Burgenland houses, ablaze with a riot of flowers and displaying the characteristic dried sheaves of maize. Window-boxes bright with geraniums and large tubs overflowing with blossoming oleander conjure up a Mediterranean atmosphere, redolent of warm sunshine in long alleys and courtyards bordered by gleaming whitewashed houses.

Heading west now, away from the lake, the next place of interest is **Burg Forchtenstein** ❿ (open Apr–Oct: daily; fee for obligatory tour; tel: (0226) 81 212), situated 20 km (12 miles) southwest of Eisenstadt. It is one of the most interesting castles in Austria. Certainly no other fortress makes such a strong, multi-faceted impression. Nothing remains of the oldest section, dating from the 14th century, apart from the keep with a roof that recalls the keel of a ship. After the rest of the complex was completely destroyed, the construction of the New Castle was begun by Count Nikolaus Esterházy in 1635.

On his instructions were built the entrance tract in the inner courtyard, the vaulted passage linking it to the higher section of the ramparts, the true castle entrance, the arsenal and the chapel. In the middle of the 17th century his successor, Count Paul, continued the extensions and gave the castle its present form. From this period date many door frames and doors with exquisite hand-wrought locks, some parts of the original window glazing, tiled floors, fireplaces and the 142-metre (465-ft) deep "Turk's Well", which has a fine echo.

BELOW: boathouses beside the lake.

The town of Forchtenstein also has another claim to fame: the Gourmet Restaurant Reisner, renowned for its regional specialities.

Another 25 km (15 miles) south lies **Stoob**. This pretty roadside village is a mecca for potters. Apart from a traditional potters' guild – the original round-bellied clay pots with thin necks known as *Pluzer* are manufactured here – Stoob is home to the only specialist ceramics academy in Austria.

Map on page 168

Southern reaches

The town of **Lockenhaus** ⓫, lying in the Günstal just off Road 50, some 20 km (12 miles) south of Stoob, is first mentioned as a settlement at the end of the 9th century. The imposing Romanesque castle (open daily) – today the scene of chamber music festivals and other cultural events – once belonged to the Order of Templars, officially disbanded in 1311. Around the beginning of the 17th century, the castle was owned by the Nádasdy family, one of whose members, Erzsébet Báthory, the so-called Blood Countess, was responsible for the murder of 600 women. The Italian master builder Orsolini constructed a Baroque parish church in Lockenhaus in 1669. Today it is a place of pilgrimage.

Colourfully painted houses liven up the local villages.

Bernstein ⓬, 15 km (9 miles) west, is the world's only known source of the gleaming green semi-precious stone known as serpentine. Interested parties can learn more about Bernstein itself, the history of the village and its mining development from the laboriously executed details with which Otto Potsch, the painter and sculptor, adorned the **Felsenmuseum** (Rock Museum; open Mar–Dec: daily; Jan–Feb: Sat pm only; entrance fee). The Chinese astronomical sphere on display is also his work.

The castle, which dates from the 13th century, was of great strategic importance in the border skirmishes between Austria and Hungary – in contrast to **Schloss Schlaining**, 12 km (7 miles) south (open Apr–Oct: Tues–Sun; entrance fee), which was originally in the possession of the Babenbergs and predominantly involved in local plots and treachery.

Bad Tatzmannsdorf, just west of Schlaining, offers a comprehensive range of treatments for patients suffering from rheumatism or coronary, circulatory, spinal, metabolic or vascular disorders. As long ago as the 17th century the medicinal baths in this spa town – previously a Magyar and before that a Croatian settlement – were popular with the aristocracy.

The most important centre in southern Burgenland is **Oberwart**, the next town to the south. Half of the population here is Hungarian, as evidenced by the presence of a Calvinist church, rare in Austria. Finally, **Güssing** ⓭ – an additional 35 km (21 miles) south on Road 57 – is famous for its pretty situation and mineral water. The town itself is dominated by a magnificent castle perched high on a hillside (open mid-Apr–Oct: Tues–Sun; entrance fee). Dating from the 12th century, it contains a museum, an ancestral portrait gallery containing some pictures attributed to Brueghel, and an armoury. Its chapel houses the oldest organ in Burgenland. West of Güssing, the village of Gerersdorf has an open-air museum with farm buildings dating from the 18th and 19th centuries (open Apr-Oct: daily; entrance fee). ❑

BELOW:
a Burgenland smile.

STYRIA

Known as the "Green Province", Styria combines majestic mountains with fertile wine-growing regions, thermal spas and gently rolling hills reminiscent of Tuscany

Maps:
Area 182
City 180

The "green heart of Austria" is an appropriate slogan for Styria (Steiermark). The second-largest Austrian province includes alpine landscape such as perpetual ice and deeply cut ravines, as well as extensive expanses of forest which give way to rolling ranges of hills skirting the lower Hungarian plains.

For some Styria may at first seem exotic: dark pumpkin-seed oil, ruby-red Schilcher wine, and a dialect that may be unintelligible to unpractised ears. But, in fact, here Austria shows itself at its best: pithy and natural. Two factors – a genuinely hospitable attitude to visitors and affordable prices – unite the mountainous north, with its countless opportunities for active and adventure holidays, and the green hills of the romantic south. These favourable conditions are underlined by the fact that the Austrians themselves regard the "Green Province" as their favourite holiday region within their own borders.

PRECEDING PAGES: the wine country of southern Styria. **LEFT:** Graz and its clocktower. **BELOW:** a Graz market trader.

The Styrian capital

With a population of 240,000, the province's capital, **Graz ❶**, is the second-largest city in Austria. Situated on the Mur River, it is an economic and cultural centre settled as long ago as AD 800, but first mentioned in records in 1128. The town was awarded special privileges under the Habsburg King Rudolf I, who seized it from his arch rival Ottokar, and from 1379 it became the chief residence of the Leopoldine line. A bastion against the Turkish threat, Graz was fortified between the 15th and 17th centuries and withstood a succession of sieges. The Italian influence on the architecture is unmistakable.

The starting point for a walking tour should be the Old Town. Its appearance is characterised by numerous gabled houses dating from the 17th and 18th centuries, some of which still display fine stucco decorations. A favourite meeting place is the **Erzherzog-Johann-Brunnen ❹** (Archduke Johann Fountain) on Hauptplatz. The four female figures on the bronze fountain are allegorical depictions of the Enns, Mur, Drau and Sann – the four principal rivers of Styria before the partition. The neo-Renaissance **Rathaus ❸** (Town Hall; built in 1888) also stands on the busy Hauptplatz and is a classic example of historicist architecture.

Of particular interest is the **Landhaus ❻**, behind the Rathaus, built by Domenico dell'Allio between 1557 and 1565. It is considered one of the finest intact Renaissance buildings in the south German-speaking area. The highlight is the stunning courtyard with its three tiers of arcades and bronze well-canopy. Also not to be missed are the Rittersaal (Knights' Hall) and Landstube (Parliament Chamber), with their magnificent stucco ceilings depicting the four elements, signs of the zodiac and scenes from local history.

Armour for a medieval army

On the south side of the Landhaus stands the 1645-built **Landeszeughaus**  (Arsenal; open Mar–Dec: Tues–Sun; entrance fee), which contains a unique collection of weapons. In the 17th century it could easily have equipped a 28,000-man army of mercenaries. Experts consider this historic arsenal to be the finest in the world; 15th-century suits of armour, old guns, warhorses, two-handed swords, chain mail, shields, muskets and rifles are all on view here.

The social focal point of the Old Town is the **Herrengasse**, a fashionable shopping street with a number of noteworthy townhouses. The Herrengasse eventually leads to the square Am Eisernen Tor, with the **Türkensäule**, the Turks' Column (also known as the Virgin's Column) in the middle. North of here are a number of architectural jewels. The 15th-century **Burg** ❺ (Castle) on Hofgasse now contains government offices, but a double spiral staircase dating from 1499 survives in the the northwest wing. Opposite the Burg is the late 15th-century **Domkirche** ❻ (Cathedral) whose interior combines Gothic and Baroque features. Beside the cathedral is the magnificent **Mausoleum of Ferdinand II** ❼ (open Mon–Thur and Sat; entrance fee), a Mannerist-Baroque construction begun in 1614. The interior contains some eye-catching stucco and frescoes by Johann Bernhard Fischer von Erlach, and a red marble sarcophagus of Ferdinand's parents, Charles II and Maria. Three fine Baroque palazzi can be found on Sackstrasse, to the west – **Palais Herberstein** (at No. 16), **Palais Attems** (No. 17) and **Palais Khuenburg** (No. 18).

Not to be missed by any visitor to Graz is the **Schlossberg** ❽. This dolomite rock is 470 metres (1,540 ft) high and can be ascended by funicular (in three minutes) or by foot (in 20–25 minutes). It is crowned by the 28-metre (90-ft)

BELOW: statue of St Peter in the Mausoleum of Ferdinand II.

Uhrturm (Clocktower) ❶, a city landmark that is visible for miles around. Facing the Schlossberg and the Old Town, on the west bank of the Mur, is a new exhibition hall, the **Kunsthaus Graz**. A shimmering, blue, biomorphic bubble, it opens in September 2003 for exhibitions of contemporary art.

Graz is also a student town (it has two universities and a music conservatory). It has an active cultural life. Every autumn it hosts the avant-garde arts festival Steirischer Herbst, and in summer, the Styriarte, devoted to classical music.

As expected, Graz can offer a wide range of gastronomic pleasures. Those in need of refreshment after an extended exploration of the city on foot will find it in one of its many fine restaurants. In recent years the Old Town has also become an attractive rendezvous for night owls. There should be something to suit all tastes among the numerous "in" places, many of which have live music.

The environs of the Styrian capital are also worth exploring. Approximately 2 km (1 mile) west of the main station stands **Schloss Eggenberg** (1625–35) (grounds open daily; entrance fee) with its characteristic four towers. The public rooms are decorated with magnificent stucco and ceiling paintings. Apart from housing a museum of prehistory and antiquity, the castle contains a hunting collection and a coin collection belonging to the provincial museum, the Joanneum (museums open Mar–Dec: daily; entrance fee; tel: (0316) 8017 4830).

Some 40 km (25 miles) west of Graz and 3 km (2 miles) northeast of Köflach, lies the **Piber Stud Farm ❷** (open Apr–Oct: daily; fee for obligatory tours). This is where the Lipizzaner stallions of the Spanish Riding School in Vienna *(see page 124)* are bred and trained. Of Spanish origin, the horses were first brought here from Lipica in Slovenia. Don't be surprised to see foals with black coats; Lipizzaners do not acquire their characteristic grey colour until fully grown.

Maps:
Area 182
City 180

Every year about five Lippizaner stallions are sent from Piber to the famous riding school in Vienna.

BELOW: a cherub in the sun in Graz.

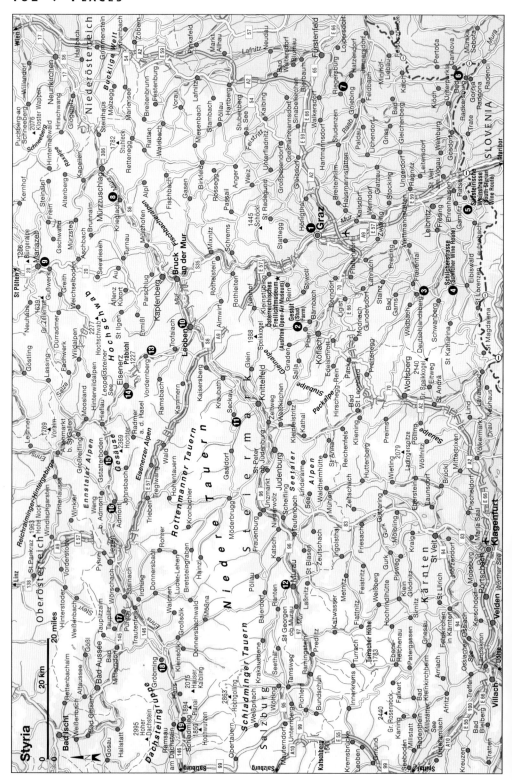

The nearby town of **Barnbach** is worth visiting to see a church that was given a unique make-over in 1987 by Viennese architect Friedensreich Hundertwasser. Pfarrkirche St Barbara now has irregular windows, a golden onion dome, a bowed roof and other typical Hundertwasser touches.

Map on page 182

Where the Schilcher grows

South of Graz lies Styria's principal wine-growing district. At present, more than 3,000 hectares (7,400 acres) of land are devoted to viticulture in the province. This means that it only contributes around 5 percent of the national total wine production. However, the 4,000 wine-growing concerns produce predominantly high-quality vintages. The wines produced here are in the main piquant Rhine Riesling and Welschriesling varieties. However, the Schilcher, the Styrian speciality produced in the western part of this region, is not so much a wine as a staple of life.

The Schilcher claims to be the oldest Styrian wine; it was probably first cultivated from a wild vine stock by the Celts. Pope Pius VI reported on the occasion of his journey to Vienna in 1782, that he had been served at the foot of the Koralpe mountain a "light-red, sharp-tasting wine, agreeable and refreshing". In the 16th and 17th centuries the Wildbach grape was widely grown in Styria. Archduke Johann, the popular younger brother of Franz I and an enthusiastic supporter of Styrian wine-growing, had the Wildbach grape bred in his own vine nurseries. At the end of the 19th century, however, the vine louse destroyed most of the Schilcher stocks; the continuation of the strain could only be assured by grafting the Wildbach grape on to an American stock. In the middle of the 1960s this ancient Styrian grape species was rediscovered and cultivation along modern lines was begun.

South Styrian grapes ready for harvest.

BELOW: workers on the steam railway in Stainz, north of Deutschlandsberg.

The Schilcher, whose name derives from the word *schillert* (shining) – as its colour shimmers from light pink to dark red – is one of the rarer Austrian wine varieties. Its production is the only one to be protected by law and restricted to a specific area. It is characterised by a fruity yet lively sharpness, a mild yet distinctive bouquet and a balanced, slightly acid taste.

The central village in the Schilcher District is **Deutschlandsberg ❸**, 35 km (22 miles) southwest of Graz. Dominated by the fortified Landsberg Castle, it is an excellent place for resting in one of the numerous rustic taverns. Those who prefer to live more healthily should pay a visit to the neighbouring spas or the mudbaths at **Schwanberg**. Castles and country houses are scattered across the area. The Renaissance **Schloss Hollenegg** is just to the south, as is Schloss Limberg; to the north, there are castles at Frauental and **Stainz**, the latter being the magnificent ancestral home of the Counts of Merano. Another castle in the area that should not be overlooked is at **Wildbach,** near Frauental. Franz Schubert stayed here in 1827. Schilcher is pressed here too, from the Blue Wildbacher Grape.

The Schilcher lends its name to the panoramic **Schilcherstrasse ❹** (Schilcher Wine Route). It leads across attractive ranges of hills and past pretty wooden vintners' houses, winding from Ligist (in the north) via Greisdorf to Stainz, Bad Gams, Deutschlandsberg and thence to Eibiswald, almost on the Slovenian

*Colourful doorway in
St Veit am Vogau,
near Ehrenhausen.*

BELOW:
a wine estate in
southern Styria.

border, where it joins the South Styrian Wine Route *(see below)*. Way down south, where the route approaches the national frontier, you should not be surprised to notice men in Yugoslavian uniforms. It does not mean that you have unknowingly strayed across the border; they are neighbouring frontier guards who cross over to sample the local wine.

More wine country

To the southeast of the Schilcher region is the South Styrian Wine Country, which stretches from **Leutschach**, near the Slovenian border east and north through **Ratsch**, **Gamlitz** and many other famous wine-growing villages to **Frauenberg** near Leibnitz. Gamlitz, with a total of 350 hectares (865 acres) under cultivation, is regarded as the largest wine-growing village in the province.

This region is served by the **South Styrian Wine Route ❺**, which takes you through a land of hills that radiates peace, calm and a salubrious air. The vineyards cascade down the hillsides to the valley floors; farmhouses are scattered as if by some caprice across the scene; and the graceful poplars recall the cypresses so familiar in the Tuscan landscape. In fact, "The Styrian Tuscany" is the nickname given to this corner of the Green Province. Visitors enjoying the 40-km (25-mile) drive or rail journey south from Graz via Leibnitz to **Ehrenhausen**, the gateway to the South Styrian Wine Country, may find themselves making this comparison.

Maize, another important component of the local economy, is also much in evidence; only the olive trees are missing. In their place grow sweet chestnuts, known here as *maroni* and roasted over the countless stoves that proliferate beside woodland and roadway when they are harvested. The chestnuts are especially good accompanied by grape juice, which can be sampled at the long tables placed

near the chestnut stoves or in the kitchens of the farmhouses. Musicians perform on accordion and dulcimer by some chestnut stands until well into October.

The *klapotetz*, a kind of windmill, is a regular sight in the area. Six or eight slanting wings, fixed to a powerful shaft, each carry small hammers positioned to hit an anvil – either furiously if a strong wind is blowing or intermittently if only a breeze is stirring. The actual purpose of the contraption is to scare away the starlings, which may have designs on the grapes. Each of the bird-scarers has its own individual sound. The vintners start up their *klapotetz* each year on St Jacob's Day, 25 July, and shut them down on St Martin's Day, 11 November.

The land of spas

The southeastern corner of Styria is one of the healthiest regions in Austria. Here, thermal spa resorts invite the visitor to undertake a health tour. **Bad Radkersburg** ❻ lies right in the southeast corner of this region, some 75 km (46 miles) southeast of Graz via Road 69. The River Mur, flowing along the southern side of the town, marks the border with Slovenia.

Bad Radkersburg is an attractive town, characterised by well-preserved merchants' and noblemen's houses from the Gothic, Renaissance, Baroque and art nouveau periods – it was recently given a European Gold Medal for Historic Preservation. Today the town is devoted to health and fitness. The spa buildings, which lie a short distance from the centre, contain warm spring waters which are considered beneficial for health complaints of all kinds.

The Styrian spa with the longest tradition retains its elegant mid-19th century Biedermeier character. **Bad Gleichenberg**, 25 km (15 miles) north of Bad Radkersburg, was highly esteemed during Imperial times for its efficacy in the treatment of circulatory and pulmonary disorders. In recent years cure programmes for children suffering from respiratory disorders have been available here. The village is surrounded by a 20-hectare (50-acre) nature park in which no motor traffic is permitted. Bad Gleichenberg also offers an excellent golf course.

North of Bad Gleichenberg, **Riegersburg** ❼ is home to a monumental castle (open Apr–Oct: daily; entrance fee). Standing majestically on a basalt cliff, it was built in 1170 on the site of a Roman fort. It received its present appearance in the 17th century. The castle, which became the country's main bulwark against Turkish invasion, is today one of the best-preserved medieval castles in Europe. Since 1987 it has housed a number of temporary exhibitions.

Walkersdorf Therme, a little further north, specialises exclusively in relaxation and fitness. In addition to the wide range of curative facilities on offer, there are walks through peaceful woods, past vineyards, fishponds and fairy-tale castles.

In Rosegger's forest home

North of Graz, on the right bank of the Mur near Stübing, is the **Austrian Open-Air Museum** (open Apr–Oct: Tues–Sun; entrance fee; tel: (03124) 53 700). It is home to a collection of old farmhouses, barns and mills from the nine provinces. There are more than 70 exhibits, from cattle troughs to a complete farmyard.

Map on page 182

The village of Blumau, about 30 km (18 miles) northeast of Riegersburg, was transformed in 1997 by the construction of a spa resort by visionary architect Friedensreich Hundertwasser. His signature bright colours and crazy paving are unmistakable here.

BELOW:
Riegersburg castle.

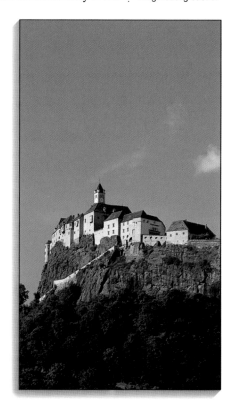

North again and you will eventually reach Bruck an der Mur, at the confluence of the Mur and Mürz rivers. A 30-km (18-mile) detour east on Road S6 to **Krieglach**  ❽ is strongly recommended. Here, at Roseggerstrasse 44, is the house where Peter Rosegger, the celebrated Styrian poet, lived and died. It is now a museum (open Feb–Dec: Tues–Sun; tel: (03855) 2375). A memorial recalls the famous local son, whose grave you'll find in the village cemetery. Krieglach is also the starting point for walking tours through "Rosegger's native country".

A side road south to **Alpl** will transport the visitor into a woodland landscape that could have come straight out of a Grimm's fairy tale. The Austrian Walkers' Museum (open Apr–Oct: Tues–Sun; entrance fee; tel: (03855) 8238), Peter Rosegger's country home birthplace (also a museum; open Apr–Dec: Tues–Sun; entrance fee; tel: (03855) 8230) and the famous woodlands make the village an attractive stopping point.

Northern pilgrimage

If, however, you continue your exploration of Styria in a northerly direction from Bruck an der Mur, you will soon enter the **Hochschwab** region. Of note here is the resort village of **Aflenz**, 18 km (11 miles) north of Bruck, often referred to as "the Davos of Styria". Those wishing to recuperate here can either take a Kneipp cure or simply enjoy the healthy, bracing air by taking a long walk – the Hochschwab is a designated conservation area. The region also provides the headwaters for the freshwater supply network of Vienna.

The village of **Mariazell** ❾ is 40 km (25 miles) north of Aflenz and almost on the provincial boundary between Styria and Lower Austria. This northernmost part of the province is the country's major point of interest for religious

BELOW: an outdoor feast.

pilgrims, thanks to a simple wooden statue of the Virgin Mary *(see box)*. She is kept in the town's basilica, which was built to display her (basilica open daily; treasury open May–Oct: Tues–Sun; entrance fee; tel: (03882) 25 950). Fischer von Erlach created the magnificent Baroque high altar (1704) of various coloured marble, dominated by a larger-than-life silver Crucifixion group.

Mariazell also offers a variety of attractions that make it suitable for a longer stay. These include a Kneipp cure complex, tennis courts, fishing facilities, canoeing, riding and various excursions – to **Lake Erlauf**, to the **Grünau-Maria Waterfall**, to **Lake Hubertus**, up via a cable-car to the **Bürgeralpe** or into the Hochschwab mountains.

Southwest of Bruck is **Leoben ⑩**, the second-largest town in Styria (37,000 inhabitants) and the centre of the province's iron industry. Here we find not only the seat of an iron and coal university with a worldwide reputation, but also much to appeal to the culturally-interested traveller. Visitors passing through the "Mushroom Tower" – as the local populace lovingly calls the 17th-century **Mautturm** (Customs Tower) in reference to its toadstool-shaped roof – emerge onto Kärntner Strasse, which winds through the entire town centre. A little further on, on the right-hand side, is the Municipal Theatre (founded in 1791). It is one of the oldest public theatres in Austria, but no longer has a resident troupe of players. Apart from productions from the stages of Vienna and Graz, it also hosts touring groups from Germany and Switzerland.

The Kirchgasse leads to the **Municipal Museum** (open daily; entrance fee), housed in what was formerly the castle of the local prince. One section of the museum is devoted to fine examples of wrought-ironwork of past centuries; another commemorates the "French period" in Leoben.

Map on page 182

BELOW: a wayside shrine near Mariazell.

THE VIRGIN OF MARIAZELL

Mariazell is a place with an importance out of all proportion to its small size. This scenic mountain village takes in a deluge of visitors every year, particularly in August and September – all because of a single wooden statue believed throughout Austria, Hungary and the Balkans to possess both healing and protective powers.

Mariazell's basilica, Romanesque in origin, was rebuilt in the 14th century as a Gothic-style hall church before being transformed into a larger Baroque edifice between 1644 and 1683. The goal of all pilgrims, however, is the late-Romanesque, wooden statue of the Virgin Mary, a plain rendering which in 1157 was claimed by a local monk to have delivered his party from danger. Soon a small chapel was constructed in the woods, and a cult began to develop. In 1377, the Virgin of Mariazell was given direct credit for preventing a Turkish victory over the Hungarians.

Today she is housed within the basilica in the Gnaden-kapelle (Chapel of Miracles) behind a Viennese silver grille. Two important religious holidays, Assumption Day and Mary's birthday (8 September) bring even more than the usual throngs to see her, as do Saturday evenings in summer, when the village streets are lit by torches and filled with processions.

The Murtal

If you are heading west from Leoben, you should include an excursion through the **Upper Mur Valley**. The countryside here is mountainous and houses idyllic little villages where old traditions are still cultivated. The setting is ideal for a more restful holiday. Protected by the Schladminger and Rottenmanner mountains, many of the village resorts here are renowned for their healthy climate. Walking enthusiasts will find excellent conditions at any time of year.

First stop is the famous **Benedictine Abbey** in **Seckau** ⓫. It was founded in 1140 and, following a fire, rebuilt in the original style in 1259. The abbey is one of the finest Romanesque buildings in Central Europe. A cloister courtyard with Tuscan-style pillars, a basilica which retains its Romanesque character, the Imperial Hall, the Homage Hall and the so-called Black Hall are all worth seeing.

Some distance to the southwest lies the village of **Zeltweg**, internationally known as the site of the Österreichring, the national motor racing circuit. **Judenburg**, St **Peter** and **Unzmarkt-Frauenburg** – all west along Road 96 – are all good starting points for walking tours through the Seetaler Alps or the Niedere Tauern.

Castle fanatics should not fail to visit **Teufenbach**, further up the valley. The village has a population of barely 600, but houses a whole series of castles: **Alt-Teufenbach** (12th century), **Neu-Teufenbach** (16th century), the ruins of **Stein Castle** (12th century) and **Pux Castle** (12th–14th century), and two spectacular rarities: the only two remaining medieval underground castles – find them in the caves at Pux.

Murau ⓬, a few miles west, is a centre for Nordic sports. The village contains a number of ancient trees dating from medieval times. In the neighbouring village of **St Georgen** stands the Styrian Wood Museum (open daily;

The kürbis *(pumpkin) is a Styrian speciality whose seeds provide* kürbiskernöl, *an oil used in local cooking.*

BELOW: a bellowing stag near Seckau.

entrance fee; tel: (03534) 2202), which documents the links between the province's inhabitants and their lush green forests.

Those wishing to continue their journey towards Carinthia – or rather, towards Klagenfurt – should turn left on to Road 95 near Predlitz. It leads steadily uphill through the romantic Turracher Graben between the Gurktaler Alps. The summit is the **Turracher Höhe**, at 1,780 metres (5,840 ft), which forms the natural boundary between Styria and Carinthia. A trio of lakes, the **Turracher See**, the **Grünsee** and the **Schwarzsee**, invite the visitor to explore the district on foot. In winter the area is a favoured ski centre; in summer, the mountain pastures and forests attract almost as many visitors.

An industrial past

Back at Leoben, the road northwest (No. 115A) leads to **Trofaiach**, an archetypal summer resort. It was once the main resting place along the so-called Styrian Iron Road that ran northwest from Leoben to Steyr in Upper Austria. Today, thanks to its castles – Möll, Stibicchofen (open Sat and Sun) and Oberndorf – it is an attractive goal for excursions.

Beyond Trofaiach is **Vordernberg** ⓭, once a centre for iron production. Archduke Johann was largely responsible for the development of the Vordernberg coal and steel industry, the history of which can still be traced in numerous places. Vordernberg is one of the foremost towns in the history of European iron manufacture. Apart from numerous old mineworkers' houses and the **Meran House** (Archduke Johann's house), there are several wheelwrights' shops, a rack railway museum, an iron-smelting plant and an old blacksmith's shop to see.

The **Präbichl Pass**, which reaches 1,230 metres (4,035 ft), links Vordernberg

Map on page 182

TIP

The Murtalbahn, a private narrow-gauge railway, runs steam-train trips in the summer from Murau up the idyllic Mur Valley to Tamsweg in Salzburg Province.

BELOW: the Erzberg, scarred by open-cast mining.

and Eisenerz via 12 km (7 miles) of twisting road. The Erzberg railway, which traverses the pass through a series of tunnels, was not completed until 1892. As recently as 1978 steam engines still puffed up the steep rack railway over the pass. Nowadays the Präbichl is held in high regard as a first-class ski resort.

The town of **Eisenerz** ⑭, another important mining centre, lies in a wild valley basin, at the mouth of the Krumpen and the Trofeng valleys. Rising more than 700 metres (2,300 ft) above the valley floor is the 1,470-metre (4,820-ft) Erzberg, or "ore-mountain", its slopes scarred by open-cast mining methods into ochre-coloured ridges and terraces. Tours of the mountain and mining works, including a 90-minute journey underground and a ride around the terraces in a huge dumper truck, are offered in town (May–Oct: daily).

The town's present-day appearance owes much to its economic heyday in the 15th and 16th centuries. There are a number of sights worth visiting: the **Schichtturm** bell-tower (1581); the **Bergmannsplatz** with its fine miners' union houses; the remains of the Rupprechta furnace; the Kammerhof (once the seat of the mining overseer), which now contains the **Municipal Museum** (open May–Oct: daily; Nov–Apr: Tues–Fri; entrance fee); the Kaiser-Franz-Stollen, where the ore was prepared for smelting; remains of the ore consignments at the railway station; and the huge slag heaps in **Münichthal**.

In addition Eisenerz has a well-developed infrastructure for tourists: camp site, climbing school, fitness circuit, footpaths and a lake for bathing (with boat rental and windsurfing opportunities).

Northwest of Eisenerz is the **Leopoldsteiner See**, 1,500 metres (4,920 ft) long by 500 metres (1,640 ft) wide. A mountain lake impressively surrounded by craggy rock walls, it recalls the fjords of Scandinavia. According to local

The parish church in the mining town of Eisenerz features a relief over the doorway which depicts Adam and Eve as miners!

BELOW:
the Eisenerz Alps from Präbichl Pass.

legend a malevolent water sprite was once bringing bad luck to the lake's fishermen. Eventually they gathered up their courage and caught the wicked fellow, but the sprite, somewhat subdued, made his captors a proposal: "A golden river, a silver heart or an iron hat" in exchange for his release. His captors wisely chose the iron hat, whereupon the sprite pointed at the nearby Erzberg mountain. It is said that this incident marked the beginning of the history of ore mining in Upper Styria.

Map on page 182

The Gesäuse Ravine

About 15 km (9 miles) northwest of Eisenerz is **Hieflau**, the principal traffic intersection in the Gesäuse region. At this point Road 115 (the Iron Road) meets Road 146 (the Gesäuse Road), and the Amstetten-Selzthal railway line meets the Erzberg line to Leoben. Hieflau marks the eastern end of the **Gesäuse Ravine**. Here, between mountains that rise up to 2,400 metres (7,870 ft) high, the River Enns laboriously carves its way through precipitous rock faces. The rushing torrents and majestic mountains make this countryside some of the most bizarre and fascinating in Austria.

A few miles along Road 146 we are in the middle of a wildly romantic mountain world. **Gstatterboden** ⓯ deserves its epithet of "Capital of the Gesäuse". It lies exactly in the middle of the Enns corridor between the Hochtor Range in the south and the Buchstein Group and the Tamischbachturm in the north. Gstatterboden is a good starting point for a variety of Alpine pursuits. Walkers, mountaineers, climbers, ski tour enthusiasts, wild-water canoeists and fishermen are all well catered for here.

Johnsbach, south of the main road, is regarded as the second most important climbing centre in the Gesäuse. It is linked with the Enns valley by a 6-km (4-mile) long gorge, lying in an idyllic high-altitude valley between the Hochtor range in the northeast and the gentler Eisenerz Alps and the Admonter Reichenstein to the south and west. Many visitors to Johnsbach consider it to be the prettiest of all Alpine villages. Not to be missed are the **Mountain Church** (14th century), with its world-famous climbers' cemetery, the **Wolfbauer Waterfall** and the **Odelstein Stalactite Caves**.

One of the highlights of any tour of Upper Styria is a visit to **Stift Admont** ⓰, Austria's oldest male monastic institution. The Benedictine monastery (open Apr–Oct: daily; entrance fee; tel: (03613) 231 2601) was founded by Archbishop Gebhard of Salzburg in 1074 and was for centuries the artistic and cultural centre of the Enns valley.

The abbey library is one of the finest examples of Baroque architecture in the world, with superb ceiling frescoes by Bartolomeo Altomonte. It contains more than 150,000 volumes, 1,600 manuscripts, 900 early printed works and 123 12th-century codices, making it the largest and most valuable monastery library in the world. The foundation buildings also house a museum of the history of art, an exhibition of curiosities and, perhaps not for the phobic, an insect collection consisting of no fewer than 252,000 exhibits.

The capital of the Styrian section of the Enns valley

BELOW: a miniature painting in the library at Stift Admont.

Map on page 182

is **Liezen,** a town with over 7,000 inhabitants located to the west on Road 146. It is a winter paradise for skiers thanks to the nearby Wurzeralm; in summer, it is also a centre for mountain activities.

Southwest of Liezen the next important centre is **Stainach,** a railway hub, with express train connections to Bad Aussee, Leoben, Salzburg, Vienna and Graz. Just before Stainach is the town of **Bad Wörschach** with its famous sulphur springs. The **Wörschach Gorge** is one of the most striking in the land, and there is a fine panorama from the ruins of Wolkenstein Castle (1186), which overlooks the town. Beyond Stainach is the romantic 13th-century **Trautenfels Castle** (open Easter–Oct: daily). It was built to defend the Enns valley and acquired its present-day appearance in 1670. Some sections of the colossal structure date from around 1520. Frescoes, a two-storey Knights' Hall and the Enns Valley Museum can all be seen here.

Just northwest of Trautenfels is **Pürgg** ⓱, site of some of the oldest surviving frescoes in Austria, completed around 1160. They decorate the Romanesque Chapel of St John, set on a hill on the edge of town. Among the subjects portrayed are the *Annunciation,* the *Nativity* and the *Feeding of the Five Thousand.* If you continue beyond Pürgg on Road 145, you soon arrive in the Styrian part of the Salzkammergut *(see page 213).*

(see page 213).

Carry on in a southwesterly direction along Road 146 and you will reach **Gröbming** ⓲. The village is a popular holiday resort because of its sunny climate; the late-Gothic parish church (15th century) contains the largest altarpiece in Styria. Families with small children are particularly welcome in Gröbming. Childcare and babysitting services have been set up to relieve parents of some of the strain of holidaymaking.

BELOW: the Dachstein Massif from the south.
RIGHT: Styrian fare – bread, apple wine and schnapps.

Around the Dachstein

If you follow Road 146 still further southwest, you soon arrive in the town of **Schladming** ⓳ (population 4,000), and the area surrounding the **Dachstein Massif.** Schladming has the largest Lutheran church in Styria, built in 1862 but containing a much older altarpiece from around 1570. Today it is a textile manufacturing town, specialising in loden, the heavy green wool of the overcoats beloved by Germans and Austrians.

In 1982, Schladming and the neighbouring village of **Haus im Ennstal** were the venue for the Alpine Skiing World Championships. The winter-sports infrastructure is correspondingly well developed. Linking the ski centres of **Reiteralm, Planai-Hochwurzen** and **Hauser Kaibling** are 90 km (55 miles) of avalanche-free pistes, a cable-car network and chair and drag lifts. For those wishing to sample these snowy pleasures in summer – in a bathing costume – ample opportunities are available on the Dachstein glacier.

Ramsau, a neighbouring village reached by a twisting road north, has meanwhile developed into a fine resort for Nordic skiers. And in the warmer months the entire region is ideal for mountain and walking tours. **Ramsau-Rössing** is the site of the oldest loden-dyeing factory in Austria; Germany's and Austria's loden coats (green with a short pile) are world-famous for their warmth and hard-wearing qualities. ❑

Bernhard
Scheffenberg

UPPER AUSTRIA

*Between the Baroque monasteries of St Florian and Kremsmünster
and the historic towns of Steyr and Freistadt, Upper Austria hides
large swathes of remote countryside untouched by tourism*

Map
on page
198

From the Dachstein peaks in the south to the Bohemian woods in the north, from the Inn River to the Enns River – these are the boundaries of Upper Austria (Oberösterreich). The province is also sub-divided into regions: the Mühlviertel, the Innviertel, the Hausruck Forest and the Traunviertel. The most scenic region, the Salzkammergut, is covered in the next chapter.

Upper Austria can offer its visitors a wide range of holiday facilities: adventurous souls, for example, will get their money's worth hang-gliding (Windisch-Garsten), potholing (Dachstein Caves), wild-water canoeing (on the Steyr) or scaling one of the region's many peaks. The more than 70 lakes in the Salzkammergut cater to every type of water sport. If you prefer a more tranquil atmosphere, the Mühlviertel will prove a paradise for extended cycle tours and walking holidays, while those whose interests lie more on the cultural side will find much to explore in the countless monasteries and convents, and in the pretty villages with their quaint houses.

PRECEDING PAGES:
colourful houses
in Mauthausen,
east of Linz.
LEFT: stained glass
at Stift St Florian.
BELOW:
arcade in Linz.

Linz, the capital

A popular rhyme, claiming that "It all begins in Linz", arouses the new arrival's curiosity about the provincial capital of Upper Austria. **Linz ❶** proves to be a city that at once invites the visitor to stroll through its streets, to watch the world go by, to eat, drink and shop. The third-largest city in the country has been the capital of the "Land around the Enns" since 1490.

The city's roots stretch back to before the time of the Romans, whose records mention "Lentia" for the first time in AD 410. The name is of Celtic origin, and it is even claimed that the site was settled in Neolithic times. In approximately 700 Linz became the eastern base of the Bavarian kingdom.

At the start of the 13th century it came into the possession of the Babenbergs and received its town charter soon afterwards; at the end of the 15th century Linz even became the royal seat for a short while. In 1672 a wool factory (which later employed as many as 50,000 home workers) was founded. In 1832 Austria's first (horse-drawn) railway commenced operations between Linz and Budweis, and 1842 saw the foundation of the shipyard, which made the first iron ships in Europe. Thanks to the nitrogen works and the VOEST steelworks, Linz has become one of the principal industrial cities in Austria.

Within the city, the attractive **Old Town** has preserved its predominantly Baroque appearance, inviting the visitor to take a leisurely stroll followed by a *kleiner Brauner* (a coffee) in one of the many welcoming cafés – perhaps with a piece of *Linzer torte*, the traditional local cake.

The town's landmark, the white marble **Plague Column**, was dedicated in 1723. It dominates the **Hauptplatz**, whose dimensions – 220 by 60 metres (720 by 195 ft) – make it the largest enclosed square in Austria. Between the stately patrician houses with their Baroque and Biedermeier facades stands the imposing Renaissance **Old Town Hall**. South of Hauptplatz are the sophisticated shops of the pedestrianised Landstrasse.

The fact that Linz was long the seat of the local bishop and hence a town of considerable importance explains the presence of the numerous churches. Worthy of special mention is the Jesuit church just off Hauptplatz, known as the **Old Cathedral**, where the composer Anton Bruckner was once organist. Bruckner, "God's musician", as he was dubbed, is a great favourite among the Austrians. The citizens of Linz honoured him by naming the **Brucknerhaus** after him. Opened in 1974, this concert hall beside the Danube has since become one of the most famous in Europe. Just north of the river is the **Ars Electronica Museum** (open Wed–Sun; entrance fee; tel: (0732) 72 720), devoted to the

TIP

If want to catch a film in English in Linz, head for Moviemento, at Damtezstrasse 30, where movies are often shown in their original language.

internet, virtual reality and other cyber-trickery. It's definitely worth a look if you're tiring of more traditional culture. An art and technology festival with same name, Ars Electronica, takes place in Linz every September.

Elsewhere in town, you can admire paintings by Klimt, Kokoschka and Schiele at the **Neue Galerie** (Blütenstrasse 15; open daily; Thur until 10pm; entrance fee); ride the **Pöstlingbergbahn**, the steepest tramway in Europe; and see a fine cactus collection in the **Botanical Gardens** southwest of the city centre (open daily; entrance fee).

Ecclesiastical glories

An easy day-trip southeast of Linz takes you 15 km (9 miles) to the beautiful Baroque abbey **Stift St Florian** ❷ (open Easter–Oct: daily; fee for obligatory tour; tel: (07224) 890 20), built in 1686, where composer Anton Bruckner first rose to prominence and is now buried. Regular tours take in the heavily stuccoed and frescoed abbey church, the remarkable library (with a ceiling fresco by Altomonte) and other highlights such as the grand Marmorsaal and the world's largest collection of paintings by Albrecht Altdorfer (1480–1538). The abbey's patron saint was a Roman official drowned in the nearby Enns River as punishment for his conversion to Christianity; he is believed to protect from both drowning and fires, and is usually depicted as a boy throwing water onto a fire.

Another building of outstanding beauty is **Kremsmünster Abbey** ❸ (founded in 777) which overlooks the Krems Valley about 35 km (22 miles) southwest of Linz (open Easter–Oct: daily; Nov–Easter: Tues–Sun; entrance fee). It was remodelled in the Baroque style in the late 17th century. The frescoes are well worth a visit, as are the library and the Kaisersaal. The 8th-century

Map on page 198

A collection of Gothic-era stained glass is on display at Stift St Florian.

BELOW: the large courtyard at Stift St Florian.

Tassilo Chalice – the most valuable exhibit – is made of gilded copper and housed in the treasury. Also worth visiting is the Sternwarte (Observatory Tower), which has a varied museum collection; and the Fischkalter – five fish ponds dating from the late 17th century, complete with statues and arcades.

A detour west of Kremsmünster brings you to **Lambach**, whose Benedictine abbey contains some unique treasures (open Easter–Oct: one tour daily, at 2pm). The highlights are the Romanesque Adalbero Chalice, an unusual Rococo theatre and, best of all, a series of extremely well-preserved Romanesque frescoes dating from the 11th century.

Ornate shop signs adorn the Stadtplatz in Steyr.

Steyr and the Iron Road

About 20 km (12 miles) south of St Florian is the old iron town of **Steyr ❹**, situated where the Steyr River flows into the Enns. Here the medieval Old Town offers an impressively harmonious countenance. The **Bummerlhaus** (1497), on the Stadtplatz, and the **Parish Church** (15th–17th centuries) are real jewels of Gothic architecture. Between 1886 and 1894 Anton Bruckner put his finishing touches to his last great compositions in the Priest's House next door to the church. Only a few yards away from the Stadtplatz, across the Grünmarkt, is the **Innerberger Getreidestadel** (1612). This former granary now contains the Municipal Museum (open Wed–Sun; free) and the Steyrer Kripperl, a famous mechanical puppet theatre (performances held only in December and January).

The **Wehrgraben** district, north of the River Steyr, has retained all its fine 16th–18th century architecture, making it an enchanting setting for a stroll. It also contains a museum of the "World of Work", which displays industrial history in a lively manner (open Mar–Dec: Tues–Sun; entrance fee).

BELOW: Steyr's Michaelerkirche, with its frescoed gable.

SCHUBERT IN STEYR

The Viennese composer Franz Schubert came to the wealthy industrial city of Steyr in 1819 at the invitation of a fellow musician, opera singer Johann Vogl, a native of the city. He was instantly smitten with the place, located at the confluence of two rivers, and stayed the better part of a year. While here, he gained a commission to write what would become one of his best-known works, the *Trout Quintet*, and set a number of poems to music.

It was a time of creative growth for Schubert. He met painters, musicians and writers, was trailed briefly by intelligence authorities (he ran with an impetuous university crowd) and generally had a good time, while staying with an assortment of doctors and other patrons. One dispatch home stated, "The country around here is extremely beautiful. In Steyr I've always had good conversations.... [and] in the house where I live there are eight girls, nearly all of them pretty. You can see that there's much to be done." His spirits seemed to rise above the malaise of what had been a rather diffuse life back in Vienna.

Schubert returned to Steyr twice more, in 1823 and 1825. Today his stay here is commemorated by a stone plaque on the side of the so-called "Schuberthaus", where he sometimes resided while composing.

A worthwhile short excursion into the surrounding countryside is to the pilgrimage church of **Christkindl**, situated only 3 km (2 miles) from Steyr and constructed during the 18th century by the Baroque master builders Carlone and Prandtauer. The special post office set up every year at Christmas in the town sends letters bearing the coveted special stamp to all the corners of the earth.

The so-called Iron Road in Styria *(see page 189)* continues into Upper Austria and winds through the province's southeast corner to reach Steyr. After the decline in the European steel industry, this part of the province was largely forgotten but in recent years new life has been injected into this once-important trading route. South of Steyr the Iron Road (No.115) runs along the Enns through densely wooded Alpine foothills. **Losenstein ⑤**, the highlight of the Enns valley, lies beneath the peak of the Schieferstein. Perched on a cliff above the village stand the ruins of a castle. Worth seeing are the Gothic parish church (*circa* 1400), the Castle Tavern and the Klausgraben ravine. Nearby is **Laussa**, one of the prettiest and neatest villages in Austria.

The next town, **Reichraming**, was once an industrial centre with hammer mills and a brass factory; today it is above all the gateway to the popular but unspoiled countryside of the **Reichraminger Mountains**. Brunnbach, in the hills to the south, is a good starting point for mountain walks through the hinterland.

Further up the valley, the former "golden market" of **Weyer Markt ⑥** was reputedly founded in the 13th century, receiving its charter as a market town as early as 1460. Nowadays the resort area is a perfect base for walking tours, riding holidays, fishing, and in winter both Alpine and cross-country skiing. Visitors who are interested in the town's past should view the impeccably restored market place, the late-Gothic Church of St John and Egerer Castle.

Map on page 198

About 25 km (16 miles) northeast of Weyer Markt, over the border into Lower Austria, is the famous pilgrimage church of Sonntagberg. Built on a hill long associated with miracles, the present church was completed in 1733.

BELOW: a family outing in the woods.

Also of interest is nearby **Kastenreith**. Formerly known as Kasten and today the site of the **Enns Museum**, it was an important trade centre when the rafting and boat traffic on the Enns was in its heyday. The Iron Road continues via Kleinreifling to Altenmarkt, by which time it has crossed the provincial border into Styria.

The Mühlviertel

The name of this remarkable region derives from its two principal rivers, the **Greater** and **Lesser Mühl**. It stretches out to the north of Linz, between the Danube and the Czech border, and consists of a granite plateau whose densely wooded slopes remain largely untouched, even by tourism. The rural scene is interspersed with the occasional castle or ruined fortress and little market towns which look as though they have been nestling in the hills since time immemorial.

Kefermarkt ❼, about 40 km (24 miles) northeast of Linz, is famous for the huge Gothic altarpiece in the **Church of St Wolfgang** (open daily; free; tel: (07947) 6203). Carved from limewood by an unknown master, it measures 14 by 6 metres (44 by 20 ft). The village is dominated by **Schloss Weinberg** to the north, which is now an art and music school.

Freistadt ❽, 11 km (7 miles) north of Kefermarkt, is regarded as the capital of the lower Mühlviertel and one of the most interesting sights in Austria. Founded by free merchants in 1200, today the town retains its medieval fortifications: the double defensive wall, moats, circular towers and the late-Gothic town gates – the **Linzertor** and the **Böhmertor**. The former merchants' houses surrounding the main square still have their original Gothic interiors behind magnificent Renaissance and Baroque facades. Also of note is the parish church, the so-called **St Catherine's Cathedral**, with two masterpieces of late-Gothic

Freistadt's brewery has been in operation since 1777 and, unusually, is owned communally by all the households within the medieval town walls. A share in the brewery comes with ownership of a house (and in no other way), making a takeover effectively impossible.

Below: traditions continued by the next generation.

architecture: the chancel and the baptism chapel (1483–1501). To the north-east is the **Schloss** – the former residence of the local rulers – whose medieval keep is well preserved (14th century). It contains the Mühlviertel Museum, which houses an extensive collection of stained-glass pictures (open daily; Sat & Sun pm only; entrance fee). The 15th-century **Church of Our Lady** stands outside the Böhmertor. The town is also home to an outstanding local brewery – try some of the thick, dark Freistädter Bier.

Map on page 198

Sandl, some 15 km (9 miles) northeast of Freistadt, is a destination which is still a closely-kept secret amongst winter sportsmen. The 1,110-metre (3,645-ft) Viehberg offers some very acceptable Alpine ski pistes, whilst the network of cross-country ski runs has made the town a centre for Nordic skiing.

There are also a number of worthwhile destinations west of Freistadt. **Bad Leonfelden** is a peat and Kneipp spa about 20 km (12 miles) away. The nearby Sternstein (with winter-sports facilities) is, at 1,125 metres (3,690 ft), the high-est peak in the entire Mühlviertel. By continuing through **Rohrbach**, which is encircled by the dense pine and spruce forests of the Bohemian Woods, our tour brings us to **Aigen-Schlägl** ❾. Here a highlight is the Premostratensian monastery in Schlägl, rebuilt in the Baroque style in the 17th century.

Austria's only Trappist monastery is at Engelhartszell, on the Danube east of Schärding.

South of Rohrbach lies another of the Mühlviertel's special attractions: the **Altenfelden-Mühltal Nature Park**. Its 80 hectares (200 acres) house over 700 animals, including ibexes, wild horses, antelopes and deer.

The Innviertel

The northwest part of Upper Austria is separated from Germany by the River Inn. **Schärding**, a little town perched high above the river, is famous today as the home of the largest Kneipp cure clinic in Austria. Its appearance is characterised by its medieval sil-houette, which is dominated by a ruined castle (15th century) and the town ramparts and gates.

BELOW: farmhouse in the Mühlviertel.

In **Reichersberg** ❿, 18 km (11 miles) south, stands an imposing Augustinian abbey. Founded in 1084, the buildings were badly damaged by fire in 1624 and rebuilt over the course of the rest of the century. During summer months a variety of craft courses and cul-tural events are held in Reichersberg.

Turning away from the river, Road 143 brings us to **Ried im Innkreis**, the economic focal point of this region, the Innviertel. A number of scenic roads from Ried thread through the **Hausruck** forest to **Franken-burg**. This town was the setting for a macabre spec-tacle in 1625; citizens and peasants alike were forced to throw dice to decide which of them would die and which would live. As a reminder of this gruesome event dating from the Peasant Wars, the Frankenburg Game of Dice is staged every year.

Ampflwang, a little further to the east, has earned a reputation during the past few years as an equestrian centre. The entire village has dedicated itself to the sport all year round, and novices and professionals alike will find a wide range of activities to suit them.

To the south of here is Upper Austria's most beau-tiful region, the **Salzkammergut**, which is covered in full in the next chapter. ❑

THE SALZKAMMERGUT

Lofty peaks and placid lakes provide the Salzkammergut with an endless succession of postcard-perfect scenes. But the region is also a paradise for sightseers, sailors and winter-sports enthusiasts

Map on page 208

The Salzkammergut is famous for its lakes, which provide unequalled possibilities for summertime recreation. There are 76 of them altogether, strung out like a necklace of pearls, each possessing its own inimitable charm. There are lakes for bathing in, like the Mondsee and the Wolfgangsee; yachting centres (the Attersee or the Traunsee), apparently bottomless gleaming "emeralds" (the Grundlsee and the Hallstätter See), and romantic retreats like the Gosausee and the Altausseer See. The area is also known for its numerous salt mines (Salzkammergut means "salt chamber estate"), at one time an important source of revenue.

It is difficult to encompass the Salzkammergut within a single geographical term, but it extends from the Fuschlsee and Wolfgangsee in Salzburg Province to the Toplitzsee in Styria. If Salzburg is your point of departure, the quickest route to the lakes is the motorway leading via Thalgau to Mondsee. If you have sufficient time at your disposal, however, a short detour to the south is recommended. The **Fuschlsee ❶** lies only minutes away from the busy main road, its dark, cold waters nestling between forested slopes. The pristine hills surrounding the lake were used for the famous opening scene in *The Sound of Music (see pages 214–15)*.

Not far from the road stands the **Fuschl Hunting Lodge**, with a museum containing a number of rare trophies (open daily). The nearby **Schlosshotel Fuschl** stands on a promontory above the northwest end of the lake. It was built in 1450 as a hunting lodge for the archbishops of Salzburg, and in the 20th century it became the property of the Nazi politician Ribbentrop. It is now a luxury hotel offering guests every imaginable facility: beach, fishing jetties, indoor swimming pool, tennis court and one of the most scenic golf courses in Austria. Walking through the castle's magnificent grounds, the visitor follows in the footsteps of the many monarchs, film stars and politicians (Nixon and Khrushchev, for instance), who have slept or conferred here.

Wolfgangsee and Mondsee

Skirting the south side of the Fuschlsee we soon reach **St Gilgen** on the **Wolfgangsee**. Of particular interest here is the birthplace of Mozart's mother, Ann Maria Pertl (1720–78). Today the building houses the local courthouse, but includes a Mozart memorial room (open Jun–Sept: Tues–Sun; entrance fee). One should not miss a boat trip on the lake itself, which covers an area of 13 sq. km (5 sq. miles).

The excursion to the village of **St Wolfgang ❷**, on the northern shore, is highly recommended. The landing stage is near the Weisses Rössl, the "White Horse Inn", made famous in an operetta by Ralph Benatzky. Strolling along delightful alleys, the visitor arrives at the village's main attraction, the **Pilgrimage Church**

PRECEDING PAGES: boathouses on Hallstätter See. **LEFT:** St Gilgen, on the edge of Wolfgangsee. **BELOW:** ornate bay window in St Gilgen.

(open daily; free; tel: (06138) 2321), which contains one of the most remarkable examples of Gothic art in Austria. The magnificent winged altar, created by Michael Pacher between 1471 and 1481, has 16 panels, depicting scenes from the lives of Christ, the Virgin Mary and St Wolfgang. The central sculpted scene shows the Coronation of the Virgin, flanked by saints Wolfgang and Benedict.

The village is also the starting point for a unique highlight. A steam-driven train (commissioned in 1893) chugs along unhurriedly to the summit of the 1,785-metre (5,855-ft) **Schafberg**. From here there is a breathtaking panorama of the Lake District, a stunning view of 12 lakes: Wolfgangsee, Fuschlsee, Attersee, Mondsee, Zeller See, Wallersee, Obertrumer See, Niedertrumer See, Grabensee, Abtsdorfer See, Chiemsee and Waginger See.

The Wolfgangsee, with an average water temperature of 23°C (73°F), is a paradise for those who like water sports: with fishing jetties, diving schools, boat rental (rowing, sailing, pedal and motor boats), windsurfing and sailing schools, it offers a range of water-borne activities for every taste.

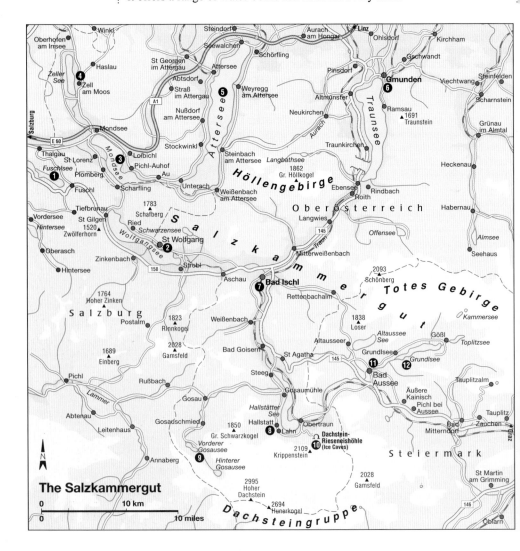

The Salzkammergut

Map on page 208

Those who choose St Gilgen as their base for further exploration of the Salzkammergut can take Road 154 north to the **Mondsee ❸**. The lake lies in the shadow of the dominant silhouettes of the Drachenwand and the Schafberg; 11 km (7 miles) long and over 2 km (1 mile) wide, its waters are among the warmest in the region. Lakeside bathing beaches and sailing schools lend the lake a carefree holiday atmosphere.

The village of Mondsee, founded in 748 by Odilo II, a Bavarian count, when a Benedictine monastery was established here, offers a number of historical sights. The local museum, for example, has a display of finds dating from the Mondsee's prehistoric culture (open May–Oct: Tues–Sun; entrance fee), while the market place is surrounded by well-preserved houses dating from the 16th–18th centuries. The **Parish Church** was redesigned in the Baroque style at the end of the 17th century and contains some particularly fine altars carved by Meinrad Guggenbichler. Retained Gothic elements include a beautiful sacristy doorway. The wedding scene in the film *The Sound of Music* was filmed here *(see pages 214–15).*

The villages surrounding the Mondsee offer yet another attraction: gourmets will discover more illustrious restaurants here than in almost any other region of Austria – creative nouvelle cuisine of the highest quality, with strong local influences, can be found almost everywhere.

Baroque figures adorn the pulpit in St Wolfgang's church.

The lakes beyond Mondsee

Continuing from Mondsee you are spoilt for choice between the vast eastern waters of the Attersee and the Traunsee and the untamed romanticism of the south – the Hallstätter See, Grundlsee, et al – quite apart from the enchanting lakes of the Alpine foothills to the north. To get a better perspective, make a detour north into the neighbouring flatlands and the Salzkammergut catchment area.

BELOW: blue water and craggy peaks.

Road 154 leads off in a northerly direction from Mondsee, reaching **Zell am Moos ❹** some 6 km (4 miles) later. The village lies on the eastern shores of the **Zeller See** (or Irrsee), a nature conservation area. The lake's waters reach temperatures of 27°C (80°F) during the summer months, allowing bathing between May and September. There are accessible bathing areas all round its perimeter. Zell am Moos is a particularly attractive holiday destination for families – playgrounds, activity programmes and a children's bathing area on the lake ensure variety.

Returning to our original starting point, the Mondsee, you can then take Road 151 to **Unterach**, on the **Attersee ❺**. The lake's dimensions – 20 by 3 km (12 by 2 miles) – make it the largest in the Salzkammergut. It is an El Dorado for sailors and is encircled by a succession of picturesque villages ideal for holidaymaking: **Unterach**, **Nussdorf** and **Attersee** on the western shore, **Seewalchen** and **Kammer** to the north and **Weyregg**, **Steinbach** and **Weissenbach** to the east. Most have camp sites, sailing and windsurfing schools and boat rental. The Attersee is the only lake in the Salzkammergut which never freezes in winter. Its waters are also considered to be very clean, and the underwater topography makes it ideal for divers (courses available).

Those wishing to explore the **Traunsee**, yet another jewel of the Salzkammergut, should follow the road round the southern tip of the Attersee before continuing via **Neukirchen** to **Gmunden**  (population 12,000). Lying in a picture-postcard setting on the northern shore of the Traunsee and offering a wide variety of water-sports facilities as well as traditional cures (salt-water baths), Gmunden is a typical summer resort. Architecturally, it also has much to offer: there is the Renaissance-era **Town Hall** with its porcelain-tiled glockenspiel, as well as a number of fine townhouses and numerous castles (Cumberland, Württemberg and Freisitz-Roith). Southwest of town is the so-called **Landschloss Orth**, which is linked by a 130-metre (425-ft) long wooden bridge to the **Seeschloss** (Lake Castle), built in the 14th century on an artificial island.

One should also make a point of visiting the town's famous porcelain factory, with its characteristic green-glazed china (Keramikstrasse 24; tours Mon–Sat am; entrance fee). Gmunden, once the salt capital and residence of the local prince, documents its close links with the "white gold" in a museum in the **Kammerhof**, which was for centuries the seat of the Salt Authority (open May–Oct: Mon–Sat; Sun am only; entrance fee; tel: (07612) 794 244). It contains displays tracing the development of the salt industry and that of the local pottery. In addition there is a collection of original manuscripts by the town's famous sons Johannes Brahms and 19th-century playwright Friedrich Hebbel.

The famous salt town of **Ebensee** lies at the southern end of the Traunsee. As early as 1607, its townfolk were refining brine from the salt mined in the area. Ebensee is a good starting point from which to make excursions into the nearby **Totes Gebirge** and **Höllengebirge** mountains. Particularly recommended is a visit to the romantic **Langbathsee** lakes, 8 km (5 miles) to the west.

In Traunkirchen, a former fishing village on the Traunsee's western shore, the parish church has an unusual Baroque pulpit from 1753. It is in the form of a fishing boat and is carved with the New Testament scene of the miraculous haul of fish.

BELOW: the Seeschloss Orth, on an island in the Traunsee.

THE GISELA

A particular attraction in Gmunden is a trip on the oldest coal-fired paddle steamer in the world. The 52-metre (170-ft) long *Gisela* was built in Vienna and then taken apart and transported to the Traunsee, where it was reassembled for its maiden voyage in 1872. It has been ploughing through the waters of the Traunsee ever since.

The steamer even transported Emperor Franz Joseph to his cool summer retreat in the heart of the Salzkammergut every year. (Gisela, not coincidentally, was the name of his first daughter.) In fact, the Habsburgs used it as a transport link between Vienna and Salzburg – at the time there were no roads between Gmunden (at the head of the lake) and Bad Ischl (en route to Salzburg) – and an especially luxurious "Kaiserkabine" was designed for their exclusive use.

It seemed in 1980 that the *Gisela* was doomed to an ignoble death as, dilapidated and rusting, it appeared in imminent danger of breaking up. Only an initiative of the Association of Friends of Gmunden saved it from the scrap heap. First of all the ship – the only one of its kind in Austria – was declared an historic monument; later, when the necessary funds had been raised, it was restored to its original splendour. And so today the *Gisela* still puffs merrily across the Traunsee every summer.

Map
on page
208

Following the course of the River Traun southwest from Ebensee, the visitor will duly arrive in **Bad Ischl ❼**. This spa town, where the emperor used to come for a cure, is still well worth a visit today. Its inimitable late 19th-century aura greets the traveller everywhere, not only in the **Kaiservilla** (Imperial Villa; open May–Oct: daily; Nov–Apr: Wed pm; entrance fee) and the **Lehárvilla** (open May–Sept: Wed–Mon; entrance fee), the summer home of operetta composer Franz Lehár. The oldest saline baths in Austria now have ultra-modern therapeutic equipment; even a short cure is relaxing. It is pleasant to follow such a session with a stroll along the esplanade beside the Traun and then to sample coffee and cakes at **Café Zauner**, the legendary pâtisserie at Pfarrgasse 7.

Thus fortified, the 11-km (7-mile) journey south to **Bad Goisern** will prove child's play. A resort with sulphur and brine baths, the town is also the shopping centre of the Salzkammergut. Manufactured here and nowhere else are the "Original Goiserer" mountain boots – one of the best of their kind in the world.

Baroque jewel

If there is a single village which fully deserves to be the subject of a postcard, then it must be **Hallstatt ❽**, to the south. Predominantly Baroque in style, the pastel-coloured houses cling precariously to the steep mountain slopes on the edge of the Hallstätter See. The historic part of the town looks as if, by some superhuman effort, it has reclaimed a narrow strip of land from both the mountains and the lake. From the village church there are numerous hikes into the surrounding hills.

There are no cars allowed through central Hallstatt, which has helped to preserve its character. If you do drive here, you'll be required to park your car in one of two parking lots; one is in a tunnel, while the second is a little further along the road.

BELOW: the lakeside town of Hallstatt.

The past 4,500 years have left their mark here. Salt was the basis of wealth in the town even for the Celtic and Illyrian tribes. An entire epoch, marking the first phase of the European Iron Age, between 800 and 400 BC, has been christened the "Hallstatt Period". Sophisticated artefacts were produced by this ancient culture, and Hallstatt achieved world fame when many were unearthed from a 2,500-year-old burial site. Some can be seen at the new **Hallstatt Museum** in the village (open May–Oct: daily; Nov–Apr: Tues–Sun; entrance fee).

Visitors with an interest in the macabre should take a look inside the **Beinhaus** (charnel house) beside the parish church. Since space is at a premium here, the bones have to be removed from the tiny cemetery after 10 years. They are stacked up, but not before the skull has been artistically labelled and painted.

The **Hallstätter See** is very popular with people who are into fresh-water diving, shipwrecks and the recovery of sunken treasure. Gerhard Zauner, proprietor of the diving school and Divers' Inn in Hallstatt, spends almost more time underwater than above it. Even experts can learn from his classes. He offers more than 20 courses, from a basic introduction to diving, to such esoteric topics as "Fish Language" and "Cutting and Welding Under Water".

Dachstein delights

Opinions are divided, but the **Gosausee** ❾ – 17 km (11 miles) southwest of the Hallstätter See – can certainly lay claim to be the loveliest lake in the Salzkammergut. Whether you are visiting it for the first or fifth time, you will not fail to be captured by an indescribable emotion as you gaze upon the view of the lake set against the slopes and glaciers of the Dachstein Massif. It is best to stay here until the late afternoon, taking the last funicular to **Zwieselalpe**. The benches in front

The hundreds of skulls in Hallstatt's Beinhaus are labelled with the names of their former owners.

BELOW: cross-dressing antics in Bad Aussee on Shrove Tuesday.

of the shelter are perfectly placed for watching the Alpine pyrotechnics at sunset.

Obertraun, at the southeastern tip of the Hallstätter See directly across from Hallstatt, is regarded by winter-sports enthusiasts as a place where snow is assured. A funicular leads up the 2,110-metre (6,920-ft) **Krippenstein** facing the lake's southern shore, providing another impressive view of the Dachstein.

From Schönbergalm, the intermediate station, one can visit the famous **Dachstein Ice Caves ⑩** (open May–Oct: daily; entrance fee). Here, imposing vaults and corridors lead into the interior of the mountain. The highlight of this chilly excursion is undoubtedly the **Mammuthöhle** (Mammoth's Cave), which consists of several storeys with a total combined height of 300 metres (985 ft). Equally impressive is the **Koppenbrüllerhöhle**, with its fantastically-shaped stalactite sculptures.

Into Styria

From Obertraun, the road climbs steeply and crosses into the Styrian Salzkammergut. Here the regional capital is **Bad Aussee ⑪**, which lies between the Dachstein foothills and the Totes Gebirge. It is a lively town with a number of architectural jewels: the 15th-century **Parish Church of St Paul,** the **Spital Church** (14th century), with a very fine altarpiece (1449), and the Gothic **Kammerhof,** once the office of the salt works in the region, and now housing the local museum (open Jun–Sept: daily; Apr–Jun and Oct: Tues, Fri and Sun; entrance fee). A sleepy enchantment hangs over the place; some houses give the impression that time has stood still. The modern spa complex is a stark contrast.

From Bad Aussee it is well worth seeking out a panoramic view of the nearby **Altausseer See.** The best one is reached by heading northwards from the lake itself towards the **Loser.** This brilliantly-engineered toll road requires 15 hairpin bends to reach an altitude of 1,600 metres (5,250 ft). From this height one has a magnificent eagle's-eye view of the entire lake and its fairy-tale surroundings. If you are lucky, you may even see a hang-glider or parasailing enthusiast launching himself towards the glittering depths below.

Northeast of Bad Aussee is the **Grundlsee ⑫**, whose emerald waters shimmer like a jewel. The largest lake in the Styrian Salzkammergut, it is 6 km (4 miles) long and popular with sailors and windsurfers; anglers, too, like to try their luck from its shores. A three-hour boat trip from Bad Aussee gives great views of the lake.

In summer, a horse-drawn post coach (tel: (03622) 8666 or 72 160) plies the route between Gössl (at the far end of Grundlsee) and the next lake, **Toplitzsee.** Gerhard Zauner *(see page 212)* has salvaged large quantities of treasure buried here during World War II. His activities have also contributed to the lake's fame. The visitor surveying its dark waters, secluded shores, steep rocky cliffs and roaring waterfalls will understand why he chose this lake to search in rather than any other.

A 10-minute walk through the forest beyond Toplitzsee, including a steep track with 71 steps, leads to the tiny, idyllic **Kammersee.** Eerie reflections, utter peace and a sense of seclusion engender a delusion of having escaped from the world. ❏

Map on page 208

BELOW: carnival time in Altaussee, just north of Bad Aussee.

ART IMITATES LIFE: THE SOUND OF MUSIC

Hollywood immortalised the von Trapp family and their English governess in a film, and now the hills are alive... with the sound of tourists

Salzburg's touristic fortunes took a tremendous upturn the moment the enduringly popular Hollywood film *The Sound of Music* was released in 1965. Although the cast of "Austrians" oddly sing and speak in flawless British accents the film does succeed in displaying the splendid Salzkammergut scenery, working in a love story, earth-shattering world events and an ethical conflict all at once.

Maria (Julie Andrews) was a real-life nun-in-training at Stift Nonnberg *(see page 223)* who met and married Captain von Trapp – an Austrian naval officer angered by Hitler's rise to power, portrayed by a tough-yet-tender Christopher Plummer – in 1927. The two are forced to escape with the Captain's children or be shipped off to (gasp) Bremerhaven by the Germans.

The film took 11 weeks to make, and was shot on location in Salzburg – well, almost. The producers occasionally eschewed actual locations of events and substituted more camera-friendly ones, ranging as far out of town as Mondsee and St Gilgen, for the fields of wildflowers.

THE TOUR VAN COMETH

Each summer, "Do-Re-Mi"-singing tourists dutifully pour into Salzburg seeking vestiges of the von Trapps. These pilgrims are rewarded by two competing tour companies, each offering more or less the same experience – a somewhat kitschy van tour of the film sites.

▷ **HORSING AROUND**
This statue of Pegasus in Salzburg's Mirabell Gardens, was the site of a scene in which Maria teaches the children pitches of the seven-tone scale.

▷ **AWARD-WINNING FILM**
The film, based on the real Maria von Trapp's book and a subsequent German theatre production, won five Academy Awards. It is still shown on US and British television today.

△ **MIRABELL GARDENS**
When Mirabell Gardens was laid out by Fischer von Erlach *(see page 224)*, he could not have imagined that Maria and the kids would one day prance around its statuary.

△ **QUICK STUDY**
On the silver screen the von Trapp children were musical prodigies: Maria taught them to sing perfect seven-part harmonies in just one afternoon.

▷ **FINAL CURTAIN**
The film's tense final scene is of the von Trapps hiding out in St Peter's cemetery *(see page 222)* as Nazi officers search for them.

ROBERT WIS

RODGERS and HAMMERSTEIN'S
SOUND OF MUSIC

PRODUCED IN
TODD-AO®
AND
COLOUR
DE LUXE

EXILES OF CONSCIENCE

Beyond the obvious love story, *The Sound of Music*'s central conflict is one of conscience; and the real-life von Trapps' opposition to Hitler did in fact place their lives in great danger.

Hitler's rise to power was slow but continual, and by the time German troops entered Austria in 1938 there was little resistance as he swiftly moved to fold the country into the Third Reich. At first, Austrians carried out Hitler's orders by harassing Jews into leaving. Groundbreaking psychoanalyst Sigmund Freud was among those forced to flee as the rhetoric – and violence – escalated. Later Jews were simply rounded up and sent to the death camps. It has been estimated that some 110,000 Jews escaped Austria between 1938 and 1940, but that 60,000 perished in the camps.

Religious and political leaders of the time stood by and did little, others seemed to jump to aid Hitler. Open resistance such as that of the von Trapps was unusual, and the risk the family took was real indeed.

▽ **POETIC LICENCE**
The "Salzburg" church where Maria and the Captain tie the knot in the film is actually in the lakeside town of Mondsee *(see page 209)*. Visitors can walk down the aisle if they want to.

△ **AUSTRIAN TRADITIONS**
The real von Trapps escaped Austria and eventually settled in Vermont, USA. As befits their origins, the family's descendants now operate an Austrian-style ski lodge.

▷ **HOUSE OF GLASS**
The glass gazebo depicted in the film was located at Schloss Hellbrunn, a 17th-century hunting estate *(see page 224)*. The present gazebo was added later to oblige the tourists.

SALZBURG

Home to both the sublime Mozart and the irrepressible Von Trapps, Salzburg is popular with visitors from all over the world. The city's combination of splendour and intimacy enchants them all

Map on page 220

Many towns in Austria are blessed with fine churches, squares and ornamental fountains. In none but Salzburg, however, do they enjoy such a vibrant, cosmopolitan atmosphere and such magnificent surrounding scenery. Salzburg is one of the most visited cities in Austria, especially during the Salzburg Festival, its annual tribute to local hero Wolgang Amadeus Mozart (1756–91), when music lovers flock here from all corners of the globe.

The **Mönchsberg** and the **Kapuzinerberg** – the two mountains within the city boundaries – tower over the narrow alleys of the **Old Town,** with their tall, narrow merchants' houses, hidden arcaded courtyards, Baroque-domed churches and the palaces and spacious squares of the prince-bishops' quarter. Clinging to the side of Mönchsberg, and dominating the Old Town, is the fortress of Hohensalzburg, a symbol of the power base that shaped so much of the city's history.

Princes and archbishops

The Celts were the first to recognise the region's attractions; and it was here that the Romans built Juvavum ("the seat of the god of heaven"), their administrative centre. Over the course of a few hundred years, the monastery founded by St Rupert shortly before AD 700 grew into the mightiest spiritual principality in South Germany. In the 13th century its archbishops were given the title of Princes of the Holy Roman Empire. Thanks to their considerable income from the salt and silver mines of the area they were able to express their power in fine buildings. Three bishops in particular, all possessing an awareness of aesthetics as well as of their own might, stamped the town with the characteristics it still bears today.

Wolf Dietrich von Raitenau (archbishop from 1587) was a typical Renaissance prince, who dreamed of creating a "Rome of the North". He charged the Italian architect Scamozzi with the task of constructing a cathedral larger than St Peter's in Rome. At the same time he commissioned Mirabell Palace for his mistress Salome von Alt, by whom he had 12 children. His successor, Marcus Sitticus von Hohenems (archbishop from 1612), reduced the cathedral to a more modest scale, but commissioned a summer residence, Schloss Hellbrunn, set in an extensive park and surrounded by an elaborate system of fountains. Paris Lodron (archbishop from 1619) was finally able to dedicate the cathedral in 1628; it was during his term of office that the new Residenz (Bishop's Palace) was also completed.

In Renaissance and Baroque times, the starting point for the building activity of the prince-bishops was the **Residenzplatz**, an excellent place to begin a tour of the town. In the square stands the 15-metre (50-ft) Baroque Residenzbrunnen (Residenz Fountain; 1661).

PRECEDING PAGES: Mirabell Gardens in spring.
LEFT: sundial facing Mozartplatz.
BELOW: street entertainer on Kapitelplatz.

Grouped around this focal point – partly following the dictates of history and partly the whims of the prince-bishops – stand the most important episcopal buildings. On the south side is the **Dom ❶** (Cathedral), begun according to Renaissance precepts in 1614 and completed in the Baroque style in 1655. If you walk across from the Residenzplatz to the **Domplatz**, you will gain a view of the West Front, built of light-coloured Salzburg marble and framed by twin towers topped with cupolas, which are themselves surmounted by lanterns.

As a result of the annual performances of Hofmannsthal's *Jedermann (Everyman)* here, the three arcaded porticos with their four statues have achieved worldwide fame. The latter depict the apostles St Peter and St Paul flanked by two local saints, St Rupert and St Virgil. Watchfully surveying the scene are statues of the four evangelists, plus Moses and Elijah, while a statue of Christ dominates the ensemble. The contemporary bronze doors are dedicated to the themes of Faith, Hope and Charity. The baptismal font in the left aisle, dating from 1321, is a relic from the previous Romanesque church. So, too, is the crypt, in

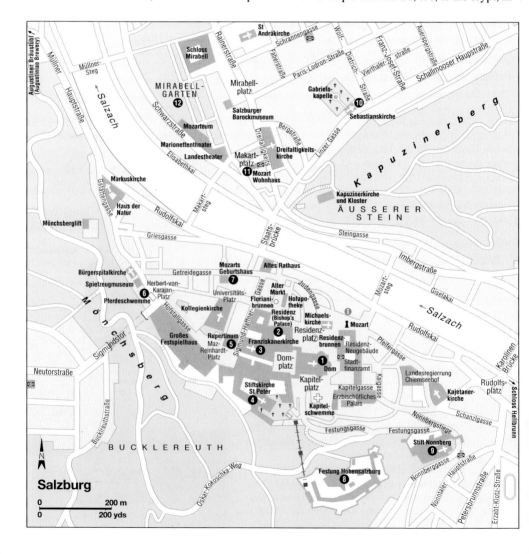

Salzburg

0   200 m
0   200 yds

which traces of the original walls have been exposed. The mosaic-tiled floor shows the ground plans of the three cathedrals built in succession upon this site. The priceless treasures assembled by the bishops across the centuries can be seen in the **Cathedral Museum** (open mid-May–Oct: daily; entrance fee).

Map on page 220

Palaces and churches

Forming the western boundary of the Residenzplatz is the **Residenz ❷** (Bishop's Palace; open daily; entrance fee; tel: (0662) 8042 2690). Archbishop Wolf Dietrich von Raitenau had it constructed from 1595 to replace the previous 12th-century building. The state apartments of the Residenz are predominantly decorated in late-Baroque and Classical style. A total of 15 rooms are lavishly appointed with murals, stucco, paintings, tapestries and statues. The young Mozart frequently performed in what is now the Conference Hall. The **Residenzgalerie** on the floor above (open Apr–Sept: daily; Oct–Mar: Thur– Tues; entrance fee; tel: (0662) 840 4510) contains paintings from the 16th–19th centuries. Opposite the Residenz, on the east side of the square, is the **Glockenspiel**, erected in 1705 and containing 35 bells cast in Antwerp. It sounds several times daily.

The city owes its early Baroque look to the dreams of Wolf Dietrich von Raitenau (1559–1617).

To the west of the Domplatz stands the **Franziskanerkirche ❸** (Franciscan Church), dedicated in 1221 and demonstrating an interesting transition between the Romanesque and Gothic styles. The nave is still completely Romanesque, and creates a rather austere impression due to the massive columns and capitals decorated with stylised foliage and animal figures. The late-Gothic chancel dates from the 15th century and features stellar vaulting supported by cylindrical pillars with palm-tree capitals. Of the late-Gothic winged altarpiece created by Michael Pacher in 1496, only the Madonna remains; it is integrated into the Baroque high altar.

BELOW: view across the rooftops.

A wrought-iron shop sign on bustling Getreidegasse.

BELOW: the city capitalises on its favourite son.

Tucked into the north side of the Mönchsberg, and accessed from Franziskanergasse, are **Stiftskirche St Peter** and its cemetery. The church itself is a Romanesque triple-aisled basilica dating from 1147, but in the 18th century it was completely redesigned and as a result acquired the Baroque ostentation – elaborate frescoes and ornate stucco – that makes it so striking. The nave vaulting contains frescoes depicting scenes from the life of St Peter; the walls above the great arches are decorated with a Passion and a Crucifixion scene. Beneath the clerestory are scenes from the life of St Benedict on the left and St Rupert on the right.

The cemetery is flanked on three sides by arcades housing family tombs; hewn from the rock face above are the catacombs (tours daily), in which early Christians celebrated Mass during the 3rd century. In the church's courtyard is the entrance to an atmospheric, subterranean restaurant and watering hole. Said to be Austria's oldest, it has been a tavern for some 1,200 years.

Mozart's birthplace

Just west of the Franziskanerkirche is the **Rupertinum** (open daily; Wed until 9pm; entrance fee), an art gallery with a permanent collection of 20th-century work and space set aside for temporary exhibitions. Highlights include pieces by Gustav Klimt and Oskar Kokoschka.

West again and you reach Hofstallgasse, which leads past the Festspielhaus (a concert venue used during the Salzburg Festival) to the **Pferdeschwemme** . What appears to be a fountain was actually a pool for washing horses, built in 1700. It is decorated with equine frescoes. To the northwest is the Gstattengasse lift up the Mönchsberg. From the top of the ridge, the views are splendid, and there are wooded walking trails leading along the ridge to Festung Hohensalzburg *(see page 223)* and the Burgweihr café.

Not far away is the **Getreidegasse**, one of the principal thoroughfares of Old Salzburg. The houses lining the street were built between the 15th and 18th centuries; they are characterised by lovely arcaded courtyards, wrought-iron signs and carved stucco window frames. Passageways occur at regular intervals; the people of Salzburg call them *Durchhäuser* (through houses). The house at Getreidegasse 9 is the **Mozarts Geburtshaus** (open daily; entrance fee; tel: (0662) 844 313), where the child prodigy Wolfgang Amadeus was born on the third floor on 27 January 1756. It was while living here that Mozart composed almost all of his juvenile works. Today the house contains many mementoes of the composer's childhood, as well as instruments.

The Getreidegasse leads on in an easterly direction towards the **Rathaus** (Town Hall) and the **Alter Markt** (Old Market), with its St Florian Fountain. At Alter Markt 6, the Rococo interior of the **Hofapotheke**, founded in 1591, retains the fittings of the original chemist's shop.

Shortly after this, the Getreidegasse joins the **Judengasse**, once the centre of Salzburg's thriving Jewish quarter; it, too, is characterised by numerous, elaborate, wrought-iron shop signs.

Map on page 220

Wealth and power

For many the **Festung Hohensalzburg** ❽ (open daily, entrance fee, tel: (0662) 8424 3011) is the highlight of a trip to Salzburg. It stands south of the old town, 15 minutes up the hill by foot, or a short ride up the Festungsbahn funicular. A symbol of the worldly power of the prince-bishops, the fortress was begun by Archbishop Gebhard on the site of a Roman *castrum* in 1077 and was continuously extended until the 17th century. It was Leonhard von Keutschach, Archbishop of Salzburg from 1495 to 1519, who had the most significant influence on its present structure and furnishing. Conducted tours around the state apartments, dungeons and torture chamber take place throughout the day. One particularly interesting item is a monumental porcelain tile stove, dating from 1501, kept in the so-called Golden Room. It portrays Biblical scenes and the princes of the time.

To the east of the fortress lies **Stift Nonnberg** ❾, a Benedictine convent founded at the beginning of the 8th century by St Rupert, which makes it one of the oldest convents still in existence. Its late-Gothic church dates from the end of the 15th century. Look out in particular for a Gothic winged altarpiece, created by Veit Stoss in 1498, and remarkable 12th-century frescoes to the rear of the nave.

The right bank

If you cross the river on the Staatsbrücke and continue straight on, you'll find yourself on Linzergasse. The street is lined with shops and always bustling with activity. The **Sebastianskirche** ❿, at No. 41, is worth visiting for its arcaded cemetery, the highlight of which is Archbishop Wolf Dietrich's late-Renaissance mausoleum (1603). Its tiled interior is decorated with delicate paintings by Elias Castello, who is buried nearby. Also in the cemetery are the tombs of

TIP

If you visit the church at Stift Nonnberg in the late afternoon, you may be lucky enough to hear the nuns singing Evensong – an experience that greatly enhances the beautiful Gothic interior.

BELOW: Festung Hohensalzburg, standing sentinel over the city.

Map on page 220

Dramatic statues decorate the Baroque Mirabell Gardens.

BELOW: the church of Maria Plain.

Mozart's father and widow, as well as that of Paracelsus, the 16th-century doctor, alchemist and, according to many of his contemporaries, quack.

Back towards the river, at Makartplatz 8, is the **Mozart Wohnhaus ⑪** (open daily; entrance fee), where the composer lived for seven years from 1773. It now houses original manuscripts, period furniture and, most interesting, various multimedia displays covering his life and times.

The nearby **Mirabell Gardens ⑫** form the most attractive park in Salzburg. Designed by Fischer von Erlach at the beginning of the 18th century, they enchant visitors with their statues, fountains and well-tended flowerbeds. One of the loveliest views is towards Hohensalzburg fortress from the terrace of the former palace, which now houses government offices. The original palace, built here in 1606, was the Altenau, commissioned by Wolf Dietrich to accommodate his celebrated Jewish mistress, Salome von Alt. Between 1721 and 1727 it was rebuilt by J. Lukas von Hildebrandt, but this structure was destroyed by a catastrophic fire in 1818. The present palace is a reconstruction of that building by Peter von Noble.

In the evening head back to the Linzergasse and its many vibrant restaurants. Alternatively, younger folk gravitate towards nearby pubs such as Zum Fidelen Affen (at Priesterhausgasse 8), with its good simple meals, or across the river to the raucous, monk-owned Augustiner Bräu (Augustinergasse 4) – a big, open-air courtyard where thick, dark steins of beer wash down cuts of pork.

On the outskirts

The pilgrimage church of **Maria Plain** stands on a hilltop about 5 km (3 miles) north of the city. Built in 1674, it has a facade framed by two towers. The interior is exceptionally attractive, representing the transition from Baroque to Rococo.

Schloss Hellbrunn (open Apr–Oct: daily; entrance fee; tel: (0662) 820 3720), 5 km (3 miles) south of Salzburg proper, symbolises pleasures of a primarily worldly nature – even though the complex, surrounded by a spacious park, was the summer residence of Archbishop Marcus Sitticus. It was designed by Santino Solari, the architect who was also responsible for Salzburg's cathedral (an unfinished sketch of this is kept in the castle's dining-room). The most interesting aspect of the interior appointments are the ballroom's *trompe-l'oeil* paintings by Arsenio Mascagni. The main attraction of Hellbrunn, however, is undoubtedly the collection of fountains in the park. Elaborate waterspouts and grottoes with countless figures, scenic representations and a mechanical theatre in which no fewer than 113 marionettes are set in motion by water power, were designed for the prince-bishop's private amusement.

Southwest of the city, the **Untersberg** makes a good day-trip. Begin by renting a bicycle at the train station, then take it with you on a bus to Moosstrasse on the western side of Mönchsberg. Here, climb onto the saddle and head straight down Moosstrasse. You soon leave the city behind and roll down a perfectly straight road past farmhouses, schools and cows. After a time, the road brings you to the base of the Untersberg. Here, you can hike or, more sensibly, take the cable-car to a mountain-top restaurant with excellent views. ❑

Mozart and the Salzburg Festival

Two annual festivals in Salzburg highlight the genius of Wolfgang Amadeus Mozart. Born in the city in 1756, Mozart was pushed into music at an exceptionally early age by his court-musician father, who recognised his son's abilities at once. The boy began composing and performing while practically a toddler, and first toured Europe at the age of six. He later moved to Vienna, where he wrote such classics as *The Magic Flute* and *The Marriage of Figaro*.

Despite wide acclaim, he never knew enduring wealth and security – his gambling and philandering suggest he had little time for such bourgeois virtues. The archbishop of Salzburg would not countenance his applications for prestigious positions, and he was later hounded by unappreciative music critics. At 35 he died of fever and was buried a pauper in an unmarked grave.

In 1848, supported by donations from the Mozart family, a group of enthusiasts formed the International Mozarteum Foundation to "perform and propagate Mozart's music and music in general, to broaden the public's knowledge of Mozart and his creative work and to preserve the memory of Mozart, his work and his family". Today the foundation runs two Mozart museums in Salzburg. Its extensive collections include the composer's original letters and sheet music and numerous performances of his work.

But the foundation is best known for its two long-running concert series. For almost half a century, it has kicked off each year with Mozart Week *(Mozartwoche)* in late January. This 10-day presentation of the composer's works marks his birthday – 27 January. The idea is to present the entire oeuvre through successive years. Performances usually include traditional concerts by the Vienna Philharmonic Orchestra and concertos performed by star pianists.

In July and August every year, the foundation's Mozart concert series forms an integral part of the annual Salzburg Festival *(Salzburger Festspiele)*. The festival dates from 1920 and the decision of local theatre director Max Reinhardt to keep his performers employed during the traditionally slow summer holiday season. Supported by the composer Richard Strauss and the poet Hugo von Hofmannsthal, he initiated an annual programme of opera, drama and music, performed in spectacular settings around the city. Venues include Domplatz (in front of the cathedral), the Mozarteum, the Landestheater, the Kollegienkirche, the Grosses Festspielhaus and the Kleines Festspielhaus. Particularly oustanding are the Marionettentheater's ornate puppets, which sing opera in perfect pitch beneath the Mirabell's fine ceilings. Huge crowds arrive in the city to see it all.

For Mozart Week information and tickets, contact the Mozarteum Foundation's Ticket Office at Theatergasse 2 (tel: (0662) 873 154; fax: (0662) 874 454). For Salzburg Festival schedules and tickets (available from November), visit the festival website at www.salzburgfestival.at. ❏

RIGHT: Rehearsal of a Berlioz opera at the Salzburg Festival.

SALZBURG PROVINCE

Away from the well-known attractions of its capital, Salzburg Province is where the Alps begin for real. In the south are winter resorts, spa towns and the soaring peaks of the Hohe Tauern

Map on page 230

Most visitors to the province will begin with the capital **Salzburg ❶** *(see pages 219–25),* the Baroque city that spawned both Mozart and *The Sound of Music.* But the rest of the province deserves some exploration, starting with the so-called German Corner, a pocket of Bavaria that juts provocatively into Austrian territory just south of Salzburg.

To reach it from the capital, take Road 160, which soon crosses into Germany and the beautiful foothills of the Bavarian Alps, heading towards the town of **Berchtesgaden ❷**. There was once an important Augustinian priory here, which served as one of the bastions of the Bavarian House of Wittelsbach against the predations of the archbishops of Salzburg. The Wittelsbachs themselves appointed three powerful prince-provosts to the priory between the 16th and 18th centuries. The entire region was finally ceded to the Kingdom of Bavaria in 1809, which explains why this territory now belongs to Germany and not Austria. The town today contains the former priory, with its 13th-century cloisters and Gothic dormitory. The monastery's salt mine is still in operation and can also be viewed.

The main attractions nearby are the **Königssee**, with its remote Church of St Bartholomä; the panoramic drive via the Rossfeld-Ringstrasse to the **Obersalzberg**, the site of Hitler's infamous Eagle's Nest; and the ascent to the **Kehlsteinhaus**, Hitler's former "tea house", at 1,834 metres (6,015 ft). All these destinations afford spectacular views of the surrounding countryside.

Salt and water

Hallein ❸, which lies east of Berchtesgaden and back in Austria, was one of the most prized possessions of the archbishops of Salzburg. From the 13th century onwards they refined salt from the brine extracted from the Dürrnberg, a practice that had been carried out at various points in history. Even the Celts had exploited this source of "white gold"; traces of their civilisation can be seen in the **Museum of Celtic History** (Pflegerplatz 5; open Apr–Oct: daily; entrance fee; tel: (06245) 80 783).

The salt mine is still in operation today, and is open to visitors (open Apr–Oct: daily; entrance fee; tel: (06245) 852 8515). Part of the tour includes riding on a toboggan down the salt miners' wooden slide, a trip in a punt across a salt lake and a thundering journey on the underground train. It is strongly recommended; both children and adults thoroughly enjoy it.

Opposite the parish church in the picturesque Old Town is the house where the organist Franz Xaver Gruber (1778–1863) lived. He it was who in 1818 composed the world-famous carol *Silent Night, Holy Night* for the Christmas Mass in Oberndorf, north of Salzburg.

South of Hallein, the **Salzach Valley** is increasingly

PRECEDING PAGES: winter fuel. **LEFT:** stained glass in the Church of St Leonhard, Tamsweg. **BELOW:** rushing waters in the Salzachöfen.

dominated by flowing water. The karst water from the 2,523-metre (8,276-ft) **Hoher Göll** plunges in an awe-inspiring curtain of water, foam and mist known as the **Gollinger Waterfalls**. Schwarzenberg, a prince-archbishop of Salzburg, commissioned the construction of the footpath to the top of the falls.

Further south, the **Salzachöfen** and **Lammeröfen** are two narrow gorges carved through the limestone rock over many millions of years by the rivers Salzach and Lammer. In the case of the Lammer, the walls of the gorge, known locally as *öfen* (ovens), are only 1 metre (3 ft) apart in some places. The Salzachöfen is a vast jumble of rocks, crevices, caves and erosions. It is accessible from the Lueg Pass.

Tennengebirge to the High Tauern

Beyond Golling, the Salzach is forced into narrow, forbidding ravines by the mountain ranges of the Hagengebirge in the west and the Tennengebirge in the east. Near the village of **Werfen** the naturally impregnable countryside gives

Map
on page
230

way to defences of a man-made nature: here, dominating the scene from a rocky eminence, stands **Burg Hohenwerfen** ❹ (open Apr–Oct: daily; entrance fee). As in the case of Festung Hohensalzburg *(see page 223)*, the stronghold was begun by the archbishops of Salzburg in the 11th century. It was enlarged to its present form towards the end of the 16th century by the addition of an extensive system of outer defences in the Italian manner. For the present-day visitor the fortress provides an excellent impression of medieval defences.

Opposite Hohenwerfen, hidden away between the cliffs of the Tennengebirge, lie the **Eisriesenwelt Caves** (open May–Oct: daily; entrance fee). They form one of the most extensive cave complexes in the world; to date, about 50 km (30 miles) of galleries, subterranean halls and labyrinths have been systematically explored. Since the entrance to the caves lies at an altitude of 1,641 metres (5,385 ft), the approach by bus and cable-car is an experience in itself. The cave is illuminated only by the carbide lamps of the visitors and the magnesium lamps of the guides; the effect of this is magical. Some of the individual ice structures are as much as 20 metres (65 ft) thick. From the cave entrance there is an exceptionally fine view westwards to the glaciers of the 2,941-metre (9,647-ft) **Hochkönig**.

Further south, the parish church of **Bischofshofen** is one of the finest examples of Gothic architecture in the Austrian Alps. The transept dates from the 11th century and the chancel from the 14th century, whilst the nave was built in the hall style with groined vaulting in the 15th century. On the left wall are 16th- and 17th-century frescoes depicting the Passion of Christ. The north transept contains the marble tomb of Sylvester, Bishop of Chiemsee, completed in 1462. It is the only example of a Gothic standing tomb in the Salzburg region.

The white water of the Lammer River is perfect for kayaking.

BELOW: Burg Hohenwerfen in autumn.

About 25 km (15 miles) to the east is **Radstadt ❺**, a medieval town situated at the foot of the pass through the Radstätter Tauern, which lost much of its importance following the construction of the A-10 motorway. As a result, its protected position behind moats and turrets enhances its charm for the visitor. Once upon a time, however, the ancient walls had a more crucial role to fulfil: they were built between 1270 and 1286 on the orders of the prince-bishops of Salzburg as a border defence against the neighbouring province of Styria. Furthermore, Radstadt served as a point of control over access to the northern approach to the **Radstädter Tauern Pass**.

Since the construction of the motorway, the 1,738-metre (5,700-ft) pass, which marks the boundary between the Low and the High Tauern ranges, has become a quiet country road once more. Encouraged by the excellent walking possibilities in summer and the reliable snow conditions in winter, a holiday village has grown up at the top. On both sides of the village there are cable-cars for the journey to the summit and the ridge.

On the southern side of the pass is the town of **Mauterndorf ❻**. King Henry II gave Archbishop Hartwik not only possession of the area, but also the right to levy customs duties. Thus the first occupied toll-booth in the Eastern Alps was founded. As a result, Schloss Mauterndorf was built at the beginning of the 14th century. It was extended in about 1500 by Archbishop Leonhard von Keutschach. The residential apartments, the chapel and the frescoes on the wall of the triumphal arch are of particular interest (open May–Oct: daily; entrance fee).

BELOW: Tamsweg's Church of St Leonhard.

Schloss Moosham, just south of Mauterndorf, was also once a stronghold of the prince-bishops of Salzburg. It served as a bastion of local defence in the Lungau, this remote but strategically important region. As the seat of the ordinary court in the 17th and 18th centuries, the fortress achieved notoriety through numerous trials of witches, sorcerers, beggars and other "miscreants". The judicial procedure was usually extremely brief, thanks to the intervention of the executioner (on the instructions of the bishop). Today the castle functions as a local history museum (open daily; entrance fee).

To the east is the principal town in the Lungau, **Tamsweg ❼**, first mentioned as Tamswick in 1160. The town's most famous monument is the ancient pilgrimage **Church of St Leonhard**, situated on one of the foothills of the Schwarzenberg. Its turretted surrounding wall lends it the appearance of a fortified church. It houses a number of notable treasures, including stained-glass windows, manufactured between 1430 and 1450. Most famous of all is the church's "gold window", composed almost entirely of blue and gold pieces. Hardly less precious is a choir stall dating from around 1415 and decorated with intricate carvings and inlaid woodwork.

The Pongau

It is only upon reaching **St Johann im Pongau ❽**, 6 km (4 miles) south of Bischofshofen, that the Salzach, which in its upper reaches flows in a precise west-easterly direction, finally decides to change its course towards the north. Characteristic of the entire upper stretch are the tributaries, some of which flow through deeply cut north–south valleys. They all descend from the main Alpine crest and were previously the cause of frequent flooding. The area surrounding the elbow of the Salzach was once the domain of the counts of the Pongau, who also gave it their name.

In the immediate vicinity of St Johann, the Grossarl Valley branches off before opening into the remarkable **Liechtensteinklamm**. This gorge is reached by a path which in many places has been blasted through solid rock; after passing through the first section of the gorge, it opens out into a basin enclosed by 300-metre (985-ft) high walls of rock. Then the gorge narrows down again, becoming sometimes no more than 2 metres (6 ft) wide; finally, in order to reach the 60-metre (212-ft) high waterfall at the end of the gorge, one must pass through a tunnel which is a good 50 metres (165 ft) long.

Perched up high above the left bank of the Salzach stands **Schloss Goldegg**, built in the 12th century by the counts of the Pongau in the centre of their area of feudal jurisdiction, in their capacity as ministers of the prince-bishops of Salzburg. The present-day fortress and its outer wards both date from the years 1320–23. In 1527 the castle passed into the possession of Graf Christoph von Schernberg. He had it decorated with frescoes and tempera paintings on wood and canvas. Today the castle houses the Pongau Museum of Local History.

Healthy radioactivity

The largest and also the wealthiest of the side valleys of the Salzach is the **Gastein Valley**. It is a district that has always possessed the right basis for wealth at the right moment in time. First of all, gold and silver mined in the area brought the local princes riches and prestige. Later, the healing powers of the local hot

Map on page 230

TIP

A good time to visit the Pongau is in early January, when the bizarre Perchtenlauf ritual takes place. Men dress up (in costumes and masks) as spirits who bring good fortune and bumper harvests. They parade the streets waving sticks and ringing cowbells.

BELOW: rolling hills in the Pongau.

springs made the valley famous, and in 1434, when Emperor Friedrich III became the first prominent visitor of his time to take a cure here, its reputation as a spa flourished. In recent years, the snow itself has become a marketable commodity, and the population has put their efforts into the skiing industry. Consequently, the fact that mining is no longer lucrative is unimportant.

The "Court at Gastein", as **Bad Hofgastein** (30 km/18 miles south of St Johann) was originally called, belonged first of all to the dukes of Bavaria, subsequently to the counts of Pongau and finally to the diocese of Salzburg. Even in the 16th century the bishops were able to have gold and silver extracted here. Hofgastein first became known as a spa town in 1828, following the laying of water mains to divert some of the thermal waters from Badgastein itself.

Nonetheless, **Badgastein** , 8 km (5 miles) to the south, remains pre-eminent as the centre of spa facilities in Austria. Its thermal springs contain radon – the therapeutic waters are drunk and used for bathing, and the steam is inhaled. Particularly favoured are the steam baths in the radioactive thermal tunnels, where the water temperature climbs as high as 41°C (106°F). A little train transports patients and visitors down into the tunnels, where they inhale the rare radon gas. Unfortunately, some scientists now consider radon to be carcinogenic.

In spite of its position at an altitude of more than 1,000 metres (3,280 ft), Badgastein seems in some respects to have many of the characteristics of a miniature international metropolis, with its tall hotel buildings, elegant shops and bustling atmosphere. The spa and congress complex, situated near the upper waterfall, is the centre of activity. It contains the congress centre, pump room, spa pool and museum. The **Kaiser-Wilhelm-Promenade** is the most attractive place for a stroll, affording fine views of the valley basin.

Savoury Krapfen *(similar to doughnuts) are a speciality of the Pinzgau (the upper Salzach Valley).*

BELOW:
Salzburger kids.

The numerous chair lifts providing access to the mountains around Badgastein were erected primarily to serve skiing enthusiasts. They also provide an easily-reached starting point for delightful mountain walks. Further up the valley, in **Böckstein**, cars are loaded on to the train for transport through the 8-km (5-mile) Tauern Tunnel, the shortest link between Salzburg and northwest Carinthia or East Tyrol. (However, a tragic fire in the tunnel in 1999 has prompted the authorities to rethink its single-bore design.) In winter, **Sportgastein** – up a tunnelled mountain road from Bockstein – attracts mountain sports enthusiasts with its facilities for ski-touring and downhill and cross-country skiing.

Zell am See and the Saalach Valley

Along the entire length of the Upper Salzach Valley there is only one fork that is open at both the northern and southern ends. During the Ice Age this was the only place where the Salzach glacier managed to carve out an exit to the north – a course which the river itself did not follow. The build-up of moraine deposits at this spot prevents the waters of the **Zeller See** from flowing away to the southeast into the Salzach or northwards into the Saalach. Even today, no meltwater flows into the lake; for this reason, in summer the temperature of the water rises exceptionally quickly for an Alpine lake.

Map
on page
230

Perched on a small alluvial hill in a pretty setting on the western lake shore is **Zell am See ❿**, the principal town in the Pinzgau and a gateway to Hohe Tauern National Park *(see page 238)*. As the epicentre of the so-called **European Sports Region Kaprun-Zell-Saalbach** it has plenty of attractions to offer – although admittedly most of them are in nearby Saalbach or Kaprun. Within Zell itself there is only the cable-car to the 1,964-metre (6,445-ft) **Schmittenhöhe**, which nonetheless affords an excellent view of the Pinzgau, and the mighty snow peaks of the High Tauern and the Grossglockner.

The Salzburg monks discovered this picturesque lakeside setting and founded a "Cella in Bisontio" (Pinzgau) in AD 743. This expanded to become an Augustinian priory, whose church – dedicated to St Hippolytus – has been the **Parish Church** since 1217. Its squat fortified tower, dating from the middle of the 15th century, can be seen for miles around. The interior contains frescoes from the 13th, 14th and 16th centuries, the most impressive of which include the *Madonna in Glory* (13th century) in the apse of the north aisle, and the *Martyrdom of St Catherine* (14th century) in the porch. The delicate tracery on the balustrade of the west gallery dates from 1514, and the fine representations of St George and St Florian on the west gallery wall are from 1520.

In the winter months, Zell am See belongs first and foremost to ski enthusiasts. In summer – apart from the walkers and climbers – it is gliding fans who find optimum conditions here. Thanks to the east–west orientation of the Pinzgau, the southernmost chain of the **Kitzbühel Alps** provide more than 50 km (30 miles) of south-facing slopes producing the thermals gliders need to attain height. What is more, the pilots of the Alpine Gliding School are willing to take guests up with them.

TIP

Between the Gastein Valley and Zell am See is Taxenbach Gorge, which is famous among white-water rafters. Tour operators in Zell am See can arrange trips for you to try a white-knuckle ride for yourself.

BELOW: Zell am See, perched on the lakeside.

Smoked trout, another speciality of the Pinzgau region.

BELOW: climbing near Saalfelden.

A footpath across 11 peaks

A few miles north of Zell am See, the road meets the Saalach as it flows eastwards from the Kitzbühel Alps. If you follow the course of the river westwards you will arrive in the skiing community of **Saalbach-Hinterglemm ⑪**. The local tourist managers take pride in their 60 lifts and 200 km (125 miles) of pistes. From the 2,200-metre (7,205-ft) **Schattberg**, the intrepid and fit can trek across no fewer than 11 mountain peaks to the **Schmittenhöhe**, and enjoy stunning views across to the summits of the High Tauern Range.

To the north (and lying immediately to the south of the "German Corner" and Berchtesgadnerland) is **Saalfelden ⑫**, which has developed at the point where the Saalach Valley is at its widest. It was once an important market town where horses and cattle were traded. Today it is above all a good starting point for climbing expeditions up the 2,941-metre (9,648-ft) **Hochkönig** and the vast limestone plateau of the **Steinernes Meer**. It is a beautiful trek across to the **Königsee** in Germany, dominated by the mighty, 2,713-metre (8,900-ft) Watzmann rising almost vertically from its western shore.

East of Saalfelden lies the Urslau Valley, which extends as far as the western slopes of the Hochkönig. The prettiest village in the valley is undoubtedly **Maria Alm**. Its Gothic pilgrimage church houses not only a Madonna dating from 1480 but also a graceful spire, which at 84 metres (275 ft) is higher than the towers of Salzburg's cathedral.

Further to the north, the Saalach Valley becomes narrower, closed in as it is on the western side by the Leoganger Steinberge and to the east by the precipices of the Hochkalter. Near **Weissbach** it is worthwhile climbing up to the Seisenbergklamm or visiting the Lamprechtsofenloch.

St Martin bei Lofer is a village of historical interest some 25 km (15 miles) north of Saalfelden. Until 1803 its parish church belonged to the Augustinian Priory of St Zeno in Reichenhall (in Germany). The church, a late conversion to the Baroque style, contains fine 17th- and 18th-century altar paintings, the work of Wilhelm Faistenberger, Johann Friedrich Pereth and Jakob Zanusi.

West of St Martin, hidden away at the top of a high-altitude valley, nestles the pilgrimage **Church of Maria Kirchental**. It was built between 1694 and 1701 according to the plans of no less a celebrity than Johann Bernhard Fischer von Erlach. It is interesting above all for the two marble side altars, completed in 1700. The pulpit, too, dates from 1709. An early 15th-century *Madonna in Glory* is venerated as possessing miraculous powers. Of interest to the visitor are the numerous votive gifts. They are collected in an *ex voto* chapel.

Zell am See to the Grossglockner

The valley of the **Fuscher Ache**, branching off south of Zell am See near **Bruck**, is both lonely and wild, but from earliest times it attracted travellers seeking a mountain pass to the south. Even the Romans knew of this particular pass – a 17-cm (7-inch) bronze figure dating from the 1st century AD was found at an altitude of 2,570 metres (8,430 ft) near the Hochtor during the construction of the **Grossglockner Hochalpenstrasse** (High Alpine Road). The south side of the pass was also of interest to the Romans, for they mined gold in the region of Heiligenblut. In the Middle Ages the "Blood Pilgrimage" to Heiligenblut drove the faithful from the Pinzgau into these hostile mountains.

The metre-high walls of snow which border the road until well into the summer relay an unequivocal message. In winter, the snow here lies an average of over

One old chronicle describes the perils of the Grossglockner peaks as they were perceived in medieval times: "There is a region up there where the demons reside, threatening with falling rocks and avalanches every mortal who ventures into the vicinity."

BELOW: the road to Grossglockner, the country's highest peak.

5 metres (16 ft) deep. On approximately 99 days every year a stormy wind blows with gusts of up to 150 kph (93 mph); on 250 days of the year it snows. The climate along the crest of the Grossglockner Road is equivalent to that of Siberia.

The summit of the panoramic road is marked by the **Edelweissspitze**, at 2,577 metres (8,450 ft), which also offers the best view. Despite the fascination of the Edelweissspitze, this observation post does not mark the southern pass proper. Instead, our journey continues downhill again to the **Fuscher Törl**, at 2,405 metres (7,890 ft), down again to the Fuscher Lake, and then along the eastern sides of the Brennkogel and uphill again past a long section of scree slopes to the **Hochtor Tunnel**, at 2,505 metres (8,220 ft).

From the car park at the southern tunnel entrance there is a quite splendid view far to the south, towards Carinthia and East Tyrol: across to the Schober Range and down into the Möll Valley *(see pages 255–57)*.

In the Upper Pinzgau

The main attraction of the European Sports Region around Zell am See is the largest year-round ski slope in Austria – the **Schmiedinger Kees**, which lies beneath the jagged peak of the 3,203-metre (10,508-ft) **Kitzsteinhorn**. It has brought renown (at least in the skiing world) to the little Alpine village of **Kaprun** ⑭, which lies a few miles south of Zell am See, at the entrance to the valley of the same name. In order to provide access to this sporting paradise it was necessary to build a glacier cable-car in three sections; it leads via the intermediate stations at the Salzburger Hütte (1,897 metres/6,223 ft) and the Alpine Centre (2,452 metres/8,044 ft) to the Mountain Station (3,029 metres/9,937 ft) on the ridge of the Kitzsteinhorn. Since the cable-car soon proved inadequate to cope with

The Tauern Power Station is one of the most ambitious in the Alps. Some 200 million cubic metres (7 billion cubic ft) of water are stored in two vast reservoirs, which are dammed by three barrages, each over 100 metres (328 ft) high. The plant can generate a total of 220,000 kW.

BELOW: a view of Grossvenediger, in the Hohe Tauern National Park.

HOHE TAUERN NATIONAL PARK

Little of Europe remains wild today, and that makes the presence of Hohe Tauern National Park all the more remarkable. The tremendous variety of mountain, meadow, pasture, forest, riverine and even glacial landscapes here are all worth experiencing.

The park began as a series of relatively small land acquisitions in the Stubach and Amer valleys. Parcels were steadily added in such important areas as the Glockner Massif until, by the 1950s, the growing preserve aroused enough support among locals that they turned out en masse to halt the damming-up of the Krimml River for hydroelectric power. In 1971, leaders of the three provinces within the park's boundaries – Salzburg Province, Carinthia and Tyrol – signed an agreement to create the park.

Hiking and nature-watching are the preferred activities here. The park is home to a wide variety of flowers such as the Alpine aster, alpenrose, edelweiss and orchids; trees include the famous Arolla pine, spruces and firs. Animal life is similarly diverse: you might spot anything from swallowtail butterflies to vultures, wild horses, ibex or lynx.

More than a million visitors come to the park each year. Tourist offices in Zell am See, Badgastein and other centres can provide information on hiking trails, flora and fauna.

the traffic, a 4-km (2.5-mile) long funicular train was constructed parallel to the two lower sections. This partially underground funicular was the site of a catastrophic fire in November 2000, which claimed the lives of 155 skiers.

Access to the Pinzgau's most famous mountain provides even visitors without mountaineering aspirations with a spectacular experience of the Alps. From the Mountain Station of the cable car there is a footpath to the summit of the Kitzsteinhorn. Its exposed position affords views of the Glockner massif, the Wiesbachhorn and the Grossvenediger. Lined up to the north stand the Kitzbühel Alps, the Steinernes Meer with the Hochkönig, the Tennengebirge and the Dachstein ranges. Far down below are the vast green reservoirs of the **Tauern Hydroelectric Power Station**, at the head of the Kaprun valley.

Back in the valley, visitors can tour the power station complex, which includes two huge reservoirs, the higher of which is at 2,036 metres (6,680 ft). Private cars cannot be used all the way – the last stretch is covered by bus. At the upper reservoir, the Mooserboden, the road peters out by the so-called **Heidnische Kirche** (Heathen Church), claimed by archaeologists to be a Celtic religious site. The high spot – literally – of this impressive mountain tour is the 2,108-metre (6,916-ft) Höhenburg, between the twin dams of the Mooserboden reservoir. From here one can see both lakes at the same time, and there is a breathtaking panorama of the mountain peaks and glaciers flanking the Karlinger Kees.

Devilish masks are used in the local Krampus festival in early December.

The **Stubachtal**, which forks off southwards near **Uttendorf**, west of Kaprun, has also been exploited by the construction of a power station and cable-cars. On this occasion one can drive right down to the floor of the valley and up to the first stage: the **Enzingerboden** (1,468 metres/4,816 ft), which is set in spectacularly forested scenery. The Stubach-Weisssee cable-car climbs from here to the Weisssee, at an altitude of 2,323 metres (7,620 ft). The best view can be obtained from the **Rudolfshütte**, the Austrian Alpine Association Centre on the Hinterer Schafbühel, at 2,352 metres (7,716 ft).

BELOW: traditional outfits are not just for the tourists.

An ancient mountain pass

Further west, the route across the **Felber Tauern** was an important one for Austrians long before the construction of the 5.2-km (3¼-mile) tunnel. Back in the Middle Ages it was a much-used trade route, crossing the Alpine crest at an altitude of 2,481 metres (8,139 ft) at precisely the point where the St Poltner refuge is situated today. In those days pack-horses carried velvets and silks, barrels of wine and citrus fruit northwards and copper, iron, leather and salt in the opposite direction.

Of corresponding significance was the town of **Mittersill** ⓯, just west of Uttendorf, which marks the start of the climb on the northern side. The town itself came into the possession of the counts of Matrei in the 12th century as a Bavarian fief. They called themselves the counts of Mittersill from 1180, and in 1228 they became subject to the archdiocese of Salzburg. The castle here has been rebuilt complete with massive corner towers and battlements. The triple-bayed Gothic castle chapel was rebuilt in its present form in 1553. It houses a winged altarpiece dating from the middle of the 15th century. The

Map on page 230

Church of St Leonhard was completed in 1749 and contains interesting stained-glass windows designed by Hans Hauer and Franz Sträussenberger.

Even from afar, the **Church of St Anne** stands out from the usual Salzburg Baroque by virtue of its curved gable facade. This is hardly surprising, since the architect was Jakob Singer, from Schwaz in Tyrol, who completed the church in 1751. Also a native of Schwaz was Christoph Anton Mayr, who, in 1753, painted the frescoes adorning the interior. The visitor should be sure to see St Anne's Gothic daughter church, **St Nicholas in Felben**, on the outskirts of town, which has a high altar dating from 1631, depicting a series of highly expressive late-Gothic figures of the 14 auxiliary saints.

Beyond Mittersill, the Salzach Valley gradually becomes narrower and more typically Alpine. The peaks fringing the horizon are dominated by the 3,674-metre (12,050-ft) **Grossvenediger**. There are two ways of approaching this majestic giant. The first is to make the ascent through the Obersulzbach Valley to the Kürsinger Refuge, which lies at 2,549 metres (8,362 ft). This involves a journey on foot of several hours. An easier route is by chair lift from **Neukirchen**, 20 km (12 miles) west of Mittersill. By this means one is transported to the Alpine Ridge west of the Wildkogel, at a height of 2,093 metres (6,866 ft). From this point one has a perfect view across the Salzach Valley towards the ridge dominated by the Grossvenediger.

BELOW: Krimml Falls, near the border with Tyrol.
RIGHT: early morning mist near Salzburg.

The waterfall of the twelve glaciers

A unique natural phenomenon awaits the traveller in the uppermost reaches of the Salzach Valley, another 12 km (8 miles) west, near the town of Krimml. The **Krimml Falls** ⓰ are the most spectacular in the entire Alps, deserving

superlatives on several counts. First, there is the sheer volume of water of the Krimmler Ache, which is fed by no fewer than 12 glaciers in the Venediger Massif to the south. Then there is the total height of the falls, which, divided among the three great cascades, totals 380 metres (1,246 ft), with the longest free-fall being one of 65 metres (213 ft). And finally there is the variety of settings and wealth of natural features which the thundering water passes through on its path. The entire site is marked by well-signposted footpaths which make exploration of the area by foot surprisingly easy. As an added bonus, opposition from Alpine hiking and parks groups has so far prevented the exploitation of these magnificently thunderous falls for hydroelectric purposes.

Starting at Krimml, the Gerlos Pass Toll Road leads up and over the 1,507-metre (4,944-ft) **Gerlos Pass**, and descends on the other side into the Ziller Valley in Tyrol *(see page 276)*. On the way up, it describes a large loop around the Tratenköpfl, thereby offering an excellent view of the cascading Krimml Falls.

Shortly after the top of the pass, and just before one reaches the Tyrol border, the traveller can expect to see another remarkable sight. Immediately below the road lies the Durlassboden Reservoir, and dominating the scene, towering proudly above other less lofty peaks, are the soaring summits of the Gerlosspitze and the Reichenspitze. ❏

CARINTHIA AND EAST TYROL

*The country's southernmost province and its remote western
neighbour are relatively unknown outside Austria, but they offer
relaxed lakeside holidays and spectacular alpine scenery*

**Map
on pages
246–7**

Warm lakes and clear rivers, majestic mountains and secluded valleys,
gently rolling meadows and dense woodlands have given the people
of Carinthia (Kärnten) a happy disposition which often expresses itself
in song. An above-average amount of sunshine makes the snow-clad slopes
glisten in winter, melts the ice in spring, warms lake waters – and hearts – in
summer, and illuminates golden landscapes in autumn.

Klagenfurt

Today it is hard to imagine that this region was once rough marshland. Legend
tells of a winged dragon that struck terror into the hearts of the local inhabitants.
Its statue is immortalised as the emblem of **Klagenfurt ❶**, the capital of
Carinthia. It stands in the middle of **Neuer Platz**, which is actually anything but
new. Most of the lovely old houses around its perimeter date from the 17th century, as does the **Town Hall**. A number of picturesque inner courtyards can be
glimpsed off Kramergasse and Alter Platz, which adjoin Neuer Platz to the
north. In the vicinity are the Trinity Column (1680), the Palais Goess (18th
century) and the **Landhaus**, dating from the 16th century, with its famous
Grosse Wappensaal (Great Heraldic Hall; open Apr–Oct: daily; entrance fee; tel:
(0463) 57 757-102), which displays 665 coats of arms.

At the western end of Alter Platz is the **Haus zur
Goldenen Gans** (Golden Goose), which is listed in
records of 1489 and was originally planned as an imperial residence. In return, the emperor handed over his
former castle and its park to the estates for the erection
of a country house. The estates of the realm was an
influential body in Klagenfurt, and at their request, in
1518, the Emperor Maximilian I formally handed over
the town to them, a situation unique in German constitutional history. Naturally they cherished their jewel
with all their combined strength, creating a chequer-
board street layout which was unique at the time, and
which characterises the town plan to this day.

Klagenfurt has also retained its traditional function
as a shopping centre. Whether you seek traditional
costumes or jewellery, gourmet delicacies, fine china,
books or exquisite linen, shopping or just browsing
through the town's elegant shops is always a delight.
There are plenty of cultural attractions too: the **Cathedral Church**, the **Church of the Holy Ghost** (14th
century), the **Parish Church** on the Pfarrplatz and,
north of town, the 9th-century Carolingian Church in
St Peter am Bichl. There are also no fewer than 22
castles within a radius of a few miles.

No-one should fail to visit **Minimundus** (open
Apr–Oct: daily; entrance fee; tel: (0463) 211 940), the
miniature world beside Wörther See, 3 km (2 miles)

PRECEDING PAGES:
the Karawanken
Mountains, south
of Klagenfurt.
LEFT: carving in
Gurk Cathedral.
BELOW: quiet
courtyard in
Klagenfurt.

west of the city. Many thousands of people, large and small, visit the exhibition annually. There are more than 150 replicas of famous buildings, all constructed to a scale of 1:25, as well as a miniature railway and a harbour with model ships.

There is no shortage of restaurants in the Carinthian capital. Visitors with a sweet tooth, gourmets, wine buffs and beer drinkers, devotees of spaghetti and chop suey, will all find establishments to suit their tastes. Worthy of particular mention are the café and restaurant in the romantic **Hotel Musil**, at 10-Oktober-Strasse 14.

Wörther See

This sculpture of a dwarf – a character in local legends – is in Klagenfurt's Kramergasse.

BELOW: pumpkin field near Maria Saal, north of Klagenfurt.

Klagenfurt's advertising campaign claims that "A town by a lake has twice as much feeling for life". Surveying **Wörther See ❷**, it's difficult not to agree. The town is justifiably proud of the largest lakeside bathing area in Europe and one of the most modern camp sites in the country. In spite of a depth of 85 metres (275 ft) in places, the water temperature can reach 28°C (82°F) – making it irresistible for swimmers.

The five ships of the Wörther See fleet are available for pleasure cruises from the beginning of May until the beginning of October. One of them, the *Thalia*, is the last propeller-driven steamer in Austria. The *Muse of Grace* has had a very varied life since she was launched in 1909. After being destroyed by an explosion in 1945, she was rescued several years later by high-level politics. Restored by the governement, she hosted the US and Soviet ambassadors for the preparatory discussions leading to the SALT-1 agreement.

Heading west from Klagenfurt, the first landing jetty on the north shore is at **Krumpendorf**. The atmosphere of this resort community with 7 km (4 miles)

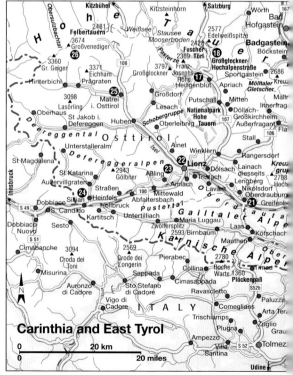

Carinthia and East Tyrol

of sunny beaches can best be described as informal. Lakeside promenades, bathing beaches, shady avenues and green parks provide the setting for a restful holiday; the requisite amenities are also all here: water skiing, windsurfing, diving and an 18-hole golf course at nearby Moosburg.

The bronzed Adonises of the area can be found at the bathing areas, boulevard cafés or tennis courts in **Pörtschach,** 6 km (4 miles) west. Here a peninsula of land with old trees, flower-bordered paths and little bays juts far out into the lake. Nowadays it seems hardly possible that until the middle of the 19th century this was just a sleepy fishing village.

It was the Southern Railway that brought the wealthy citizens of the Habsburg monarchy to Pörtschach and it was here that they built their summer residences in order to escape the bustle of the cities. Johannes Brahms was another summer visitor. Inspired by the beauty of the lake, he composed his *2nd Symphony* and celebrated *Violin Concerto* here. Those wishing to follow in the great composer's footsteps are advised to visit the **Weisses Rössl** – the White Horse Inn. The parlour with his favourite table has not changed since his time.

Velden ❸, the next town west, is the local high-life arena, for it is the resort favoured by the rich and the beautiful, the sailors and the golfers. This is the home of the sailboard and the convertible. Playground of the jet set, Velden's yacht marina, golf course and casino attract the rich and sporty from across the globe.

The Illyrians, and later Baron von Khevenhüller, had quite different reasons for settling in Velden. The Renaissance **Schloss Velden** the baron built here in 1590 was a favoured rendezvous for the aristocracy at the end of the 16th century. In 1920 it was converted into a luxury hotel. Visitors can sleep in the royal chambers. If you can't afford that, a stroll through the castle park must suffice.

Map on pages 246–7

Schloss Velden was used as a backdrop for a popular 1980s soap opera, Schloss am Wörther See.

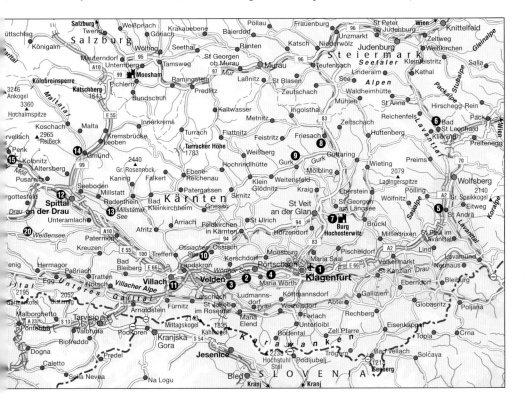

**Maria Wörth **, set on a peninsula on the southern shore of the lake, is an idyllic spot. The character of the village stems from the church, which dominates the peninsula (an island until the water level sank because of the ford on the River Glan). It was built in AD 890 by Bishop Waldo of Freising (in Bavaria) and later extended. The former presbytery church stands on the highest spot; it was rebuilt in the Gothic style following a fire and houses a number of art treasures: a Baroque likeness of St Christopher on the exterior wall, a Baroque high altar, an exquisite statue of the Madonna and Baroque carved wooden altars. Maria Wörth has enjoyed considerable political and economic importance over the centuries, giving its name to the lake in the process.

More bathing lakes

The **Keutschach Valley**, just south of Lake Wörther, is the setting for four large lakes. Camp sites and bathing areas fringe the shores of **Hafnersee** and **Rauschelesee**. The idyllically situated **Bassgeigensee** is shaped like its namesake (*Geige* means violin). And then there is **Keutschacher See** itself; its 1.4-sq. km (0.5-sq. mile) expanse and water temperatures which reach 26°C (79°F) in the summer entice visitors to swim or hire a rowing, sailing or pedal boat. Its shores are ringed by bathing areas, camp sites, tennis courts, mini-golf ranges and even football pitches. The Keutschacher See Children's Summer is always popular, featuring play festivals, do-it-yourself workshops and "children's gastronomy".

Keutschach, beside the lake, is the focal point of the valley and offers two cultural attractions in the form of its 17th-century Baroque castle and the late-Romanesque **St George's Chapel**, which has a Carolingian-era stone depicting

TIP

If you're spending some time in Carinthia in the summer, it may be worth paying €32 for a Kärnten Card. Available from tourist offices, it allows free use of all public transport and free entry to the majority of museums and attractions, all for three weeks.

BELOW:
the peninsula and church of Maria Wörth.

a symbol of the Resurrection. Remains of pile dwellings, Neolithic implements and Stone-Age caves bear witness to the region's long history of settlement.

Map on pages 246–7

The Lavant Valley

The eastern part of Carinthia is dominated by the idyllic Lavanttal. First stop in the valley en route from Klagenfurt is the ancient diocesan town of **St Andrä ❺**, which grew up around the pilgrimage **Church of Maria Loreto**. The town enchants the traveller with its lovely setting amidst verdant meadows, encircled by castles and palaces. Gourmets flock here in May and June for the so-called Asparagus Sundays. In autumn, fruits are pressed amidst scenes of great merriment, and a culinary walking tour covering local specialities takes place. The Lavant Valley local museum, in nearby **St Ulrich**, is also worth visiting. It provides a well-displayed insight into the life and traditions of the region.

St Paul im Lavanttal, a 10-km (6-mile) detour down Road 69 to the south, is often referred to by locals as "Carinthia's treasure chest", a name it owes to its **Benedictine Abbey** (open May–Oct: daily; entrance fee; tel: (04357) 201 922), founded in 1091. The museum here displays collections featuring masterpieces from a number of eras. When the exhibitions are open to the public, guided tours are conducted round the abbey.

In all senses of the word, **Wolfsberg** – about 10 km (6 miles) north of St Andrä – is the centre of the Lavant Valley. Its mountain parks, the Saualpe and the Koralpe, invite the visitor to wander at leisure, to tarry awhile, or to fly – by motorised aircraft, glider or hang-glider.

It was in Schloss Waldenstein in **Preitenegg**, further north, that the Carinthian anthem was composed in the 19th century. This little community on

BELOW:
the Church of Maria Loreto in St Andrä.

THE SLOVENES OF CARINTHIA

Official estimates place Austria's Slovene population at around 30,000, making them the country's second largest ethnic group. Most live in southeastern Carinthia, in a strip of land that runs along the Slovenian border from Faakersee, near Villach, to Bleiburg, east of Klagenfurt.

There has long been a Slav influence in Carinthia. (Most town names ending -ach are Slavic in origin.) However, when Yugoslavia invaded Carinthia in 1918, tensions between Slovenes and locals rose to a boiling point. They have never completely simmered down since. Jörg Haider's ascension to governorship of the province, running on an anti-immigrant platform, is only the most recent manifestation of decades-old unease.

Over the years, the Slovenes have pushed for recognition and autonomy, and in 1955 a treaty granted them official minority status in Austria. Today the various groups in the province speak a number of dialects of their original language – some of them mutually unintelligible. Interestingly, the number of Carinthians who describe themselves as Slovene on census forms has dropped sharply in recent decades, even as their population has held steady – a sign they have become Austrian in their own minds, if not in those of other Carinthians.

The unusual Hotel St Veit in St Veit an der Glan was designed by Viennese artist Ernst Fuchs and built in 1998.

BELOW: church on the Magdalensberg, near Burg Hochosterwitz.

the Packsattel Mountain Road has a late-Gothic parish church with a Baroque interior and a small collection of notable paintings.

Bad St Leonhard ❻, further up the valley, offers excellent spa facilities. Its sulphur springs provide rejuvenation and relaxation from mid-May to mid-October. In addition to numerous folklore festivals there is a fine Gothic parish church and, in the surrounding area, 100 km (60 miles) of signposted footpaths leading up to an altitude of 1,800 metres (5,905 ft), plus an excellent network of mountain refuges.

Burg Hochosterwitz

Northeast of Klagenfurt, Road 92 leads to the town of Brückl. Just to the west of Brückl is the stunning fortress of **Burg Hochosterwitz** ❼, a Carinthian landmark (open Apr–Oct: daily; entrance fee). The path to the castle up the 160-metre (525-ft) cone-shaped rock passes through no fewer than 14 gate towers. Next to the eighth stands the chapel, with an unusual bronze altar. The castle museum houses an imposing collection of weapons. On the **Magdalensberg**, south of Hochosterwitz, is the site of the largest archaeological excavations in Austria – a Romano-Celtic town, with an open-air museum and display rooms (open May–mid-Oct: daily; entrance fee; tel: (04224) 2255).

The road from Brückl continues to **St Veit an der Glan**. Before you reach the latter, there is a fork to the right leading to **St Georgen am Längsee**. The waters of Langsee, nestling between densely wooded mountain slopes, reach summer temperatures of 26°C (79°F). Here are all the ingredients for a varied holiday: sailing, rowing, riding, cycling and fishing (thanks to careful stock management), not only for pike and carp, but also zander.

Road 83 from St Veit an der Glan heads north to the old town of **Friesach ❽**. It's worth stopping here awhile – you won't often find three castles, a fort and a still-extant moat in one town, but here they are – testament to Friesach's former importance as a trading post on what was once the main road from Vienna to Venice. The town's enormous basilica is one of half a dozen churches, several with important carvings or altar work.

Map on pages 246–7

The Gurk Valley

South of Friesach, the entrance to the Gurk Valley at Zwischenwässern is marked by **Pöckstein Castle**, a late-Baroque bishop's residence. Its magnificent audience rooms make it a much-visited architectural curiosity. This is also the starting point of the **Gurk Valley Museum Railway**, which puffs westwards to Glödnitz from early June to late September – a unique experience for railway fanatics, romantics and keen photographers. You can even apply for an amateur engine-driver's certificate.

Strassburg, to the west, is dominated by the castle of the same name, which is visible for miles around (open Apr–Oct: Mon–Fri; entrance fee). The original building dates from the year 1131; between the 14th and 17th centuries it was constantly altered and added to, and served as the summer residence of the bishops of Gurk until 1780. Apart from viewing the exquisite arcaded courtyard and the castle chapel, the visitor should not miss the church in the nearby village of **Lieding**, an architectural gem with a 1,000-year history.

Countess Emma, the consort of the ruler of Carinthia and the region's patron saint, founded the Romanesque cathedral in **Gurk ❾** during the 12th century. The priory courtyard was built in the 15th century. The crypt, supported by 100

The area between Magdalensberg and Klagenfurt, known as the Zollfeld, is the historic heart of Carinthia. The Celts and Romans settled here, and it is the site of the Herzogstuhl, a double throne used in medieval times for ducal investiture ceremonies.

BELOW: *Garden of Eden fresco in the Bishop's Chapel at Gurk Cathedral.*

pillars, the Gothic paintings and the most important Romanesque series of frescoes in the German-speaking world give it architectural and artistic significance. The celebrated Raphael Donner immortalised his memory with the transept altar and a set of lead reliefs on the pulpit. When the sun is shining brightly, the 13th-century stained-glass windows in the West Porch transform the light into cascades of colour.

The Kranzlreiten *horserace is a survivor from medieval times, when the plague took its toll on the population. Young men would compete in such races to see who could marry the village's surviving virgins.*

Further west, **Weitensfeld** is a village that appeals to the visitor on second sight. It is a centre in which ancient Carinthian customs, such as the *Kranzlreiten* (a horserace which takes place at Whitsun), are still observed. The district also has a rich artistic heritage. Austria's oldest item of worked glass, the Magdalene Windowpane, originated in a church in Weitensfeld. The church in the neighbouring village of Zweinitz houses frescoes in the apse which are real jewels of sacred art.

The road soon forks off to the right towards **Flattnitz**, a resort village situated at an altitude of 1,400 metres (4,600 ft). Here, where once the Roman legions crossed the Alps, walkers gather in summer and skiers in winter. The Spitzeralm and the Pfandlhütte are popular goals. The Pass Church contains magnificent frescoes which provide a moving reminder of the faith of early Christians.

Back at the fork, take a left turn instead to reach the road to **Deutsch-Griffen**, the site of one of the few remaining medieval fortified churches in the entire Alpine region. A flight of 200 steps leads up to the sacred edifice, picturesquely situated on a hillside and housing a collection of 15th-century frescoes.

BELOW: traditional baking in the Carinthian hills.

Standing at the point where the Gurk Valley becomes increasingly wild and romantic is **Sirnitz**. Nearby **Albeck Fortress**, today a romantic ruin, experienced its Golden Age at the time of Barbarossa, later becoming the administrative seat of the bishops of Gurk. Visitors are captivated by the octagonal

Map on pages 246–7

form of the late-Gothic charnel house attached to the medieval parish church. After a detour via Hochrindl, which lies at 1,600 metres (5,250 ft) in the middle of the Gurktaler Alps, the road crosses the Gurk once more near **Ebene Reichenau** before climbing a gradient of 1 in 4 up to the **Turracher Höhe** (1,780 metres/5,850 ft), at the top of the valley *(see page 189)*. Here, the spectacular panorama is enlivened by the emerald-green waters of the mountain lakes, and the air seems to taste of the pine woods. There are plenty of choices for a mountain walk. For those preferring not to exert themselves too much, there are two chair lifts climbing to 2,010 and 2,240 metres (6,590 and 7,350 ft). A mineral museum (open Mon–Sat), a summer toboggan run and a total of 800 hotel beds also tempt visitors to stay a day or so.

Ossiacher See

South of Sirnitz, the main road leads to Feldkirchen and then turns southwest to **Ossiacher See** , a lake that offers sports enthusiasts a wide choice of activities. There are 13 schools of sailing, windsurfing and water-skiing. Bold spirits can even attempt parasailing from a motorboat. Overcoming initial fears will be rewarded by an extra-terrestrial floating sensation and a bird's-eye view of the surrounding countryside. Even the inevitable soft, wet landing is no hardship, for here the water reaches a temperature of 26°C (79°F).

Culture addicts can enjoy the events of the Carinthian summer in the monastery of **Ossiach**, on the south side of the lake. Anglers are in their element catching the catfish, pike, tench, trout, eel and many other fish that abound in the lake. For others there is the attraction of a summer sledging run, while an attractive diversion for the young at heart is **Elli Riehl's Puppenwelt** (Puppet World; open Easter–Oct: daily; entrance fee; tel: (04248) 2395) in Treffen.

BELOW: Petersberg Castle in Friesach.

South of Ossiacher See is the Drau (Drava) River, and straddling the river is the chic and historically important town of **Villach** . The Romans built a fort and a bridge here during the first century AD, constructing paved roads as they did so. It was not until 1759 that the town and its surrounding area were ceded to Austria from the Bishopric of Bamberg. They were purchased by Maria Theresa. In the 16th century, when Paracelsus spent his youth here, the town was the economic and cultural centre of Carinthia. He later described the healing power of the springs which were to move Napoleon to rapturous enthusiasm.

Even today, the warm waters offer relaxation and healing to guests from all over the world in a number of well-planned cure and bathing centres.

The Drau Valley

Road 100 leads northwest from Villach through the lower valley of the Drau. Beyond Kellerberg and Feistritz, **Paternion** nestles between sunny mountain slopes and shady woodland, offering a range of amenities for the holidaymaker. Between swimming, fishing, walking, skating, curling and cross-country skiing there is the opportunity to witness the lovely altars of the pilgrimage **Church of St Paternianus** as well as, on an eminence, a 16th-century castle complex. A

A brightly painted sundial on a wall in Spittal an der Drau.

rewarding detour away from the main road is the trip up the Weissenbach Valley to **Stockenboi** to see the remarkable architecture of the local farmhouses.

Back on Road 100, **Spittal an der Drau** is an exceptionally pretty little town. It lies on the boundary between the upper and lower Drau valleys. Its fine houses, historic monuments and elegant shops make it worth visiting whether one's interests lie in sightseeing or shopping. Stately **Schloss Porcia** unites the civilisations of past and present: not only does it house a fascinating museum of local history (open May–Oct: daily; Nov–Apr: Mon–Thur; entrance fee), but its pretty arcaded courtyard serves a as setting for the drama festival held in August and September each year.

Just north of Spittal, **Millstätter See** is idyllically situated amid gentle countryside, offering – in addition to its exceptional beauty – excellent facilities. Its unspoilt southern shore, densely wooded, is a nature reserve with free access for the public. The sandy beaches and warm, clear waters make the lake ideal for bathing. Parasailing and diving, illustrated lectures and fashion shows, evenings of traditional music and piano recitals are typical of the region's leisure activities. Rounding out the picture is the Kneipp circuit and footpath in **Kaning**, where six flour mills dating from around 1800 can be seen clattering away within a stretch of 3 km (2 miles), inviting passers-by to a bread-baking session or to a tot of *Mühlengeist*, the local schnapps.

There is another, slightly longer excursion which all visitors should undertake. Taking the E 55 route from Spittal to **Gmünd** , the traveller should make a point of pausing for long enough to visit the **Porsche Museum** (open daily, entrance fee, tel: (04732) 2471). Between 1944 and 1950 the revolutionary car designer's workshop was situated here, and in 1948 the legendary Porsche 356

was born on this very spot. A road branches off to the northwest towards **Malta**. Beyond the village, a toll-booth marks the beginning of a remarkable section of road between Malta and Hochalm, which passes through the so-called **Valley of Falling Waters**. A new panorama opens up after every hairpin bend – another waterfall, or a glimpse of the 200-metre (656-ft) high wall of the **Kölnbrein Barrage**, the highest dam wall in Austria. Soon we reach the reservoir, which lies amidst mountain peaks at an altitude of almost 2,000 metres (6,600 ft). A hotel stands beside the dam. A night spent here, with an evening and morning walk, is an unforgettable experience. Walkers can set off after breakfast to the Osnabrück Hut or even go on a wild-animal safari.

The valley of the Möll

Starting back at Spittal, head northwest and then take Road 106 towards the north for an exploration of the **Mölltal** ⓯ (Möll Valley), which twists and turns before bringing you eventually to Austria's highest peak. The first diversion in the valley is in **Kolbnitz**, about 20 km (12 miles) from Spittal. Here it is possible to climb from 800 to 2,000 metres (2,600 to 6,600 ft) without exerting oneself unduly and in a short space of time; or when the weather is fine, take the trip by funicular and underground railway up to the **Reisseck-Lake Plateau**. You are bound to want to prolong your stay here, so be prepared. The invigorating mountain air, good range of accommodation and signposted walks of all grades of difficulty make Reisseck ideal for a short holiday.

The road through the Möll Valley leads on past the ruins of Schloss Falkenstein, arriving next in **Obervellach** with its pretty townhouses and 16th-century tower. Art connoisseurs will enjoy the 400-year-old parish church with its early Dutch altar paintings and Gothic carvings. Also worth visiting is the Baroque **Trabuschgen Castle**.

Road 105 branches off at Obervellach towards **Mallnitz**, a high-altitude resort lying at 1,190 metres (3,900 ft) and marking the southern end of the Tauern Tunnel. Day by day, a car-ferry train system passes on a 10-minute journey through the 8-km (5-mile) tunnel, carrying thousands of cars between Carinthia and Salzburg Province each year *(see page 234)*.

Castles, glaciers and waterfalls

Continuing up the Möll Valley, castle addicts will be in seventh heaven when they reach **Schloss Groppenstein**, whose roots reach back to the 13th century. It stands majestically over the countryside, next to the waterfall of the same name.

We soon reach **Flattach** ⓰ – a small village, but one of the most important centres in the Möll Valley. It is the starting point of the magnificent panoramic road leading up to the **Möll Valley Glacier**. Every bend opens up new perspectives, each more breathtaking than the last, until, at 2,200 metres (7,210 ft), the road reaches the valley station of a mountain railway. This takes you across the glacier itself up to the mountain station, situated at 2,800 metres (9,180 ft). If you don't feel inclined to jump on your skis (forgetting them is no problem, for all equipment can be rented here) or to climb a 3,000-metre (9,800-ft) peak,

Map
on pages
246–7

BELOW:
statue in Gmünd.

you may prefer to enjoy the intoxicating mountain air, the blue sky and the glittering snow from the sun terrace of the mountain restaurant.

Also near Flattach lies the counterpart to the panoramic view of the Möll Valley Glacier: the wildly romantic **Ragga Gorge**, carved over millennia. A meticulously constructed system of bridges and steps permits the visitor to traverse the remarkable site without difficulty, admiring the eight thundering waterfalls formed by the Ragga torrent as it plunges downhill.

Typical of the resorts of the central Möll Valley, beyond Flattach is the village of **Rangersdorf**, which has the ruins of a castle first mentioned in 1278. **Lainach**, too, with its miniature iron and sulphur spring, is a good choice for a restful holiday. **Winklern**, nestling between meadows and fields at the junction with Road 107, lies in a conservation area. The village's landmark, the **Toll Tower**, was built in about 1500 on foundations which are thought to date back to Roman times.

From this point onwards the course of the cheerfully babbling Möll (the name is of Celtic origin) turns northwards alongside Road 107, passing through pretty villages on the way to **Döllach-Grosskirchheim**. The settlement – known even in Roman times – was the gold-mining centre of the Tauern in the 15th and 16th centuries. As many as 3,000 miners extracted the precious metal from 800 different sites. A museum of gold mining, housed in Kirchheim Castle, contains interesting displays on the subject. A walk through the nearby **Zirknitz Valley** affords views of two magnificent waterfalls, the Neunbrunnen (Nine Springs Falls) and the Gucklöcher des Lindwurms (Dragon's Peepholes).

The Upper Möll Valley Mountain Road leads on from here via various villages to Heiligenblut, where it joins the Grossglockner High Alpine Road.

BELOW: the Alps attract daredevils of all kinds.

The long and winding road

Before venturing onto the hairpin bends and up the mountain, however, there are two sights worth visiting in **Heiligenblut** ⓱.

The first is the Gothic **Parish Church of St Vincent**, dating from the 15th century. It contains the most important winged altarpiece in Carinthia and an equally renowned, elaborately decorated sacramental shrine.

The second recommendation is to join the local gold- and silver-panning society. This entitles you to search for the precious metals at three different places using the traditional hand-washing method. All equipment is provided, all finds may be kept, and the goldrush atmosphere even extends to an evening camp-fire. There is no doubt about your chances of striking it rich – the mountains behind the Fleisstal are called the **Goldberge**.

The discussions are endless as to which high-altitude mountain road is the most beautiful in the world. Definitely deserving of a place on the short list is the **Grossglockner Hochalpenstrasse** ⓲ (High Alpine Road), a curvaceous beauty that is inaccessible for long periods each year, and only open to traffic between May and October. Even in summer there may be times when the road is impassable. But visitors who make allowances for its unpredictable conditions – a course strongly recommended in the interests of safety – will be rewarded with a succession of truly unforgettable vistas. This major project, planned by civil engineer Hofrat Franz Wallack, employed more than 3,000 workers between 1930 and 1935. The impressive result, known at the time as the Dream Road of the Alps, is 50 km (30 miles) long and 7.5 metres (25 ft) wide, with a maximum gradient of 12 percent.

On top of the world

The first spectacular view after you leave Heiligenblut is of the 3,105-metre (10,185-ft) **Hoher Sonnblick**, topped with the highest weather station in Austria. About 6 km (4 miles) further on, the route forks off to the left on to the glacier road leading to **Franz-Josephs-Höhe**. From the plateau, which at an altitude of 2,360 metres (7,740 ft) lies above the tree line, you can see across the **Pasterze Glacier** to the summit of the **Grossglockner**, Austria's highest mountain at 3,797 metres (12,455 ft).

The Pasterze, the biggest glacier in Austria, was recently surveyed by scientists, who came to the conclusion that it was 220 metres (720 ft) thick. With a surface area of 180 sq. km (70 sq. miles), that represents a vast amount of water. A funicular transports visitors directly to the edge of the ice sheet. If you are wearing suitable shoes, you can venture on to the slippery surface.

Another worthwhile excursion is the **Gamsberg Nature Path**, which can be tackled with ease and leads alongside the Pasterze to an idyllic waterfall. Noticeboards provide information about the glacier, the marmots and the ecological state of the biotope.

Returning to the fork along our main route, turn left for the **Hochtor**. Here, at 2,575 metres (8,450 ft) above sea level, is the boundary between Carinthia and

Map on pages 246–7

TIP

There is a hefty toll imposed for use of the Grossglockner Road. The frequent buses that make trips along the road include a small fraction of the toll in the cost of a ticket.

BELOW: Grossglockner, Austria's highest peak, at sunrise.

Salzburg Province. The Grossglockner Road continues through the unique **Hohe Tauern National Park**, the largest continuous stretch of unspoiled countryside in Austria *(see page 238).*

The Upper Drau Valley

If instead of exploring the Mölltal, you continue west from the confluence of the Möll and Drau rivers (12 km/7 miles northwest of Spittal), the Drau Valley soon becomes very narrow, and is known here as the Sachsenburg Defile. Ruins of several castles and fortresses dating from the 13th century testify to the valley's strategic importance in those days.

Greifenburg ⓳, 20 km (12 miles) west, is known as the Heart of the Upper Drau Valley. As early as the 2nd century, this market town in the shadow of its castle was an important staging post on the Roman road to Gurina. Today, there is a newly constructed artificial lake for bathing, with a 400-metre (1,310-ft) beach.

The **Weissensee ⓴**, in the hills southeast of Greifenburg, has its own distinctive charm. The fact that the two ends of the lake are not connected by road makes it a quiet and peaceful holiday destination. The crystal-clear waters are a shimmering turquoise hue due to the white sandy shores – which also gave the lake its name. In the shallow sections near the bank one can see the stems of the water lilies right down to the lake bed – an unusual sight, also due to the white sand. Lying at an altitude of 930 metres (3,050 ft) above sea level, the Weissensee is the highest Alpine lake in which bathing is still possible; the waters reach temperatures of 25°C (77°F) in summer.

BELOW: mountain pastures near the Weissensee.

The best amenities are available on the western approaches, on the **Techendorf** shore. Apart from fishing, sailing and water-skiing there are also archery

and canoeing facilities. A local speciality is *schlurfen*, a sort of water-borne cross-country skiing on polystyrene boards. There is also golf in summer and curling in winter. The countryside here was used as a location in the James Bond film *Licence to Kill*.

Berg im Drautal, back in the Drau Valley and west of Greifenburg, appeals to even the most discriminating traveller, offering a good choice of hotels with indoor and outdoor swimming pools and a wide variety of restaurants. For walking enthusiasts there are the Gaisloch and Ochsenschluchtklamm, two unspoiled, romantic gorges nearby. Adventurous souls might enjoy a boat trip on the Drau in an inflatable raft.

A short distance further on, a minor road branches off to the right towards **Irschen**, an attractive resort village on the southern slopes of the Kreuzeck Range. The local **Parish Church of St Dionysius**, originally Romanesque in style, was rebuilt in the 15th century. It contains an exceptionally fine winged altarpiece and murals dating from the 14th century.

Oberdrauburg ㉑, a few kilometres west, is the last bastion of the Carinthian section of the Drau Valley before the border with East Tyrol. A market town lying at the foot of the Lienzer Dolomites, Oberdrauburg was first settled in the 13th century. Today it offers the traveller a number of historic sights as well as a full range of tourist amenities. The castle on the eastern side of the town dates from the 16th century. It was badly damaged during World War II and subsequently rebuilt, losing much of its original character in the process. However, the **Church of St Leonard**, in the village of Zwickenberg, north of town, houses a 16th-century winged altarpiece and 15th-century murals, and has retained its aura of historic charm.

Map on pages 246–7

TIP

One of Austria's best restaurants, the Kellerwand, is in the town of Kötschach-Mauthen, in the Gail Valley 14 km (9 miles) south of Oberdrauburg. It specialises in authentic local cuisine.

BELOW: the dark crags of the Lienzer Dolomites.

East Tyrol is the country's smallest and most isolated province.

Into East Tyrol

West of Oberdrauburg, the main road follows the Drau Valley into East Tyrol (Osttirol). This remote region was once connected to Tyrol, its more famous namesake, but became separated when South Tyrol was ceded to Italy in 1919. Since then the province's connections with the rest of Austria have been improved by the construction of new transport links such as the Felbertauern Tunnel.

Nikolsdorf marks the beginning of the East Tyrolean section of the Drau Valley on the way to Lienz. There is a woodland swimming pool where you can splash and sunbathe in glorious surroundings. Not far beyond, **Lavant** – a detour south off Road 100 – is recognisable from a distance by its pretty **Pilgrimage Church of St Peter and St Paul**. Since 1948, the foundations of settlements dating from various different eras have been discovered here. A kilometre or so further on lies *Aguntum*, an excavated Roman town and a diocesan city until 622. Many rare and interesting exhibits are on display here.

Not far away is **Dölsach,** a resort village at 740 metres (2,430 ft) above sea level. Like the villages of **Amlach** and **Tristach** – situated on a pretty little lake just west of it – Dölsach lies in the Lienzer Dolomites resort area, the starting point in summer for delightful mountain walks and in winter for skiing trips, curling and cross-country skiing.

Lienz ㉒ is the capital of East Tyrol. It was an Illyrian settlement as long ago as 500 BC. In fact, at several points in history the region surrounding Lienz acquired considerable importance. Between 1250 and 1500, the counts of Görz resided at **Schloss Bruck** (open May–Oct: daily; entrance fee; tel: (04852) 62 580) near Lienz. At this time the town was subject to planned development. Later, it passed to the counts of Wolkenstein and finally to the Convent of Halle.

BELOW:
waiting for a bite.

In 1798 the town centre was destroyed by a major fire; only on the right bank of the Isel did there remain traces of the old city defences. The war memorial chapel in the cemetery of the **Parish Church of St Andrä** was built by Clemens Holzmeister and contains the tomb of the painter Albin Egger-Lienz, as well as that of artist Franz Defregger – a native of East Tyrol.

Map on pages 246–7

The Puster Valley

Southwest of Lienz, beyond the Lienz Defile, is the **Puster Valley**. One way of getting a preview of this breathtaking countryside, is to climb the **Sternalm** – the first half of the ascent as far as Hochstein is accessible by twin chair lift – from which you will have a magnificent panoramic view. Shortly after Leisach the mountain road forks off to **Bannberg**; from here, a toll road leads almost as far as the Hochstein refuge. **Assling ㉓**, the largest village in the area, also lies on the "sun terrace" on the mountain road, further up the valley. It has a Game Park with rare native animals (open May–Oct: daily). In winter, Assling can offer a ski area that includes a 1,300-metre (4,260-ft) lift.

Down in the valley again, on the Road 100, is **Thal**. Here the Gothic parish church of St Korbinian, dedicated in 1486, contains a late-Gothic Crucifixion group dating from 1490, three altars of considerable artistic merit and two paintings by Pacher (*circa* 1500). On the sunny north slopes of the valley nestle four idyllic villages: **Unterried**, **Wiesen**, **Anras** and **Asch**. Accessible by means of a narrow road, they all lie at altitudes of 1,000 metres (3,280 ft) or more.

Traversing **Strassen**, with its late-Gothic church of St James, the road reaches Heinfels and Panzendorf. The name of **Schloss Heinfels**, the valley landmark and the property of the ancient Görz family, is derived from the Hunnenfels –

BELOW: a Corpus Christi procession near the village of Strassen.

Map
on pages
246–7

Kayaking on the Isel River, near Matrei.

BELOW: waterfall in the Virgental, west of Matrei.
RIGHT: the Grossglockner High Alpine Road.

Huns' Rock. During the Venetian Wars, Emperor Maximilian I surrounded it with a defensive wall to protect the arsenal.

Sillian ㉔ is a sports resort dominating the end of the Austrian section of the Puster Valley. Only a short distance beyond lies the Italian border, which already makes its presence felt here in the mild climate. Each season has its own particular charms: the magnificent colours of the blossom in spring, the luxuriant green of the mountain pastures in summer, the riot of rusts and golds in autumn and the picture-postcard whiteness of the snow in winter. The village itself, with a population of 2,000, presents a broad range of leisure amenities: indoor swimming pool and sauna, tennis courts, hang-gliding school, shooting range, fitness circuit, library and reading room, cycling paths, toboggan run, skating and curling rinks, Alpine and cross-country ski schools and a number of facilities for children.

Matrei

About 30 km (18 miles) northwest of Lienz, in a spectacular setting against the background of the High Tauern mountains, is the little town of **Matrei ㉕**. Majestically dominating the scene from a high crag is the landmark **Schloss Weissenstein**, which dates from the 12th century but was modified in the 19th. Standing in solitary splendour is the 800-year-old **Church of St Nicholas**, which houses some remarkable Romanesque wall paintings. *The Healing* evokes memories of the frescoes in the cathedral of Gurk. In the tower are three stone sculptures dating from the first half of the 15th century. The impressive **Parish Church** originally dates from the 14th century, but acquired its present form between 1768 and 1784, when it was rebuilt by Wolfgang Hagenauer.

Every year in September the charming St Matthew's Market takes place in Matrei, but most visitors actually come for the mountains. Over 100 with peaks above 3,000 metres (9,840 ft) can be tackled from here. The **Mountain Climbing Advisory Office** on Rauterplatz offers guided tours of the entire region and provides information, touring tips and meteorological information. The mountaineering tradition is an important part of life here. On 11 August 1865 an expedition starting in Matrei conquered the **Grossvenediger ㉖** (3,675 metres/12,055 ft) from its most attractive side – via the Innergschlöss-Alm. Nowadays the "Grossvenediger Adventure" is offered as part of a package in a number of variations by the Mountain Climbing Office.

Matrei has more to offer than just mountain walks: trekking to the isolated High Tauern miners' huts, mountain biking, paragliding, climbing and kite flying are just some of the attractions in this pretty village community. Alpine rafting on the River Isel is a classic adventure for lovers of water sports. Fly-fishing enthusiasts can also indulge in their hobby here. Information can be obtained at the Hotel Rauter on Rauterplatz.

Visitors who would like to try one of these activities, but have left their equipment at home, will be delighted to discover that the Mountain and Sports Gear Rental Service can supply most needs. Another pleasant surprise is the kindergarten for visitors' children situated in Schloss Goldried. ❏

TYROL

The precipitous peaks and highly developed ski resorts of this famous western province draw millions of visitors each winter, but peace can still be found in the more sedentary summer months

Maps:
Area 272
City 268

According to a popular song, **Innsbruck ❶**, the capital of Tyrol (Tirol), is a "beautiful Alpine town". As long as one restricts one's observations to its breathtaking location surrounded by mountains and to the medieval Old Town itself, the description holds true. Now, as during the reigns of the Emperor Maximilian and Empress Maria Theresa, the encircling chain of unspoiled peaks ensures that nothing changes much: the town is contained by the **Karwendel Range** to the north, towering more than 2,000 metres (6,600 ft) above the town itself, and the twin landmarks in the south, the **Patscherkofel** and the **Nockspitze**.

It was no less a personage than Emperor Maximilian I who first recognised the many-faceted charms of this town nestled in the mountains. Although the residence of the Tyrolean branch of the Habsburgs was transferred from Merano (in what is now Italy) to the River Inn as early as 1420, Maximilian was the first monarch really to hold his court here, when he ascended the throne in 1493. He left his most lasting mark on the city in the magnificent Renaissance funerary monument he commissioned for himself in the Hofkirche. Maria Theresa also brought the splendour of court life to Innsbruck. She had the ancient royal residence (the Hofburg) extended and had the Triumphal Arch erected to mark the marriage of her son.

PRECEDING PAGES: peaceful Tyrolean valley.
LEFT: Hasegg Castle.
BELOW: Defregger's *Das Letzte Aufgebot* shows Tyrolean freedom fighters in the 1809 struggles.

Tyrolean idol

The year 1805 marked the beginning of a dark but heroic period of history, after the Habsburgs had been forced to cede Tyrol to Bavaria in the Treaty of Bratislava. The Tyroleans, under Andreas Hofer, rebelled and in 1809 made Innsbruck the seat of a civilian government following their victory in the Battle of Bergisel. Andreas Hofer ruled Tyrol "in the name of the Emperor". The resistance was broken in November 1809, and a year later, the Tyrolean popular hero was betrayed and shot in Mantua. Since then the Bergisel Mountain on the southern boundary of the town has symbolised the Tyrolean love of freedom.

Innsbruck's late-Gothic centre has been preserved largely intact. Pedestrians can easily explore the compact area between the **River Inn** and the beginning of Maria-Theresienstrasse. **Herzog Friedrichstrasse**, enclosed by arcades, fans out in front of the famous **Goldenes Dachl ❷** (Golden Roof), providing an insight into the intimacy that must have characterised life at court. This magnificent balcony was built to provide a fitting stage for the ruling family to see and be seen. It was erected on the orders of Emperor Maximilian I and completed in 1500. The balustrade of the upper section, which juts out slightly, is decorated on the front and sides with carved reliefs. The two middle sections represent Maximilian with his two

wives, Maria of Burgundy and Maria Bianca Sforza, and Maximilian with his chancellor and court jester. The remaining panels portray Morris dancers. The structure was the work of Nikolaus Türing the Elder, the Innsbruck court builder. It is to him that the balcony owes its roof, which was covered with gold-plated copper tiles.

Old-fashioned postboxes are still used in Innsbruck.

Diagonally opposite the Goldenes Dachl is the **Helblinghaus ⑧**, a late-Gothic building to which a Rococo facade was added in the 18th century by Anton Gigl. The window frames, oriels and tympana are painted in pastel colours and lavishly decorated. A little further on, near the River Inn, stands the **Goldener Adler ⑨** (Golden Eagle) – the oldest inn in the town – dating from the 16th century. The German poet Goethe (1749–1832) stayed here twice. The **Ottoburg ⑩**, diagonally opposite, was originally built as a residential tower in 1495. Still furnished in period style, it serves today as a wine bar.

The **Domkirche St Jakob ⑤** (Cathedral of St James) is hidden away to the north of the Goldenes Dachl. It was completed in the Baroque style in 1722 in accordance with plans drawn up by Johann Jakob Herkommer. The interior space is enclosed by a series of domes: three domed vaults spanning the nave and a dome with lantern above the chancel. The frescoes adorning the vaulting – dedicated to St James the Intercessor – are the work of Cosmas Damian Asam, whilst the stucco was decorated by his brother, Egid Quirin.

BELOW: the Leopoldsbrunnen fountain opposite the Hofburg.

The **Hofburg ⑥**, extended during the reign of Maria Theresa, adjoins the cathedral on the north side (open daily; entrance fee; tel: (0512) 587 186). Inside, the **Riesensaal** (Giant's Hall), over 30 metres (100 ft) long, is one of the main attractions. Its walls are clad with magnificent stucco panels with a marble finish. The grand ceiling was painted in 1776 by Franz Anton Maulbertsch.

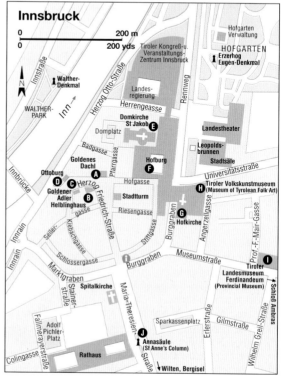

Austria's greatest Renaissance monument

Opposite the southeast corner of the Hofburg, the **Hofkirche** (open Mon–Sat; entrance fee; tel: (0512) 584 302) was completed in 1563. It was built in the late-Gothic style with a Renaissance porch, and was designed to house the Tomb of Emperor Maximilian I, the Habsburg whose talents as a matchmaker ensured that there was a member of his family in every royal house in Europe at his death. In 1502, 17 years before he finally expired, the emperor commissioned his own mausoleum. It was to become the most outstanding work of art in Tyrol, and the most moving imperial monument in the Western world.

Gilg Sesselschreiber, a Munich artist, was asked to produce sketches for the tomb. He proposed a bronze edifice with 40 larger-than-life statues of the most important ancestors and kinsmen of the emperor. The ensemble was to be completed by two rows of statuettes and busts of patron saints of the Habsburgs and Roman emperors. Of the 40 statues originally planned, 28 were actually cast, between 1509 and 1550. The two most famous represent King Arthur and Theodoric and were cast in 1513 in Nuremberg by Peter Vischer. It was not until 1550 that the idea arose of erecting a cenotaph bearing the statue of Maximilian as the focal point of the monument. Its construction, in accordance with the design of Alexander Colin, was completed in 1583.

Beside the Hofkirche is the **Tiroler Volkskunstmuseum** (Museum of Tyrolean Folk Art; open daily; entrance fee; tel: (0512) 584 302), which contains an important collection of local costumes, tools and peasant furniture. Nearby, on Museumstrasse, the newly refurbished **Tiroler Landesmuseum Ferdinandeum** (Provincial Museum; open May–Sept: daily; Oct–Apr: Tues–Sun; entrance fee) records the development of painting and sculpture in Tyrol.

Map on page 268

BELOW: view of the Domkirche across the River Inn.

Hiking near Innsbruck

Set at the heart of some of Austria's most spectacular scenery, Innsbruck is the nerve centre of the country's large hiking community. Here you will find the national hiking club, virtually all the major trail associations, an alpine school and an astonishing range of useful, well-organised programmes for visitors.

Hotel guests in Innsbruck or the adjacent towns of Igls and Patsch are eligible for a free "Club Innsbruck Card". From early June until the end of September, this card gives access to mountain walks, shuttle buses into the mountains, a guidebook and equipment such as walking shoes and rucksacks.

The Austrian Alpine Club (Oesterreichischer Alpenverein; Wilhelm-Greil-Strasse 15, 6010 Innsbruck, tel: (0512) 59 547) teams up with the local Innsbruck Alpine School to guide trips such as the Sunrise-Mountain Hut Trek,

offered every Tuesday and Thursday, from July to September. On this guided tour through the Karwendel nature reserve, you climb the 2,250-metre (7,380-ft) Nordkette and the 2,215-metre (7,065-ft) Stempeljoch, visit a mining museum and sleep in a mountain hut.

Day hikes from Innsbruck start at 8.30 each morning. Alpine School guides take guests on moderate three-to-five-hour walks chosen from more than 40 routes in the Stubai, Tuxer, Karwendel and Mieminger ranges. Children are welcome – indeed the Monday Hiking Day programme is designed specifically for them. Parents and children are paired with guides for local nature walks, a picnic and a camp fire.

For an alternative family outing, the Zirbenweg trail is an easy walk through pine forests. Another easy option is to take the cable-car up to the 2,000-metre (6,600-ft) Patscherkofel station, which has great vistas of the Inn Valley. If you have time while you're here, check out the Alpine Garden Patscherkofel, Europe's highest botanic garden, with 400 kinds of tree, flower and other mountain plant life (open Jun–Sept: daily; free). It is a quite easy 7-km (4-mile) walk from the cable-car station.

The most romantic option is a Lantern Walk. These take place every Tuesday and Thursday night in the summer. Present your club card at a depot in Innsbruck or Igls, then ride a free bus to the trailhead, where, led by guides bearing lanterns, you ascend in a quiet, easy hike to a rustic lodge, where a hut party with food and drink awaits. You are ferried back to your hotel before midnight. The pick-up point in Innsbruck is just outside Congress Innsbruck at 7.45pm. The shuttle stops at about 8pm at the Igls Tourist Office.

Note that, while guided hiking programmes are free, if you put together your own itinerary, the cost of train journeys can add up. Consider buying a hiking pass for unlimited passage on the Patscherkofel and Nordkette mountain railways, and discounted lifts up the Axamer Lizum and the Glungezer.

If you're here in winter, there are free ski shuttles to downhill and cross-country resort areas, reductions on ski passes, day tickets and single-run prices, and cheap family tobogganing programmes. ❑

LEFT: hikers passing through a village on their way to the Karwendel Mountains.

Maria-Theresienstrasse runs south from the Old Town. It is dominated by St Anne's Column ❶, erected in 1706 in memory of the retreat of the Bavarian troops from Tyrol during the War of the Spanish Succession. Surmounting the slender pedestal is a statue of the Virgin Mary. St Anne stands next to St George (the patron saint of Tyrol), and St Vigilius and St Cassianus (the patron saints of the dioceses of Trent and Bressanone), symbolise the political unity of Tyrol. The southern end of the street is marked by the **Triumphal Arch**.

If you continue south you soon reach **Wilten**, a district of Innsbruck and once the site of the Roman town of *Veldidena*. **Wilten Abbey** was founded in 1128 under the jurisdiction of the Premonstratensians. Until 1180 they controlled the entire area as far as the Inn. Only after this date did they permit settlers to leave the northern bank of the Inn and to make their homes in what is now the Old Town. The present Abbey Church is a Baroque edifice dating from the 17th century, with an imposing facade completed in 1716.

Nearby **Wilten Parish Church** was completed in 1756 in accordance with the plans of the Tyrolean priest-architect Franz de Paula Penz. Its Rococo interior was the work of Franz Xaver Feichtmayr, the stuccoist of the Wessobrunn school, and Matthäus Günther, the Augsburg painter. The high altar has a statue of the Virgin under a baldachin supported by marble columns. "Our Lady of the Four Pillars" has been venerated as a source of miraculous powers since the Middle Ages.

Wilten is overlooked by the **Bergisel** hill, site of the famous battle. Today it features a ski jump erected for the 1964 Winter Olympics. The Imperial Light Infantry Memorial here commemorates the élite Tyrolean corps disbanded in 1919.

Perched on a mountainside southeast of the centre is **Schloss Ambras**, the favourite residence of Archduke Ferdinand and his lovely wife Philippine Welser (open Apr–Oct: daily; Dec–Mar: limited; entrance fee; tel: (0512) 348 446). Ferdinand had the castle extended to its present size from 1564. Today visitors can admire a comprehensive arms collection, an exhibition of paintings and curios and the **Spanish Hall**, with its magnificent Renaissance coffered ceiling.

The **Bergisel Panorama**, situated near the Hungerberg funicular station north of the town centre, depicts the Battle of Bergisel as a moment of glory for the freedom fighters of the province.

Leaving the capital

The prosperity of the salt-water spa of **Hall in Tirol** ❷, northeast of Innsbruck, comes from its salt deposits. The latter are guarded by **Hasegg Castle**, in which Archduke Ferdinand II set up the first mechanical mint in 1567. For this reason the fortress's distinctive tower is known to this day as the Mint Tower. The parish church of St Nicholas was completed in 1437 and remodelled in the Baroque style in 1752. The nearby village of **Wattens** is home to the popular **Swarovski Kristallwelt** (Crystal World), a series of sound-and-light installations and a showcase for the nearby Swarovski cut-glass factory (open daily; entrance fee; tel: (05224) 51 080).

A further 18 km (11 miles) to the northeast, alongside the Inn River, is the town of **Schwaz**. At the start of the 16th century there were 20,000 miners working

Maps:
Area 272
City 268

The bobsleigh run at Igls, just south of Innsbruck, was used in the 1976 Olympics.

BELOW: the steeple of Wilten Abbey Church.

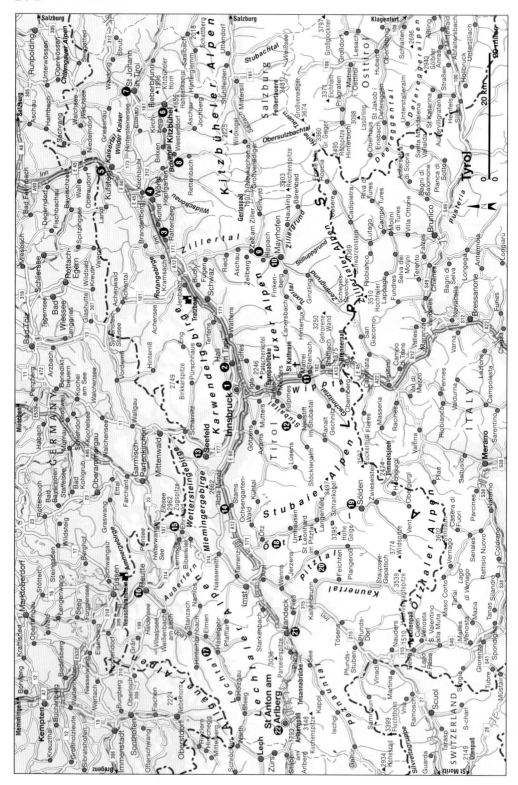

underground here. The town's parish church dates from this period. It was begun in 1460 and completed after 1492 by Erasmus Grasser, the Munich architect. The largest Gothic hall church in Tyrol, it has a roof covered in 15,000 hammered copper tiles and is known as the Mountain Blessing.

Around 7 km (4 miles) to the northeast is **Schloss Tratzberg** (open Apr–Oct: daily; entrance fee). It was built in 1296 as a stronghold on what was then the Bavarian frontier. The extensive complex consists of four main wings and received its present form during the 16th and 17th centuries at the instigation of the Fugger banking family. Beyond **Tratzberg** the fortresses of **Matzen** and **Lichtwer** recall the era of medieval chivalry. Unfortunately they are closed to the public.

Family fortune

Rattenberg ❸, another 11 km (7 miles) to the northeast, owes its prosperity to the mining rights that Maximilian awarded to the Fugger family. From here they controlled all silver mining operations in the entire province. The town itself has managed to retain its medieval splendour. The late-Gothic **Parish Church of St Virgil**, which has a magnificent Baroque interior, testifies to the great wealth Rattenberg once enjoyed.

Kramsach lies on the opposite bank of the Inn, a village surrounded by a trio of lakes that are all ideal for bathing: the Buchsee, the Krummsee and the Reintaler See. The nearby **Brandenberg Valley** is delightful walking country, and includes the Kaiserklamm Gorge and the Archduke Johann Hermitage. A chair lift from Kramsach provides access to the **Rofan Mountains**.

Further to the northeast lies the little hamlet of **Kundl**, which had a church as long ago as 788. Nonetheless, the most interesting religious building here is

Map on page 272

Fresco on the outside wall of the parish church in Eben, north of Tratzberg.

BELOW: the Wilder Kaiser peaks, east of Wörgl.

Tyrol's many winter resorts are heaven for snowboarders.

not really the Parish Church of the Assumption itself but rather the pilgrimage **Church of St Leonhard in the Meadows**, lying just outside the village proper. Reputedly founded by Heinrich I in 1012, it was dedicated in 1020 by Pope Benedict VIII. The present building dates from 1512. Walkers will enjoy the wild and romantic footpath through the **Kundlerklamm**, which affords direct access to the Wildschönau Mountains.

Carry on in the direction of Kufstein and you will come across the busy little village of **Wörgl ④**, the centre of the Tyrolean Lowlands. The Baroque parish church houses the Virgin of Wörgl, dating from about 1500. Perched up on a terrace above the village stands the medieval **Castle and Chapel of Mariastein.** The keep, with its pentagonal ground plan, was built in around 1350 to defend the Inn Valley route, which in those days ran past its door. The Chapel of Miracles containing a venerated image of the Virgin is tucked away on the upper floor.

Kufstein ⑤ lies just on the Austrian side of the border with Bavaria, 16 km (10 miles) northeast of Wörgl. The town itself changed hands between Tyrol and Bavaria on many occasions. Maximilian was the first to fortify the stronghold, first mentioned in 1205, to any great extent. At his behest the Kaiserturm (Emperor's Tower) in **Kufstein Fortress** acquired walls which were up to 7.5 metres (25 ft) thick. Today the fortress houses a museum of local history and the Heroes' Organ, the largest in the world, built in 1931 in memory of the Tyrolean freedom fighters (open mid-Mar–mid-Nov: daily; entrance fee).

Sporting Kitzbühel

BELOW: a colourful street in Kitzbühel.

The reputation of **Kitzbühel ⑥** (40 km/25 miles southeast of Kufstein) as a chic winter sports centre dates at least from the triple Olympic victory of local boy Toni Sailer – the "Kitz Comet" – in the 1956 Winter Games in Cortina. Apart from that, the famous Hahnenkamm Races ensure that the Kitzbühel skiing area attracts top enthusiasts from all over the world. It has more than 50 slopes and countless first-rate descents.

The mountains surrounding Kitzbühel have contributed most to the town's sporting reputation, especially the **Kitzbüheler Horn** to the east and the **Hahnenkamm** to the west. In summer, the relatively tame Kitzbühel Alps afford a range of mountain walks. For those who prefer it steeper, rockier and more challenging, there are the vast limestone peaks of the **Wilder Kaiser** to the north. The charms of the broad Kitzbühel Basin can best be experienced when the wall of mountains are lit by the setting sun and reflected in the dark waters of the moorland **Schwarzer See**, just north of town.

The **Parish Church**, dating from 1435, is a relic of Kitzbühel's earlier period of prosperity. The triple-naved Gothic structure with its slender tower and overhanging single roof blends in harmoniously with its Alpine setting. The nearby **Church of Our Lady** has an unusual two-storey design. The lower church is mentioned in records as early as 1373. The upper storey was adorned in the Baroque manner in 1735. Its most attractive feature is the series of frescoes by Simon Benedikt Faistenberger, thought to be his finest work. The painting adorning the high altar is a copy of

Our Lady of Succour, the Lukas Cranach (1472–1553) masterpiece in Innsbruck Cathedral. The rose grille in front of the high altar was created in 1781.

Barely 8 km (5 miles) south of Kitzbühel, the parish church of **Jochberg** also contains frescoes by Faistenberger. The apostles St Peter and St Paul, and St Wolfgang are portrayed as vividly as in a Rubens painting. Works by the same artist can also be seen in the Parish Church of the Assumption in **St Johann in Tirol ❼**, a scattered village lying in the valley between the Kitzbüheler Horn and the sheer face of the Wilder Kaiser, 10 km (6 miles) north of Kitzbühel. The church's most notable feature is the protruding west front, completed in 1728 and flanked by twin towers capped by Baroque cupolas.

St Johann is first and foremost the central starting point for walking and mountaineering in the Wilder Kaiser. Those seeking a grandstand view of the region can take the route from Griesenau into the **Kaiserbach Valley**, and from there up to the Griesener Alm. From here one has only to climb a further 580 metres (1,905 ft) to the legendary **Stripsenjoch**. Those who prefer more romantic scenery can travel west to the picturesque **Hintersteiner See**.

There is more art and culture in the **Brixental ❽** (Brixen Valley), west of Kitzbühel. In **Kirchberg**, the first village in the valley, the Baroque parish church houses some fine ceiling frescoes by Faistenberger. That **Brixen im Thale**, 5 km (3 miles) west, was once a prosperous place is apparent from the twin-towered **Parish Church of the Assumption**, which has a nave roofed by three domes. It was constructed by the master-builder Andrä Hueber between 1789 and 1795.

The third important church in the Brixen Valley is in **Hopfgarten**. Begun in 1758 by Kassian Singer, it was completed by Andrä Hueber. Once more we see a twin-towered facade with an extravagantly curved gable. The ceiling

Map on page 272

BELOW: winter transport.

frescoes here are the work of Johann Weiss. Ensuring that mountaineering addicts are not left in the lurch in the Brixen Valley is the **Hohe Salve**, accessible by cable-car and providing the best views of the Wilder Kaiser.

Ziller Valley contrasts

On the first weekend of May, Zell am Ziller marks the beginning of summer with the 400-year-old Gauderfest. Folk rituals, processions and contests are accompanied by the consumption of huge amounts of lethal Gauder beer.

Heading back west towards Innsbruck, the first important valley south of the Inn is that of the Ziller. There is no other region that has become so associated with Tyrol as the Ziller Valley, and this despite the fact that the area has only been part of Tyrol since 1816. Previously it had belonged to the Duchy of Salzburg. At the end of the 17th century Archbishop Johann Ernst of Salzburg erected a hunting lodge in Floitengrund. Today the valley is one of the best-known in the entire Alps. But while Mayrhofen, at the head of the valley, offers more hotel beds than Salzburg, the valley still contains many remote nooks which remain unspoilt. The glaciers, precipitous mountain faces and razor-edge ridges, combined with the height of the mountains have ensured that the beauty of this pristine landscape has remained intact.

The valley extends some 30 km (18 miles) in a north–south direction, from **Strass** on the Inn River to Mayrhofen. Over this distance, however, it only rises some 100 metres (330 ft). This gentle incline made it possible to open up the valley by means of a narrow gauge railway, still sometimes served by a steam train.

Near Strass, you will be able to view the remains of early 14th-century frescoes in the late-Gothic parish church of **Fügen**, and the **Pilgrimage Church of St Pancratius**, built above the village at the end of the 15th century; its altars date from the 17th century.

BELOW:
a Tyrolean in his rifleman's uniform.

Further up the valley, the **Zillertal Mountain Road** branches off to the west and weaves its way at a height of 1,700–2,000 metres (5,600–6,600 ft) along the side of the valley, offering the best panoramic views of the main ridge of the Zillertal Alps and its remarkable glaciers. Access points are from Ried, Aschau, Zellberg and Hippach, so that visitors can plan their ascent and descent via different routes if they so wish. The highest point on the road (2,050 metres/6,725 ft) lies just below the summit of the **Arbiskopf** (2,130 metres/7,000 ft). From here you will experience the best view of the main Alpine ridge.

Zell am Ziller ❾, the principal village in the valley, lies at the junction with the road to Gerlos Pass. Its name is derived from the monk's cell which was reputedly founded here in the 8th century by St Rupert. The present parish church was finished in 1782 by the Kitzbühel master-builder Andrä Hueber. The main construction is Rococo, although the pointed tower was retained from the original Gothic building.

Mayrhofen ❿, further up the valley, stands at the head of the four *Gründe*, as the highest mountain valleys are known. The **Zillergrund** stretches from Mayrhofen for 15 km (10 miles) in a southeasterly direction as far as the Bärenbad Hut (1,450 metres/4,760 ft). The **Stilluppgrund** is the most deeply eroded and sparsely inhabited of the four mountain valleys.

The **Tuxer Grund** is the most accessible of the four valleys. It has the most inhabitants and is popular among skiers as the Hintertux Glacier affords fine opportunities until well into the summer. The last valley, the **Zemmgrund**, leads into the heart of the Zillertal Alps. The construction of the Schlegeis reservoir means that there is now a good road leading up to the Dominikus Refuge in the Zamser Valley. The latter branches off from the Zemmgrund near the Breitlahner Hut, thus enabling the traveller to drive right up to the reservoir, which lies at 1,780 metres (5,850 ft).

Map on page 272

Whilst the Ziller, Stillupp and Zemm high-altitude valleys have remained virtually untouched, the Tuxer Grund has become a lively tourist centre. **Tux**, **Lanersbach** and **Hintertux** have developed rapidly since the construction of the Hintertux Glacier Railway. The cable-car opens up good skiing opportunities until well into the summer, and after that it provides access to an extensive high-altitude region for mountain tours, including the Hoher Riffler (3,230 metres/10,600 ft), the Olperer (3,475 metres/11,400 ft) and the Hoher Wand (3,060 metres/10,035 ft). Those who prefer rather warmer temperatures than these heights afford will enjoy the radioactive thermal spring.

The spectacular Europa Bridge was built between 1959 and 1963.

From the Wipp Valley to the Stubai

South of Innsbruck, between the Tux Alps in the east and the Stubai Alps in the west, the Wipptal leads to the **Brenner Pass** (1,375 metres/4,510 ft), the lowest-lying cleft in the entire Alpine Ridge and as such the easiest and also the oldest Alpine pass. The Illyrians used a mule track here, and the Romans had a chariot road. In the Middle Ages the pass was used by emperors and kings on pleasure journeys or with their armies. Today, the old main road, the motorway and the railway attempt to cope with the route's ever-increasing traffic.

BELOW: the soaring Zillertal Alps seen from the Zillertal Mountain Road.

A brilliant example of modern technology is the **Europa Bridge**, which crosses

BELOW: the Tyrolean
riflemen recall the
19th-century
liberation struggles.

the valley of the Sill near Schönberg. With a span of 800 metres (2,625 ft) it stands at over 190 metres (625 ft) high, making it the tallest motorway bridge in Europe.

The first village in the Wipp Valley, **Matrei** , is also the oldest. Oriel-windowed houses with overhanging roofs, Gothic entrances and ground-floor vaulted ceilings characterise the appearance of this typical linear village. The parish church, which dates from the 12th century, was refurbished in the 18th century with brightly coloured Baroque frescoes.

The Navis Valley branching off to the left beyond Matrei, contains the **Chapel of St Kathrin**, built on the remains of Aufenstein Castle. The chapel houses the two oldest known wooden statues in Tyrol, dating from the early 14th century.

Following a major fire in **Steinach** in 1853, only the chancel remained of the old parish church but it was integrated into the new construction. Its most impressive feature is the fine altar by the South Tyrol artist Johann Perger.

The **Gschnitz Valley** leads off westwards from Steinach. North of Trins, the first village in the valley, a road climbs towards the Blaser (2,245 metres/7,360 ft), the Tyrolean mountain with the richest carpet of flowers in spring.

About 10 km (6 miles) south of Innsbruck is the beginning of the **Stubaital** (Stubai Valley), the largest subsidiary valley leading off the Wipp. It leads eventually to the massive **Stubai Glacier**, a year-round skiing area with a wide range of pistes. By taking the Stubai Glacier Railway summer visitors can venture onto the icy surface.

In the valley, Mieders, Telfes, Fulpmes and Neustift are not merely lively tourist villages. They all have parish churches built during the 18th century by Franz de Paula Penze, the parish priest of Telfes. The loveliest of his churches is in Neustift. **Fulpmes** was in former times the home of the most famous iron

workers in Tyrol. Their hammers were driven by hydraulic power derived from the Plövenbach stream. Even today, a few riverside workshops continue to ply their trade. Ice axes and crampons from Fulpmes are famous the world over.

Heading back towards Innsbruck, the northern exit of the Wipptal is marked on the eastern side by the Patscherkofel and to the west by the Nockspitze. At their feet extends a broad upland plateau with sleepy villages like **Mutters** and lively ones like **Axams**. Between the two, in **Götzens**, stands what rates as perhaps the loveliest Baroque parish church in Tyrol. It was completed in 1780 by Franz Singer. Colourful late-Rococo frescoes by Matthäus Günther enhance the master-builder's fine stucco.

The Karwendel and the Wetterstein

North of Innsbruck are the gigantic cirques and grey limestone walls of the **Karwendel Range**, which runs from Achensee in the east to the Seefeld Ridge in the west. To the north, the foothills peter out into the Bavarian uplands. To the south, the 2,000-metre (6,600-ft) peaks plunge steeply into the Inn Valley.

The highest mountain in the range is the **Birkkarspitze** (2,749 metres/9,019 ft). The most convenient cable-car access is via the Northern Cable-Car from Innsbruck, which climbs to the peak of the **Hafelekar** (2,330 metres/7,645 ft). The Karwendel covers an area of 900 sq. km (350 sq. miles) all told, two-thirds of which lie within the boundaries of Tyrol.

The mountainous region is subdivided by four long mountain ranges running from west to east. Correspondingly long are the valleys in between, some deeply eroded and all inaccessible to traffic. For this reason the Karwendel has remained as it always was: a remote and lonely mountain region with pre-

Map
on page
272

BELOW: wintertime in the Wetterstein Mountains.

The cable-car from Ehrwald to the Zugspitze, Germany's highest mountain.

cipitous limestone cliffs, silent high-altitude cirques and numerous pine-fringed Alpine meadows. The threat to the ecology of the area has been averted by the establishment of a national park covering the entire area.

Forest life and death

Many of the trees in the Alps look perfectly healthy, and herds of chamois give the impression that there are no real dangers. Appearances are deceptive, however. Even here, every other tree suffers from a fatal disease, the pine trees no longer give off their characteristic scent and the crystal-clear streams are not infrequently as acid as dilute car battery fluid. And yet, the Karwendel remains an apparently unspoilt mountain wilderness offering walkers, mountaineers and climbers a high-altitude experience which is second to none.

Despite the almost 3,000 metres (9,840 ft) attained by the **Zugspitze**, its highest peak, the **Wetterstein Range**, to the west, has less to offer the visitor. It consists of a single vast mountain ridge, of which only the south side lies in Tyrol. This is actually no real disadvantage, for the **Mieminger Mountains**, with the prominent Hohe Munde (2,662 metres/8,733 ft), rise up parallel to the Wetterstein Range to the south. This, in conjunction with the western slopes of the Karwendel, creates a high-altitude triangle in which the austerity of the mountain scenery is interspersed by rolling hills, idyllic lakes and vast tracts of unspoilt natural beauty.

The centre of this plateau is marked by **Seefeld ⓭**, famous as a winter sports resort and the Tyrolean centre for Nordic skiing. During the summer months, mountain walkers will find extensive touring routes of all grades here.

Back in the Inn Valley southwest of Seefeld is the Cistercian abbey at **Stams ⓮** (open May–Sept: Mon–Sat; entrance fee; tel: (05263) 6242). Together with Göttweig and Melk, it is one of the finest monastery complexes in Austria. Founded in 1268 to mark the death of Konradin, the last of the Hohenstaufen, the monastery became so important within the next century that in 1362 Charles VI had the Imperial jewels deposited here for safe-keeping. The abbey church, 80 metres (265 ft) long, was rebuilt in 1699 and has recently been superbly restored, displaying a breathtaking array of stucco, ornamentation, colourful frescoes and finely worked choir stalls. The high altar features a limewood *Tree of Life*, carved with the figures of Christ, the Virgin, Adam and Eve, and 84 saints.

Travel about 35 km (22 miles) northwest and a unique high-altitude basin opens up at a height of 1,000 metres (3,280 ft), on the periphery of which lies a succession of resorts: Biberwier, Lermoos and **Ehrwald ⓯**. All three are excellent starting points for extended mountain tours. Here, a completely flat meadow unfolds like a single bright-green clover leaf between the rock walls of the Mieminger Range, the Zugspitze, the Daniel and the Grubigstein. Dark forested slopes rise up continuously on all sides, surmounted by 1,000-metre (3,300-ft) high limestone cliff faces: the western escarpments of the Schneefernerkopf and the Zugspitze Massif. From Ehrwald it is possible to reach the Tyrol side of the Zugspitze by cable-car.

BELOW: Zugspitze, the Wetterstein's highest peak.

Head northwest again and you enter a region known as the Ausserfern. The focal point here is the village of **Reutte** ⓰, set beside the Lech River. The village grew up as a typical ribbon development along the valley road. Even today, it is dominated by the squat, low-lying houses with overhanging gables. Particularly noteworthy are the elaborately painted outside walls, dating from the 18th century, the work of the Zeillers, a family of local artists. The highly decorative and figurative murals on the Zeiller family house were painted by Franz Anton Zeiller. Johann Jakob Zeiller executed the vast ceiling fresco in the Parish Church of St Nicholas in **Elbingenalp**, further up the Lech Valley.

The Lech Valley

The main "landgrabber" in the Tyrolean stretch of the **Lechtal** ⓱ (Lech Valley) is the untamed Lech itself. The torrent acquired this nickname from the inhabitants, for stretches of the valley have frequently been flooded by detritus which centuries of carefully tended meadowland have only been able to cover after a fashion.

At first glance, this region, the Ausserfern, may not look interesting. In fact, geologically-speaking, it is fascinating. To the northwest the valley is hemmed in by the **Allgäu Alps**; to the south lie the **Lechtal Alps**. Whilst only the southern and southeastern slopes of the Allgäu mountains belong to Tyrol – and the northern section disperses into Bavaria – the Lechtal Range forms the longest independent mountain ridge in the northern limestone Alps. The summits form a single ridge of countless 2,000-metre (6,560-ft) peaks, except for one single 3,000-metre (9,800-ft) mountain – the **Parseier Spitze**, at 3,035 metres (9,955 ft).

The best view of this unique mountain ridge can be gained from the summit of the **Valluga** (2,810 metres/9,220 ft), accessible by cable car from St Anton

Map on page 272

The frescoes at Stift Stams have been carefully restored.

BELOW:
snowboarding in the powder snow.

(see page 285). From this vantage point one can begin to comprehend the forces which once pushed the layers of rock across each other and into a vertical position, and how the subsequent weathering gouged out cracks and clefts, thus forming the jagged mountain peaks. This is ideal countryside for a high-level walk across the peaks and ridges since the latter are uninterrupted by deep valley clefts, and the shelters lie at convenient distances from each other.

Meadows and lakes

The position on the north side of the Lech Valley is quite different. Here the terrain is dominated by flysch, which consists of alternating layers of clay, slate, marl and limestone, which, lightly weathered, acquires a less jagged profile. Verdant meadows, dense forests, marshy water meadows and highland moors are the external characteristics of this "soft", easily weathered stone.

Limestone also contributes to the appearance of the mountain world of the **Allgäu**. The variety of rocks explains the wealth of flora, for different plants flourish on different geological foundations. Only in the Allgäu, where the mountains are clothed up to their summits in a thick carpet of grass and the alpine meadow flora blooms in such a riot of colours, can such myriad species be found.

The most attractive part of the Tyrolean section of the Allgäu Alps lies behind the **Gaicht Pass** (1,095 metres/3,590 ft), accessible via **Weissenbach am Lech**, which is about 6 km (4 miles) southwest of Reutte. On the other side of the pass is a valley where turquoise lakes contrast with green pastures and ochre-coloured dolomite rock. Two lakes, the **Haldensee** and the **Vilsalpsee**, are as yet virtually unknown but offer an ideal starting point for an expedition into the **Tannheim Mountains** or along the Allgäu Jubilee Path.

BELOW: clearing snow from a roof in Kühtai, above the Ötztal.

The Ötztal Alps

Retracing your route back to the River Inn, head for the **Ötztal** ⑱ (Ötz Valley), the Inn's longest and most imposing side valley. Obergurgl, at the far end, is at least 50 km (30 miles) from the valley mouth. The difference in altitude, 1,235 metres (4,050 ft), corresponds to that of quite a considerable mountain ascent. The valley opens up like a staircase in distinct steps which mark the stages of the retreating glaciers. Steep narrow sections with a deeply cut river bed alternate with broad, almost level fertile valley areas, on which villages and agricultural lands are located.

The village of **Ötz** is dominated by the silhouette of the parish church, which overshadows historic houses with painted facades. The most attractive of the latter is the Gasthof Stern, whose frescoes date from 1573. High above the village is the popular bathing spot of **Piburger See**.

The most important spa in the Ötztal – thanks to its sulphur springs – is **Langenfeld**. Here, too, is the highest church tower in the valley (75 metres/245 ft). The late-Gothic parish church was completed in 1518. On the other side of the valley stands a votive chapel erected in 1661 to commemorate local plague victims.

Sölden ⑲, which lies at an altitude of 1,380 metres (4,525 ft) about 30 km (18 miles) south of Ötz, is primarily a winter sports resort. Skiers are attracted in hordes to Hochsölden, which lies 700 metres (2,300 ft) higher still, and to the glacier road to the Rettenbachferner, where skiing is possible well into the summer months.

In the upper reaches of the valley, at Zwieselstein, the Ötztal divides into two: the Gurgltal and the Ventertal. Here lie the two highest villages in the eastern Alps: **Obergurgl** (1,920 metres/6,300 ft) and **Vent** (1,895 metres/6,215 ft). Vent is popular with mountaineers. From here they can easily reach many of the surrounding

Map on page 272

TIP

Glaciers such as those accessible from Sölden are in constant, but hardly noticeable motion. Consequently, glacier skiing can be hazardous – one should never stray from the marked trails.

BELOW: the idyllic Ötztal, with the village of Ötz in the foreground.

3,000-metre (9,840-ft) peaks. Both valleys continue upwards until they reach the glaciers of the main Alpine ridge. It was here, by the Italian border, that the famous "Ötzi", a Celt who died in this icy region 5,500 years ago, was discovered in 1991.

Obergurgl and nearby **Hochgurgl** are both ski resorts. From here cable-cars fan out in all directions towards the surrounding peaks. The toll road to the **Timmelsjoch**, the 2,474-metre (8,115-ft) pass connecting the valley with Italy, begins in Hochgurgl. The best view can be had from **Windegg**, at 2,080 metres (6,822 ft), which affords a panorama extending over the entire Gurgl Valley and part of the Gurgler Ferner. To the north one can see extensive sections of the Ötz Valley.

Since the Ötz Valley merely marks the eastern boundary of the Ötztal Alps, the **Pitztal** ⑳ (Pitz Valley) – which branches off from the upper Inn Valley some 8 km (5 miles) to the west – provides the first route into the heart of the mountains themselves. For long stretches it is a forbiddingly narrow gorge, only occasionally opening out into a sunny basin. The villages of **Wenns**, **Jerzens** and **St Leonhard** owe their new prosperity to skiing enthusiasts and the Glacier Road, constructed to provide access to the Mittelbergferner. The principal sight in the valley is the **Platzhaus** in Wenns, which is adorned with fine Renaissance murals.

The **Kauner Valley** in the west runs in a north–south direction through the Ötztal Alps. It branches off from the Inn Valley in an easterly direction south of Landeck near Prutz, soon turns towards the south and offers at its far end – near the Gepatsch reservoir – another glacier with skiing facilities beneath the slopes of the **Hochvernagtspitze** (3,540 metres/11,610 ft).

In the valley, the parish church in **Kaltenbrunn** was a place of pilgrimage as long ago as 1285. The Gothic chancel was completed in 1502, and the nave contains a domed Chapel of Miracles with a carved votive statue of the *Madonna with Child* (1400).

From Landeck to the Arlberg

Even in pre-Roman times there was a settlement at present-day **Landeck** ㉑, at the confluence of the rivers Sanna and Inn. During the 13th century, Duke Meinhard II of Tyrol had the existing fortress rebuilt in its present form. The fortress chapel, which dates from the same period, was adorned with frescoes during the first half of the 16th century. Today the castle houses a museum (open Jun–Oct: Tues–Sun; entrance fee). The most important architectural monument in the town is the parish church, in the Angedair district. The elaborate tracery of its windows and the network vaulting make this the most harmonious Gothic church in Tyrol. Inside there is the late-Gothic Schrofenstein Altarpiece.

Beyond Pians, a few kilometres west, the valley forks again; to the left opens up the **Paznaun Valley** with the Trisanna River, whilst the **Rosanna Valley** leads straight ahead, climbing towards the Arlberg. At the river confluence, the railway crosses the valley at a height of 85 metres (280 ft) by means of the famous **Trisanna Bridge**. In former times the Paznaun Valley was virtually cut off from the rest of the world. Nowadays, thanks to the tourism within the region, it has been opened up with the construction of the **Silvretta Alpine Road** (with a pass at an altitude of 2,035 metres/6,675 ft), and the development of skiing around Ischgl.

After the discovery of Ötzi, the well-preserved Stone-Age man, in the Ötztal Alps, several women asked to be impregnated with his 5,500-year-old frozen sperm. Unfortunately his preservation did not stretch that far, and the authorities were unable to oblige.

BELOW: church in the Ötztal.

The Arlberg

Skiers have also brought world fame to the **Arlberg**, which was once just a mountain with pine-covered slopes, Today it is a gigantic winter sports paradise, including **St Anton am Arlberg** ㉒ (30 km/18 miles west of Landeck), **Zürs** (15 km/9 miles further west) and **Lech** (5 km/3 miles beyond Zürs).

One hundred years ago the rural, farming existence – which for centuries had functioned satisfactorily on the Arlberg – was on the verge of extinction. Only technology and the development of skiing as a sport brought about the region's renaissance. First came the construction of the railway through the Arlberg, followed by the building of the Flexen Road (which reached Lech in 1900). But it was really the invention of skiing which led to the boom. A priest named Müller, from the Lech Valley, was the first to try out the new sport. Progress in the footsteps of the daring priest was rapid. The Arlberg Ski Club in St Christoph was founded in 1901, and Hannes Schneider from Stuben started to adapt techniques from Scandinavia to suit Alpine conditions. Stefan Kruckenhauser developed the parallel turn – now practised all over the world – and the *wedel* (a short, rapid turn), which makes skiing seem like child's play.

The skier's delight was until recently the bane of the driver. In winter the Arlberg Pass, which lies at 1,795 metres (5,885 ft), was frequently closed due to snowdrifts or the danger of avalanches. Only since the end of 1978 has the road tunnel, almost 14 km (9 miles) long, provided a year-round link.

So now motor travellers, too, can enjoy, in peace, the broad alpine meadows as well as the tunnels and avalanche galleries on the Flexen Road. They can also enjoy breathtaking views down into the **Klostertal** and towards the pretty village of **Stuben am Arlberg** *(see page 301).* ❏

Map on page 272

BELOW: off-piste skiing in the Arlberg.

THE KANDAHAR RACE

The Kandahar is one of the year's most anticipated World Cup downhill races – a breakneck affair of near-vertical skiing down the steep lower section of the Gampen/Kapall wall at St Anton. Curiously, it was an Englishman who helped to get the event started.

Sir Alfred Lunn, a ski enthusiast and travel agent who devised the sport of slalom racing, came to St Anton in 1927 at the invitation of local ski instructor Hannes Schneider. Schneider was himself a legendary figure: he had developed the modern feet-together, crouched-down style of downhill racing, taught Austrian troops to ski, written an early textbook and made an influential film on ski techniques.

Lunn and Schneider set to work developing the rules of a downhill event, and races began the following March. Snow conditions, organisational problems and World War II conspired to shift the event around and even to cancel it for a time. The Kandahar eventually returned to St Anton for good in the 1950s. (The exotic-sounding name, actually a city in Afghanistan, was a tip of the cap to the Earl of Kandahar, an acquaintance of Lunn's father.)

People in the Arlberg still remember the flying runs of local skier Karl Schranz, who used his local knowledge to beat the world's best nine times between 1957 and 1972.

VORARLBERG

Map
on page
290

*Reaching from the shores of the Bodensee to the Silvretta peaks,
this small state – Austria's western outpost – is home to a multitude
of religious buildings and magnificent mountain scenery*

or the Irish missionary Columban, who came to **Bregenz**  on the Bodensee
(Lake Constance) in AD 610 to convert the region to Christianity, the town
of *Brigantium* lay "as in a golden dish". What he described so vividly in
words is the same impression gained by a modern-day traveller approaching Bregenz in one of the ships of the Lake Constance Line, or surveying the town, lake,
Rhine Valley and Swiss Alps from the summit of the Pfänder.

The capital of Vorarlberg lies on a gently rising terrace on the shores of a wide
bay on the Bodensee. To the east the shell-shaped intrusion is sheltered by the
slopes of the Pfänder. To the southwest lies the Rhine, which once provided the
necessary protection against enemy attack from the plains beyond. It was precisely this protected position which encouraged the Celts to settle on the site.
Their village, *Brigantioi*, later became *Brigantium* under Roman occupation,
complete with forum, basilica, baths and temple. The Romans were the first to
build a fortified harbour. Following attacks by the Alemanni in the 3rd century
the Romans withdrew up the hillside to the strategically more easily defensible
site of what is now the Upper Town; here they built themselves a new fort.

After the retreat of the Romans in the middle of the 5th century, the Alemanni captured the town and with it the main and subsidiary valleys of the
Rhine. The new conquerors did not, however, establish
their rule from the town itself but chose Feldkirch, to
the south, where – as the counts of Montfort – they
built a fortress, the Schattenburg. In 1860 Bregenz
became the nominal capital of Vorarlberg, by virtue of
the creation of the first local parliament for the region,
which at that time was still a part of Tyrol. Only in
1918, however, did Bregenz become the official capital of the province.

The Lower Town

Bregenz's greatest claim to fame – and one for which
the town is now known all over the world – is the annual
Bregenz Festival, held on a specially constructed
floating stage *(see page 291)*. Nearby, the **Lower
Town** huddles on a mound of land deposited by the
lake. Apart from the railway station, it is characterised
by a series of Neoclassical local government buildings,
the regional military headquarters and the **Museum of
Vorarlberg** (Kornmarkt 1; open Tues–Sun; entrance
fee). In the Middle Ages the lake waters actually reached
as far as the foundation walls of the **Seekapelle** (Lake
Chapel), at the junction of Rathausstrasse and Anton-
Schneider-Strasse. In 1445 the first memorial to the
fallen soldiers of the Appenzell Civil War was erected
here. The present church was built in 1698 according
to the plans drawn up by Christian Thumb. Externally
its most remarkable feature is an octagonal tower with

PRECEDING PAGES:
pastoral idyll.
LEFT: the faces
of Vorarlberg.
BELOW:
Lech am Arlberg
in the spring.

BELOW: Bregenz,
on the edge of
the Bodensee.

an onion dome; inside, its high altar is an unusual example of late-Renaissance craftsmanship. The work, completed in 1615, has a central shrine decorated with a Crucifixion group; on the upper section you can see the figures of St John the Baptist and St John the Evangelist.

A granary was built on to the north side of the chapel in 1686 by Hans Kuen. The chapel was then converted into the **Town Hall**, completed in 1810. Only in 1898 did the broad front acquire its present-day neo-Renaissance facade.

The most impressive building in the Lower Town is without doubt the **Herz-Jesu-Kirche** (Sacred Heart Church). It stands near the Pfänder cable-car station and is characterised by twin pointed spires. The largest neo-Gothic building in Vorarlberg, it was built under the supervision of Stuttgart architect Joseph Cades, and was completed in 1908. The harmonious design of the west front reveals the inspiration of the medieval brick churches of north Germany. Within, too, the architect has followed these examples, constructing a basilica with ribbed vaulting in accordance with the strict rules laid down by the church designers of the past.

The Upper Town

If you stroll along Maurachgasse towards the **Upper Town**, you will pass the site of the former Roman port. Passing through the **Unteres Tor** gateway, you will enter the medieval town centre. Haug von Tübingen, later known as Hugo of Montfort, had this area laid out in a regular pattern on the ruins of the Roman fortress. Sections of the town wall which formed part of medieval Bregenz have survived to this day.

The most notable building in the Upper Town – **Martinsturm** (St Martin's Tower) – also serves as the local landmark. The first count of Bregenz used it

Map on page 290

as a tithe barn – in other words, as his tax office. During the 14th century two storeys were converted into a double chapel. Finally, by 1601, Benedetto Prato from Roveredo had added the flamboyant canopy to the tower and topped it with its lantern-festooned onion dome.

Passing along the Meissnersteige, we come down to the Thalbachgrund, opposite which stands the **Parish Church of St Gall**. Its origins date from an early church founded here by the missionaries St Gall and St Columban. The present building was completed by 1737 under the supervision of Franz Anton Beer, using some structural elements from the older edifice. The West Tower, constructed in 1480, acquired its Baroque gable in 1673. The single-naved interior seems exceptionally wide because of its relatively low ceiling; it was elaborately decorated in the Rococo style by Abraham Bader.

The location of the Upper Town betrays the fact that, at least in early times, the citizens of Bregenz had no strong links to the lake in spite of the town's picturesque situation on the eastern bay. No important buildings were erected on the lake shore, and at the end of the 19th century few protests were voiced when a jungle of railway tracks wormed their way on to the land between the town and the lake. Since that time, those wishing to visit the lakeside or board one of the white ships of the Lake Constance Line must use the only railway crossing. A 9-km (5-mile) path along the lakeshore from Lochau in the north to the mouth of the Bregenzer Ache in the west has proved little compensation.

Nestled in the meadowland to the west of town (and beyond the Seebühne) is the former Cistercian **Abbey of Mehrerau**, founded in 1097 and a bastion of the Counter-Reformation. The neo-Romanesque abbey church, rebuilt in 1962, is a high-ceilinged hall with a transept and a semicircular chancel, impressive

Empress Maria Theresa donated 1,500 Gulden for the high altar in the Parish Church. As a token of gratitude, one of the shepherdesses in the altarpiece of the Adoration of the Magi *was painted in her likeness.*

BELOW: an opera production on the Seebühne.

THE SEEBÜHNE

Reaching out onto the Bodensee just behind the Bregenz casino, the Seebühne (lake stage) is famous throughout Austria and one of Europe's most interesting opera venues. The tiered banks of seats, which can accommodate 6,800, rest firmly on dry land, but the square performance space itself floats on the lake – creating a stage with the entire Bodensee (and its weather) as a rather dramatic backdrop to the operas being sung upon it.

In 1946 the director of the Vorarlberg State Theatre constructed the stage on a raft anchored in one of the old harbour basins. Mozart's lyrical drama *Bastien and Bastienne* was performed, as well as a ballet to his *Eine Kleine Nachtmusik*. The little raft was later replaced by a floating stage 60 metres (200 ft) wide and 40 metres (130 ft) deep, some 25 metres (85 ft) from the shore.

The designers here put great care into the construction of sets on the stage, spending months hammering and painting away before unveiling them to appreciative crowds at the Bregenz Festival each summer. In 1999, they erected an enormous (and startlingly lifelike) skeleton holding open the pages of a giant book – the book of human accounts, perhaps – for the two-year-long run of Verdi's opera *Un Ballo in Maschera*.

Angelika Kauffmann (1741–1807), who spent her youth in Schwarzenberg, was one of the few famous pre-20th-century women artists. At the peak of her success in London, she was a founder member of the Royal Academy and was rumoured to have had an affair with Joshua Reynolds.

in its simplicity. The right aisle wall is broken up by three chapels, each containing an important work of art: a triple portrait of St Anne (*circa* 1515), an *Annunciation* (second half of the 15th century) and a triptych with Crucifixion scenes from the end of the 15th century.

In the Bregenzerwald

In 830 the abbot of Reichenau Abbey, Wahlafried Strabo, described the Bregenz hinterland and the primeval forests along the Bregenzer Ache as far as the Hochtannberg Pass as a "wilderness devoid of human habitation". It was not until the middle of the 10th century that the counts of Bregenz started to use these forests as hunting grounds and permitted settlers to make their homes here.

In the first half of the 19th century a systematic network of footpaths was finally created, although proper access was not guaranteed until 1912, when the Bregenzerwald Railway reached as far as Bezau. The present-day road network was not built until after World War II. Today it is possible to drive from Dornbirn across the Bödele to Schwarzenberg, across the Furka Ridge or the Faschina Ridge to Damüls or from the Lech Valley across the Hochtannberg into the Valley of the Bregenzer Ache. From Bregenz there is a direct link across the gorge of the Schwarzbach torrent to **Alberschwende**, which sits at the base of the Brüggelekopf. The village square in front of the church is adorned by a linden tree that is reputedly 1,000 years old.

Hittisau, which possesses more than 100 privately-owned meadows, and **Sibratsgfäll** – the youngest community in the Bregenzerwald, reached by a 10-km (6-mile) detour southeast – are ideal destinations for holidaymakers in search of a relaxing atmosphere. **Langenegg ❷**, just west of Hittisau, has an exceptionally

BELOW:
village musicians.

fine church. Built in 1775, the interior was decorated during the following year by Johann Michael Koneberg. The nave contains murals depicting the Nativity, the Marriage and the Assumption of the Virgin Mary. The fresco under the balcony, depicting Christ expelling the money-changers from the temple, includes (somewhat incongruously) the figure of a woman carrying a basket of eggs and dressed in the unmistakable traditional costume of the Bregenzerwald.

In the village of **Schwarzenberg**, 10 km (6 miles) southwest on the road to the Bödele summit, stands the house where the artist Angelika Kauffmann lived as a child. In 1757, when she was 16 years old, she painted the pictures of the apostles on the walls of the nave of the Parish Church of the Trinity. In 1802 she presented the village church with a picture that adorns the high altar to this day, the *Coronation of the Virgin by the Holy Trinity*.

The market town of **Bezau**, southeast across the mountain, is one of the principal communities of the Bregenzerwald. Its Museum of Local History is worth visiting for its exhibition of folklore. The terminus of the Bregenzerwald Railway, long since axed, is marked today only by an old steam locomotive. **Mellau**, which lies a little further up the valley, is overshadowed by the lofty summit of the Kanisfluh. Its five rock faces, with a total length of 6 km (4 miles), fall precipitously down to the valley from a height of 1,300 metres (4,265 ft).

Damüls ❸, at the foot of the Glatthorn, was first and foremost a Walser settlement. According to a document dated 1313, the Walser people received the mountain valley in fief from the counts of Montfort. In 1484 they had the massive stone **Parish Church of St Nikolaus** built by Rolle Maiger from Röthis. The flat wooden coffered ceiling was decorated in 1693 by Johann Purtscher with scenes from the Life of the Virgin. The walls are a poor man's bible:

Map on page 290

BELOW: dawn on the Bodensee.

frescoes on the north wall depict the Passion of Christ; the apse portrays Christ at the Last Judgment with the Sword of Justice; scenes on the south wall depict Miracles of Compassion. The early Baroque elements in the church date from 1630 onwards. Erasmus Kern created the high altar and its figures, as well as the Plague Altar in the north wall.

Back on Road 200, the last village of any size in the valley of the Bregenzer Ache is **Schoppernau** ❹. The desolate nature of this upland valley is reflected in the name, which means "naked meadows". Even in early times its inhabitants were forced to seek their living elsewhere. Nonetheless, the woodland dwellers had a grand church built during the second half of the 18th century. Its frescoes and stucco date from 1796.

The final hamlet within the valley proper is **Schröcken**, 10 km (6 miles) southeast, which is also an old Walser settlement dating from the 14th century. In 1863 all the buildings were destroyed by a fire – even the church did not remain unscathed. Beyond Schröcken the road winds uphill to the 1,675-metre (5,495-ft) **Hochtannberg Pass**. On the other side lies Warth, in the Lech Valley, the last village before the Tyrol border. Providing there is no danger of avalanches when you arrive, you can drive from here into the bustling world of the Arlberg.

A Bavarian valley in Austria

The **Kleines Walsertal** ❺, situated north of the Hochtannberg Pass, is accessible from Austria only by foot. By road it can be reached through the Bavarian section of the Allgäu, via Oberstdorf. Because of its location, in 1871 Hungary and the German Reich agreed that the Kleines Walsertal should become part of the German Customs Union. Today the valley appears more German than Austrian in character, although it remains officially part of Austrian territory.

BELOW: the Kleines Walsertal in winter.

The largest village in the Kleines Walsertal is **Riezlern**, located 18 km (11 miles) southwest of Obertsdorf; it contains a Museum of Walser History, a casino and various mountain lifts. Hirschegg and Mittelberg, just southwest, are also primarily tourist centres. The oldest parish church in the valley can be found in Mittelberg. Dedicated in 1390, it was extended in 1463 and 1694. Its 15th-century frescoes depict the Creation of the World and scenes from the Life of Christ.

Along the Rhine

The first town up the Rhine from Bregenz is also the biggest and youngest in Vorarlberg. **Dornbirn** ❻ was formed in 1901 by the amalgamation of four villages. For this reason, between townhouses and factories you will repeatedly come across single farms, large gardens and open fields. The name Dornbirn was first mentioned as long ago as 815, when it was known as Torrinpuirron. The present centre is dominated by the **Parish Church of St Martin**, completed in the Neoclassical style in 1840. It has a temple-like porch with six Ionic columns. The fresco in the nave portrays the Last Judgment. Near St Martin's stands the **Rotes Haus** (Red House), the town landmark. Built in 1634, it is a typical Rhine valley dwelling with a brick-built base surmounted by an ornate log-cabin construction.

For nature-lovers Dornbirn can offer two attractions: firstly, the refurbished **Vorarlberg Exhibition of Natural History** (open daily; entrance fee; tel: (05572) 23 235-0) – a remarkable collection explaining the area's geology as well as its wealth of fascinating flora and fauna – and secondly the **Rappenloch Gorge**, a 60-metre (200-ft) deep ravine that was gouged out by the Dornbirner Ache when the Rhine glacier melted.

In the early Middle Ages, the Alemanni advanced as far as **Hohenems ❼** – 7 km (4 miles) southwest on Road 190 – in their struggles against the Rhaeto-Romanic tribes. As early as the 9th century a fortress was built here to guard the frontier. The Emperor Barbarossa gave it to the knight of Ems, who extended it into a mighty Imperial castle. As the castle itself grew in importance, so too did the Ems family, until Marcus Sitticus became prince-archbishop of Salzburg in 1612. As bishop of Konstanz, long before he was summoned to the Salzach, he began to build a new palace in the valley.

The centre section of the present palace (**Schloss Hohenems**) was completed in 1576. The two side wings and the curtain wall on the rock side were finished in 1610. The magnificent main facade is divided into 11 sections; the doorway in the centre bears the arms of Marcus Sitticus.

Connected by a passageway to the palace is the **Parish Church**, completed in 1581. The most important element in its interior is a Renaissance high altar with a late medieval *Coronation of the Virgin* in the central shrine. **Glopper Castle** is what is left of the former fortress on the mountainside. The late-Gothic complex consists of an inner fortress protected by an outer castle, moat and ramparts. The **Town Hall**, too, owes its origins to Marcus Sitticus. He commissioned its construction in 1567 as a guesthouse on the occasion of a synod in Konstanz.

Map on page 290

TIP

Every summer, as part of the Bregenz Festival, Schloss Hohenems plays host to a series of concerts. They are performed in the castle's beautiful Renaissance courtyard.

BELOW: the centre of Dornbirn, with the Church of St Martin.

Five kilometres (3 miles) to the south, **Götzis** ❽, first mentioned in 842 as *Cazzeses*, owed its early economic importance to its trading rights, dispensed by the Montforts. What is known today as the **Old Parish Church** was thus dedicated in 1514. It enchants the visitor even now with its richly decorated frescoed walls. The left wall of the nave displays scenes from the Life of Christ and the choir arch has a rather grim *Last Judgment*. The tabernacle is the work of Esaias Gruber from Lindau and dates from 1597. The nearby daughter church, dedicated to St Arbogast, has a wooden porch containing a cycle of pictures by Leonhard Werder, painted in 1659 and portraying scenes from the legendary life of the saint, who became bishop of Strasbourg and died in 1550.

The market community of **Rankweil** ❾, further south, has grown up around a picturesque hill, which was a holy place for the Rhaetians as long ago as 1500 BC and subsequently supported a Celtic and then a Roman fort. At the start of the 9th century the bishops of Chur had the first chapel built here. From then until the end of the 15th century, it was extended to form the present **Castle Church**. Its most valuable treasure is the silver cross in the chancel apse.

Medieval Feldkirch

It was Louis, king of the East Franks, who gave the next town, **Feldkirch** ❿, its name. In the year 909 he gave "*ad Veldkirichum*" – the settlement at the forking of the roads to the Arlberg and the canton of Grisons – to the monastery of St Gallen. The village only began to prosper, however, when Hugo of Montfort moved his residence from Bregenz to Schattenburg Castle in Feldkirch, and then, around the year 1200, had a brand new town built in the shadow of his fortress.

In spite of a colourful political past, Feldkirch has been able to retain its regular medieval plan as well as the picturesque squares enclosed by ancient houses with creeper-clad arbours. The town wall has suffered from the passage of time since the Middle Ages, but its course can still be made out everywhere by virtue of the numerous towers. The finest example of the old fortifications is the **Cats' Tower**, built in 1500. It is 40 metres (130 ft) high and has a circumference of 38 metres (125 ft). It was originally crowned by battlements, which gave way to a belfry during the 17th century. The bell, weighing 7.5 tonnes, is the largest in the whole province.

The square in front of the cathedral – now one of the busiest centres of life in the town – was until 1380 the site of the local cemetery. The **Cathedral of St Nicholas** is a double-naved late-Gothic construction with an asymmetrically placed tower at the end of the north aisle. The church was completed in 1487 by Hans Sturn, the master-builder from Göfis. The chancel as we know it today has a number of Renaissance features and was added to the church in about 1520. The most notable treasure contained within is a picture showing the Descent from the Cross painted in 1521 by Wolf Huber.

Schattenburg Castle was built by Count Haug von Tübingen in 1185. In 1200, in line with his new place of residence, he changed his name to Hugo of Montfort. He was responsible for the 23-metre (75-ft) high keep which forms the heart of the complex as it stands

BELOW: in the courtyard at Schattenburg Castle.

Map on page 290

today. In 1436, after the Montfort family died out, the castle came into the possession of the Habsburgs. Emperor Maximilian I had it extended to its present aspect in about 1500. The castle now houses a **Museum of Local History** (open Dec–Oct: Tues–Sun; entrance fee; tel: (05522) 71 982).

The Walgau

Beyond the Ill gorge lies the **Walgau**, the basin-shaped section of the Ill Valley between Feldkirch and Bludenz. Hemmed in to the south by the Rätikon Massif and to the north by the Walser Ridge and the foothills of the Lechtaler Alps, the valley's name recalls the Rhaeto-Romanic tribes who were the first settlers, for they were known to the Alemanni as the Walser. They built their homesteads on the cones of scree deposited by the gushing mountain streams, or on the mountain terraces formed by the glaciers.

The best example of such a settlement is **Göfis**, mentioned in a document of 850 as *Segavio*. Even in those days it had its own church and was part of the king's property. In 1450 local son Hans Sturn, who built the cathedral in Feldkirch, was allowed to build a new church for his fellow-citizens. In 1972, however, the edifice, with the exception of the chancel, was demolished to make way for a new building. This is a particularly good example of a successful symbiosis between ancient and modern building styles.

Just south on Road 193, once-strategic **Bludenz ⓫** lies at the end of the Walgau, a short distance before the **Kloster Valley** branches off from the Ill. It was founded by Count Rudolf von Werdenberg, who gained lands in the Grosses Walsertal, in the Kloster Valley and the Montafon when the Montfort family heritage was divided up. To protect his domain he built a fortress in Bludenz

TIP

Just north of Bludenz a cable-car climbs to the Muttersberg, which, at 1,384 metres (4,541 ft), affords breathtaking views of the towering Rätikon and Silvretta mountains to the south.

BELOW: the streams of Vorarlberg are a paradise for kayakers.

and – in the manner established by his relatives in Feldkirch – started to lay out a town according to a regular grid pattern. His goal was to extract certain advantages from the traffic passing through the Arlberg. In 1394 the last of the Werdenbergs was forced to sell his seigneurial rights to the Habsburgs.

The Werdenbergs' fortress stood on the rock which is crowned today by the Baroque-style **Schloss Gayenhofen**. It was completed in 1752 by an Austrian governor on the site of the earlier stronghold. Today it houses the district officers' quarters. The prominent position on the castle rock was also chosen as the site of the **Parish Church of St Laurence**. Since the church was mentioned as early as 830, it seems to have an even earlier claim to the place than the castle. The present building was completed in 1514, the tower dating from 1670.

More typical of the historical aspects of the Walgau is the small-scale **Church of St Martin** in nearby **Ludesch**. Completed in 1480 in the Gothic style, the building has a fascinating collection of treasures which make it one of the most interesting examples of sacred architecture in Vorarlberg. The high altar was created in 1629 and combines various Gothic elements with Renaissance details.

Where the Walser once lived

The high-lying valleys to the west of the Arlberg were inhabited at the beginning of the last millennium by Rhaeto-Romanic farmers and hunters, although their settlements did not extend beyond the valley floors. This pattern did not change until about 1400, when Germanic Walser tribes from the Upper Rhône Valley drove out the Rhaetians, taking possession of their lands and building their own settlements not only in the valleys but also on the upland slopes.

BELOW: hang-gliding in the Vorarlberg.

Many of their villages were situated in the **Grosses Walsertal** ⓬, a valley

some 25 km (15 miles) long, which extends in a northeasterly direction from Ludesch. It is demarcated on its sunny side by the Walser Ridge, and on the shadow side by the Lechtaler Alps. The valley gradually climbs from the depths of the Walgau to the 1,850-metre (6,070-ft) **Schadona Pass**, through which one can reach Schröcken on the Hochtannberg Pass. Two roads provide access to the Grosses Walsertal. One winds along the shadow side of the valley from Ludesch to Raggal; the other opens up the sunny side from Thüringen to the Faschina Ridge and the way to Damüls on the edge of the Bregenzer Wald.

Up the Walsers' valley

The hamlet of **Raggal**, 7 km (4 miles) north of Bludenz, is one of the Rhaetian settlements which was taken over by the Walser. Its **Parish Church** has its origins in a Rhaetian chapel dating from the 12th century. The Gothic chancel is the result of an extension added in 1460. The stucco ceiling, elaborately decorated with painted creepers, was completed in 1899.

The remote **Priory of St Gerold** is worth a detour. It marks the site of a hermitage to which a nobleman once retired. In the year 949 he was pardoned by the abbot of the Abbey of Einsiedeln (in Switzerland). As a counter-gesture the hermit gave his cell to the abbey, which founded a monastic settlement on the site. The priory experienced its Golden Age in the 18th century when it was even able to purchase the High Court from the emperor in Vienna. Today, there are seminars, concerts and theatrical productions put on here.

The principal village in the valley is **Sonntag**, which consists of a number of districts, hamlets and isolated settlements. House 17 in the Flecken district contains the Grosses Walsertal **Museum of Local History**. The furnished rooms

Map
on page
290

In spring the cattle are put out to pasture on the lower slopes.

BELOW: skiers heading for the hills.

The Arlberg is one of the country's prime locations for snowboarding.

and workshops provide an excellent insight into the rural life of the Walser as well as their customs and costumes. **Buchburg** is the best starting point for mountain walks in all directions. The surrounding area is regarded with good reason as the largest nature conservation area in Vorarlberg.

Here you will still find flower-covered mountain meadows, where edelweiss and gentians of every variety grow, and where you may even find wild orchids in bloom. On the rocky slopes above, are the homes of the golden eagle and the chamois – all talk of a threatened ecology seems far away.

The highest settlement in the Grosses Walsertal is the scattered village of **Fontanella**, about 2 km (1¼ miles) north of Sonntag. Until 1806 it formed a part of the parish of Damüls, on the other side of the Faschina Ridge. Until the middle of the 17th century its inhabitants had to attend the larger village's church. In 1673, however, they were allowed to build their own place of worship. In recent years the district of Faschina has become a popular ski centre.

The Brandner and Kloster valleys

Brandnertal, which lies south of Bludenz, opposite the Grosses Walsertal, was formerly colonised by the Walser. A community of 12 families received the valley in fief in 1347. They built the hamlet of **Brand**, 10 km (6 miles) southwest of Bludenz and close to the three-country point – where the borders of Austria, Liechtenstein and Switzerland meet. It has become a popular tourist centre thanks to the nearby **Lünersee**, which lies at an altitude of almost 2,000 metres (6,560 ft), and the 2,965-metre (9,725-ft) **Schesaplana**, the highest mountain in the Rätikon range.

From Bludenz the main valley seems to continue in a straight line southeast. This is true geographically, for the River Ill does indeed spring from this part of the valley. However, it is the shorter **Klostertal** ⑬ (Kloster Valley), which runs from east to west that is the route taken by the railway, the main road and the motorway heading for the **Arlberg Pass**. Only 1,795 metres (5,885 ft) high, the pass was for a long time the only east–west link between the Rhine and the Inn, and the only route from the Austrian motherland to Vorarlberg.

It is clear that the traffic to the pass dominated life in the Klostertal from the earliest times. As the way was difficult and dangerous, Hugo of Montfort instructed the Knights of St John of Jerusalem to establish and maintain a hospice near the pass to provide travellers with accommodation and assistance. This hospice was called **Klösterle**, and soon gave its name to the entire valley and the village which sprang up in its shadow. Heinrich Findelkind followed this good example in 1386 with the foundation of the St Christopher Brotherhood, which organised searches to find travellers who had strayed from the path.

The real link to the modern world came in 1884, when the **Arlberg Railway** from Bludenz to Landeck was inaugurated. The section between Langen and St Anton required a 10-km (6-mile) tunnel. It provided the first all-weather link between Tyrol and Vorarlberg. The road followed the trail blazed by the railway with the opening of the **Arlberg Road Tunnel** in 1978. Its length of 14 km (9 miles) makes it the longest road tunnel in Austria.

BELOW: hikers in the Arlberg.

Since the approach road to the Arlberg Road Tunnel is a motorway that bypasses the villages of the Klostertal, the latter have returned to their former tranquillity, affording sufficient leisure to enjoy the sights they have to offer. The first of these can be found in **Braz**, the oldest permanent settlement in the valley, just east of Bludenz. The name comes from the Rhaetian *Prats*, which means "broad meadow". The **Parish Church of Innerbraz** was rebuilt in the Baroque style at the end of the 18th century by Tyrolean artists. The frescoes on the vaulting are the work of the artist Carl Klausner.

As long ago as the 9th century, **Dalaas**, to the east, was the centre of the Rhaetian iron mining industry. The Walser took over the excavations, but decided to dig for silver instead. They smelted their finds in **Danöfen**, further up the valley. The village's name is directly derived from the location "by the ovens".

In **Langen,** another 10 km (6 miles) east, both the railway and the main road disappear into the mountain, leaving **Stuben am Arlberg** ⓮, an attractive, sleepy place, a little further east up the valley. The village's name stems from the room maintained by the Knights of St John as a place where travellers could warm themselves. The little church has a Gothic chancel, a Baroque nave and a lovely *Madonna* dating from about 1630. Above Stuben, the road finally wends its way to the crest of the Arlberg. To the north, the Flexenpass provides access to **Zürs** and **Lech am Arlberg** across almost vertical rock faces.

The Montafon

If instead of taking the Klostertal you continue up the Ill River southeast of Bludenz, you enter a region known as the Montafon, which the commercially-minded Vorarlberg community claims, with some justification, to have made

Map on page 290

BELOW: misty view of the Flexenpass above Lech.

TIP

A good one-day hike from Bielerhöhe (the top of the Silvretta Road) takes you past the Silvretta Reservoir to the Wiesbadener Hütte, surrounded by 3,000-metre (9,840-ft) peaks. Here you can have lunch on the terrace, and then head back to the road.

into an Alpine Park. **Schruns-Tschagguns**, **St Gallenkirch**, **Gaschurn** and **Partenen** sport pretty Montafon-style houses, ski-lifts of all descriptions – and, in every season, an assortment of Austrian and foreign holidaymakers.

The Montafon lies directly in front of the impassable barrier formed by the giants of the Silvretta Range. In former times the region was poverty-stricken despite the existence of iron ore and silver deposits in the mountains. The profits from mining filled the coffers of the local feudal lords, the bishops of Chur and the Fugger clan of Augsburg. For this reason the area contains few major architectural masterpieces or works of art.

The one exception is the ancient community of **Bartholomäberg** ⓯. Not only is it the oldest village in the region, it also possesses the most important church in the valley. The **Parish Church of St Bartholomew** existed even in Roman times. Its 12th-century processional cross is the most valuable Romanesque work of art in Vorarlberg. The present church is Baroque in style and was completed in 1743.

Nearby **Schruns** was the seat of the local court during Maria Theresa's reign. It was also once the terminus of the railway line. Today this is unused except on special occasions when trips are arranged on old steam engines. There are, however, plenty of cable-cars and hotels in the town. The **Montafon Museum of Local History** (open Jun–Oct: Tues–Sat; Nov–May: Tues, Fri & Sat; entrance fee) provides an insight into the natural and human history of the valley.

Mule tracks and Alpine roads

BELOW:
traditional outfits in the Montafon.

The highest permanently inhabited village in the Montafon today is **Gargellen** ⓰, at 1,423 metres (4,669 ft). It is situated in a side valley, about 15 km (9 miles) south of Schruns on Road 192. Its name, derived from the Romansch language,

means mountain torrent. What was once a miners' summer encampment has become a popular holiday village, bearing not the slightest sign of its former poverty. In any case, the path up to the 2,200-metre (7,220-ft) **Schlappinerjoch** follows an ancient shepherds' trail, which continues across the Swiss border to Klosters in the Prättigau. The valley and ridge represent the geographical boundary between the Rätikon and Silvretta mountains.

There were also once ancient footpaths leading from **Partenen**, further up the Montafon Valley. One mule track led across the Zeinisjoch to the Tyrol; a second, via the Vermuntpass, into Switzerland. The Romans used the Zeinisjoch, whilst Swiss farmers drove cattle across the Vermuntpass to summer pastures in the meadows of the Montafon. Mountain ramblers follow in their tracks to this day.

Hydroelectric power stations are as important to the Montafon as road traffic is to the Klostertal. In 1953 the Montafon and the Paznaun Valley in Tyrol were linked by the **Silvretta Reservoir**, which lies at an altitude of 2,036 metres (6,680 ft). The reservoir is located exactly on the watershed between the two valleys. Here the River Ill, fed by the Silvretta glaciers, runs precisely along the European watershed between the Rhine and the Danube. As it seemed unable to make up its mind in which direction to flow at this point, it was necessary to construct dams on both sides. The road built to serve the station, the **Silvretta Hochalpenstrasse** ⓱ (High Alpine Road), has become a real attraction. It is constructed to a very high standard and leads into a magnificent section of the High Alps, where rocks and glaciers form a harmonious unity seldom encountered in these mountains. South of the reservoir no fewer than 74 peaks rise above the 3,000-metre (9,840-ft) mark. The top section of the High Alpine Road is a toll road maintained by the Vorarlberg Ill Power Authority. ❑

Map on page 290

Shepherding skills are expected at a very young age.

BELOW:
not recommended
for beginners.

INSIGHT GUIDES
Travel Tips

✴ INSIGHT GUIDES Phonecard

One global card to keep travellers in touch. Easy. Convenient. Saves you time and money.

It's a global phonecard

Save up to 70%* on international calls from over 55 countries

Free 24 hour global customer service

Recharge your card at any time via customer service or online

It's a message service

Family and friends can send you voice messages for free.

Listen to these messages using the phone* or online

Free email service - you can even listen to your email over the phone*

It's a travel assistance service

24 hour emergency travel assistance – if and when you need it.

Store important travel documents online in your own secure vault

For more information, call rates, and all Access Numbers in over 55 countries, (check your destination is covered) go to **www.insightguides.ekit.com** or call Customer Service.

JOIN now and receive US$ 5 bonus when you join for US$ 20 or more.

Join today at

www.insightguides.ekit.com

When requested use ref code: **INSAD0103**

OR SIMPLY FREE CALL 24 HOUR CUSTOMER SERVICE

UK	0800 376 1705
USA	1800 706 1333
Canada	1800 808 5773
Australia	1800 11 44 78
South Africa	0800 997 285

THEN PRESS ⓪

For all other countries please go to "Access Numbers" at **www.insightguides.ekit.com**

* Retrieval rates apply for listening to messages. Savings based on using a hotel or payphone and calling to a landline. Correct at time of printing 01.03

(INS001)

powered by ◉ *ekit*

"The easiest way to make calls and receive messages around the world"

CONTENTS

Getting Acquainted

The Place

Area: 83,838 sq. km (32,370 sq. miles).
Capital: Vienna.
Highest Mountain: Grossglockner. 3,797 metres (12,455 ft).
Population: 8 million, of which around 1.6 million live in Vienna.
Language: German.
Religion: Predominantly Roman Catholic; smaller numbers of Protestants and Muslims (5 percent each).
Time zone: Central European Time (GMT plus one hour).
Currency: Euro.
Weights & Measures: Metric.
Electricity: AC 220 volts.
International dialling code: 43.

Austria borders Germany and the Czech Republic in the north, Hungary in the east, Slovenia and Italy in the south, and Switzerland and Liechtenstein in the west. It has a total surface area of 83,838 sq. km (32,370 sq. miles) and extends over 525 km (326 miles) from east to west, and from north to south between 46 km (28 miles) at its narrowest point and 265 km (165 miles) at its widest. Vienna, the federal capital, has a population of around 1.6 million.

Topography

The Alps cover as much as two-thirds of the country, tapering off into the plateau of Upper and Lower Austria and the plains of Burgenland.

Eastern Austria consists mostly of plains, hills, forests and the green, vineyard-covered valley of the Danube River. The Central Alps, of which the Grossglockner at 3,797 metres (12,455 ft) is the highest peak, constitute a stunning display of the country's natural beauty, not to mention the lovely lakes of Salzkammergut and Carinthia; this is where skiing, hiking and touring are most prevalent. To the west, the mountains and valleys sometimes become sharp, dark and foreboding (as in the Ötzal) before dropping away at Lake Konstanz just before the Swiss and German borders. Southern Austria consists of still more ranges of limestone mountains, including a group of Alps which share the border with Italy. Warm-water lakes are characteristic of this region.

Climate

The Alps cover most of the land in Austria and play a decisive role in determining the country's different climatic conditions. The weather on the northern edge of the Alps is Central-European for the most part, which means that even during the usually lovely summers you can expect quite a bit of precipitation. South of the Alps, in Carinthia, the climate is almost Mediterranean – warmer temperatures and less rainfall. In the Alps themselves summers are hot and winters are cold and snowy, closing many routes; proceed with caution whenever driving in the high mountains. Also note that late winter and early spring bring dangerous avalanches to the mountains. The eastern part of the country has a continental climate – Burgenland is under the influence of the Panonian Plain, which causes hot summers and freezing winters.

Government

Austria is divided into nine provinces: Vienna, Lower Austria, Burgenland, Upper Austria, Styria, Carinthia, Salzburg, Tyrol and Vorarlberg. The country is a democratic republic governed by two houses: the National Assembly, composed of 185 members, and the Upper House with 58 members. Together, they constitute the Federal Assembly. The voting system is based on proportional representation and every four years the government is elected into office by secret ballot.

Austrian provinces enjoy a large amount of autonomy; each is led by an official elected by the provincial parliament. Whereas the president is the head of state, the government is led by the federal chancellor.

The Economy

The tourism industry is vital to the economic well-being of the country. Without its income, the balance of trade would certainly show a deficit.

Austria has a modern and well-developed industrial base: the electronic, chemical and textile industries are flourishing. Food and forestry are also important.

On the Styrian Erz Mountain near Leoben, iron ore is mined; it is then processed into iron and steel in the VOEST-Alpine, Austria's largest industrial complex.

Although oil has been found north of Vienna, most of the country's energy is produced by hydroelectric power stations. The abundance of power allows Austria to export electricity.

Vienna Average Temperatures

These are average figures for the city. In summer, the temperature can reach 35°C (95°F) and in winter it can get as low as –20°C (–4°F).	**May:**	14°C (57°F)
	June:	18°C (64°F)
	July:	19°C (66°F)
	August:	19°C (66°F)
January: −1°C (30°F)	**September:**	15°C (59°F)
February: 2°C (36°F)	**October:**	9°C (48°F)
March: 4°C (39°F)	**November:**	3°C (37°F)
April: 7°C (45°F)	**December:**	–1°C (30°F)

Planning the Trip

Visas & Passports

Austria relies heavily on tourism, and immigration and customs formalities are fairly relaxed. Citizens of most European nations are not required to possess a visa in order to enter the country, only a valid passport. Non-European visitors also require a passport, but many (from Canada, the US and Australia for example) don't need a visa; contact the Austrian embassy in your home country for specific details.

You can also find information at www.traveldocs.com/at/index

Customs Regulations

Austria applies the same customs regulations as those in other European Union nations. There is no customs duty on items intended for personal use and gifts up to a total value of €175. This can include two cameras, a video camera, a laptop computer, a radio, a portable television set and a portable stereo.

The following free import allowances are for persons over 17:

Entering from another country:
200 cigarettes or 50 cigars or 100 cigarillos or 250 grs tobacco. 2 litres of alcohol max. 22 vol. percent, or 1 litre of more than 22 vol. percent, and 2 litres of wine. 50g of perfume and 0.25 litres of toilet water.

Entering from an EU country where the goods were bought with tax paid:
800 cigarettes, 400 cigarillos, 200 cigars or 1 kg of tobacco; 10 litres of spirits, 90 litres of

wine (for sparkling wine the maximum is 60 litres) and 110 litres of beer.

Visitors entering Austria by car are not required to obtain any special customs documents for their vehicles. The import and export of Austrian and foreign currency is unrestricted, although sums above €10,000 must be declared if they are not to be used for tourist purposes.

Health & Insurance

Austria is, generally speaking, a very safe, clean and healthy country; no special vaccinations are necessary, water won't need to be boiled, and healthcare is free to EU residents. Nevertheless, it's always prudent to buy health and travel insurance with medical cover prior to a trip – especially since reimbursement for medical expenses involves mounds of paperwork.

If you are going to ski, hike, do water sports, etc, check that your insurance covers accidents in such sports – you may need to purchase a "rider" covering these activities. The same holds true for travel with a laptop computer. Bring proof of your insurance policy in case you need to show it to doctors, police, hospital attendants, etc. Also carry a list of emergency numbers in your wallet or purse *(see page 312).*

Embassies Abroad

Australia: 12 Talbot St, ACT 2603, Canberra, tel: (02) 6295 1533.
Belgium: Place du Champ du Mars 5, 1050 Ixelles, tel: (02) 289 0700.
Canada: 445 Wilbrod Street, Ottawa, K1N 6M7, tel: (613) 789 1444.
Denmark: Solundsvej 1, 2100 Copenhagen, tel: 3929 4141.
France: 6 Rue Fabert, F 75007 Paris, tel: (01) 4063 3063.
Germany: Stauffenbergstrasse 1, 10785 Berlin, tel: (030) 20287-0.

Great Britain: 18 Belgrave Mews, London, SW1X 8HU, tel: (020) 7235 3731.
Italy: Via Pergolesi 3, 00198 Rome, tel: (06) 844 0141.
Netherlands: Van Alkemadelaan 342, The Hague, 2597 AS, tel: (070) 324 5470.
Switzerland: Kirchenfeldstrasse 77–79, 3006 Bern, tel: (031) 356 5252.
USA: 3524 International Court NW, Washington DC 20008, tel: (202) 895 6700.

Public Holidays

- **1 January** New Year's Day
- **6 January** Epiphany
- **April** Easter Monday
- **1 May** May Day
- **May** Ascension Day
- **May/June** Whit Monday
- **May/June** Feast of Corpus Christi
- **15 August** Day of Assumption
- **26 October** National Holiday
- **1 November** All Saints' Day
- **8 December** Day of the Immaculate Conception
- **25 December** Christmas Day
- **26 December** St Stephen's Day

Money Matters

In January 2002, the Austrian Schilling was replaced by the European single currency, the Euro (€), which was made equivalent to 13.76 Schillings. 1 Euro equals 100 cents. Banknotes are available in denominations of 500, 200, 100, 50, 20, 10 and 5 Euros. The coins come in denominations of 2 and 1 Euro, and 50, 20, 10, 5, 2 and 1 cent. Coins minted in the different countries will match on one side but differ on the other. However, they can all be used in all EU countries.

The main credit cards and travellers' cheques are widely accepted by major hotels and many shops in cities. For those that do not, ATMs are by far your best option for obtaining local currency; cash dispensers at most banks accept Eurocheque cards. When travelling to remote destinations in rural areas you might need to change money at a train station. Banks (usually open Monday–Friday 8am–12.30pm and 1.30–3pm, often to 5.30pm Thursday) and exchange offices will change foreign currency at the current rate of the Viennese stock exchange.

There is no limit to how much local money visitors may bring into or take out of Austria.

What to Wear

Bring comfortable clothes and sensible shoes. More formal wear is expected at the theatre and concerts. Those walking in the mountains should be well prepared with proper footwear and equipment.

Be prepared for weather fluctuations that are normal in a country with this much topography. Pack something light for Vienna or Carinthia in summertime, as it can get quite hot, but also bring sweaters and perhaps an emergency poncho if you'll be in the high mountains whatever the season. The Alps require cold-weather gear of the highest order in winter, as well as appropriate expertise. Most parts of the country (other than the south) get a fair amount of rain, so bring an umbrella and a bit of rain gear.

Airline Offices in Vienna

Air Canada, 1, Kärntner Ring 18, tel: (01) 503 6181-17633
Air France, 1, Walfischgasse 1, tel: (01) 50 222 2400
Alitalia, 1, Kärntner Ring 2, tel: (01) 505 1707
Austrian, Lauda, Tyrolean, 1, Kärntner Ring 18, tel: (01) 051 789
British Airways, 1, Kärntner Ring 10, tel: (01) 7956 7567

Delta Airlines, 1, Gredlerstrasse 3, tel: (01) 7956 7023
El Al, 1, Opern Ring 1/E/7, tel: (01) 58 536 3215
KLM, 3, Löwengasse 3, tel: (01) 0900 359 556
Lufthansa, 1, Kärntner Ring 18, tel: (01) 081 0102-58080
Quantas, travel agents or tel: (01) 587 7771

Getting There

BY AIR

Austria's national carrier, Austrian Airlines, operates direct services to most European capital cities on a several-times-daily basis from Vienna's Schwechat airport, and less frequently from the other principal international gateways of Salzburg, Graz, Linz, Klagenfurt and Innsbruck. Dozens of other carriers, including most European airlines, also fly between Vienna and national capitals. From London, for example, BA has four daily London–Vienna flights, with less frequency to Klagenfurt and Graz. Austria's Lauda Air flies an increasing number of routes from London, Manchester and continental Europe to Austria at very competitive rates.

Austrian Airlines' route network is principally within Europe and the Middle East, but it has direct non-stop daily flights to New York's JFK airport and Atlanta's Hartfield International as well as less frequently to Tokyo. A host of other airlines also connect the US and Vienna, with a change of planes in Germany or Switzerland. Lufthansa connects New York with Munich.

Schwechat airport is located 15 km (9 miles) to the east of the city (25 minutes' drive on the motorway). Its terminals were modernised in 1988, and its information booth – tel: (01) 70 072 2233 – in the arrival hall is open 24 hours daily. An express bus service that operates approximately every half hour from 5am–midnight, links the airport with Vienna's two main railway stations and the City Air Terminal next to the Hilton Hotel. For information, tel: (01) 93 000 2300. A train service operates between the Südbahnhof and the airport approximately every hour from 6am to 9.30pm.

Tourist Offices Abroad

Austria: Österreich Werbung, Margaretenstrasse 1, 1040 Vienna, tel: (01) 587 2000 or (01) 588 660; www.austria-tourism.at
Australia: Austrian National Tourist Office, 1st Floor, 36 Carrington Street, Sydney, NSW 2000, tel: (2) 9299 3621.
Belgium: Office National Autrichien du Tourisme/Ostenrijkse Dienst voor Toerisme, Tourisme BP/Postbus 700, B-1050 Bruxelles, tel: (02) 646 0610.

Canada: 2 Bloor Street East, Suite 3330, Toronto, M4W 1A8, tel: (416) 967 3381.
France: Office National Autrichien du Tourisme, BP 475, 75366 Paris Cedex 08, tel: (01) 5383 9520.
Germany: Österreich Information, Postfach 701580, D-81315 München, tel: (089) 6667 0100, fax: (089) 6667 1201.
Great Britain: Austrian National Tourist Office, PO Box 2363, London W1A 2QB, tel: (020) 7629 0461, fax: (020) 7499 6038.

Italy: Ente Nazionale Austriaco per il Turismo, Casella Postale 1255, 20185 Milano, tel: (02) 4399 0185.
Netherlands: Oostenrijks Toeristenburo, Postbus 94285, 1090 CG Amsterdam, tel: (20) 468 4793.
Switzerland: Österreich Information, CH 8036 Zürich, tel: (1) 451 1551.
USA: Austrian National Tourist Office, PO Box 1142, New York, NY 10110–1142, tel: (212) 944 6880, fax: (212) 730 4568.

BY TRAIN

For travellers from the UK and northern Europe, there are two options. If you're travelling by Eurostar to Paris, the *Orient Express* night train leaves Paris-Est station at 5.49pm each evening and pulls into Vienna at 8.30am the next morning. If you're travelling via Belgium, the *Donauwalzer* departs from Brussels at 7.10pm every evening, arriving in Vienna at 10.58am the following morning. Bookings from London are made through DER, tel: (020) 7408 0111.

Other major international trains include the *Prinz Eugen* (Hamburg and Hannover to Vienna), the *Donauwalzer's* Amsterdam leg and the *CityNightLine Donau Kurier* (Dortmund, Bonn and Frankfurt to Vienna).

There are two main stations in Vienna: the Westbahnhof serves Germany, France, Belgium and Switzerland, and the Südbahnof serves Italy, the Balkans, Greece and Hungary. For passenger information in Vienna tel: 051 717.

BY ROAD

By Bus/Coach

If you want to make the journey by bus, it's a brutal 22-hour haul from London to Vienna for approx £100/ $150 return. Another alternative is to travel to Munich (at roughly the same fare), then use local services to connect to Salzburg or elsewhere. Not all these long-distance services operate daily, however. Contact Eurolines in the UK, tel: (08705) 808 080 or www.eurolines.com, for the latest schedule and pricing details.

By Car

Travelling to Austria by car from northern Europe is a long and arduous journey, best achieved via Germany's excellent toll-free motorway network. Beware of attempting to enter the country via the less busy alpine passes, which may be closed at night and in winter.

To drive on motorways in Austria you need to buy a 'vignette', which you then attach to your windscreen. A vignette can last anything from 10 days to a year, with a 10-day pass costing around €8. They can be bought at petrol stations, post offices and tobacconists.

A Green Card for insurance purposes is not mandatory, but it is advised; a red accident triangle, seat-belts and first aid kit are mandatory, however, for all vehicles travelling on Austrian roads.

Petrol and diesel prices are similar to those in the rest of Europe.

Tour Operators

There are numerous Austrian-holiday specialists in the UK and North America; some are German- or Austrian-owned, giving them special insight into the culture.

Austrian Holidays/Austrian Airlines Vacations, 10 Wardour Street, London W1D 6BQ, tel: (020) 7434 7399; in USA, tel: (1800) 377 1889. Owned by national air carrier Austrian Airlines, this tour company runs the usual Vienna and Salzburg tours plus spa and sports tours in the countryside.

Danube Travel, 6 Conduit Street, London W1R 9TG, tel: (020) 7493 0263. The usual Vienna packages, as well as some combining the city with Budapest and Prague.

DER Travel, 9501 West Devon Ave, Rosemont, IL 60018-4832, USA, tel: (1800) 782 2424, fax: (1800) 782 7474; in London, tel: (020) 7408 0111. Easily the most comprehensive operator in North America. A large number of themed tours, including ski packages, city packages and Christmas Market tours.

Habsburg Heritage Tours, 158 Rosendale Road, London SE21 8LG, tel: (020) 8761 0444. This company specialises in art- and music-based tours. Classical-music and river-cruise themes are two of its offerings.

Practical Tips

Business Hours

In general, shops and businesses are open Monday–Friday 8am–6pm and on Saturday 8am–12 noon. Banks are open Monday–Friday 8am–12.30pm and again from 1.30–3pm, often to 5.30pm on Thursday.

Media

Television

There are two official channels, (ÖRF1 and ÖRF2), both of which are German-language, plus a cable package, largely controlled by the Telekabel consortium, that includes some programmes in other languages. Your hotel might well subscribe to the package that includes CNN and BBC World News. There's a glut of German TV with its focus on sport, business news and slightly racy films, as well as some programming from France and Switzerland. The advent of satellite television in a growing number of higher-priced Austrian hotels improves your chances of catching news and sport in English.

Press

There's only one regular English-language publication in all of Austria, and it's certainly not comprehensive: *Austria Today* is sold weekly at newsagents. International newspapers and magazines are available in city centres. The *International Herald Tribune* and the *Financial Times*, along with various other foreign-language newspapers, are available early in the morning. Newsagents, called *Tabak Trafik*, are recognisable by the sign of a red ring with a cigarette in the middle. In addition to newspapers and magazines they also sell stamps and bus and tram tickets.

Radio

The Austrian Radio Network broadcasts a brief daily news report in English and French on Channel 1 (Ö1) at 8.05–8.15am. The Blue Danube Radio programme to which expatriates had turned for years to hear English news and opinion is, sadly, no more.

Local Tourist Offices

Austria (National Office)
4, Margaretenstrasse 1, Vienna, tel: (01) 587 2000 or 588 660.
Vienna
1, Albertinaplatz/Ecke Maysedergasse, tel: (01) 24 555; email: info@info.wien.at
www.wien.info
Open daily 9am–7pm.
Lower Austria
1, Fischhof 313, Vienna, tel: (01) 536 100.
Burgenland
Schloss Esterházy, 7000 Eisenstadt, tel: (02682) 63 384-0.
Styria
St Peter Hauptstrasse 243, Graz, tel: (0316) 4003-0;
www.graztourism.at
Upper Austria
Schillerstrasse 50, 4010 Linz, tel: (0732) 662 020.
Salzkammergut
Wiverstrasse 10, 4820 Bad Ischl, tel: (06132) 69 090.
Salzburg
Auerspergstrasse 7, tel: (0662) 889 870;
www.salzburginfo.or.at
Salzburg Province
Wienerbunderstrasse 23, 5300 Hallwang bei Salzburg, tel: (0662) 6688;
www.salzburgerland.com
Carinthia
Casinoplatz 1, 9220 Velden, tel: (04274) 52 100.
Tyrol
Maria-Theresien-Strasse 55, 6010 Innsbruck, tel: (0512) 5320.
Vorarlberg
Römerstrasse 7, 6900 Bregenz, tel: (05574) 425 250.

Addresses & Phones

Vienna has 23 numbered districts. The district number *precedes* the street name; the house number comes after the street name. You can ascertain the district of any given address from the postcode – the middle two numbers represent the particular district. A single street number can refer to a number of adjacent buildings.

Phone numbers don't all have the same number of digits, and extensions are often included as part of the number. In this book, any digits following a hyphen refer to an extension number.

Postal Services

Post offices are open 8am–noon and 2–6pm. Railway post offices in the main cities are open 24 hours, though not all services may be available around the clock. In Vienna, the Main Post Office is at Fleischmarkt 19, tel: (01) 515 090, open 24 hours. Dial (0810) 010 100 for general post office enquiries. Courier services are also available in major cities. In Vienna, try **Der Bote**, tel: (01) 486 1686, or **Blitzkurier**, tel: (01) 409 4949-0.

Telecommunications

Austria has a modern communications network and direct dialling is available to the majority of countries. In addition to telephoning from your hotel, you can also make international calls from post offices or from

many telephone booths. Note that, when dialling Vienna numbers from outside the city, you must include the area code 01 (within Austria) or 1 (outside Austria).

Tipping

It is customary to leave a 10–15 percent tip for good service. Bills at hotels and restaurants include a service charge but porters and maids expect a gratuity. Taxi drivers, tour guides, cloakroom attendants and hairdressers also expect a 10 percent tip. In general, rounding up the bill seems to be good form.

Travelling With Kids

Children are highly regarded in Austria – some trains even have playrooms – and they tend to go on the same sort of outings as their parents. There are a number of child-geared attractions throughout the country, of course – everything from Vienna's Prater amusement park to an array of zoos, nature parks and slightly kitschy attractions such as Minimundus in Klagenfurt.

There is a children's hospital in Vienna with emergency services: **St Anna Kinderspital**, 9, Kinderspitalgasse 6, tel: (01) 401 700.

Religious Services in Vienna

Anglican, 3, Jaurésgasse 12, tel: (01) 714 8900.
Catholic Mass (in English) Votivkirche, 11am, tel: (01) 402 1830.
Jewish, 1, Seitenstättengasse 4, tel: (01) 531 040.

Dialling Codes to Foreign Countries

Australia: 00 61
Belgium: 00 32
Denmark: 00 45
France: 00 33
Germany: 00 49
Hungary: 00 36
Italy: 00 39
Netherlands: 00 31
Switzerland: 00 41

United Kingdom: 00 44
USA: 00 1

For directory enquiries:
Dial 11 88 77 (Austria)
(0900) 11 88 77 (international)
or (0800) 100 190 (telegrams).
For operator-assisted long-distance calls: dial 11 816

Embassies in Vienna

Australia: Mattiellistrasse 2–4, tel: (01) 5128 5800.
Canada: Laurenzerberg 2, tel: (01) 5313 8300-0.
Germany: Metternichgasse 3, tel: (01) 71 154-0.
Great Britain: Jaurésgasse 12, tel: (01) 7161 3151 (consulate), (01) 716 130 (embassy).
Ireland: Rotenturmstrasse 16–18, tel: (01) 715 4246.
Switzerland: Prinz-Eugen-Strasse 7, tel: (01) 795 050.
USA: Gartenbaupromenade 2, tel: (01) 31 339-0 (consulate), Boltzmanngasse 16, tel: (01) 31 339-0 (embassy).

Methodist, 15, Sechshauserstrasse 56/2/6, tel: (01) 895 8175.
Viennese Islamic Centre, 21, Am Hubertusdamm 17–19, tel: (01) 263 0918.

Medical Treatment

Austria's standard of medical care is generally good. If you need help, visit the local pharmacy for minor aches, pains and sniffles; most stay open to 6pm weekdays and noon on Saturday and usually post a list of 24-hour pharmacies nearby.

For more serious matters, call the emergency number (141) or go straight to a hospital. In Vienna, lots of hospitals maintain 24-hour walk-in emergency services – the Allgemeines Krankenhaus (AKH), an enormous hospital at Alserstrasse and Spitalgasse with its own U-Bahn stop, is excellent; tel: (01) 40 400-0.

Security & Crime

Austria is uniformly safe, except for a few areas in Vienna – and the chief threat here is the pickpocket. Keep a hand on your hip in such crowded and/or seedy areas as the Westbahnhof, Naschmarkt, the Prater and especially Karlsplatz – a noted haunt of thieves and drug-dealers at night. Keep valuables in your hotel safe.

Getting Around

Public Transport

BY TRAIN

The Austrian Federal Railway System maintains approximately 5,800 km (3,600 miles) of track and is connected with both the Eastern and Western European railway networks. Passengers are required to pay a surcharge on certain InterCity trains; the price of reserved seating is within this additional charge.

Trains travelling between Vienna and Graz, and between Vienna and Salzburg, depart at one-hour intervals; between Vienna and Innsbruck, and Vienna and Villach they leave at 2-hour intervals.

Children up to seven go free if they don't need their own seat.

Railway Nostalgia

There are a number of narrow-gauge railway lines in Austria that are still – or once again – in operation and that have evolved into tourist attractions. Some are serviced by steam engines. The **Steyr Valley Railway** makes its way from Steyr along the Steyr River valley into Grünburg. The **Gurk Valley Railway** plies its way through the Nock area in Carinthia, from Treibach-Althofen to Pöckstein-Zwischenwässern. The **Feistritz Valley Railway** chugs from Weiz to Birkfeld in Eastern Styria.

Payerbach-Hirschwang, a local train, operates south of Vienna. From here you can also take the **Schneeberg Railway**, which transports passengers to the

Nearly all day trains have dining cars; night trains have sleeping compartments and *couchettes*. For local train details, dial 51717 in any city.

BY BOAT

From the beginning of April until the end of October boats operate on regular schedules along the Danube River. Vienna is connected to Budapest and Passau.

There are also boats running on a regular basis on all larger lakes in Austria. Along the stretch from Vienna to Budapest, the Donau-Dampfschiffahrts-Gesellschaft Blue Danube (the Danube Steamship Company), Handelskai 265, operates the hydrofoil to Budapest. The hydrofoil makes three trips form Vienna to Budapest and three return Budapest–Vienna trips daily. For details, tel: (01) 588 800, or visit www.ddsg-blue-danube.at

DDSG also offer a Vienna–Bratislava hydrofoil service. Boats leave Vienna at Reichsbrücke from Wednesday to Sunday at 9am and 9.30am and arrive in Bratislava at 10.30am and 11am. The hydrofoil leaves Bratislava at 5pm and

highest railway station in Austria at 1,795 metres (5,890 ft).

The **Mariazeller Railway** connects St Pölten with Mariazell, a Styrian place of pilgrimage.

In Vorarlberg the **Montafon Railway** runs from Bludenz to Schruns-Tschagguns and in Tyrol you'll find the world-famous **Ziller Valley Train**.

In the area along the border of Upper Styria and Salzburg the **Mur Valley Railway** makes its way from Unzmarkt to Tamsweg.

In addition to these, there is also the privately-operated railway **Vöklamarkt-Attersee** in Salzkammergut, and the **Stainzer Flascher Train**, which runs from Preding-Wieseldorf to the Stainz Palace.

5.30pm, arriving in Vienna at 6.45pm and 7.15pm.

BY BUS

Some 70 international bus lines connect Austria to other countries. The Austrian public bus service primarily links places not served by the railway network. Nearly all tourist areas offer bus excursions into the surrounding countryside.

Private Transport

TAXIS

All taxis are equipped with calibrated meters. They park at taxi stands and cannot be hailed from the street.

BY CAR

Driving in Austria
Traffic regulations in Austria correspond to those of other continental European countries. Driving is on the right. In snowy conditions (mid-November–mid-April) winter tyres, chains or studded tyres are required. ARBÖ (Austrian Motoring Association) and ÖAMTC (Austrian Automobile, Motorbike and Touring Club) run over 100 agencies throughout the country from which you can rent chains for your car. On main roads the speed limit is 100 kph (about 60 mph), on motorways 130 kph (80 mph), and in populated areas 50 kph (30 mph).

The blood alcohol limit is 0.8 parts per thousand; a driver caught

Important Numbers

Fire Brigade, tel: 122.
Police, tel: 133.
Ambulance, tel: 144.
Doctor (emergency), tel: 141.
Rescue Services (in mountainous areas), tel: 140
Breakdown Services
ÖAMTC, tel: 120.
ARBÖ, tel: 123.

exceeding this limit can expect to have his or her licence suspended and be fined at least €600. It is illegal for children under the age of 12 to sit in the front seat, and wearing a seat-belt is mandatory. Drivers must have proof of liability insurance; a Green Insurance Card is advisable.

In many cities where you are required to pay a fee for short-term parking, it is first necessary to obtain a parking certificate, available at tobacco shops, banks and petrol stations.

Breakdowns & Accidents
The police must be called to the scene of all car accidents in which any persons are injured. Foreigners should fill out the accident form entitled *Comité Européen des Assurances*. ÖAMTC and ARBÖ maintain vehicle breakdown services along the most important thoroughfares; non-members may also take advantage of these services for a somewhat higher price than members.

Traffic Reports
Traffic reports are broadcast on Channel 3 (Ö3) every hour following the regular news bulletin. Programmes may be interrupted by announcements about especially nasty traffic conditions.

Car Rental
Most international car rental agencies have offices in Austria. In addition to these, there are also a number of local rental businesses. You'll find offices located in larger cities, at airports and in main railway stations. In Vienna try:
Avis, 1, Opernring 5 and airport, tel: (01) 587 6241.
Budget, 3, Vienna Hilton and airport, tel: (01) 714 6565-0.
Europcar, 1, Schubertring 9, tel: (01) 714 6717.
Hertz, 1, Kärntner Ring 17, tel: (01) 512 8677.
Star-Caravan (camper rental), 22, Wagramer Strasse 198, tel: (01) 258 1660.
Rent a Bus, 12, Assmayergasse 60, tel: (01) 813 3223.

Blecha, Exclusive Rent a Car (Rolls-Royce, Bentley, Mercedes), 16, Lienfeldgasse 37, tel: (01) 486 1321-0.

Tour Suggestions

The following itinerariesoffer breathtaking views of the Austrian countryside:

A tour across the Alps
Away from the major routes, along the ridge of the Alps from Bregenz to Vienna, you can organise a spectacular trip across the countryas follows:
Bregenz – Bregenzer Wald – Schröcken – Hochtannenbergpass – Lechtal – Holzgau – Reutte – Leermos – Ehrwald – Fernpass – Nassereith – Mieminger Plateau – Innsbruck – Hall – Schwaz – Zillertal – Gerlos-Pass Strasse – Krimml – Zell am See – Saalfelden – Mühlbach am Hochkönig – St Johann im Pongau – Radstadt – Schladming – Gröbming – Admont – Hieflau – Mariazell – Lilienfeld – Vienna.

Vienna
Höhenstrasse: The road to Klosterneuburg with city views.

Carinthia
Villacher Alpenstrasse: This road from Villach to Rosstratte presents a view of the Dachstein and the Grossglockner.

Salzburg
Grossglockner-Hochalpenstrasse: The Bruck–Heiligenblut (Carinthia) road with a view of Grossglockner and Edelweiss peaks.

Tyrol
Timmelsjoch-Hochalpenstrasse: High road from Sölden to Meran (Italy); views of the Ötztal Alps.

Vorarlberg
Arlberg-Pass-Strasse: The road from Langen to St Anton (Tyrol).

Where to Stay

Private Accommodation

On just about every street in tourist-oriented towns you'll find a *Zimmer frei* (vacancies) sign. Alternatively, tourist information offices can give you a list of local private accommodation, probably the most reasonably-priced lodgings you'll find anywhere in Austria.

Hotels

Austrian hospitality enjoys worldwide recognition (many hotels throughout the world are under Austrian management). Even the country's smallest inns offer excellent service.

Hotels in Austria are divided into five categories, each distinguished by a number of stars. In the following list you'll find hotels belonging to the top three categories, plus Vienna *pensions*.

In the tourist season (in July and August, and over Christmas and Easter), you should book hotel rooms in advance as most hotels and inns are fully booked. Bookings can be cancelled up to three months before the date of arrival. On shorter notice a cancellation fee will apply.

Besides the excellent hotel industry, Austria is known for inexpensive family vacations. These are offered through a system of vacations on farms and in villages, and through the many *pensions*, guest houses and private accommodations throughout the country. The Austrian National Tourist office has two brochures – *Dorfurlaub in Österreich* and *Preisgünstiger Urlaub in Österreich* – that list the many possibilities.

VIENNA

Arenberg
1, Stubenring 2
tel: (01) 512 9249-0
fax: (01) 513 9356
email: arenberg@ping.at
The doyen among *pensions* (part of the Best Western group), with a plush, elegant atmosphere and excellent location. All rooms have satellite TV and direct-dial telephones. €€

Astoria
1, Kärntner Strasse 32–34
tel: (01) 51 577-0
fax: (01) 51 577-82
email: astoria@austria-trend.at
A civilised old hotel immediately behind the Staatsoper. Some rooms are accessible to physically disabled guests. €€€

Baltic
8, Skodagasse 15
tel: (01) 405 6266-0
fax: (01) 405 6266-130
Family hotel with 27 rooms. Double beds are actually two single beds joined together in clean but antique-looking rooms. Some rooms can accommodate disabled guests. €

Biedermeier im Sünnhof
3, Landstrasser Hauptstrasse 28
tel: (01) 71 671-0
fax: (01) 71 671-503
email: hotel.vienna@dorint.rogner.com
A unique, attractive set of restored Biedermeier-style buildings, with original shopping arcade. Specially outfitted rooms for guests with disabilities. €€€

Bristol
1, Kärntner Ring 1
tel: (01) 51 516-0
fax: (01) 51 516-550
email: hotelbristol@westin.com
An art nouveau building dating from 1884 that is rather more intimate than many other five-star hotels. Its restaurant, the Korso, is known for its light Viennese cuisine and distinguished wine list. There are non-smoking rooms and wheelchair facilities for guests. €€€€

Cyrus
10, Laxenburger Strasse 14
tel/fax: (01) 604 4288
email: hotel-pensioncyrus@aon.at
Families are particularly welcome at

this small hotel with 20 rooms, eight with bath or shower. €

Haydn
6, Mariahilfer Strasse 57–59
tel: (01) 587 4414-0
fax: (01) 586 1950
email: info@haydn-hotel.at
Simple, mid-range *pension* in a noisy area. Only a few minutes from the city centre by U-Bahn. There is cycle storage space available to guests, and breakfast is included. €

Price Categories

€€€€ = more than €300
€€€ = €140–300
€€ = €90–140
€ = less than €90
Prices are for a double room in high season; off-season rates are often considerably lower.

Im Palais Schwarzenberg
3, Schwarzenbergplatz 9
tel: (01) 798 4515-0
fax: (01) 798 4714
email: palais@schwarzenberg.co.at
Wonderfully furnished, and located in one wing of a Baroque royal palace with a superbly romantic view of the park, all just a stone's throw from the city centre. Some rooms can be used by guests with physical disabilities. €€€€

Imperial
1, Kärntner Ring 16
tel: (01) 5010-0
fax: (01) 501 0410
email: hotelimperial@ luxurycollection.com
Official guests of state, actors and leading pop stars stay in the Imperial, with its 128 elegant rooms and suites. Definitely the place to be seen, and the Zur Majestät restaurant is one of the best and most expensive in Vienna. All rooms can accommodate guests with wheelchairs. €€€–€€€€.

Kärntnerhof
1, Grashofgasse 4
tel: (01) 512 1923-0
fax: (01) 513 2228-33
email: kaerntnerhof@netway.at
Pleasantly quiet, despite its central location. A range of services is offered by the

multilingual staff. Though the hotel is very popular, some might find the hand-held showers to be as outdated as the furniture. All rooms have satellite TV and telephones; some are outfitted for wheelchairs. €€

König von Ungarn
1, Schulerstrasse 10
tel: (01) 51 584-0
fax: (01) 51 584-8
Centrally located only metres from the Stephansdom, and over 400 years old, this hotel is full of old-fashioned charm. It has everything you would expect of a four-star hotel, and the glass-roofed inner courtyard is particularly attractive. All rooms are wheelchair-friendly and guests with cycles have access to repair and storage facilities. €€€

Kugel
7, Siebensterngasse 43
tel: (01) 523 3355-0
fax: (01) 523 3355-5
email: hotel.kugel@netway.at
Good location in the middle of the shopping district, and small, clean rooms. Enthusiastic owners make the experience more enjoyable. Some rooms are outfitted for wheelchair use. €

Mailbergerhof
1, Annagasse 7
tel: (01) 512 0641
fax: (01) 512 0641-10
An old building with a modern interior, in the pedestrian area of the city centre. A full breakfast is included in the rate. €€€

Marriott Vienna
1, Parkring 12a
tel: (01) 51 518-0
fax: (01) 51 518-6736
email: mhrs.vieat.gm@marriot.com
A postmodern glass building opposite the park. All rooms are air conditioned, have televisions and are outfitted for wheelchairs; some are for non-smokers. €€€

Nossek
1, Graben 17
tel: (01) 533 7041
fax: (01) 535 3646
Small, cosy *pension* in the heart of Vienna's shopping district. Credit cards are not accepted and reservations are highly

recommended in the high season. Also available is an apartment for those wishing to stay longer. €–€€

Parkhotel Schönbrunn
13, Hietzinger Hauptstrasse 12
tel: (01) 87 804-0
fax: (01) 87 804-3220
email: parkhotel.schoenbrunn@austria-trend.at
Very close to the palace and gardens of Schönbrunn, this hotel formerly housed the kaiser's guests and is still redolent of the Imperial past. Amenities include an indoor pool, satellite TV, and phones with voice mail as well as some rooms outfitted for wheelchair use. Rates include a generous breakfast. €€€

Price Categories

€€€€ = more than €300
€€€ = €140–300
€€ = €90–140
€ = less than €90
Prices are for a double room in high season; off-season rates are often considerably lower.

Penta Renaissance
3, Ungargasse 60
tel: (01) 71 175-0
fax: (01) 71 175-8145
email: atvpr003@ibm.net
One of the city's architecturally most striking hotels (with a lavish reception area), but slightly off the beaten track, 10 minutes by tram from the Ringstrasse. All rooms can accommodate wheelchair users, and there are telephones, satellite TVs and minibars in all rooms. €€€

Plaza Vienna
1, Schottenring 11
tel: (01) 31 390-0
fax: (01) 31 390-160
email: business.center@vienna-plaza.telecom.at
A recently built and very elegant art nouveau-style hotel. Catering to the business traveller, rooms are equipped with modems and satellite TV. Wheelchair users can be accommodated in any room. €€€

Rathaus
8, Lange Gasse 13
tel: (01) 406 4302-0

fax: (01) 408 4272
email: rathaus@inthotels.com
Inexpensive quiet rooms right in the middle of the lively Josefstadt district, with its many small bars. €

Sacher
1, Philharmonikerstrasse 4
tel: (01) 51 456-0
fax: (01) 51 457 810
email: hotel@sacher.com
Archdukes, ministers and senior army officers used to stay here, and the Sacher is still the city's most famous hotel. Past its heyday, perhaps, but you can still be sure of top-class service. Some rooms outfitted for wheelchair users. €€€€

Schild
19, Neustift am Walde 97–99
tel: (01) 440 4044-0
fax: (01) 444 000
email: schild@atnet.at
This 20-room hotel is a paradise for wine connoisseurs, since it is surrounded by *Heurigen* – bars selling new wine made on the premises. The country location is also appealing to cyclists as the hotel offers cycle storage and repair facilities. Wheelchairs are welcome in some rooms. €€

Schweizerhof
1, Bauernmarkt 22
tel: (01) 533 1931-0
fax: (01) 533 0214
email: office@schweizerhof.at
Relatively inexpensive, despite its very central position. A generous breakfast buffet is served with salmon and champagne on Sunday. All rooms have en-suite facilities and satellite TV. €€

Wandl
1, Petersplatz 9
tel: (01) 53 455-0
fax: (01) 53 455-77
email: reservation@hotel-wandl.com
Located immediately behind the Peterskirche, and thus very much at the hub of things. Nice rooms and moderate rates. €€–€€€

Wild
7, Lange Gasse 10
tel: (01) 406 5174-0
fax: (01) 402 2168
email: info@pension-wild.com
A popular *pension* in Josefstadt with modern rooms with or without

en-suite facilities. There are kitchenettes on every floor for light meals. **€**

Zur Wiener Staatsoper
1, Krugerstrasse 11
tel: (01) 513 1274-0
fax: (01) 513 1274-15
email: office@zurwienerstaatsoper.at
Newly renovated and, as its name suggests, close to the opera and thus popular with singers. Small rooms, most with en-suite facilities, all facing a quiet, residential street. Advance reservations are strongly recommended. **€€**

LOWER AUSTRIA

Krems
Gästehaus Anna-Maria Rameis
Steiner Landstrassse 16
tel: (02732) 85 169 or 87 013
fax: (02732) 85 169-8
email: gaestehaus-rameis@aon.at
16th-century inn located outside Krems in Stein with recently renovated rooms. Near ferry terminal. Longer stays are encouraged. Cycle storage. **€**

Gourmet-Hotel Am Forthof
DonaulAnde 8
tel: (02732) 83 345
fax: (02732) 83 345-40
email: hotel.foerthof@netway.at
The only Krems hotel overlooking the Danube, this civilised inn is festooned with window-boxes. Ask for an off-street room for peace and quiet. Bikes available to all guests. Restaurant for gourmets, as the name of the hotel implies. **€€–€€€**

Hotel-Pension Unter den Linden
Schillerstrasse 5
tel: (02732) 82 115
fax: (02732) 82 115-20
email: hotel@udl.at
Spacious rooms with antique wooden beds and shiny parquet floors. There's an extra charge for one-night stays. **€**

Kremsleithenhof-Familie Felsner
Kraxenweg 15
tel: (02732) 85 671
Apartments with cooking facilities, cycle hire and home-made brandies. Parking is available. Guests are required to stay for a minimum of three days. **€**

Melk
Gasthof Wachauerhof
Wienerstrasse 30
tel: (02752) 52 235
fax: (02752) 53 229
email: wachauerhof@pvg.at
Large, comfortable inn with spacious rooms. **€**

Gasthof Goldener-Stern
Sterngasse 17
tel: (02752) 52 214
fax: (02752) 52 214-4
A good resting place for cyclists, this *pension* features clean rooms with shared facilities. **€**

Gasthof zum Fürsten
Rathausplatz 3–5
tel: (02752) 52 343
fax: (02752) 52 343-4
email: cafe.madar@netway.at
Small, family-run hotel with a view of the town square and abbey. **€**

Hotel Zur Post
Linzer Strasse 1
tel: (02752) 52 345
fax: (02752) 52 345-50
email: ebner.post@netway.at
Cheerful building in city centre. En-suite rooms and fine restaurant. **€€**

St Pölten
Gasthof Graf
Bahnhofplatz 7
tel: (02742) 352 757
fax: (02742) 352 757-40
Facing the train station, this hotel is a good, clean place convenient for early-morning departures. **€**

Hauser Eck
Schulgasse 2
tel: (02742) 73 336
fax: (02742) 78 386
email: m.hauser@eunet.at
Warm, inviting hotel close to train station. All rooms are furnished with TV and direct-dial phones. **€**

Metropol
Schillerplatz 1
tel: (02742) 707 000
fax: (02742) 70 700-133
email: metropol@austria-trend.at
Modern, city-centre hotel with standard, comfortable rooms equipped with TV and air conditioning. Some rooms for use by guests in wheelchairs. There's also a golf course available to hotel residents. **€€€**

Semmering
Panoramahotel Wagner
Hochstrasse 267
tel: (02664) 25 120
fax: (02664) 2512-61
email: panoramahotel.wagner@netway.at
Small and tidy, with a good restaurant. **€€–€€€**

Panhans Grand Hotel
Hochstrasse 32
tel: (02664) 81 81
fax: (02664) 818 1513
email: hotel@panhans.at
This once-great resort is somewhat faded now, and is consequently surprisingly affordable. **€**

BURGENLAND

Eisenstadt
Gasthof Familie Ohr
Rusterstrasse 51
tel: (02682) 62 460
fax: (02682) 62 460 9
email: hotel.ohr@burgenland.org
Golden stucco hotel run by a friendly family. Close to transport links and city centre. On-site restaurant. **€€**

Hotel Burgenland
Schubertplatz 1
tel: (02682) 696-0
fax: (02682) 65 531
email: burgenland@austria-hotels.co.at
Modern structure featuring doubles as well as apartments, and cycle hire and breakfast are included. **€€€**

Neuseidl am See
Hotel Wende
Seestrasse 40–42
tel: (02167) 81 11
fax: (02167) 81 11-649
email: anfrage@hotel-wende.at
Lakeside hotel that's great for health-conscious and active guests – there are cycles for hire and swimming and fitness facilities. **€€**

Rust
Apartment-Restaurant Rusterhof
Rathausplatz
tel: (02685) 6416
fax: (02685) 6416-11
email: office@rusterhof.at
Old town-centre house with restaurant and apartments. **€€€**

Hotel Sifkovits
Am Seekanal 8
tel: (02685) 276
fax: (02685) 36 012
email: hotel@sifkovits.at
Small, lakeside hotel with large,
comfortable rooms. Pets are
accepted, credit cards are not. €€

STYRIA

Graz
Hotel Erzherzog Johann
Sackstrasse 3
tel: (0316) 811 616
fax: (0316) 811 515
email: office@erzherzog-johann.com
Charming grand hotel in the centre of
town with 19th-century furnishings.
Spacious rooms with high ceilings.
Excellent restaurant. €€€
Ibis
Europaplatz 12
tel: (0316) 778-0
fax: (0316) 778 300
email: h1917-re@accor-hotels.com
This full-facility business hotel
enjoys a prime location next to the
train station. All rooms are en-suite
and have satellite TV. Some
wheelchair-friendly rooms. €€
Gasthof Häuserl im Wald
Roseggerweg 105
tel: (0316) 391165
fax: (0316) 392277
email: legenstein@aon.at
Country inn with a fine restaurant in
a peaceful setting near the forest.
Good for wildlife spotters. Well
appointed rooms. €
Pension Iris
Bergmanngasse 10
tel: (0316) 322 081
fax: (0316) 322 081-5
This suburban apartment building
has a lovely location near the park
and university. Large, well-furnished
rooms, some with sitting area. Get
an off-street room to avoid noise. €
Rosen-Hotel Steiermark
Liebiggasse 4
tel: (0316) 3815 03
fax: (0316) 3815 0362
On the university campus, but close
enough to the centre, this college
residence hall becomes a hotel in
summer. Open July–September.
All rooms have baths. €

Mariazell
Hotel Schwarzer Adler
Hauptplatz 1
tel: (03882) 286 30
fax: (03882) 286 350
email: adler-mz@kom.at
Posh hotel with four fully
functioning apartments for
travellers needing longer stays.
Great views of the cathedral and
town. Good facilities for guests in
wheelchairs. €€–€€€
Pension Maria Zechner
Wienerstrasse 25
tel: (03882) 60 40
fax: (03882) 60 40-20
Perfectly positioned between the
centre and the rail station, this
spotless *pension* goes the extra
mile with all en-suite rooms. €

UPPER AUSTRIA

Freistadt
Austria Classic Hotel-Goldener Adler
Salzgasse 1
tel: (07942) 72 112-0
fax: (07942) 72 112-44
email: goldener.adler@hotels-
freistadt.at
A pale-yellow building containing
just 80 beds, but lots of amenities
such as a pool and gym. At the
on-site restaurant, you're advised
to skip the main menu and go
straight for the legendary
desserts. €
**Gasthof Deim Zum Goldener
Hirschen**
Böhmergasse 8–10
tel: (07942) 72 258 0
fax: (07942) 72 258 40
email: goldener.hirsch@hotels-
freistadt.at
Historic, hospitable hotel. The
bright, airy reception hall's
stonework and vaulted ceilings lend
it a medieval look. Bikes are
available to guests as well. €€
Pension Pirklbauer
Höllgasse 2/4
tel: (07942) 72 440
fax: (07942) 72 440-5
email: pension.pirklbauer@aon.com
Well situated for sightseeing and
famous for its breakfasts (which
you must order ahead). All rooms
are equipped with shower/toilet. €

Linz
Goldenes Dachl
Hafnerstrasse 27
tel: (0732) 775 897
This fairly spacious *pension* is not
particularly exciting but provides
value for money and is centrally
located. Friendly management. €
Hotel Drei Mohren
Promenade 17
tel: (0732) 772 626-0
fax: (0732) 772 626-6
email: hotel@drei-mohren.at
An excellent location and modern
rooms – all complete with toilet and
shower – make for a pleasant stay
at this 300-year-old hotel. Great
breakfast buffet. €€
Hotel Mühlviertlerhof
Graben 24
tel: (0732) 772 268
fax: (0732) 772 268-34
Modern hotel centrally located in
the downtown area. Amenities
include all en-suite rooms. €
Pension Wilder Mann
Goethestrasse 14
tel/fax: (0732) 656 078
This homely *pension* has a great
location – a 10-minute walk from
the railway station – and cosy
rooms. Breakfast costs extra. €

Steyr
Gasthof Bauer
Josefgasse 7
tel: (07252) 54 441
fax: (07252) 51 936
email: bauersgasthof@aon.at
Inexpensive rooms some distance
away from the city centre. €
Landhotel Mader
Stadtplatz 36
tel: (07252) 533 580
fax: (07252) 533 586
email: mader@mader.at
This central Renaissance building
has quite small rooms but the
restaurant is outstanding and there
is a traditional German wine bar on
site. €€–€€€

THE SALZKAMMERGUT

Bad Ischl
Goldenes Schiff
Stifter-kai 3
tel: (06132) 24 241

fax: (06132) 24 241-58
email: office@goldenes-schiff.at
Riverside hotel offering
comfortable rooms, some with
pleasant balconies, all recently
renovated. €€€
Haus Stadt Prag
Eglmoosgasse 9
tel: (06132) 23 616
email: stadt-prag@aon.at
Pink building not far from the train
station. Spacious rooms; most with
balconies (which cost extra). €
Waldesruh
Kaltenbachstrasse 43
tel: (06132) 24 558
Contemporary chalet-hotel not far
from the centre. En-suite rooms
throughout the building. €

Fuschlsee
Hotel Schloss Fuschl
5322 Hof bei Salzburg
tel: (06229) 22530
fax: (06229) 22 53 531
email: schloss.fuschl@arabella
sheraton.com
Smart hotel in a stone complex
overlooking the pretty lake of Fuschl
See, with short but scenic golf
course adjacent. €€€

Hallstatt
Gasthof Zauner Seewirt
Markplatz 51
tel: (06134) 8246
fax: (06134) 8246-8
email: zauner@hallstatt.at
A historical hotel with all the
modern conveniences. €
Gasthof Simony
Wolfenstrasse 105
tel/fax: (06134) 8231
email: susanna.scheutz@
multikom.at
Small, lakeside hotel with some
rooms sharing shower facilities.
Friendly management. Good-value
restaurant on premises. €

Mondsee
Gästhof Schwarzes Rössl
Raisnerstrasse 32
tel: (06232) 22 35
fax: (06232) 22 355
In addition to its good location –
not far from the centre – this
comfortable hotel offers great
value for money. €

Hotel Seehof
Loibichl am Mondsee
tel: (06232) 5031
fax: (06232) 5031-51
email: seehof@nextra.at
Lakeside luxury hotel that looks like
a farmhouse. Breakfast buffet,
beach access. €€€
Seegasthof-Hotel Lackner
Gaisberg 33
tel: (06232) 2359
fax: (06232) 2359-50
email: office@seehotel-lackner.at
A pristine location on the lake is
the setting for this family-run
resort. Features cycles and
sailboats for guests, and non-
smoking rooms. €€

Price Categories

€€€€ = more than €300
€€€ = €140–300
€€ = €90–140
€ = less than €90
Prices are for a double room in
high season; off-season rates
are often considerably lower.

St Gilgen
Parkhotel Billroth
Billrothstrasse 2
tel: (06227) 2217
fax: (06227) 221 825
email: office@billroth.at
Luxury resort within spacious park.
Facilities include tennis courts and
massage/sauna. €€–€€€
Pension Falkensteiner
Salzburger Strasse 11–13
tel: (06227) 2395
fax: (06227) 7298
email: pension-
falkensteiner@aon.at
Pleasant family-run *pension*
featuring comfortable rooms, some
of which are en-suite. Relax in the
adjacent garden or hire a cycle from
reception. €

SALZBURG (CITY)

Amadeus
Linzergasse 43–45
tel: (0662) 871 401
fax: (0662) 871 401-7
email: salzburg@hotelamadeus.at

Good location on highly-trafficked
Linzergasse, this hotel offers
functional en-suite rooms and
has a lift. €€
Bergland
Rupertgasse 15
tel: (0662) 872 318
fax: (0662) 872 318-8
email: pkuhn@sol.at
A hotel run by gracious hosts
who provide rooms ranging from
comfortable to posh. You can
choose rooms with just toilet, just
shower or (more expensive) both. €
**Best Western Hotel-Restaurant
Elefant**
Sigmund-Haffner-Gasse 4
tel: (0662) 843 397
fax: (0662) 8401 0928
email: reception@elefant.at
Partake of the breakfast buffet
included in the rate. Children are
well catered for by staff attendants
who will help supervise them while
you shop. Catch up on local and
international news via the TVs that
are supplied in every room. €€€
Blaue Gans
Getreidegasse 41–43
tel: (0662) 842 4910
fax: (0662) 842 4919
email: office@blauegans.at
The location is this hotel's finest
feature – it is firmly entrenched in
the Altstadt. But following close
behind are the simply appointed
rooms – decorated in warm tones
and with contemporary art – which
come with or without private toilet
and shower. €€–€€€
Cordial Theater-Hotel
Schallmooser Hauptstrasse 13
tel: (0662) 88 168-10
fax: (0662) 88 168-692
email: chsalzburg@cordial.co.at
Staff ensure you're well looked
after here, and a variety of
amenities, such as an Austrian-style
breakfast, are included in the rate.
There's a restaurant and bar, a non-
smoking public area, lift, parking,
TVs, sauna, solarium, suites and
studios. €€–€€€
Goldener Krone
Linzergasse 48
tel: (0662) 872 300
fax: (0662) 872 300-66
Expect a warm welcome at this
relaxed family hotel. Ask for a quiet

room if you want to sleep, and a room without a toilet or shower if you're on a budget. €

Haus Ballwein
Moostrasse 69
tel/fax: (0662) 824 029
Pleasant bed-and-breakfast establishment featuring farm-style accommodation outside the city limits. Rooms range from the simple, with the use of shared bath facilities down the hall, to those featuring basic cooking facilities for longer stays. If you don't have a car, you'll have to rely on the buses (No 1 from train station and No 60 from F-Hanusch-Platz) to get there. €

Hinterbrühl
Schanzlgasse 12
tel: (0662) 846 798
fax: (0662) 841 859
email: hinterbruehl@aon.at
This hotel just east of Alstadt is good value and is often full. Situated near the bus station and the Salzburg Festival. Don't expect en-suite facilities in the plain but functional rooms. €

Hotel Restaurant Weisses Kreuz
Bierjodlgasse 6
tel: (0662) 845 641
fax: (0662) 845 6419
email: weisses.kreuz@eunet.at
Small hotel located at the foot of Hohensalzburg Castle with a good restaurant featuring food from the Balkans. €

Hotel Bristol
Makartplatz 4
tel: (0662) 873 557-0
fax: (0662) 873 557-6
email: hotel.bristol@salzburg.co.at
Located in a stately building flanked by gorgeous gardens, and with an impressive facade, this hotel fulfills your every need with a comprehensive series of services ranging from childcare to a beauty parlour. The hotel's luxuries extend to antique furnishings and wonderful thick pile carpets. €€€€

Hotel Goldener Hirsch
Getreidegasse 37
tel: (0662) 8084-0
fax: (0662) 843 349
email: welcome@goldenerhirsch.com
This hotel frequently serves as the meeting point for the stars of the Salzburg Festival, which is reflected

in the prices. The glamorous and wealthy are attracted by comfortable yet old-fashioned furnishings and the staff's attention to detail. Expect to be pampered, and an air-conditioned room complete with TV. €€€€

Institut St-Sebastian
Linzergasse 41
tel: (0662) 871 386
fax: (0662) 871 386-85
email: office@st-sebastian-salzburg.at
Located in the centre of Linzergasse, complete with kitchens, laundry facilities and private rooms with balconies overlooking the city. Be sure to confirm reservations in advance at this hotel. €

Price Categories

€€€€ = more than €300
€€€ = €140–300
€€ = €90–140
€ = less than €90
Prices are for a double room in high season; off-season rates are often considerably lower.

Pension Adlerhof
Elisabethstrasse 25
tel: (0662) 875 236
fax: (0662) 873 663
email: adlerhof@pension-adlerhof.at
Great location for early-morning trains because the hotel is very close to the Hauptbahnhof. The furnishings are a mixed bag, ranging from the modern to the traditional. There is also the option of cheaper rooms without private facilities. €

Schloss Mönchstein
Mönchsberg Park 26
tel: (0662) 848 555-0
fax: (0662) 848 559
email: salzburg@monchstein.at
Fairy-tale castle, overgrown with vines and overlooking the city. Nestled in a garden with sculptures and a winding path, this hotel serves those for whom money is no object. Features include tennis courts and meals tailored to meet individual dietary needs. €€€€

Überfuhr
Ignaz-Rieder-Kai 43
tel: (0662) 623 010
fax: (0662) 623 0104
email: ueberfuhr.sbg@aon.at
Not close to town, but in a peaceful setting. Welcoming rooms with and without private facilities. €

SALZBURG PROVINCE

Zell am See
Gasthof Schmittental
Schmittenstrasse 42
tel: (06542) 72 332
fax: (06542) 723 328
email: info@schmittental.at
Traditional Austrian chalet with window-boxes. Relax in adjacent garden. Rooms are all en-suite. €

Hotel Lebzelter
Dreifaltigkeitsstrasse 7
tel: (06542) 7760
fax: (06542) 72 411
email: zell@hotel-lebzelter.at
Hotel in city centre with large, comfortable rooms, en-suite facilities and television. €

Salzburgerhof
Auerspergstrasse 11
tel: (06542) 765
fax: (06542) 765-66
email: 5sterne@salzburgerhof.at
Full-facility resort nestled in the mountains. Good for active travellers, as it provides bicycles, a spa and health-related courses such as yoga. €€€–€€€€

CARINTHIA AND EAST TYROL

Klagenfurt
Hotel Musil
10-Oktober-Strasse 14
tel: (0463) 511 660
fax: (0463) 511 660-4
email: reservation@musil-hotels.co.at
Romantic spot with a good restaurant. €€€

Moser-Verdino
Domgasse 2
tel: (0463) 57 878
fax: (0463) 516 765
email: moser-verdino@arcotel.at
Guests staying here on business have computer access, satellite TV

and decent bathrooms, which make this hotel recommended for any working traveller. €€€

Blumenstöckl
10-Oktober-Strasse 11
tel: (0463) 57 793
fax: (0463) 57 793-5
email: mail@blumenstoeckl.at
Great central location with en-suite facilities, satellite TV and attractive courtyard. €

Sandwirt
Pernhartgasse 9
tel: (0463) 56 209
fax: (0463) 514 322
email: hotel@sandwirth.com
An idyllic lakeside location and reliable, inexpensive rooms are among the many features of this family-run hotel. €€

Hotel-Pension Aragia
Völkermarkter Strasse 100
tel: (0463) 31 222
fax: (0463) 31 222-13
email: hotel@aragia.net
This wheelchair-friendly *pension* is some distance from the city centre and isn't particularly spectacular, but it does have a restaurant. €€

Lienz
Hotel Haidenhof
Grafendorfer Strasse 12
tel: (04852) 62 440
fax: (04852) 62 440-6
email: info.@haidenhof.at
Country manor some distance from the city centre but close to the natural beauty of the Tyrolean green hills and golden meadows. €

Romantikhotel Traube
Hauptplatz 14
tel: (04852) 64 444
fax: (04852) 64 184
email: hotel.traube@tirol.com
Four-star hotel includes many extras such as golf, bike rentals, great restaurant, swimming pool and very comfortable rooms. Located right on the main square. €€

Matrei
Hotel Rauter
Rauterplatz
tel: (04875) 6611
fax: (04875) 6613
email: hotel.rauter@netway.at
Full-service resort for sports-oriented guests. €€€€

Villach
Hotel Goldenes Lamm
Hauptplatz 1
tel: (04242) 24 105
fax: (04242) 24 105-56
email: hotel.goldeneslamm@utanet.at
Centrally located, comfortable hotel with annex containing less expensive rooms with fewer amenities. Facilities available for wheelchair users. €€

Hotel Mosser
Bahnhofstrasse 9
tel: (04242) 24 115
fax: (04242) 24 115-222
email: info@hotelmosser.at
Upmarket, friendly establishment that caters to those seeking straightforward rooms and spa treatments. There are non-smoking rooms also. €€–€€€

TYROL

Innsbruck
Austria Classic-Hotel Zach
Wilhelm-Greil-Strasse 11
tel: (0512) 589 667
fax: (0512) 589 667-7
email: info@hotel-zach.at
City centre hotel with large, well-decorated rooms. Abundant breakfast buffet, and televisions and telephones in all rooms. €€

Binder
Dr-Glatz-Strasse 20
tel: (0512) 33 436-0
fax: (0512) 33 436-99
email: hotel@binders.at
Twee little hotel with simple rooms in a good location. Hospitable reception. €

City Hotel Goldene Krone
Maria-Theresien-Strasse 46
tel: (0512) 586 160
fax: (0512) 580 1896
email: goldene-krone@aon.at
Contemporary, central hotel but with small rooms. €€

Goldener Adler
Herzog-Friedrich-Strasse 6
tel: (0512) 571 1110
fax: (0512) 584 409
email: office@goldeneradler.com
Grand Austrian hotel featuring large, comfortable rooms and a convenient central location. €€€

Hotel Helga
Brandlweg 3
tel: (0512) 261 137
fax: (0512) 261 137-6
email: hotel.helga@tirol.com
Not close to town, but rooms have TVs and en-suite facilities. Pool. €€

Internationales Studenten Haus
Rechengasse 7
tel: (0512) 5010
fax: (0512) 501 905
email: office@studentenhaus.at
Large, dorm-like rooms, open July–Oct. Accepts all credit cards. €

Weisses Kreuz
Herzog-Friedrich Strasse 31
tel: (0512) 59 479-0
fax: (0512) 59 479-90
email: hotel@weisseskreuz.at
Though the exterior of this Altstadt hotel has been preserved for greater authenticity, the rooms have been renovated to modern standards. Choice of en-suite or shared facilities in the hall. Guests can use storage rooms for winter sports equipment. €€

Kitzbühel
Hörl
Josef-Pirchler Strasse 60
tel/fax: (05356) 63 144
Inexpensive hotel near the station, good for early morning departures. It's cheaper still if you choose a room with facilities down the hall. €

Hotel Weisses Rössl
Bichlstrasse 5
tel: (05356) 625 410
fax: (05356) 63 472
email: info@weisses-roessl.com
Central locale whose wide range of bright, tasteful rooms (that include a separate sitting area) is reflected in the diversity of prices. Features a restaurant, indoor pool and bar. €€€–€€€€

VORARLBERG

Bregenz
Hotel Deuring Schlössle
Ehre-Guta-Platz 4
tel: (05574) 47 800
fax: (05574) 478 0080
email: deuring@schloessle.vol.at
A classy hotel that is popular with the casino crowd. Rooms feature

contemporary art. Rooms for non-smokers available. €€€

Hotel Garni Bodensee
Kornmarktstrasse 22
tel: (05574) 42 300-0
fax: (05574) 45 168
email: hotel.bodensee@telemax.at
Comfortable accommodation at affordable prices, this central hotel has a restaurant and parking. €€

Pension Sonne
Kaiserstrasse 8
tel: (05574) 42 572
fax: (05574) 425 724
email: office@bbn.at
Pleasant, affordable rooms (more expensive in summer) in the centre of Bregenz's pedestrian zone. €

Feldkirch

Best Western Hotel Alpenrose
Rosengasse 6
tel: (05522) 721 750
fax: (05522) 721 755
email: hotel.alpenrose@cable.vol.at
A uniquely shaped rose-coloured building that has wheelchair-friendly rooms, a restaurant/bar, cycles and a posh penthouse suite. €€–€€€

Hotel-Gasthof Löwen
Kohlgasse 1
tel: (05522) 3583-0
fax: (05522) 3583-55
email: office@hotel-loewen.at
This hotel, housed in a cheery building, offers guests special touches including a shuttle service from the train station, cycles and a breakfast buffet. €–€€

Lech am Arlberg

Hotel Berghof
tel: (05583) 2635
fax: (05583) 2635-5
email: info@berghof-lech.com
A chalet-like hotel catering to active travellers, especially skiers, the

Berghof doubles its rates in the winter. Amenities include a restaurant/bar, exercise room, cycles and golf course. €€–€€€€

Hotel Restaurant Aurelio
tel: (05583) 22 14
fax: (05583) 34 56
email: aurelio@aurelio.at
Pleasant, mid-range hotel with clean, comfortable rooms, many with sitting areas. Open December–April only. €

Haus Brunelle
tel: (05583) 29 76
email: brunelle@aon.at
Simple *pension* for travellers sticking to a budget. Breakfast included in the rate. Open in summer and December–April only. €

Campsites

The Austrian Tourist Office Publicity Department, tel: (01) 587 2000, will send you a detailed map of all the country's camping sites on request. If you are planning to travel with a caravan, you should ascertain in advance the roads and passes on which these vehicles are prohibited. Trailers need a *carnet de passage*.

Österreichischer Camping Club (ÖCC), 1, Wien, Schubertring 1–3
tel: (01) 71 199-0.

Youth Hostels

Austria has about 100 youth hostels dotted around the country. Information can be obtained from:
Österreichischer Jugendherbergsverband,
Schottenring 28, 1010 Wien,
tel: (01) 533 5353,
fax: (01) 535 0861,
www.jgh.at

Eating Out

Where to Eat

Austrian cooking is generally rich and wholesome. Almost every large town has several nationally known restaurants. Listed here are some of the top dining establishments

VIENNA

Vienna's restaurant offerings are simply astounding; anything from continental to Asian food can easily be located. But try to sample the local cuisine. You will find a *Beisel*, or little local bar/restaurant, on just about every street corner in Vienna. Their simplicity reflects the uncomplicated culture and traditions of Vienna; the wine is basic table wine; the food is good home cooking; and the prices won't break the bank.

Some have developed into fashionable bars and top-class restaurants in recent years but others remain affordable and low-key. The best way to recognise a real *Beisel* is to check whether the owners do the cooking and pull the beer themselves, and whether the menu is written on a slate.

You also haven't seen Vienna properly until you've paid a visit to a *Heuriger*. Both *Heurigen* and *Buschenschanken* are places where new wine is sold by the wine-grower, and are recognisable by the wreaths or branches hanging outside the door. They often have beautiful gardens in which you can sample the latest vintage in the shade of chestnut trees or under the actual grapevine; most have music and a buffet.

Don't miss the wonderful open-air Naschmarkt (4, Linke und Recht

Beisln

Beisln are large, no-frills eating houses, usually family-run *(see page 84)*. The interiors are often wood-panelled, giving a warm, homely atmosphere, and the food is traditional Austrian, with meat dominating the menu.

Weinzeile, Karlsplatz), open Mon–Fri 6am–6pm, Sat 6am–5pm; this market has plenty of food stalls, and a genuine Viennese ambience.

Altes Fassl
5, Ziegelofengasse 37
tel: (01) 544 4298
Open Mon–Fri 11.30am–3pm, 6pm–1am
Beisel featuring al fresco eating in atmospheric courtyards shaded by enormous chestnut trees. €–€€

Braunsperger
19, Sieveringer Strasse 108 (in Sievering, outside the city)
tel: (01) 320 3992
Open daily Jan and alternate months. 3pm–midnight
If you have a particular interest in genuine local grape varieties, then don't miss this *Heuriger*. *Weissburgunder, roter Zweigelt* and *Grüner Veltliner* are among those on offer, while *Gemischter Satz* is a blend of different grape varieties that are picked and pressed together. €–€€

Cantinetta Antinori
1, Jasomirgottstrasse 3–5
tel: (01) 533 7722-0
Open daily noon–2pm, 6pm–midnight
A unique restaurant located in the meat district but specialising in exquisite fish dishes. Closely packed tables are not for non-smokers or the shy. Try the wines produced by the owners. €€–€€€

Do&Co
1, Stephansplatz 12
tel: (01) 535 3969-0
Open daily noon–3pm, 6pm–midnight
A city-centre venue in which to see and be seen. Wonderful view of the cathedral, colourful interior design,

friendly service and fabulous food, including a Japanese tepanyaki grill on Tues and Sat. €€€–€€€€

Enrico Panigl
8, Josefstädter Strasse 91
tel: (01) 406 5218; and
1, Schönlaterngasse 11
tel: (01) 513 1716
Open daily 6pm–2am
Arty and media types flock here for the Italian food and bar snacks, eaten at long communal tables. €–€€

Feuervogel
9, Alserbachstrasse 21
tel: (01) 317 5391
Open daily 7pm–2am, closed Aug
Excellent food from the Ukraine – most customers are recent arrivals from the Kiev area. €€€

Figlmüller
1, Wollzeile 5
tel: (01) 512 6177
Most famous for its *Wienerschnitzel (see page 121)*. €€

Fuhrgassl-Huber
19, Neustift am Walde 68 (in Neustift am Walde, outside city)
tel: (01) 440 1405
Open Mon–Sat 2pm–midnight, Sun, holidays noon–midnight
If you fancy a rustic setting, don't miss the earthy atmosphere of this *Heuriger*. On days when it's too cold to sit outside in the magnificent garden, warm yourself indoors with a plate of suckling pig, grilled chicken or other choice items from the buffet. €–€€

Gerhard Klager
21, Stammersdorfer Strasse 14 (in Stammersdorf, outside city)
tel: (01) 292 4107
Open Mon–Sat 3pm–midnight, every other month
This *Heuriger* is particularly good for children, who can play in the playground while the adults sample fine wines and high-quality food. If you're driving, try the delicious low-alcohol grape *must*. €–€€

Gulaschmuseum
1 Schulerstrasse 20
tel: (01) 512 1017
Open Mon–Fri 9am–midnight, Sat–Sun 10am–midnight
Touristy place with most of menu devoted to the heavy Hungarian stew that gives the restaurant its

name; there's also a vegetarian version with mushrooms. €–€€

Hubert Andreas
21, Russbergstrasse 88 (in Strebersdorf, outside city)
tel: (01) 290 1476
Open every other month Mon–Fri 4–11pm, Sat 3–11pm, Sun 10.30am–11pm
Wine-grower Hubert Andreas has earned a reputation for his truly excellent wine, and the meals here complement his vintages. €–€€

Kervansaray/Hummerbar
1, Mahlerstrasse 9
tel: (01) 512 8843-0
Open noon–midnight, closed Sun.
Two restaurants in one: Kervansaray serves up seafood dishes; the less expensive Hummerbar offers Turkish doner kebab and other international favourites. €€–€€€€

Koh-i-noor
1, Marc-Aurel-Strasse 8
tel: (01) 533 0080
The strains of the sitar and the hiss of the charcoal grill provide a sonorous accompaniment to the Indian meals in this elegant restaurant. €€

Price Categories

€€€€ = €50–120
€€€ = €25–50
€€ = €12–25
€ = Less than €12
Prices are based on an average three-course meal for one

Korso
1, Mahlerstrasse 2
tel: (01) 5151 6546
Open Sun–Fri noon–2pm, 7pm–1am; no lunch July, Aug
The place for connoisseurs of new Austrian cuisine, Korso offers an impressive range of dishes, from potato goulash and tripe to experimental creations such as skate "wings" and morel ravioli. Korso also has a range of rare Austrian and foreign wines. €€€€

Kulisse
17, Rosensteingasse 39
tel: (01) 485 3870
Open Mon–Sun 6pm–1am
Outskirts *Beisel* in a converted

theatre; look out for itinerant cabaret artists. €–€€

Ma Pitom
1, Seitenstettengasse 5
tel: (01) 535 4313
Open Mon–Thur lunch, dinner till 1am; Fri–Sun till 2am. No lunch Sun
Ma Pitom combines Israeli and Italian cuisine – hummus and pitta bread pitted against *zuppe pavese* and lasagne. More a part of the youthful Vienna *szene* than a restaurant. €€–€€€

Nordsee
1, Kärntner Strasse 25; also at Kohlmarkt, Naschmarkt and Mariahilfer Strasse
Café-syle joint specialising in fresh seafood, including succulent salmon, prepared in a variety of ways. Service is fast and friendly and the locations are well placed whenever you need a quick bite. €–€€

Palais Schwarzenberg
3, Schwarzenbergplatz 9
tel: (01) 798 451 5600

Open daily noon–2.30pm, 6–11pm
Enjoy an unforgettable evening's dining in the conservatory, with superb set menu, a glass of wine and the dulcet tones of the Wiener Staatsoper orchestra wafting over from the adjacent park. €€€€

Pfudl
1, Bäckerstrasse 22
tel: (01) 512 6705
Country-style atmosphere, finely prepared traditional Viennese cuisine, and speedy service. €–€€

Coffee Houses and *Konditorei* in Vienna

The Viennese coffee house tradition goes back 300 years. People take their coffee seriously here, and it is served in a wide variety of ways, always with a glass of water. *Konditorei* (cake shops) are equally indulgent – and essential to the Vienna experience.

Alt Wien
1, Bäckerstrasse 9
tel: (01) 512 5222
Open Sun–Thur 10am–2am, Fri–Sat 10am–4am
A café for the literati.

Alte Backstube (Old Bakehouse)
8, Lange Gasse 34
tel: (01) 406 1101
Open Sept–mid-July, Tues–Sat 10am–midnight, Sun 4pm–midnight.
A museum café with old utensils on the wall, and an 18th-century oven.

Bräunerhof
1, Stallburggasse 2
tel: (01) 512 3893
Open Mon–Fri 7.30am–8.30pm, Sat 7.30am–6pm, Sun 10am–6pm
Popular city-centre café with a wide selection of *Torten*.

Café Central
1, Herrengasse 14
tel: (01) 533 3763-38
Open Mon–Sat 8am–11pm, Sun 10am–6pm.
Splendid gothic painted ceiling. Busy but cosy.

Café Engländer
1, Postgasse 2
tel: (01) 966 8665
Open Mon–Sat 8am–1am, Sun 10am–1am
An all-day and late-night café.

Café Griensteidl
1, Michaelerplatz 2
tel: (01) 535 2692-0
Open daily 8am–11pm
Light and airy café in traditional style, next door to the Hofburg.

Café Museum
1, Friedrichstrasse 6
tel: (01) 586 5202
Open daily 8am–midnight
Popular with Academy of the Visual Arts students and lecturers.

Demel
1, Kohlmarkt 1
tel: (01) 535 1717
Open daily 10am–7pm
The best *tortes* in town

Diglas
1, Wollzeile 10
tel. (01) 512 5765-0
Open daily 7am–midnight
Old coffee house with huge *Torten* in the window, near Stephansplatz.

Drechsler
6, Linke Wienzeile 22
tel: (01) 587 8580
Open Mon–Fri 7am–8pm, Sat 4am–6pm
A shabby but superb place where customers are the main attraction.

Frauenhuber
1, Himmelpfortgasse 6
tel: (01) 512 8383
Open Mon–Sat 8am–midnight, Sunday, holidays 10am–10pm
The classic Viennese café.

Goldegg
4, Argentinierstrasse 49
tel: (01) 505 9162
Open Mon–Fri 8am–10pm, Sat 8am–1pm, Sept–third week in July
A place to enjoy a quiet *Mélange*.

Hartauer
1, Riemergasse 9
tel: (01) 512 8981
Open Mon–Fri 8am–2am; Sat 5pm–2am. The place for opera fans.

Hawelka
1, Dorotheergasse 6
tel: (01) 512 8230
Open Mon, Wed–Sat 8am–2am, Sun 4pm–2am. Stylish former artists' café. The famed *buchteln* (yeast dumplings) are served after 10pm.

Landtmann
1, Dr-Karl-Lueger-Ring 4
tel: (01) 532 0621-0
Open daily 8am–midnight
Hangout for thespians and media types, next to the Burgtheater.

Lehmann
1, Graben 12
tel: (01) 512 1815
Huge cakes in the window. Good for coffee and light meals.

Prückel
1, Stubenring 24
tel: (01) 512 6115
Open daily 9am–10pm
1950s café with weekend piano entertainment.

Schlosscafé Parkhotel Schönbrunn
13, Hietzinger Hauptstrasse 10–14
tel: (01) 817 5715
Open daily 9am–6pm
Regal café in the palace.

Zartl
3, Rasumofskygasse 7
tel: (01) 712 5560
Open Mon–Fri 8am–midnight, Sat–Sun 9am–6pm, closed July
Featuring evening events such as music and literary readings.

Rosenberger
1, Maysedergasse 2
tel: (01) 512 3458
Open daily 7.30am–11pm
Popular Innere-Stadt self-service
restaurant for salads, soups, juices
and coffee. Choose your meal from
assorted food stations. €

Schweizerhaus
2, Strasse des 1. Mai 116
tel: (01) 728 0152
Open daily Mar–mid-Nov,
10am–midnight
Particularly recommended if you've
just been to the Prater and the kids
have spent all your money there.
Leave them in the children's
playground to work off any energy
they may have left, and relax with a
draught beer in the tree-shaded
garden. €

Silberwirt
5, Schlossgasse 21
tel: (01) 544 4907
Open daily, lunch, dinner–midnight.
Very popular *Beisel* at weekends.
Good, traditional dishes at a decent
price. €–€€

Stiegen-Beisl
6, Gumpendorfer Strasse 36
tel: (01) 587 0999
Open 6pm–2am Mon–Sat.
Classic Austrian fare in this simple,
cosy and comfortable *Beisel*.

Trzesniewski
1, Dorotheergasse 1
tel: (01) 512 3291
also many other branches.
Open Mon–Fri 8.30am–7.30pm
Featuring the beloved Viennese
open-faced sandwich, with toppings
such as egg, red onion, salmon or
crab. Diners cluster around chest-
high tables and eat standing up;
beer is the traditional drink here. €

Weingut Reinprecht
19, Cobenzlgasse 22 (in Grinzing)
tel: (01) 3201 4710
Open daily Mar–Nov,
3.30pm–midnight
Everything that a *Heuriger* should
be: excellent local wines, a large
and varied buffet including grilled
meats, traditional Viennese
melodies in the background, and a
large terraced garden. €–€€

Witwe Bolte
7, Gutenberggasse 13
tel: (01) 523 1450

Open daily 11.30am–midnight
Viennese home cooking in the
city's oldest and most basic *Beisel*,
in the interesting Spittelberg
district. €–€€

Wrenkh
15, Hollergasse 9
tel: (01) 892 3356 and
Bauernmarkt 10
tel: (01) 533 1526
Open Mon–Sat 11.30am–2.30pm,
6pm–midnight
A place for vegetarians and healthy
eaters. First-class food, excellent
wines and a cosy atmosphere. €€

Zu den 3 Hacken
1, Singerstrasse 28
tel: (01) 512 5895
Open Mon–Sat 9am–midnight,
closed public holidays
A veritable temple for lovers of
Viennese cuisine. The menu is big,
and so are the portions. Very
popular with the locals, so advance
booking is essential. €–€€

Price Categories

€€€€ = €50–120
€€€ = €25–50
€€ = €12–25
€ = Less than €12
Prices are based on an average
three-course meal for one

Zu den drei Husaren
1, Weihburggasse 4
tel: (01) 512 1092
Open daily noon–3pm, 6pm–1am
Luxurious meals served by
candlelight, complete with waltz
music and a stylish interior. The
starters and desserts are
particularly recommended. €€€€

Zum Schwarzes Kameel
1, Bognergasse 5
tel: (01) 533 8125-0
Open Mon–Fri 9am–8pm, Sat
9am–3am
Delicatessen and art nouveau
restaurant that's full of history –
Beethoven used to eat here, but the
place has become over-trendy. €

Zwölf-Apostel-Keller
1, Sonnenfelsgasse 3
tel: (01) 512 6777
Open daily 4.30pm–midnight,
closed July

This well-known city-centre *Heuriger*
has an historic wine cellar on two
floors, and serves good wines and
hot (though average) food. €€

LOWER AUSTRIA

Joching
Weingut Jamek
tel: (02715) 2235
Open Mon–Thur lunch, Fri, Sat
lunch, dinner. Much-loved
restaurant attached to one of
Austria's most famous little
vineyards. €€–€€€

Kleinwien
Schickh
Avastrasse 2
tel: (02736) 7218-0
Open daily, lunch, dinner
Intimate venue for hearty food. €€

Krems
Gasthof Weinhaus Jell
Hoher Markt 8–9
tel: (02732) 82 345
Heuriger for hearty Austrian fare.
Sample some locally produced wine
with your meal. Rooms are also
available upstairs. €

Nordsee
Corner of Oberelanstrasse and
Der Kirkengasse
Chain fish joint; good value. €

Mautern
Bacher
Südtiroler Platz 2
tel: (02732) 82 937
Open Wed–Sun, lunch, dinner
Chef Lisl Wagner-Bacher shows why
she was awarded three tocques in
the *Gault-Millau* guide. €€€€

Melk
Hotel-Restaurant Zur Post
Linzer Strasse 1
tel: (02752) 52 345
Posh eatery featuring *haute cuisine*
Austrian style. €€€

Restaurant zum "Alten Brauhof"
Linzer Strasse 25
tel: (02752) 52 296
Sit and relax at outdoor tables
while savouring heavy
Wienerschnitzel or fresh greens
from the salad bar. €

BURGENLAND

Eisenstadt
Café Esterházy
Esterházy Platz
tel: (02682) 61 505
Posh restaurant with an after-hours bar. €€€
Burgenländische Gästehausbrauerei
Pfarrgasse 22
tel: (02682) 61 561-63
Try the beer, micro-brewed on site, to go with the basic pub fare. €

Neuseidl am See
Rathausstüberl
Kirchengasse
tel: (02167) 2883
Open 10am–midnight
A terrace that's especially pleasant in summer, and a kitchen featuring local fish and wine. €€

Podersdorf
Gasthaus Zur Dankbarkeit
Haupstrasse 39
tel: (02177) 2223
Tiny, family-owned place featuring great Jewish regional cookery. Weekends only in winter. €–€€

Rust
Romerzeche
Rathausplatz 11
tel: (02685) 332
A popular restaurant. Savour goulash for dinner at shared wooden tables in a flowery courtyard. €
Zum Alten Haus
Raiffenstrasse/Franz Josefplatz
tel: (02685) 230
Well-located restaurant serving schnitzel and other Austrian fare. €

Schützen am Gebirge
Taubenkobel
Hauptstrasse 33
tel: (02684) 2297
Open Wed–Sun lunch, dinner
Good for local fish, lamb and vegetable dishes. €€€–€€€€

Weiden am See
Blaue Gans
Seepark
tel: (02167) 7510
Fine Alsatian cuisine a long way from Alsace. Closed winter.
€€€–€€€€

STYRIA

Graz
Restaurant Hotel Erzherzog
Johann Sackstrasse 3
tel: (0316) 811 616
Dine in an atrium surrounded by leafy plants. Limited but traditional menu of Styrian specialities. €€€
Mangolds
Griesgasse 11
tel: (0316) 718 002
Open Mon–Fri 11am–8pm; Sat 11am–4pm.
Vegetarian cafeteria-style joint. €

Mariazell
Gasthof zum Jägerwirt
Hauptplatz 2
tel: (03882) 2362
Traditional Austrian restaurant, good for meat-based dishes. €€

UPPER AUSTRIA

Freistadt
Café Vis à Vis
Salzgasse 13
tel: (07942) 74 293
Jovial beer garden for hearty, local fare such as "farmer's soup". €€€
Goldener Adler
Salzgase 1
tel: (07942) 72 112
Good-value hotel restaurant; standard main dishes, great desserts.

Linz
Gelbes Krokodil
Dametzstrasse 30
tel: (0732) 784 182
Open daily 5–11pm
Eclectic dining at this everything-under-one-roof entertainment/dining complex in the Moviemento Cinema. Varied menu (including lots of vegetarian options) can be savoured while watching an avant-garde film. €€
Mangolds
Hauptplatz 3
tel: (0732) 785 688
Popular, self-service vegetarian cafeteria. Most of the food is organic, including the eggs. Juices and salad-bar offerings are the stars. €€

Ursulinenhof
Landstrasse 31
tel: (0732) 774 686
Open Mon–Sat lunch, dinner
Exquisite, creative cuisine, bland interior. €€€

Steyr
Zu den drei Rosen
Hotel Mader Stadtplatz 36
tel: (07252) 533 580
Closed Sunday. Dine on local cuisine while seated on the sunny terrace in a venerable restaurant attached to a posh hotel. Good *tagesmenü* (daily special). €€€

THE SALZKAMMERGUT

Bad Ischl
Restaurant Goldenes Schiff
Stifter-kai 3
tel: (06132) 24 241
Excellent restaurant specialising in locally caught fish dishes. Sit on the terrace in sunny weather. €€–€€€
Wirsthaus zum Blauen Enzian
Wirerstrasse 2
tel: (06132) 28 992
Upmarket restaurant serving a variety of pastas and salads. €€€
Café Zauner
Pfarrgasse 7
tel: (06132) 233 1020
Open Wed–Mon 8.30am–6.00pm
You'd be remiss to pass through Bad Ischl without trying one (or two) of the delectable pastries on offer at this venerable café. Also hot dishes and salads served on the river terrace at the Esplanade location. €

Hallstatt
Gasthof Zur Mühle
Kirchenweg 36
tel: (06134) 8318
Good-value eatery in a guesthouse. Try the pizza – the cheapest meal in this tourist town. €

Mondsee
Café-Restaurant Lido
Robert Baum Promenade
tel: (06232) 3370
Open for lunch, dinner until 10pm
Good place for dependable favourites such as boiled beef and

Wienerschnitzel. Savour an ice cream on the serene lakeside terrace. €€€

Pizzeria Nudelini
Marktplatz 5
tel: (06232) 4193
Pizzas and salads in a central location. €€

La Farandole
Schlössl 150/Tiefgraben
tel: (06232) 3475
You'll be well cared for at this gourmet establishment that specialises in its own Austrian, French and Swiss dishes. €€€€

St Gilgen

Grossgasthof Kendler
Kirchenplatz 3
tel: (06227) 2223
Fresh cuts of meat grace the menu at this welcoming guesthouse. Vegetarians can opt for standards such as spinach dumplings. €–€€

St Wolfgang

Pizzeria Mirabella
Pilgerstrasse 152
tel: (06138) 2353
Basic pizza parlour with a menu that includes pastas. Good value in a very touristy location. €€

SALZBURG (CITY)

Augustiner Bräu
Kloster Mülln
Augustinergasse 4
tel: (0662) 431 246
Open Mon–Fri 3–11pm, Sat, Sun, holidays 2.30–11pm
Huge beer hall with outdoor garden that becomes very rowdy at weekends. Choose Austrian dishes from self-service counter. €–€€

Café Bazaar
Schwarzstrasse 3
tel: (0662) 874 278
Open Mon–Sat 7.30am–11pm
Charming café on Salzach River with terrace overlooking Altstadt. A cup of coffee entitles you to an afternoon of people watching. €

Goldener Hirsch
Getreidegasse 37
tel: (0662) 8084-0
Elegant hotel restaurant featuring fine Austrian cuisine. €€€–€€€€

Nordsee
Getreidegasse 27
tel: (0662) 842 320
Open Mon–Sun 9am–8pm
Good, quick seafood meals for those who need to maximise sightseeing time. €–€€

Zum Fidelen Affen
Priesterhausgasse 8
tel: (0662) 877 361
Open Mon–Sat 5pm–midnight
Pub in heart of Linzergasse district with convivial atmosphere, outdoor seating and efficient service. Serves hearty dishes such as Hungarian goulash and *Wienerschnitzel.* €–€€

SALZBURG PROVINCE

Zell Am See

Moby Dick
Kreuzgasse 16
tel: (06542) 73 320
Open Mon–Fri 9am–6pm, Sat 8am–1pm
Fish (some from the adjoining lake) dominates a simple but satisfying menu at this unpretentious restaurant. €

Schloss Prielau
Hofmannsthalstrasse
tel: (06542) 72 609
Dine like royalty in this castle, where the menu specialises in traditional Austrian fare. Some non-smoking dining rooms; reservations recommended. €€€

Zum Hirschen
Dreifaltigkeitsgasse 1
tel: (06542) 7740
Hotel restaurant demonstrating a light touch with the local specialities. €€

CARINTHIA AND EAST TYROL

Klagenfurt

Da Luigi
Khevenhüllerstrasse 2
tel: (0463) 516 651
Open Tues–Sat 6–10pm
An Italian restaurant with the emphasis on fresh produce. Particularly recommended for its seafood. €€€

Dolce Vita
Heuplatz 2
tel: (0463) 55 499
Closed Sat & Sun
Small but highly rated Italian restaurant. €€–€€€

Maria Loretto
Lorettoweg 54
tel: (0463) 24 465
About 5 km (3 miles) west of Klagenfurt, the Maria Loretto is right on the edge of the lake and has a balcony, terrace and garden, with lovely views over the water. The emphasis is on fish, but there is a range of Austrian and international dishes. €€–€€€

Kötschach-Mauthen

Restaurant Kellerwand
tel: (04715) 269
A gourmet restaurant listed among the country's best eating establishments– proprietor Sissy Sonnleitner has picked up numerous national awards. €€€€

Lienz

Gästhof Neuwirt
Schweizergasse 22
tel: (04852) 62 101
Tyrolean restaurant known for its fish dishes. €€€

Matrei

Restaurant-Hotel Rauter
Rauterplatz 3
tel: (04875) 6611
Well-prepared Austrian cuisine for the hungry hiker. €€

Villach

Restaurant Mosser
Bahnhofstrasse 9
tel: (04242) 24 115
Located in Hotel Mosser, this restaurant offers no surprises on the schnitzel-heavy menu. Good, simple fare. €€

TYROL

Innsbruck
Alstadtstüberl
Riesengasse 13
tel: (0512) 582 347
Open Mon–Sat, lunch, dinner
In a busy pedestrian area, this
restaurant serves filling Tyrolean
meals such as *Tiroler Gröstl* and
tender *Tafelspitz*. €€€

Philippine
Müllerstrasse 9
tel: (0512) 589 157
Open Mon–Sat, lunch & dinner
An oasis for vegetarians with an
innovative menu that's not
restricted to Filipino cuisine,
despite the name. €€

Stiftskeller
Burggraben 31
tel: (0512) 583 490
Good for fish, especially trout. Quiet,
affordable restaurant in the centre
of the tourist area near Hofburg. €€

Thai-Li
Maria-Theresien-Strasse 18
tel: (0512) 562 813
Book early for this exceptional Thai
restaurant featuring favourites such
as green curries and *pad Thai*. A
refreshing change from heavy
Tyrolean fare. €€–€€€

Kitzbühel
Chizzo
Josef-Herold Strasse 2
tel: (053566) 2475
Good selection of Tyrolean cuisine.
Attractive seating outside. €€

Price Categories

€€€€ = €50–120
€€€ = €25–50
€€ = €12–25
€ = Less than €12
Prices are based on an average
three-course meal for one

VORARLBERG

Bregenz
Restaurant Deuring-Schlössle
tel: (05574) 47 800
One of the classiest restaurants in
Bregenz, ideal for those who have
an expansive budget. €€€

Zum Goldenen Hirschen
tel: (05574) 42 815
Open 10am–midnight (closed Tues)
Homely Austrian pub serving local
favourites as well as Austrian takes
on international classics such as
chili con carne. €€

Feldkirch
Restaurant-Gasthof Löwen
Kohlgasse 1
tel: (05522) 3583-0
Restaurant affiliated to a hotel,
featuring solid Austrian fare. €€€

Pizzeria-Trattoria La Taverna
Vorstadtstrasse 18
tel: (0522) 79 293
Open daily 11.30am–2pm,
5pm–midnight
Typical Italian pizza and pasta with
some choice for vegetarians. €€

Lech am Arlberg
Pizza Charly
tel: (05583) 2339
Open daily 11am–2pm,
4pm–midnight, closed June
Popular with skiers and others for
dependable, inexpensive pizzas. €

Restaurant-Hotel Krone
tel: (05583) 2551
Reservations recommended at this
classy après-ski eatery. €€€

Drinking Notes

Austria has a long tradition of
viticulture. The Romans tended
vineyards in the old region of
Vindobona, a tradition re-
established by local monasteries
1,000 years later. More than a third
of the total area used for the
cultivation of grapes is devoted to
the tangy and slightly peppery
Grüner Veltliner. Blaufränkische, a
hearty, fruity red wine, is also very
popular. Wine in Austria is
separated into four categories:
Landwein (table wine),
Qualitätswein (wine of certified
origin and quality), *Kabinettwein*
(high-quality white) and
Prädikatswein (special quality).
Vineyards are primarily cultivated
in four provinces: Vienna, Lower
Austria, Burgenland and Styria. In
most vineyard areas you can pay a
visit to one of the wine cellars for a

Heurigen

Heurigen are cosy wine bars that
serve new wine. *Heurig* means
"this year's", and it is here that
vintners have traditionally
encouraged tastings in order to
sell their white wine. Vienna's
traditional *Heurigen* can be found
in the wine-producing villages
that have now been incorporated
into the city's outer suburbs *(see
page 141)*. Others are in wine-
growing regions around the
country.

Vienna Suburbs
Mayer am Pfarrplatz
19, Pfarrplatz 2, Heiligenstadt
tel: (01) 370 1287

Reinprecht
19, Cobenzlgasse 22, Grinzing
tel: (01) 320 1471

Donnerskirchen (Burgenland)
Liesserhof
tel: (02683) 8636

Stadtheurigen
These are wine taverns within
Vienna's Inner City:

Esterházykeller
1, Haarhof 1
tel: (01) 533 3482

Zwölf Apostelkeller
1, Sonnenfelsgasse 3
tel: (01) 512 6777

little sampling. Or, better still, sit
out in the open, under the shade of
old trees and have the wine-grower
himself serve you a glass.

For further details of wine in
Austria, contact your nearest tourist
office *(see page 308)*.

WHITE WINE

Riesling – a lively, piquant wine with
a flowery bouquet; grown in Wachau.
Grüner Veltliner – full-bodied, fruity
and piquant; produced in Lower
Austria and Burgenland.
Traminer – aromatic.
Zierfandler – a rich bouquet.
Müller-Thurgau – light and sweet
with a flowery bouquet.

Welschriesling – finely full-bodied; from Burgenland and Styria.
Weisser Burgunder – a nutty bouquet.
Neuburger – full and hearty; grown in Lower Austria and Burgenland.

RED WINE

Zweigelt blau – fine and fruity.
Blauer Portugieser – mild; produced in Lower Austria.
Blauer Burgunder – fiery, with a nutty bouquet; found in Lower Austria and Burgenland.
Schilcher – fruity and sharp; the Styrian speciality, produced in the western region of the province.

Culture

Classical music was born in Austria, a fact to which a large number of annual, traditional music festivals pay tribute. The majority of these festival performances and week-long celebrations take place during the summer months. The **Austrian Tourist Information Centre**, tel: (01) 587 2000, will send you a calendar of the year's events.

Festivals

Vienna
Summer Fesival in Schönbrunn Palace Theatre (Sommerspiele im Schönbrunner Schlosstheater), 1, Fleischmarkt 24, tel: (01) 512 0100, www.wienerkammeroper.at Mid-July–mid-August.
Vienna Easter and Summer Music (Osterklang and Klangbogen), 1, Stadiongasse 9, tel: (01) 42 717, www.klangbogen.at Orchestral works, chamber music and opera. Easter & mid-July–mid-August.
Vienna Festival (Wiener Festwochen), 6, Lehargasse 11, tel: (01) 589 2222, www.festwochen.at A key event on the music scene: orchestras, opera and dance companies from around the world converge on the city for a month of performances. Mid-May–mid-June.
Viennale Film Festival, 7, Siebensterngasse 2, tel: (01) 5265 9470, email: office@viennale.at Two weeks from mid-October.

Lower Austria
Baden Summer Operettas (Badener Operettensommer), Stadttheater Baden, tel: (02252) 48 547, email: ticket@stadttheater-baden.at Mid-June–early September.

Midsummer's Night, Wachau region Bonfires and dances celebrating the summer solstice. Late June.

Burgenland
Haydn Festival (Haydn Festspiele), Eisenstadt (Schloss Esterházy), tel: (02682) 61 866, www.haydnfestival.at Second week of September.
Mörbisch Lakeside Festival (Seefestspiele Mörbisch), Mörbisch, tel: (02682) 662 100 Operettas on a stage built out over the Neusiedler See, with each performance ending in a firework display over the water. Mid-July–late August.
St Martin's Day Day of feasting and drinking to honour the patron saint of pubs and inns; roasted goose, red cabbage and plenty of spirits. 11 November.
Thousand Wine Festival, Eisenstadt Vintners from around Burgenland congregate here to offer wines of the region. Mid-August.

Styria
Feast of St Barbara, Leoben Parades and church services honouring the patron saint of miners. Mid-December.
Schladming Music Summer, (Schladminger Musiksommer), Schladming, tel: (03687) 22 508. Courses and concerts. August.
Styriarte Graz, Graz (Palais Attems) tel: (0316) 812 9410, www.styriarte.com A summer festival of music in Graz founded in 1985. Mid-June–end July.

Upper Austria
International Brucknerfest, Linz, tel: (0732) 732 7612-0, www.brucknerhaus.linz.at A celebration of Bruckner's music. Last three weeks of September.
Operetta Festival (Operettenwochen Bad Ischl), Bad Ischl, tel: (06132) 23 839, www.operette.badischl.at July–early September.
Upper Austrian Monastery Concerts (OÖ Stiftskonzerte), Linz, tel: (0732) 776 127, www.stiftskonzerte.at. June–July.

Salzkammergut

Corpus Christi, Hallstatt. Also in Lungau (Salzburg Province). Processions of firemen, pensioners, women wearing garlands, and flowery boats on the lake, combined with much singing. Early June

Salzburg and Salzburg Province

Mozart Serenades (Mozart Serenaden), Salzburg, tel: (0662) 436 870 or 828 695
Candlelight concerts. Easter to the end of the year.

Mozart Week (Mozart-Woche), Salzburg, tel: (0662) 873 154, www.mozarteum.at
Major orchestras and chamber music groups play Mozart favourites and less well-known works. Fourth week of January.

Perchtenlauf, St Johann im Pongau Townsmen dress as spirits and parade through town, blessing houses as they go. Early January.

Salzburg Culture Days (Salzburger Kulturtage), Salzburg, tel: (0662) 845 346. Last 2 weeks of October.

Salzburg Festival (Salzburger Festspiele), Salzburg, tel: (0662) 804 5500, www.salzburgfestival.at
The world-famous annual tribute to Mozart in his home town, when music lovers from all over the world come to celebrate. Mid-July–August.

Salzburg Fortress Concerts (Salzburger Festungskonzerte), Salzburg, tel: (0662) 825 858
Chamber concerts are held in the Salzburg Fortress. Year-round.

Salzburg Palace Concerts (Salzburger Schlosskonzerte), Salzburg, tel: (0662) 848 5860, www.salzburger-schlosskonzerte.at
All year round, chamber concerts are held in Schloss Mirabell.

What's On in Vienna

For details of what's on in Vienna, get hold of a copy of *Wien Programm*, which lists each day's events for a month, including opera, concerts, drama, exhibitions, lectures and walking tours with guides. It is available from all tourist information offices, or tel: (01) 24 555.

Carinthia

Carinthian Summer (Carinthischer Sommer), Ossiach, tel: (04243) 2510, www.carinthischersommer.at
July–August.

International Music in Millstatt (Internationale Musikwochen in Millstatt), Millstatt, tel: (04766) 202 235, www.buk.krn.gv.at/millstattmusik May–October.

Villach Kirchtag, Villach
Annual birthday party for the village turns into a night of non-stop drinking and revelry. Early August.

Tyrol

Alpabtrieb, Zell am Ziller
Merriment to mark the moving of local cattle to lower pastures. Early October.

Ambras Palace Concerts (Ambraser Schlosskonzerte), Innsbruck, tel: (0521) 571 032, www.altemusik.at July–early August.

Hahnenkamm Ski Race, Kitzbühel
Famous ski race on frighteningly steep downhill course. January.

International Summer Dance Festival, Innsbruck
Virtuoso dancers of various styles from around the world converge for two weeks of performance. Early July.

Vorarlberg

Bregenz Festival (Bregenzer Festspiele), Bregenz, tel: (05574) 4076, www.bregenzerfestspiele.com
A major opera production, symphony and chamber concerts, and lavish theatrical productions. Mid-July–mid-August.

Montafon Summer Concerts (Montafoner Konzertsommer), Schruns, tel: (05556) 722 530, www.montafon.at Mid-June–late August.

Schubertiade, Schwarzenberg, tel: (05576) 72 091, www.schubertiade.at
Prestigious chamber music festival. June and late August.

Theatre

For the non-German speaker, Viennese theatre will have limited appeal. However, there are a few English-speaking theatre groups,

and the Burgtheater is worth visiting for its splendid interior.

Burgtheater
1, Dr-Karl-Lueger-Ring 2, tel: (01) 51 444 4140
Vienna's most prestigious theatre, staging serious drama. Spectacular foyer and staircases.

International Theatre
9, Porzellangasse 8, tel: (01) 319 6272
This is where expats put on plays, both on the main stage and in the smaller, more intimate room downstairs.

Vienna's English Theatre
8, Josefsgasse 12, tel: (01) 402 1260-0
The well-established English Theatre (founded in 1963) attracts visiting groups from the UK and the US, as well as putting on its own shows.

Cinema

In Vienna, several cinemas screen films in English. The website www.film.at gives current listings – click the 'OV' box for English-language versions. These are some of the best venues:

Artis Kino-Treff, 1, Schultergasse/ Jordangasse, tel: (01) 535 6570
With six screens, a bar, and plenty of seating, showing mainstream hit films in their original English.

Breitenseer Lichtspiele
14, Breitenseerstrasse 21
tel: (01) 982 2173
Opened in 1909, this is one of the oldest cinemas in the world, as the wooden seats testify. Screens English films with subtitles.

Burgkino
1, Opernring 19, tel: (01) 587 8406
Cosy, centrally-located cinema with a small café downstairs. The place to see *The Third Man* (again).

Haydn English Cinema
6, Mariahilfer Strasse 57
tel: (01) 587 2262
Set on the city's main shopping street, here you can see mainstream Hollywood and British films in its three rooms.

Outside Vienna, unfortunately, there's very little chance of ever catching a film or play in English.

Nightlife

Bars and Clubs

While Vienna's club scene is rather limited, there are plenty of late-night drinking spots, mainly concentrated round Rabensteig, Seitenstätten-gasse and Ruprechtsplatz (known as the Bermuda Triangle). The majority of the city's clubs are bars which sometimes have live bands.

Elsewhere in Austria, nightlife is rather more subdued. To find out what's going on locally, ask at the tourist office.

Vienna
B72
8, Hernalser Gürtel
Stadtbahnbögen 72–3
tel: (01) 409 2128
Anything from live local indie talent to drum 'n' bass or soul DJs, all happening under a railway arch.

First Floor
1, Seitenstättengasse 5
tel: (01) 533 7866
An interesting mix of aquariums and 1930s fittings attracts a well-dressed, affluent crowd.

Krah Krah
1, Rabensteig 8
tel: (01) 533 8193
Very popular bar, with Austrian snacks and occasional live jazz.

Jazzland
1, Franz Josephs-Kai 29
tel: (01) 533 2575
Vienna's main trad-jazz venue.

Casinos

Bregenz: Symphonikerplatz.
Graz: Landhausgasse 10.
Linz: Rainerstrasse 12–14.
Salzburg: Schloss Klessheim.
Vienna: Kärntner Strasse 41.

The Gay & Lesbian Scene

You really need to go to Vienna to experience a gay scene in Austria – the country remains largely conservative elsewhere, even in large cities. The annual Life Ball fundraising dance each July is an extremely glam event, expensive and well-attended by high society (gay or not). More accessible to the masses is the Rainbow Parade, held each June – it's a wacky affair of motorcycles, drag musicians, outrageous floats and all-night partying. Pick up the *Vienna Gay Guide* at any of these spots for a quick overview of the city's gay-friendliest lodging, eating and shopping options.

Café Berg
9, Berggasse 8, tel: (01) 319 5720
Light meals, with good gay/ lesbian bookstore attached.

rhiz
8, Lerchenfelder Gürtel
Stadtbahnbögen 37–8
tel: (01) 409 2505
Cutting-edge club also offering multimedia events such as book readings.

Steh-Achterl
1, Sterngasse 3
This candlelit cellar attracts a young crowd.

Volksgarten
1, Burgring 1
tel: (01) 533 0518
Well-established club; varied mix of soul, funk, hip-hop and house; for young people

Wirr
7, Burggasse 70
tel: (01) 524 6825
Herbal tea and food on the ground floor; lounge music and a very alternative crowd downstairs.

Graz
Bier Baron
Heinrichstrasse 56
A large "pub" serving German, Austrian and Czech beer on tap.

Girardikeller
Leonhardgasse 28
Located in a cellar, this bar serves cheap Austrian fare.

Frauen Café
8, Lange Gasse 11,
tel: (01) 406 3754
Perhaps the only true lesbian bar in town. Lesbian bookstore attached.

Mango Bar
6, Laimgrubengasse 3,
tel: (01) 587 4448
Boisterous, well-known bar.

Rosa Lila Villa
6, Linke Wienziele 102,
tel: (01) 587 1789
Acknowledged nerve centre of gay and lesbian life. Restaurant, bar, other services.

Santo Spirito
1, Kumpfgasse 7,
tel: (01) 512 9998
Somewhat fancy wine bar/ restaurant with largely gay clientele and live music in the evenings.

2night
Sackstrasse 27
Club playing the standard Eurotechno and chart music.

Linz
Aquarium
Altstadt 22
Lively late-night bar.

Posthof
Posthofgasse 43
Live music and dance DJs at trendy arts centre.

Salzburg
Riff Bar
Schallmooser Hauptstrasse 46
Club nights and touring bands.

Klagenfurt
Fun Factory
Süring-Gerberweg 46
Club with predominantly techno sounds, plus occasional theme nights.

Innsbruck
Innkeller
Innstrasse 1
Bar on the west bank of the river with a young crowd and good, up-to-date music.

Sport & Leisure

Range of Activities

Besides the obvious national pastime of skiing, Austria offers a huge variety of outdoor activities, from hiking in the Alps to the latest white-knuckle adventure pursuits. The listings below are a selection of what is available around the country, with contact details of specialist operators and agencies.

BALLOON TRIPS

Balloons have long been a popular way to see Austria. Some of the regional clubs include:
Erster Oberösterreichischer Ballonfahrerverein
4693 Desselbrunn 21
tel: (07673) 37 300.
Österreichischer Alpenballonsportclub Salzburg
5033 Salzburg
tel: (06212) 7786.
Tiger-Heissluftballonclub Weinviertel
Felix-Grafe-Gasse 4/147/7
1100 Vienna
tel: (01) 688 1387.

BICYCLE TOURS

The Austrian Federal Railway has bicycles to rent at various railway stations; they can then be returned to any train station. The rental price is reduced by 50 percent if you've arrived by train. Contact the Austrian National Tourism Office for further inforrmation and a brochure on cycling. The most popular trails include:
Danube Bicycle Route: Passau-Vienna, 300 km (186 miles).

Classic riverside trail, framed by castles and vineyards.
Neusiedlersee Bicycle Route: Mörbisch-Rust-Neusiedl-Illmitz, 70 km (45 miles). Option of dipping into Hungary briefly.
Pinzgau Bicycle/Walking Route: Zell am See-Kaprun-Mittersill-Neunkirchen am Grossvenediger, 50 km (30 miles). Quite a workout.
Inn Valley Bicycle Route: Innsbruck-Hall-Wattens-Schwaz-Brixlegg-Kufstein, 75 km (46 miles). Spectacular scenery.
Ziller Valley Bicycle Route: Fügen-Zell am Ziller-Mayrhofen and back, 30 km (18 miles). More spectacular mountains, and not so crowded in summer as in winter.

CANOEING

Canoeing or rafting along Austria's many rivers have developed into popular sporting activities. Equipped with an inflatable raft (small and light enough to be transported in a knapsack), with or without a guide, you drift or paddle through white-water rivers. There are maps and literature available to inform you of the degree of difficulty of any particular river. The most popular rivers include the Zwettl (in Lower Austria), the Enns (in Styria), the Lämmer and Salzach (in Salzburgerland), and the Inn and the Lech in Tyrol. There are many more choices, as well.

GOLF

The Austrians are enthusiastic golfers, and although you'll sometimes find the greens fee for a round surprisingly high – many courses are attached to resort hotels – the scenery is splendid indeed. You'll find the most choices in the lower-altitude provinces such as Upper Austria, Lower Austria and parts of Salzburgerland.

Bear in mind that you will often need a letter of introduction, and possibly a handicap certificate, from your home course to book a round at many courses. For more information,

contact the private organisation Golf in Austria, Fürbergstrasse 44, A-5020 Salzburg, tel: (0662) 645 153 or (0800) 465 3123, fax: (0662) 648 206, email: office@golfinfo.at
Austria's public and private courses include:

Vienna & Lower Austria
Golf Club Vienna/Freudenau (18-hole), tel: (01) 728 9564-0.
Golf Club Schloss Ebreichsdorf (18-hole), Ebreichsdorf tel: (02254) 73 888.
Golf Club Föhrenwald (18-hole), Wiener Neustadt tel: (02622) 29 171.

Burgenland
Golf Club Neusiedlersee-Donnerskirchen (18-hole), Donnerskirchen tel: (02683) 8171-0.

Styria
Golf Club Schloss Pichlarn (18-hole), Irdning tel: (03682) 22 841-540.
Golf Club Bad Gleichenberg (9-hole), Bad Gleichenberg tel: (03159) 3717.

Hang Gliding

Hang-gliding is dangerous and should only be attempted after considerable instruction and practice. While there is no central organisation, there are a few clubs and facilities teaching this difficult sport:

Salzburg
Pinzgauer Drachen und Paragleitschule, General Keyes Strasse 15, 5020 Salzburg, tel: (0662) 431 486.

Tyrol and East Tyrol
Himberger Sepp, Pöllenweg 7, 6345 Kössen, tel: (05375) 6559.
Girstmaier Bruno, Beda Weber Strasse 4, 9900 Lienz, tel: (04852) 65 539.

Vorarlberg
Greber Kaspar, Bühel 853, 6863 Egg, tel: (05512) 3322.

Upper Austria

Golf Club Am Mondsee
(18-hole), St Lorenz Drachensee
tel: (06232) 3835.
Golf Club Linz-St Florian (18-hole),
St Florian
tel: (07223) 82 873.

The Salzkammergut

Jagd und Golfclub Schloss Fuschl
(9-hole), tel: (06229) 2390.
Salzkammergut Golf Club (18-hole),
Bad Ischl
tel: (06132) 26 340.

Salzburg

**Golf & Country Club Salzburg-
Klessheim** (9-hole)
tel: (0662) 850 851.

Salzburg Province

Golf Club Bad Gastein (9-hole),
tel: (06434) 2775.

Carinthia

Golf Club Austria Wörthersee
(18-hole), Moosburg-Pörtschach
tel: (04272) 834 860.
Golf Club Wörthersee/Velden
(18-hole), Velden
tel: (04274) 7045.

Tyrol

Golf Club Seefeld-Widmoos
(18-hole), tel: (0699) 1606 6060.
Golf Club Kitzbühel-Schwarzsee
(18-hole), tel: (05356) 71 645.

HORSE RIDING

There are a number of horse-riding
centres all around Austria. For
information, contact **Reitarena
Austria**, Mairfhof 4–5, 4121
Altenfelden, tel: (07282) 5992,
www.reitarena.at. This office can
direct the traveller to specific
stables and instructors.

MOUNTAIN CLIMBING
SCHOOLS

Mountain climbing in Austria is a
rather serious endeavour and
should not be attempted without
previous training and a clean bill of
health from your doctor. There are

countless instruction schools,
though not all teach classes in
English; it's best to call in advance
of your stay in order to learn more
about the programmes on offer.
Schools include:

Styria

Bergsteigerschule Dachstein-Tauern
8972 Ramsau am Dachstein 273
tel: (03687) 81 424.

Upper Austria

Alpenschule Laserer
4824 Gosau
tel: (06136) 8835.

Salzburg Province

Club Alpin Extra
5441 Abtenau
tel: (06243) 2939.
**Alpin und Bergsteigerschule
Oberpinzgau**, 5742 Wald
tel: (06565) 6574.

Carinthia

Alpinschule Mallnitz
9822 Mallnitz
tel: (04784) 290.

Tyrol

**Bergsporthochschule
Kaisergebirge**, 6353 Going
tel: (05358) 2750.
**Bergsteigerschule Piz Buin-
Silvretta**, 6563 Galtür 74a
tel: (05443) 8260.

Vorarlberg

Alpinschule Montafon
6780 Schruns
tel: (05556) 431 1445.
Bergschule Kleinwalsertal
6993 Mittelberg
tel: (05517) 5860.

RAFTING

Rafting is becoming increasingly
popular in mountainous parts of the
country. Popular destinations
include:

Styria

Pruggern (Gesäuse)
tel: (03685) 22 245.
Schladming (Enns)
tel: (03687) 23 372.

Pools & Baths

Thermal pools and baths are
among Austria's claims to leisure
fame, and the spas here are
indeed exceptional. You'll find
the highest concentration in the
Salzkammergut, but almost every
region of the country possesses
at least a few places to sit, soak
or swim. For more information on
spa treatments and
accommodation, contact the
national spa association (which
goes under the name of **Schlank
& Schön**, or Slim and Beautiful)
at Kongresszentrum Seeburg,
A-9210 Portschach, tel: (04272)
3620-40, fax: (04272) 3620-90,
email: schlankundschoen@
stw.co.at

Upper Austria

Bad Goisern (Traun, Lammer,
Koppentraun)
tel: (06135) 8254.

Salzburg Province

Abtenau (Salzach, Lammer)
tel: (06243) 2939.
Taxenbach, tel: (06543) 5352.

Carinthia

Oberfellach (Möll, Gail, Isel)
tel: (04782) 2510 or 2727.

East Tyrol

Lienz (Isel)
tel: (04853) 5231.

Tyrol

Haiming (Inn, Ötztaler Ache)
tel: (05266) 88 661.
Ötz (Ötztaler Ache)
tel: (05252) 6035.
Gerlos (Lech, Gerlos, Salzach)
tel: (05284) 52 440.

Vorarlberg

Lech (Lech)
tel: (05583) 2161-0.

SKI RESORT AREAS

People don't only come to Austria
just for conventional skiing these
days. In addition to "just skiing",

Snow Reports

You can find out by telephone just how deep the snow is in Tyrolean ski areas. In Austria, call the national tourist office in Vienna on (01) 587 2000 for latest reports. In Germany you can get this information from the **ADAC**, tel: (089) 7676 2687; in Switzerland it is available through the **Austrian Tourist Information Office** in Zurich, tel: (01) 451 1551.

If you want to do any powder-snow skiing, it is important to be well-informed as to the current avalanche situation. Information

regarding **avalanche conditions** in Tyrol are available by calling (0512) 7272 or (0512) 1588. For the weather forecast, you can call (0900) 911 566-10 or -12, though you will pay a charge for this service. There is also an **Alpine Safety and Information Centre** on tel: (05442) 61 400.

Finally, you can try the websites www.austria-tourism.at/winter or www.anto.com/snowreport for current snow reports in English. The website www.tirol.at contains avalanche report information.

they come to go tobogganing, bobsledding, cross-country skiing and curling, and even to take classes to learn how to manage a snowboard at one of the 190 snow resort areas. Tourist information centres can provide you with further information, as can the websites www.actionsites.com/skiing/austria and www.anto.com/topski.

Salzburg Province

Bad Gastein (51 lifts, 200 km/125 miles of piste)
Spa town with a surprising range of long-run pistes and expert slopes.
Obertauern (26 lifts, 150 km/93 miles of piste)
Block of holiday flats built to take advantage of reliable snow high atop Tauern pass; most runs are short and of medium difficulty. Cross-country skiing as well.
Saalbach-Hinterglemm (60 lifts, 200 km/125 miles of piste)
Many types of piste and good snow in a rustic setting; plenty of tracks.
Saalfelden (5 lifts, 14 km/8 miles of piste)
Favoured as a cross-country ski resort possessing some 80 km (50 miles) of track.
St Michael in Lungau (11 lifts, 60 km/38 miles of piste)
Modern resort near foot of Katschbert mountain and tunnel towards Italy.
West Dachstein/Tennengau (61 lifts, 195 km/122 miles of piste)

Series of resorts including St Martin and Annaberg. More than 200 km (125 miles) of cross-country tracks as well.
Zell am See-Kaprun (55 lifts, 130 km/80 miles of piste)
Beautiful lake town featuring steep and intermediate runs.

Tyrol

Innsbruck/Igls (7 lifts, 25 km/15 miles of piste)
Really more of a hiking destination, but a few lovely runs here as well.
Kitzbühel (60 lifts, 158 km/98 miles of piste)
Attractive and popular resort town with much to do off the mountain; range of medium pistes. Not the most difficult skiing.
Neustift (28 lifts, 68 km/42 miles of piste)
Rustic village in Stubai Valley; famous for glacier skiing through to summer. Snowboarding also popular.
St Anton am Arlberg (37 lifts, 260 km/160 miles of piste)
World-famous resort; excellent après-ski, annual World Cup event, and some rather expert pistes.
St Johann in Tirol (18 lifts, 60 km/38 miles of piste)
Pretty village with ski and snowboard schools and lively nightlife. Not the most difficult pistes.
Seefeld in Tirol (14 lifts, 25 km/15 miles of piste)
More notable as a cross-country ski destination, with more than 100 km (62 miles) of track.

Vorarlberg

Lech am Arlberg (85 lifts, 260 km/160 miles of piste)
Pretty, expensive resort of medium-difficulty skiing; backcountry routes as well. Famous après-ski scene.
Zürs (29 lifts, 110 km/68 miles of piste)
Chic resort for jet-setters only; quite remote, above Flexenpass road from the Bodensee. Lively at night.

SUMMER SKIING

Styria
Dachsteingletscher, 2,300–2,700 metres (7,545–8,860 ft) tel: (03687) 81 241.

Salzburg Province
Kitzsteinhorn, 2,450–3,030 metres (8,040–9,940 ft) tel: (06547) 8700 or 8621.

Carinthia
Mölltaler Glacier, 2,700–3,100 metres (8,860–10,170 ft) tel: (04785) 615 or 8110.

Tyrol
Kaunertal, 2,750–3,100 metres (9,020–10,170 ft) tel: (05475) 446.
Pitztaler Glacier, 2,840–3,440 metres (9,315–11,282 ft) tel: (05413) 86 999.
Ötztaler Glacier, 2,800–3,200 metres (9,185–10,500 ft) tel: (05254) 5100.
Stubaier Glacier, 2,600–3,200 metres (8,530–10,500 ft) tel: (05226) 8141 or 8151.

Shopping

Where to Shop

To shop in Austria generally means to go to Vienna, where the best choices are within the Ring. The shopping district in most other towns and cities will be compact and often close to the train station. Stores generally close at 6pm on weeknights, 7pm or later on Thursday, and noon (sometimes 5pm if you're lucky) on Saturday. On Sunday you will find little open.

Vienna

The winding streets of Vienna's Inner City – especially between the Hofburg, Graben and Kärntner Strasse – are the best places to find something. Some of the world's finest cakes and pastries abound at confectioners such as Demel and Oberlaa; and Adolf Loos-inspired furnishings and fixtures are well in evidence throughout the Inner City.

Elsewhere, Mariahilferstrasse is the other main shopping area: a long series of shops (including the superb Amadeus bookstore) which only peter out at the Westbahnhof. Smaller shopping districts can be found in the university district (near the Votivkirche) and Siebensterngasse, where a hip crowd takes over. Flea markets take place on Saturday in the Naschmarkt and elsewhere.

What to Buy

Look for Tyrolean costumes and walking sticks in the Innsbruck area, local wine in Lower Austria, bottles of pumpkin-seed oil and hand-blown glassware in Styria and Mozart balls in Salzburg. Salzburg's north-of-the-river streets and the pedestrianised Maria-Theresien-Strasse in Innsbruck are also good for browsing.

Language

Language Tips

The Austrian national language is German, which is spoken by about 100 million people world-wide. As well as Austria, Germany, parts of Switzerland and some small German enclaves in eastern Europe, there are also German-speaking communities in North America, South America and South Africa. German and English both belong to the West Germanic language group, together with Dutch, Frisian, Flemish and Afrikaans, but while a Dutchman and a German may be able to communicate quite effectively, an Englishman and a German are unlikely to make much progress. A glance at the numbers from one to 10 *(see page 337)* will prove that point.

If you learned Latin at school you'll be familiar with some of the difficulties that German presents: nouns have three genders and four cases, verbs are conjugated, pronouns are followed by one of

Compound Words

The German language can be restructured to create new words simply by linking words together, and very often it is, producing tongue-twisting words on schedules, street signs and the like. One good example is the firm which runs regular ferries up the Danube River from Vienna to Krems and beyond. Its name – Donaudampfschiffsfahrtsgesell-schaft – means Danube steamship company. Better to call it DDSG.

The Alphabet

Learning how to pronounce the German alphabet will enable you to spell your name:
a = ah, **b** = bay, **c** = tsay,
d = day, **e** = eh, **f** = eff,
g = gay, **h** = har, **i** = ee, **j** = yot,
k = kar, **l** = el, **m** = em,
n = en, **o** = oh, **p** = pay,
q = koo, **r** = air, **s** = es,
t = tay, **u** = oo, **v** = fow,
w = vay, **x** = icks, **y** = upsilon,
z = tset

three cases, word order is governed by some complicated rules and there are five different ways of saying "the". Pronunciation, thankfully, is perfectly consistent with spelling.

Although many young Austrians speak English and are always keen to try it out, there are many parts of the country where a smattering of German will prove very helpful.

Even if you are fairly confident in German, you may encounter some difficulties in rural Austria, as there is a remarkable diversity in regional accents and dialects. There are strong links between Austrian German and the dialects of German spoken in Bavaria, yet within Austria some dialects are not understood by fellow Austrians. While it may sometimes be difficult to understand Austrians when they are speaking to each other, almost all can switch to High German when necessary.

Words and Phrases

General

Hello *Gruss Gott*
Good morning *Guten Morgen*
Good afternoon *Guten Nachmittag*
Good evening *Guten Abend*
Good night *Gute Nacht*
Goodbye *Auf Wiedersehen*
Goodbye (informal) *Servus, Pfiat di*
Do you speak English? *Sprechen Sie Englisch?*
I don't understand *Ich verstehe nicht*
Could you please speak slower? *Könnten Sie bitte etwas langsamer sprechen?*

Can you help me? *Können Sie mir helfen?*
yes/no *Ja/Nein*
please/thank you *Bitte/Danke*
sorry *Entschuldigung*
How are you? *Wie geht's?*
Excuse me *Entschuldigung Sie, bitte*
You're welcome *Bitte schön*
It doesn't matter *(Es) macht nichts*
OK *Alles klar*
What a pity *Schade*
Thank you for your help *Besten Dank für ihre Hilfe*
See you later *Bis später*
See you tomorrow *Bis morgen*
What time is it? *Wie spät ist es?*
10 o'clock *zehn Uhr*
half past ten *halb elf*
This morning *heute morgen*
this afternoon *heute nachmittag*
this evening *heute abend*
Let's go! *Los!*
Leave me alone *Lass mich in Ruhe*
Clear off *Hau ab*
Where are the toilets? *Wo sind die Toiletten?*
large/small *gross/klein*
more/less *mehr/weniger*
now *jetzt*
later *später*
here *hier*
there *dort*

On Arrival

station *Bahnhof*
bus station *Busbahnhof*
bus stop *Bushaltestelle*
Will you tell me when to get off the bus? *Können Sie mir sagen, wann ich aussteigen muss?*

Pronunciation

Most **consonants** are pronounced as in English with the following exceptions:

● *g* as in "get", *ch* as in the German composer Bach, *j* is like "y", *k* is always pronounced, *v* more like an "f", *w* as the English "v" and *z* is pronounced as "ts". The scharfes *S* or *ß* is sometimes used to replace *ss*.

Vowels and vowels with umlauts are less straightforward:

● *a* as in "bad"; *e* as in "hay"; *i* as in "seek"; *o* as in "not"; *u* as in "boot"; *ä* is a combination of "a" and "e" as in "get"; *ö* combines "o" and "e" as in Bert; *ü* combines "u" and "e" as in "true".

Dipthong sounds:

● *ai* as in "tie"; *au* as in "sauerkraut"; *ie* as in "thief"; *ei* as in "wine"; *eu* as in "boil".

Where can I get the bus to the Adler Hotel? *Wo fährt der Bus zum Hotel Adler weg?*
Does this bus go to the town centre? *Fährt dieser Bus zur Stadtmitte?*
Which street is this? *Welche Strasse ist das?*
How far is it to the station? *Wie weit ist es zum Bahnhof?*
Do you have a single room? *Haben Sie ein Einzelzimmer?*
Do you have a double room? *Haben Sie ein Doppelzimmer?*
Do you have a room with a private bath? *Haben Sie ein Zimmer mit Bad?*
How much is it? *Wieviel kostet das?*
How much is a room with full board? *Wieviel kostet ein Zimmer mit Vollpension?*
Please show me another room *Bitte zeigen Sie mir ein anderes Zimmer*
We'll (I'll) be staying for one night *Wir bleiben (Ich bleibe) eine Nacht*

When is breakfast? *Wann gibt es Frühstück?*
Where is the toilet? *Wo ist die Toilette?*
Where is the bathroom? *Wo ist das Badezimmer?*
Where is the next hotel? *Wo ist das nächste Hotel?*

Travelling

Where is the airport? *Wo ist der Flughafen?*
Where is platform one? *Wo ist Bahnsteig eins?*
Can you call me a taxi? *Können Sie mir ein Taxi rufen?*
Where do I get a ticket? *Wo kann ich eine Fahrkarte kaufen?*
departure/arrival *Abfahrt/Ankunft*
When is the next flight/train to ...? *Wann geht der nächste Flug/Zug nach ...?*
to change (flights/trains) *umsteigen*
Have you anything to declare? *Haben Sie etwas zu verzollen?*
close/far *nah/weit*
free (of charge) *kostenlos*
price *Preis*
fee *Gebühr*
Have you got any change? *Können Sie Geld wechseln?*
bridge *Brücke*
Customs *Zoll*
entrance *Eingang, Einfahrt*
exit *Ausgang, Ausfahrt*
height/width/length *Höhe/Breite/Länge*
no stopping *Halten verboten*
one-way street *Einbahnstrasse*
picnic area *Rastplatz*
travel agency *Reisebüro*

Emergencies

Help! — *Hilfe!*
Stop! — *Halt!*
Please call a doctor — *Holen Sie einen Arzt*
Please call an ambulance — *Rufen Sie einen Krankenwagen*
Please call the fire-brigade — *Rufen Sie die Feuerwehr*
Where is the nearest telephone box? — *Wo ist die nächste Telefonzelle?*
I am ill — *Ich bin krank*
I have lost my wallet/hand-bag — *Ich habe meine Geldtasche/Handtasche verloren*

Where is the nearest hospital? — *Wo ist das nächste Krankenhaus?*
Where is the police station? — *Wo ist das nächste Polizeiwache?*
Where is the British consulate? — *Wo ist das britische Konsulat?*

On the Road

gas (petrol) station *Tankstelle*
I have run out of petrol *Ich habe kein Benzin mehr*
My car has broken down *Ich habe eine Autopanne*
Could you give me a push/tow? *Könnten Sie mich bitte anschieben/abschleppen?*
Can you take me to the nearest garage? *Können Sie mich zur nächsten Werkstatt bringen?*
Can you find out what the trouble is? *Können Sie feststellen, was das Problem ist?*
Can you repair it? *Können Sie es reparieren?*
The road to ... ? *Die Strasse nach ...?*
left *links*
right *rechts*
straight on *geradeaus*
opposite *gegenüber*
Where is the nearest car-park? *Wo ist der nächste Parkplatz, bitte?*
over there *da drüben*
Turn left/right after the bridge *Biegen Sie hinter der Brücke links/rechts ab*
Here is my driving licence *Da ist mein Führerschein*
Here are my insurance documents *Hier sind meine Versicherungsunterlagen*
brakes *Bremsen*
bulb *Glühbirne*
by car *mit dem Auto*
dead end *Sackgasse*
diesel *Diesel*
give way *Vorfahrt beachten*
headlights *Scheinwerfer*
jack *Wagenheber*
map *Strassenkarte*
no parking *Parken verboten*
one-way street *Einbahnstrasse*
petrol *Benzin*
road/street *Strasse*
slow/fast *langsam/schnell*

How to Say "You"

In most cases we have given the polite form for "you", which is Sie. The familiar form du can sometimes be used if talking to a younger person, but is normally reserved for close friends and family.

Shop Signs

open/closed *geöffnet/geschlossen*
bookshop *Buchhandlung*
butcher's *Metzgerei*
cake shop *Konditorei*
chemist/pharmacy *Apotheke*
department store *Kaufhaus*
drugstore, chemist (not medications) *Drogerie*
fashion *Mode*
fresh every day *täglich frisch*
ladies' clothing *Damenkleidung*
launderette *Wäscherei*
magazines *Zeitschriften*
newspapers *Zeitungen*
self-service *Selbstbedienung*
shoes *Schuhe*
special offer *Sonderangebot*
stationery *Schreibwaren*
travel agent *Reisebüro*

unleaded *bleifrei*
water/oil *Wasser/Öl*
windscreen wipers *Scheibenwischer*

On the Telephone

I must make a phone call *Ich muss telefonieren*
Can I use your phone? *Kann ich Ihr Telefon benutzen?*
Can I dial direct? *Kann ich direkt wählen?*
Please connect me with ... *Bitte verbinden Sie mich mit ...*
What is the code for Great Britain? *Was is das Vorwahl für Grossbritannien?*
Who is speaking? *Wer spricht da?*
The line is engaged *Die Leitung ist besetzt*
I'll call again later *Ich rufe später wieder an*

Shopping

Where can I change money? *Wo kann ich Geld wechseln?*
Where is the pharmacy? *Wo ist die Apotheke?*
What time do they close? *Wann schliessen sie?*
Where is the nearest bank? *Wo ist die nächste Bank?*
Where is the nearest post-office? *Wo ist die nächste Post?*
I'd like ... *Ich hätte gern ...*

How much is this? *Was kostet das?*
Do you take credit cards? *Akzeptieren Sie Kreditkarten?*
I'm just looking *Ich sehe mich nur um*
Do you have ...? *Haben Sie ...?*
That'll be fine. I'll take it. *In Ordnung. Ich nehme es.*
No, that is too expensive *Nein, das ist zu teuer*
Can I try it on? *Kann ich es anprobieren?*
Do you have anything cheaper? *Haben Sie etwas Billigeres?*

Sightseeing

Where is the tourist office? *Wo ist das Fremdenverkehrsbüro?*
Is there a bus to the centre? *Gibt es einen Bus ins Stadtzentrum?*
Is there a guided sightseeing tour? *Werden geführte Besichtigungstouren zur Verfügung?*
When is the museum open? *Wann ist das Museum geöffnet?*
How much does it cost to go in? *Was kostet der Eintritt?*
art gallery *Kunstgalerie*
castle *Schloss*
cathedral *Dom*
church *Kirche*
exhibition *Ausstellung*
memorial *Denkmal*
old part of town *Altstadtviertel*
tower *Turm*
town hall *Rathaus*
walk *Spaziergang*
Roman *Römisch*

Produce Markets/Delis

Can I taste it? *Kann ich einmal probieren?*
That is very nice. I'll take some. *Das ist sehr lecker/Das schmeckt sehr gut. Davon nehme ich etwas.*
What's the price per kilo? *Was kostet es pro Kilo?*
A piece of that cheese, please *Ich hätte gern ein Stück von dem Käse*
About 200g ham please *Etwa zwanzig dag Schinken, bitte*

● In Austria 100g is 10 dag (Dekagramm). So 200g is 20 dag.

Table Talk

I am a vegetarian *Ich bin Vegetarier(in)*
I am on a special diet *Ich alte Diät*
What do you recommend? *Was würden Sie empfehlen?*
I am ready to order *Ich möchte bestellen*
Enjoy your meal *Guten Appetit*
What would you like to drink? *Was möchten Sie trinken?*
Did you enjoy your meal? *Hat es Ihnen geschmeckt?*
Cheers! *Prost!*

Romanesque *Romanisch*
Gothic *gotisch*
open daily *täglich*

Dining Out

Do you know a good restaurant? *Kennen Sie ein gutes Restaurant?*
A table for one/two *Ein Tisch für eine Person/zwei Personen, bitte*
Could we order a meal, please? *Können wir bitte bestellen?*
Can we have the bill, please? *Können wir bitte bezahlen?*
evening meal *Abendessen*
lunch *Mittagessen*
children's portion *Kinderteller*
snack *Jause, Imbiss*
menu *Speisekarte*
soup/starter *Suppe/Vorspeise*
main course *Hauptgericht*
dessert *Nachspeise*
beer/wine *Bier/Wein*
bread *Brot*
bread roll *Brötchen, Semmel*
cake *Kuchen*
coffee *Kaffee*
milk *Milch*
mineral water *Mineralwasser*
mustard *Senf*
salt/pepper *Salz/Pfeffer*
sugar *Zucker*
tea *Tee*
wine list *Weinkarte*
tip *Trinkgeld*

Breakfast Frühstück

Brot **bread**
Semmel/Brötchen **roll**
Eier **eggs**
Fruchtsaft **fruit juice**
hartgekochtes Ei **hard-boiled egg**

heiss **hot**
kalt **cold**
Marmelade/Konfitüre **jam**
Orangensaft **orange juice**
Pumpernickel **black rye bread**
Rühreier **scrambled egg**
Schinken **ham**
Schwarzbrot **brown rye bread**
Speck **bacon**
Weissbrot **white bread**

Soups Suppen

Eintopf **thick soup**
Erbsensuppe **pea soup**
Fritattensuppe **consommé with strips of pancake**
Gemüsesuppe **vegetable soup**
Griessnockerlsuppe **semolina dumpling soup**
Gulaschsuppe **goulash soup**
Hühnersuppe **chicken soup**
Nudelsuppe **noodle soup**
Ochsenschwanzsuppe **oxtail soup**
Zwiebelsuppe **onion soup**

Starters Vorspeisen

Austern **oysters**
Froschschenkel **frogs' legs**
Gänseleberpastete **pâté de foie**
Geeiste Melone **iced melon**
Rollmops **rolled-up pickled herring**
Schnecken **snails**
Spargelspitzen **asparagus tips**
Wurstplatte **assorted cooked meats**

Meat Courses Fleischgerichte

Backhuhn **roast chicken**
Blutwurst **black pudding**
Bockwurst **large frankfurter**
Bratwurst **fried sausage**
Currywurst **pork sausage with curry powder**
Deutsches Beefsteak **minced beef/hamburger**
Stelze **knuckle of pork**
Ente **duck**
Fasan **pheasant**
Fleischlaibchen **meatballs**
Fleischpastetchen **rissole**
Gulasch **goulash**
Hähnchen/Huhn **chicken**
Kalbsbries **veal sweetbreads**
Kümmelfleisch **pork stew with cumin**
Lamm am Spiess **lamb on the spit**
Lammbraten **roast lamb**
Leberknödel **liver dumplings**
Ochsenschwanz **oxtail**

Räucherschinken **cured ham**
Rehrücken **saddle of deer**
Rind **beef**
Rinderbraten **roast beef**
Rinderfilet **fillet of beef**
Sauerbraten **braised pickled beef**
Schweinebauch **belly of pork**
Schweinebraten **roast pork**
Schweinefilet **loin of pork**
Serbisches Reisfleisch **diced pork, onions, tomatoes and rice**
Speck **bacon**
Szegediner Goulasch **goulash with pickled cabbage**
Tiroler Bauernschmaus **various meats served with sauerkraut, potatoes and dumplings**
Wienerschnitzel **breaded escalope of veal**

Culinary Terms

Backhendl **breaded and baked chicken**
Beinfleisch **cooked beef**
Beuschel **a lung and heart ragout**
Erdäpfel **potatoes**
Faschiertes **minced meat**
Fritatten **sliced pancakes**
Germ **yeast**
Geselchtes **smoked**
Grammeln **dripping**
Gugelhupf **ring-shaped poundcake**
Häuptlsalat **lettuce**
Karfiol **cauliflower**
Kohlsprossen **brussel sprouts**
Kren **horseradish**
Krenfleisch **boiled young pork with bacon in a horseradish sauce**
Kukuruz **corn**
Marillen **apricots**
Obers **cream**
Palatschinken **pancakes**
Paradeiser **tomatoes**
Powidl **plum sauce**
Ribisel **blackcurrants**
Ringlotten **Mirabelle plums**
Schlagobers **whipped cream**
Schöpsernes **mutton**
Schwammerl **mushrooms**
Selchfleisch **smoked meat**
Tafelspitz **a special cut of cooked beef**
Topfen **a soft curd cheese**
Zwetschken **plums**

Zigeunerschnitzel **veal with peppers and relishes**
Zunge **tongue**

Fish Fisch
Austern **oysters**
Barbe **mullet**
Bismarckhering **filleted pickled herring**
Fischfrikadellen **fishcakes**
Fischstäbchen **fish fingers**
Forelle **trout**
Garnelen **prawns**
Hecht **pike**
Heilbutt **halibut**
Heringstopf **pickled herrings**
Hummer **lobster**
Jakobsmuscheln **scallops**
Kabeljau **cod**
Krabbe **shrimps**
Lachs **salmon**
Makrele **mackerel**
Muscheln **mussels**
Sardinen **sardines**
Schellfisch **haddock**
Schwertfisch **swordfish**
Seebarsch **sea bass**
Seezunge **sole**
Thunfisch **tuna**
Tintenfisch **squid**

Dumplings & Noodles Knödel
Semmelknödel/Serviettenknödl **bread dumplings**
Leberknödel **liver dumplings**
Kasnocken/Kässpätzle/ Kasnödel **pasta balls with cheese**
Kartoffelknödel **potato dumplings**
Knödel **dumplings**
Maultasche **Swabian ravioli**
Nockerl **gnocchi**
Nudeln **noodles**
Spätzle **grated pasta**

Vegetables Gemüse
Bohnen **beans**
Bratkartoffeln **fried potatoes**
Champignons **mushrooms**
Erdäpfel **potatoes**
Kartoffelpuree **creamed potatoes**
Kartoffelsalat **potato salad**
Knoblauch **garlic**
Kohl **cabbage**
Kopfsalat **lettuce**
Linsen **lentils**
Pommes (frites) **chips/French fries**
Rohnen **beetroot**
Salat **salad**
Sauerkraut **pickled cabbage**

Numbers

0	*null*	1st	*erste(r)*
1	*eins*	2nd	*zweite(r)*
2	*zwei*	3rd	*dritte(r)*
3	*drei*	4th	*vierte(r)*
4	*vier*	5th	*fünfte(r)*
5	*fünf*	6th	*sechste(r)*
6	*sechs*	7th	*siebte(r)*
7	*sieben*	8th	*achte(r)*
8	*acht*	9th	*neunte(r)*
9	*neun*	10th	*zehnte(r)*
10	*zehn*	11th	*elfte(r)*
11	*elf*	12th	*zwölfte(r)*
12	*zwölf*	13th	*dreizehnte(r)*
13	*dreizehn*	20th	*zwanzigste(r)*
20	*zwanzig*	21st	*einundzwanzigste(r)*
21	*einundzwanzig*	22nd	*zweiundzwanzigste(r)*
30	*dreissig*	30th	*dreissigste(r)*
40	*vierzig*	40th	*vierzigste(r)*
50	*fünfzig*	50th	*fünfzigste(r)*
100	*hundert*	100th	*hundertste(r)*
1,000	*tausend*	200th	*zweihundertste(r)*
1,000,000	*eine Million*	1,000th	*tausendste(r)*

Desserts Nachspeisen
Apfelkuchen **apple cake**
Apfelstrudel **flaky pastry stuffed with apple**
Auflauf **soufflé**
Bienenstich **honey-almond cake**
Eis **ice cream**
Eisbecher **ice cream with fresh fruit**
Fruchttörtchen **fruit tartlet**
Gebäck **pastries**
Kaiserschmarrn **sugared pancake with raisins**
Käsetorte **cheesecake**
Linzer Torte **cake spread with jam and topped with cream**
Marillenknödel **apricot dumplings**
Mandelkuchen **almond cake**
Mohnkuchen **poppyseed cake**

Saying the Date

● **on the 20th October 2000:**
am zwanzigsten Oktober, zweitausend
● **yesterday** *gestern*
● **today** *heute*
● **tomorrow** *morgen*
● **day after tomorrow** *übermorgen*
● **last week** *letzte Woche*
● **next week** *nächste Woche*

Mohr im Hemd **chocolate pudding with chocolate sauce**
Obstkuchen **fruit tart**
Palatschinken **pancakes**
Pofesen **stuffed fritters**
Rote Grütze **raspberries or redcurrants cooked with semolina**
Sacher Torte **chocolate cake with jam and chocolate icing**
Schwarzwälder Kirschtorte **Black Forest gateau**

Days, Months and Seasons

Monday	*Montag*
Tuesday	*Dienstag*
Wednesday	*Mittwoch*
Thursday	*Donnerstag*
Friday	*Freitag*
Saturday	*Samstag/Sonnabend*
Sunday	*Sonntag*

January	*Januar/Jänner*
February	*Februar/Feber*
March	*März*
April	*April*
May	*Mai*
June	*Juni*
July	*Juli*
August	*August*
September	*September*

October	*Oktober*
November	*November*
December	*Dezember*
spring	*Frühling*
summer	*Sommer*
autumn	*Herbst*
winter	*Winter*

Slang

a right mess *eine Schweinerei*
bastard *Arschloch, du blöde Kuh,
du Schweinehund*
bloody hell! *verdammt noch mal!*
great, magic *klasse, super, toll,
Spitze, leiwand*
oh my God! *du lieber Gott!*
pissed *besoffen, fett, voll*
pissed off *sauer, grantig,
angefressen*
shit *Scheisse, Mist*
stupid *doof, blöd, deppert,
narrisch*
wow! *Mensch! Mah! Wahnsinn!*

Loan Words

With Germany standing at the heart
of Europe, its language has been
subjected to numerous and varied
foreign influences. For centuries,
there was a large Jewish community
in Germany, and they brought many
Hebrew words into regular usage.
Words such as *Massel* (good luck),
vermasseln (to make a mess of
things), *messchugge* (crazy) and
Mischpoche (rabble) are now part of
everyday language.

During the 17th century, the
Huguenots introduced many French
words into German, such as those
used to describe food (eg *Ragout
fin, Roulade, Frikassee, Püree,
Eclair, Petits fours*).

More recently, English has
infiltrated the German language,
mainly in popular culture. English
speakers will be on familiar ground
in the worlds of sport and leisure,
pop music, entertainment and
computers (words such as *Fitness,
Feedback, Snowboard, Mountain-
bike, Disco, Video recorder,
Groupie, Entertainer, Software*
and *Byte,* amongst others, are
used and heard frequently in
everyday conversation).

False Friends

False friends are words that look
like English words, but actually
mean something different. *Ich
bekomme ein Baby*, for example,
does not mean "I am becoming a
baby", but "I am having a baby"; *ein
Berliner* is a jam doughnut and *also*
doesn't mean "also", but usually
"so" or "therefore". Some loan
words can be very confusing, too.
Aktuell means "up-to-date" or
"fashionable", not "actual", and
Ich komme eventuell could mean
that I am not coming at all. A good
translation would be "I might
come". *Ein Knicker* is a scrooge
and *ein Schellfish* is a haddock.

Further Reading

General

Journeys, by Jan Morris. Oxford
University Press, 1984, and Replica
Books, 2000. Collection includes
an essay on Vienna.
Austrian Cooking, by Gretel Beer.
André Deutsch, 1999. Treasure-
trove of traditional recipes; not for
light eaters.

History

The Austrians, by Gordon Brook-
Shepherd. Harper Collins, 1997.
A fascinating and very readable
account that moves from 800 to
1994; particularly interesting on the
post-World War I period.
The Fall of the House of Habsburg,
by Edward Crankshaw. Penguin,
1983. Entertaining scholarly history
of one of Europe's most significant
dynasties.
**The Austrian Mind: An
Intellectual and Social History
1848–1938,** by William M
Johnstone. University of California
Press, 1983. Comprehensive
treatment of the psychologists,
artists and other figures assembled
in Vienna during an historical
moment.
**Dissolution of the Austro-
Hungarian Empire,** by J. W. Mason
and Neil Macqueen. Addis, 1997. A
textbook-sized tome on the ups and
downs of the Habsburgs.
**Freud and Beyond: A History of
Modern Psychoanalytic Thought,**
by Stephen A Mitchell and
Margaret J Black. Basic Books,
1996. Comprehensive, readable
history of the social science
Freud founded.
**A Nervous Splendor: Vienna,
1888–1889,** by Frederic Morton.
Viking, 1980. One of the better
snapshots of flourishing late-
period Vienna, just before the
end of the Empire.

Guilty Victim: Austria from the Holocaust to Haider, by Hella Pick. IB Tauris. A fascinating look at 60 years of Austrian and international politics, highlighting the degree of sympathy with and support for the Nazis within the country.

The Siege of Vienna, by John Stoye. Birlinn, 2000. A vivid account of what actually happened in the summer of 1683 when the Turks surrounded Vienna.

Biography

Maria Theresa, by Edward Crankshaw. Longman, 1970. Biographies in English of the great Empress are hard to find, but this one is well worth seeking out.

Prophets Without Honour: Freud, Kafka, Einstein, and Their World, by Frederic V Grunfeld. Kodansha International, 1996. Collection of essays recounting famous Austrian-related figures.

Mozart: A Cultural Biography, by Robert W. Gutman. Harcourt Brace, 1999. Massive (almost 900-page) volume, but an accurate portrait.

The Reluctant Empress, by Brigitte Hamman. Ullstein, 1998. Scholarly but readable account of the brilliant, beautiful and tragic Sisi, wife of Franz Joseph.

Diaries: 1898–1902, by Alma Mahler-Werfel. Cornell University Press, 2000. Fascinating extracts from the diaries of Mahler's wife, an artist and socialite in her own right. Gives new insight into swinging Vienna.

W.A. Mozart: Letters, edited by Hans Mersmann. Hippocrene, 1987. Just what it promises: largely unadorned letters of the troubled composer.

Thunder at Twilight, by Frederic Morton. Methuen, 2001. With a cast that includes Stalin, Trotsky, Freud and Hitler, this presents a vivid and sympathetic portrait of the Archduke Franz Ferdinand and his ferocious struggle for peace that ended with his assassination at Sarajevo.

Twilight of the Habsburgs, by Alan Palmer. Phoenix, 1998. A full and rounded biography of Franz Joseph,

ruler of the Austrian Empire from 1848 to 1916 and husband of Sisi, the Empress Elizabeth.

Art & Architecture

Baroque Art and the Architecture of Central Europe, by E Hempel. Penguin. Austria's Baroque treasures are covered admirably.

Vienna 1900: Architecture and Painting, by Christian Nebehay. Full treatment of the art of Vienna' Golden Age.

Art in Vienna 1898-1918, by Peter Vergo. Phaidon, 1993. Comprehensive and well illustrated review of Vienna's most exciting artistic years.

Klimt, by Frank Whitford. Thames and Hudson, 1998. A short biog of one of the key figures in Vienna's great artistic development at the turn of the 20th century.

Fiction

The Third Man, by Graham Greene. Penguin, 1999. Classic novel of intrigue set in uneasy postwar Vienna, later to become Orson Welles' classic film.

Madensky Square, by Eva Ibbotson. Arrow, 1998. A delightful and funny novel about life in Vienna in 1911, seen through the eyes of a fashionable dress-maker.

Eyes Wide Shut: A Screenplay, by Stanley Kubrick, Frederic Raphael and Arthur Schnitzler. Warner Books, 1999. Screenplay to Kubrick movie based on Schnitzler's now hard-to-find book *Rhapsody: A Dream Novel*. Faithful to original.

Embers, by Sandor Marai. Penguin Viking, 2001. A story of lost love and broken friendship set in imperial Vienna and the vast country estates of the aristocracy.

The Man Without Qualities, by Robert Musil. Vintage Books, 1996. Dense, two-volume work thoroughly mines the inner and outer worlds of an Austrian in pre-war Vienna.

The Radetzky March, by Joseph Roth. Granta, 2002. Sombre but evocative account of three generations of the Empire's servants until the First World War.

Hands Around: A Cycle of Ten Dialogues, by Arthur Schnitzler. Dover, 1995. Another of Schnitzler's morally amibiguous plays, again involving love and lust.

Amadeus, by Peter Shaffer. Harper Collins, 1985. Basis of the film *Amadeus*; somewhat simplified version of the Salzburg composer's life.

The World of Yesterday, by Stefan Zweig. University of Nebraska Press, 1964. Largely autobiographical memoir of old Vienna, and the subsequent horrors of the Anschluss, by one who was there.

Travel

The Sunny Side of the Alps: Year-Round Delights in South Tyrol and the Dolomites, by Paul Hofmann. Henry Holt, 1995. Author's travels in the borderland Alpine region straddling (mostly) Italy and Austria.

Other Insight Guides

Europe is comprehensively covered by the books in Apa Publications' three series of guidebooks, which embrace the world. *Insight Guides* provide a full cultural background and first-rate photography. Other titles in the region include *Insight Guide: Vienna, Germany, Berlin, Munich* and *Prague*.

Feedback

We do our best to ensure the information in our books is as accurate and up-to-date as possible. The books are updated on a regular basis, using local contacts, who painstakingly add, amend and correct as required. However, some mistakes and omissions are inevitable and we are ultimately reliant on our readers to put us in the picture.

We would welcome your feedback on any details related to your experiences using the book "on the road". Maybe we recommended a hotel that you liked (or another that you didn't), as well as interesting new attractions, or facts and figures you have found out about the country itself. The more details you can give us (particularly with regard to addresses, e-mails and telephone numbers), the better.

We will acknowledge all contributions, and we'll offer an Insight Guide to the best letters received.

Please write to us at:
**Insight Guides
PO Box 7910
London SE1 1WE
United Kingdom**
Or send e-mail to:
insight@apaguide.demon.co.uk

The *Insight Pocket Guide* series contains personal recommendations from a local host and comes with an invaluable full-size fold-out map. Titles in the series include *Vienna, Prague, Berlin* and *Munich*.

The *Insight Compact Guide* series, which packs easily accessible information into a small format, together with carefully referenced pictures and maps, includes titles on *Vienna* and *Salzburg*.

Insight Fleximaps combine clear, detailed cartography with essential travel information. The laminated finish makes the maps durable, waterproof and easy to fold. Titles include *Vienna, Prague* and *Munich*.

ART & PHOTO CREDITS

Picture Spreads

Cartographic Editor **Zoë Goodwin**
Production **Linton Donaldson**
Design Consultants
Carlotta Junger, Graham Mitchener
Picture Research
Hilary Genin, Britta Jaschinski

Map Production Dave Priestley
© 2003 Apa Publications GmbH & Co.
Verlag KG (Singapore branch)

Index

A
B
C
D

F
G
H
I
J
a
b
c
d

f
g
h
i
j
k
l

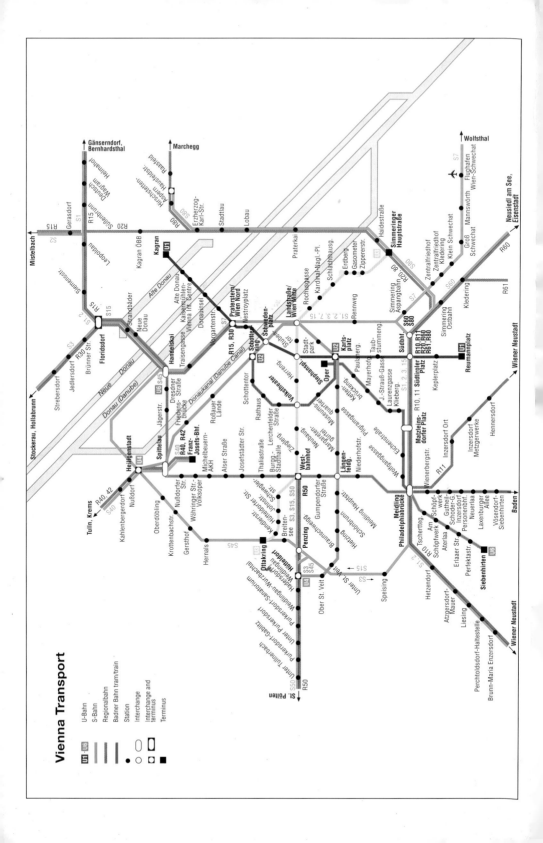

Vienna Transport

U-Bahn
S-Bahn
Regionalbahn
Badner Bahn tram/train
Station
Interchange
Interchange and terminus
Terminus